Teaching
Young
Children

CAROL SEEFELDT

University of Maryland

Teaching Young Children

Prentice-Hall, Inc., Englewood Cliffs, New Jersey 07632

Library of Congress Cataloging in Publication Data

SEEFELDT, CAROL.
 Teaching young children.

 Bibliography: p.
 Includes index.
 1. Education of children. 2. Teaching. I. Title.
 LB1025.2.S374   372.1'1'02   79-22252
 ISBN 0-13-896423-8

Editorial/production supervision and interior design by Dianne Poonarian
Cover design by Frederick Charles Ltd.
Manufacturing buyer: John Hall

Photographs courtesy of the Center for Young Children, College of Education,
University of Maryland; by Richard E. Farkas

Printed in the United States of America
10 9 8 7 6 5 4 3 2 1

PRENTICE-HALL INTERNATIONAL, INC., *London*
PRENTICE-HALL OF AUSTRALIA PTY. LIMITED, *Sydney*
PRENTICE-HALL OF CANADA, LTD., *Toronto*
PRENTICE-HALL OF INDIA PRIVATE LIMITED, *New Delhi*
PRENTICE-HALL OF JAPAN, INC., *Tokyo*
PRENTICE-HALL OF SOUTHEAST ASIA PTE. LTD., *Singapore*
WHITEHALL BOOKS LIMITED, *Wellington, New Zealand*

To Eugene, Paul, and Andrea, who continue to believe woman has the right and the responsibility to participate in the whole of life

Contents

PART III   THE CURRICULUM, 181

Preface

This is a book about teaching and becoming a teacher of young children. It is designed as a basic, introductory text in early childhood education, and combines theory, research, and practical ideas for teaching young children. It is a book based on the assumption that teaching requires a great deal of understanding, skill, and knowledge.

Teaching young children is not for the weak, but only for those persons who are strong, and who possess the willingness to continue to develop and learn. Teachers of young children must be willing to take the time to understand the past and its relation to today's early childhood education. They must also be able to develop self-understanding and become aware of their own values and feelings. An understanding of children is equally necessary. Good teachers continually work to increase their insight and understanding of children.

Part I of TEACHING YOUNG CHILDREN can assist the beginning teacher in developing these understandings. It includes an overview of the history of early childhood education in our nation, and a discussion of different philosophical approaches to teaching. The importance of understanding one's own value system and beliefs about children—boys and girls, children with special needs, or those whose cultures differ—is stressed. Suggestions are given for learning to observe children.

To become a truly effective teacher of young children a person must develop many skills. The skills of planning, evaluating, organizing the environment, and communicating are necessary. A good teacher is also skilled in using a variety of different teaching strategies.

Part II of TEACHING YOUNG CHILDREN is, therefore, concerned with helping teachers develop skills and strategies. First, strategies for developing daily and long-range plans are presented. Then, because the environment is believed to be a powerful influence on the behavior of children and adults, methods for organizing the physical environment, indoors and out, are given. An introduction to teaching strategies, such as questioning, reinforcing, and giving feedback, is included. Finally, a discussion of different verbal and nonverbal techniques for establishing effective communication with children, parents, and other faculty members concludes the section on developing strategies for teaching.

Teachers must have a broad base of knowledge. A teacher of young children must know a good deal about mathematics, music, art, science, language, health, safety, nutrition, and all of the social sciences. And, because children learn through play, it's the teacher who must know the power of play, and how children use play as their major mode of learning.

Part III of TEACHING YOUNG CHILDREN is about knowledge. It includes a discussion of the curriculum content areas of early childhood education. Goals and techniques for facilitating children's language growth, for planning experiences in art and music, and for extending children's experiences with mathematics and science are given. Suggestions for acquainting children with the social world conclude the section. Because children do learn through play, it is the premise of this section that all of the curriculum areas will be implemented as children play.

I am indebted to many people who helped in numerous ways with this book. The children and faculty of the Center for Young Children, College of Education, University of Maryland, and Richard E. Farkas, photographer, deserve special thanks. The skill and thoughtfulness of Robert Sickles, editor, and Dianne Poonarian, production editor, have been greatly appreciated. I am especially indebted to Eugene, Paul, and Andrea Seefeldt who, because they believe that all people, including women, have the right and responsibility to participate in the whole of life, cooperated, supported, and encouraged the completion of this text.

CAROL SEEFELDT

If You Would Teach Children . . .

IF ANY AMONG YOU would teach little ones, let him become as a child himself, looking at the world with faith and wonderment. Let him find pleasure in the symmetry of snowflakes, the pungency of burning leaves, the sparkle of dew, the rhythm of pattering rain, the mosaic of butterfly wings, the tang of salt spray. Let him be filled with a burning curiosity and an endless yearning to see and learn and know.

LET HIM BE TRUSTING, believing in the goodness of people and the worthwhileness of life. Let him be gentle, patient and kind, showing in every look and word and action his warm understanding and acceptance of individual and human fallibility. Let him find something good in every person, child and adult alike, confident that each will be his best self.

LET HIM LIKE CHILDREN as children like each other. Let him talk to children as children talk to each other, as one friend talks to another, in neither honeyed tones of condescension nor the sharp voice of command. Let him laugh with children, seeing through the eyes the sheer joy of living and the humor in everyday events. Let him laugh at himself, unafraid to admit his mistakes or failings, nor unable to see wherein he has appeared ridiculous to the frank eyes of childhood.

LET HIM THINK FOR HIMSELF and encourage children to think not his thoughts, but theirs. Let him be completely honest with himself and others, never sacrificing principle for expediency, never betraying the trust that children willingly give him. Let him always be able to live with himself, knowing in his heart that he has been and done the very best he knew, yet never so complacent that he sees no need for improving and growing. Let him be the kind of person that children may hope to become, as they unconsciously imitate him whom they love and respect.

THEN WILL CHILDREN who have grown tall and strong look back and call him blessed, saying to one another, "I had a teacher once who helped me find myself and learn to grow."

From Charlotte E. King, "If You Would Teach Children," in *Childhood Education*, 40, no. 8 (April 1964), 425. Reprinted by permission of Charlotte E. King and the Association for Childhood Education International, 3615 Wisconsin Avenue, N.W., Washington, D.C. Copyright © 1964 by the Association.

Teaching
Young
Children

Introduction

Part I

Introducing you to early childhood education, this part of *Teaching Young Children* discusses the historic background of early childhood education in our country, the decisions involved in becoming a teacher of young children, and the children with whom you will work. One chapter describes children who have special needs.

An understanding of the historical perspective of early childhood education is critical to fully understand early childhood education today. Chapter 1 traces the beginnings of early childhood education in our country and follows its growth to the present. The influences of individuals, as well as the social forces and changing ideas that contributed to the building of early childhood education are described.

The next chapter asks you to look seriously at yourself, your values, and attitudes before making the decision to enter early childhood education. Teaching young children is not a job for the fainthearted. Teaching demands courage, hard work, and a great deal of intelligence. Yet the joys of working with children make the job more than worthwhile.

Chapters 3 and 4 discuss the children themselves. How to get to know children using observations and information from standardized testing is described. Using this knowledge to meet the needs of children with special handicaps, who are gifted or abused, is also discussed.

A Heritage
for the Future

Many of us can recall teachers who brought out the best in us, who cared about what we knew and through this caring enabled us to build and extend our knowledge.

M. Yonemura, 1974, p. 64.

Can you recall a teacher who really cared about you, cared so much she enabled you to learn and grow? Most people, especially those who are talented and gifted, can tell of just such a teacher (Erikson 1968), one who stands out from all the rest, one whom they remember with a special fondness.

In the history of early childhood education, there is not just one such prominent teacher, but many. In fact, the history of early childhood education is the history of these special teachers. Through their caring they shaped individual children and changed and shaped the entire educational system—and society as well.

If you really care, you now have the opportunity to take your place among these special teachers. You can become a teacher who stands out from all the rest, who helps children and society grow. True, it is not a job for the weak, "It demands diligence, wisdom, courage and the acceptance of personal responsibility" (Nance 1968, p. 474), but it is an important occupation, and one that holds the promise of many rewards.

The pioneers, those memorable early childhood teachers, were strong, highly intelligent, courageous, and responsible. They created early childhood education, established it firmly in the educational system of our nation. Their

3

Do you remember a special teacher?

insight, intellectual curiosity, and resolve helped them to implement innovative ideas, and won for them the title of "dauntless women of early childhood education" (Synder 1972).

These teachers were rebels. They defied tradition as they introduced new ideas and practices into the field of education. They were idealists who were fed by the wave of humanitarianism that was sweeping the world and the idealism inherent in the new democracy of America. Their ideas came at a time when the social forces and theories being advanced by philosophers nurtured their efforts and contributed to their success. But it was, in the end, their own courage that led to permanent change in America's educational system.

The Beginnings

Even though there were many day care centers and kindergarten programs in the country, the beginnings of the early childhood education movement are often traced to Mrs. Carl Schurz. Mrs. Schurz, in order to continue her own children's German education and preserve their German heritage while in a foreign country, began a kindergarten in 1853 on the front porch of her octagon-shaped Watertown, Wisconsin home. "Here the mother-teacher used for her curriculum Friedrich Froebel's *gifts and occupations*, with the addition of the games and songs he prescribed" (Weber 1969, p. 19).

Although this first kindergarten lasted less than a year, and never enrolled more than six children, it had great impact on American education. The Octagon House in Watertown still stands. The gifts and occupations of Froebel are preserved in this museum-house, as a monument to the contribution Mrs. Schurz made to American education.

Elizabeth Peabody, reading descriptions of Schurz's kindergarten, became intrigued with the idea of the kindergarten (Garland 1924, p. 20). These descriptions, and a few fragments of the writing of Froebel, matched Peabody's interest and philosophy. Peabody, who "from early years constantly strove to express her idealism in deeds of love and service to man" (Garland 1924, p. 20), found the kindergarten—as designed by Froebel, and implemented by Mrs. Schurz—to be a perfect vehicle through which to express her idealistic love of humanity.

Based totally on the few writings of Froebel that she had read, and correspondence with Schurz, Elizabeth Peabody opened a kindergarten in Boston. By 1867 Peabody had become increasingly dissatisfied with her understanding of the works of Froebel and traveled to Europe to visit kindergartens and learn from those who had actually studied under him.

Froebel's Idealism

It was not until Friedrich Froebel (1782–1852) was twenty-seven years old that he turned to teaching as his profession after failing at a number of other occupations. Froebel's early childhood reputedly was unhappy. His mother had died before he was a year old, and his stepmother, when another baby came, found the growing Friedrich in the way.

Friedrich was restricted to the house, not permitted outside for fear that he might damage a plant or ruin his clothing. An uncle, observing Friedrich's constricted life, invited the boy to his home. At his uncle's, the ten-year-old Friedrich was given the freedom to roam where he liked, to play and spend his days outdoors in the woods and fields. These years, spent in communion with nature, are believed to have led to Froebel's conceptualization of the kindergarten. He believed that

> the kindergarten was to be a place where the child should unconsciously learn not only to express himself freely and joyfully with suitable play materials, songs and stories, but with the right kind of out of door life, to love and care for plants and animals, and through this loving and nurturing learn that the laws which govern the well-being of plants and animals also govern his body. Then, dimly, but inevitably, would stir within the child a faint feeling that somehow he and the world about him were akin. (Harrison 1924, p. 7)

At the core of Froebel's theory was the idea that learning involves activity. Froebel was not the first to express this idea. John Amos Comenius (1592–1670), Jean Jacques Rousseau (1712–1778), and Johann Heinrich Pestalozzi (1746–1827) had all advocated that the child's activity serve as the basis for all learning. Comenius, a Czech theologian, proposed that children learn by doing, through activity and concrete experiences, rather than through abstractions. Rousseau also postulated that learning should be natural, stemming from nature and things. According to Rousseau, the child should be given the opportunity to unfold naturally, learning from direct experiences in a secure, rich, inherently good environment. Pestalozzi put some of these ideas into practice, creating schools for young children that emphasized activity and doing.

These ideas, so congruent with what we believe today about children's learning through activity, led to Froebel's conceptualization of the kindergarten. In addition, Froebel's experiences in the country, and his sometimes magical, mystical idea of the unity of life, influenced the development of his curriculum. Froebel insisted that there was unity in all creation, and that it was necessary for one to understand the relationship of parts to each other and the whole, in order to be at one with God.

This idea of unity, and the belief that children learn through activity, was translated into a curriculum of gifts, occupations, songs, and games. The gifts included things such as balls, cubes, blocks, squares, triangles, paper rings, beads, and pebbles. Occupations were folding, cutting, parqueting, punching, and weaving paper, stringing beads and buttons, all to be completed by the child under exact instructions.

These gifts, occupations, songs, and activities were to bring the child to unity with God and to foster the unfolding of the child's creativity. Creative self-activity would be developed by "rendering the inner outer." "That we render visible, the invisible; that we impart an outward finite, transient to life, in the spirit" (Weber 1969, p. 31).

Looking at the exacting directions accompanying the gifts, and the nature of the gifts and occupations themselves, it is difficult to understand how they could lead anyone to creative self-activity. The Froebelian teacher-training manuals, which picture large groups of children rigidly sitting at tables, with their hands demurely folded on table top, while they patiently wait their turn for the teacher to direct them in the task of paper folding, punching, or whatever, seem totally incongruent with Froebel's writings about self-activity and creativity. Nevertheless, at the time, Froebel's ideas were revolutionary.

Peabody was especially impressed with Froebel's mystical interpretation of God, education, and creative self-activity. She returned from visiting and working in the European kindergartens originally established by Froebel, a true convert. She took up the kindergarten as others take on a religious crusade. "Kindergartening is not a craft, it is a religion; not an avocation, but a vocation from on high" (Garland 1924, p. 25). Leaving her Boston kindergarten to others, Peabody began her crusade to establish kindergartens in every part of America.

Lucy Wheelock describes this crusade as a zealous one and Peabody as "unflagging in her enthusiasm, never tiring of spreading the word" (Wheelock 1924, p. 11). With her nightgown under her street dress and toothbrush in her pocket, Peabody was prepared to sleep anywhere, go anywhere, unencumbered with a bag, to establish kindergartens across the country.

"Now and then, in the complicated affairs of man, the factors in a situation arrange themselves in such a way as to accelerate the development of some service or institution so that it makes a generation's normal growth in a few short years" (Goodykoontz 1948, p. 44). The kindergarten was one institution that benefited from social forces and made many years' progress in a short period of time. Although the first kindergartens established by Peabody were for children of the wealthy, soon children from all neighborhoods and social groups were able to attend a kindergarten program.

The massive immigration from Ireland, Asia, and Southern and Eastern Europe during the late 1800s was the social force that led to the expansion of the kindergarten. Many immigrants arrived without knowledge of the English language or American culture and settled in urban slums. These immigrants provided a pool of unskilled workers who contributed to the building of the nation, but who, because they lacked marketable skills and education, were exploited. This exploitation of the immigrant in the labor force awakened the social consciousness of the nation, leading to the development of settlement work. The kindergarten teacher, who would bring children to unity with God and provide for self-activity and creativity, found settlement work among the immigrants a fertile field.

Those involved in settlement or welfare work among the immigrant populations saw the kindergarten as a practical way to express their idealistic love of God and humanity. The children of the poor working family would be off the street, in clean, well-equipped rooms, with materials and activities to keep them occupied. The parents' gratefulness for the kindergarten would help to break down cultural barriers.

Once these barriers were broken, the settlement workers would be able to communicate with the immigrants and teach them the ways of the new country. Social settlement workers, Sunday schools, the Women's Christian Temperance Union, the Young Women's Christian Association, and other organizations supported schools for preschool children and a rapid spread of kindergartens took place. Manufacturers, "who willingly paid good salaries to efficient kindergarteners who would come and take charge of younger children of workers" (Garland 1924, p. 10), were also involved in the spread of the kindergarten.

In 1873 Susan Blow demonstrated that the kindergarten could be a successful part of the public school system. With the support of William Harris, superintendent of the St. Louis public schools, Blow initiated the first public school kindergarten. "The opening of the public kindergarten was epoch making. It was the first great and permanent step in the establishment of the kindergarten as an integral part of the school system" (Neil 1924, p. 188). Blow rigidly followed the Froebelian curriculum and philosophy, calling Froebel's *member-whole* concept the foundation of all education. By 1914 every major

American city had public kindergartens, and by 1920 kindergartens were considered a public school institution.

Another pioneer in the early childhood movement, Alice Putnam, came to kindergarten work through her own children. When her children outgrew kindergarten, Putnam maintained her interest and opened the Chicago Froebel Association for the training of kindergarten teachers. In Chicago she began working with Jane Addams, who directed the Hull Settlement House. Here Putnam initiated a kindergarten program as a part of the settlement work. Jane Addams wrote of her, "She constantly insisted that the little child of each group of the diverse nationalities represented afforded a normal and natural point of departure for the solution of the immigrant problem" (Newell 1924, p. 214).

Paralleling the work with immigrant children in the United States was the work of Maria Montessori in Italy. The first woman physician in Italy, with a doctorate in anthropology, Montessori became interested in working with retarded children. She believed that many of these children were being treated medically when their problem was one of lack of experiences, especially lack of educational experiences.

Montessori opened the Casi dei Bambini in the San Lorenzo slum district of Rome in 1907. Here she put into practice her views of education for deprived children. The major goal of the school was to keep young children busy so they would not vandalize the housing projects while their parents worked, but Montessori taught manners, cleanliness, reading, writing, and mathematics—all before the children had reached the age of five.

Jane Addams visited Montessori in Rome and saw the parallel between Montessori's work and the work of Alice Putnam in the Hull House in Chicago. "I visited Dr. Montessori's school in Rome and saw the tall figure of the founder, standing absolutely absorbed in the activities of the children and I was instantly reminded of Mrs. Putnam and her concentrated interest in our little neighbors in that early kindergarten" (Newell 1924, p. 215).

Many other American educators traveled to Rome to visit the Casi dei Bambini of Dr. Montessori. For the most part, however, Americans found the program, and its basic philosophy, at odds with Froebelian beliefs and felt that the Froebelian kindergarten was based on a deeper understanding of the child and the educative process.

Changing Ideas

Although Elizabeth Peabody and Susan Blow held rigidly to the Froebelian kindergarten, changes in the nature of the program did occur. As kindergartens reached more children, in every part of the nation, children of all economic groups and cultures, it was inevitable and natural that change would occur. The changes seemed to happen in concert with changing ideas of philosophy, of the purpose of education, and of the nature of humankind. But the changes did not occur without causing great conflict among the pioneers of early education.

Perhaps without really recognizing what was happening, Anna Bryan, of Louisville, Kentucky, made a real break with the Froebelian kindergarten. After completing her training in Chicago under Alice Putnam, she returned to Louisville and opened a free kindergarten and a training program for kindergarten teachers. The break with her Froebelian training may have stemmed from the foreignness of these concepts in Louisville, but more likely Bryan's own intellectual curiosity and creativity were responsible for the break.

Apparently Bryan approached each kindergarten and training class as an experiment in which she would work through problems, try out solutions, observe, and learn. Patty Smith Hill, one of Bryan's first students wrote, "Each kindergarten was a laboratory in which the directress was working out her individual convictions. She garnered wisdom from each school she supervised and all her experiences were turned over to the whole group at the following teachers' meeting" (Hill 1924, p. 227).

Reflecting on what was happening, Patty Smith Hill continued, "I find it difficult to explain what transpired, when the first break was made with Froebelian thought and practice. I find it difficult to analyze the processes and the results" (Hill 1924, p. 228).

Rather than giving children Froebel's gifts and occupations, Bryan gave the children practical problems relating to their own experiences. In Bryan's kindergarten children made paper dolls, doll furniture, real baskets, and experimented with a variety of materials. It seems hard to believe that making doll furniture would create such conflict among the kindergarteners. Yet these breaks with tradition, however small and minor, did draw attention to Bryan's program. People visited her to observe her in action, to analyze the program, and she was in demand as a speaker across the nation.

Anna Bryan, Patty Smith Hill, and others who adopted the methods of the new kindergarten, found the theories and philosophy of G. Stanley Hall (1846–1924) and John Dewey (1859–1952) in harmony with their concept of the kindergarten. Hall's work in studying children was especially attractive to Bryan and Hill who saw the kindergarten curriculum evolving out of the children's interests, needs, and development, rather than wholly from the prescribed gifts and occupations of Froebel.

As Dewey's writings became disseminated, and acceptance of his ideas grew, a break with Froebelian thought was the only possible result. Dewey advocated that education begin with the child's own activity and play and be based on the child's own experiences. The total environment would become the source of learning. Real life situations, not secondhand information, were preferred. The key concept of Dewey's philosophy was that the purpose of education was to prepare children to live in a democracy. As citizens of a democracy, children would need to learn to think, reason, and make decisions for themselves.

A very different type of teacher was called for to implement Dewey's ideas. These teachers, rather than merely following the prescribed directions of Froebel, would have to have an understanding of the potential of the total environment for learning. Dewey himself envisioned teachers who were active scientists, constantly evaluating and diagnosing the children's learning in order to put learning activities in sequence. But like Froebel, Dewey saw the teacher as a guide, one who would monitor each child's experience, offering assistance, encouragement, and new directions as required.

These ideas were just what the new kindergarten teachers were seeking. The basic concepts of Dewey were enough like those of Froebel to be familiar— embracing the need for children's play and activity—but they broadened the curriculum to meet the needs of America's developing democracy.

The real break with the Froebelian kindergarten came when Alice Temple spoke against those who continued to cling to the Froebelian tradition.

> We wish to make it clear that we sympathize with the idealistic motives that actuated pioneer American kindergarteners in their efforts to ameliorate the condition of young children and to bring more enjoyment and more socialized experiences into their lives. At the same time we recognize the importance of the essential social skills in reading, writing, arithmetic, which the school historically has emphasized in response to definite social needs. (Alice Temple 1925, p. 9)

Through the early 1900s both theory and practice in the kindergarten underwent constant change, revision, and reconstruction as the kindergarten pioneers merged their traditional ideas with those of Dewey.

By the 1920s and 1930s the kindergarten was a firmly established part of the American educational system. About this time the nursery school began to appear. The first cooperative nursery school was started in Chicago by a group of faculty wives from the University of Chicago. The school was begun in order to give children social experiences. Other nursery schools began to open at universities. The nursery schools of the early 1920s were designed for child study research, as well as to give young women the opportunity to prepare for their future role of wife and mother.

Nursery schools had a slower start than kindergartens. Goodykoontz (1948) reports that there were only three nursery schools in 1920, and twenty-five in 1924; most of these were supported by colleges for laboratory purposes or by private citizens for profit. While the kindergarten is firmly established as a part of the public school, the nursery school, although popular, has yet to become a regular part of all public school systems.

Even though the nursery school movement was separate from the kindergarten movement, the leaders—Harriet Johnson, Lucy Sprague Mitchell, Caroline Pratt, Eliot Pearson, and others—continued to put theory and philosophy into practice. The leaders of the nursery school movement, however, found the theories and ideas of Froebel inadequate to explain child growth and development. The ideas being advanced by current philosophers and knowledge emerging from the field of child study fed the proponents of the nursery school.

Scientific knowledge was seen as the foundation of the nursery school (Hymes 1978, p. 18). The ideas of Sigmund Freud, G. Stanley Hall, and John Dewey (as well as the child study research of Arnold Gesell), were used as the leaders developed the nursery school program.

The first nursery schools, as a result, were built on three guiding principles: (1) play is the basic mode for young children's thinking; (2) the teacher's role is to exploit daily encounters, both physical and social, as materials to stimulate the thinking process; and (3) the cognitive search for relationships should be stimulated by providing varied opportunities for children to have direct contact with the people and processes of their environment (Biber 1977, p. 47).

These principles continue today to direct and guide kindergarten, Head Start, and nursery school curricula.

Changing Times

Through the 1920s and 1930s early childhood education was available in kindergartens or nursery schools to a limited number of children. But once again changing social forces influenced the early childhood movement. The Great Depression of the 1930s brought early educational experiences to many more children. The passage of the Works Progress Administration program provided federal funding to subsidize nursery schools. There were full-day programs, with the major goal being to provide work for unemployed grade school teachers, custodians, cooks, and nurses. Although six million dollars were allocated for the WPA nursery school programs, and some 72,400 children were enrolled (with 6,770 adults employed), the effort was termed "a minor venture in relief giving" (Steiner 1976, p. 16).

But the WPA program, even if considered minor, did have impact on the growth of early childhood education. Nursery school and kindergarten teachers and leaders were hired as consultants to the program. They wrote curriculum materials and helped the upper grade, or secondary teacher, adapt to working with preschool children. "The WPA nursery schools were generally good. Children were well served from 9 A.M. to 3 P.M. Food was good. Parents were highly pleased. And for the first time many children, in all parts of the country, from all backgrounds, had a chance to go to nursery school" (Hymes 1975, p. 5).

The Lanham Programs

When the Second World War came, the need for WPA nursery school employees no longer existed. There were jobs for everyone. In fact the need for people power was so great that the federal government once again entered the child care movement by financing day care for children of working mothers. The Lanham Child Care Center program provided federal funds to factories employing working mothers for the establishment of day care centers.

With men off to war, the need for products to support the war effort increased, and women found ready employment in factories and all types of businesses. Over 229,474 children were enrolled in these programs, from all parts of the country and from all backgrounds (Hymes 1975, p. 6). When the war ended, men reentered the job market, and the federal funds for child care went back to the government "without a whimper" (Steiner 1976, p. 18). Except in a few cases, the programs initiated under the Lanham Act during the Second World War quickly disappeared.

Both the WPA and Lanham programs were short-lived, but both were designed only to fulfill specific goals and meet the needs of a nation in crisis. Both, however, did demonstrate that early education was not only feasible on a national scale, but also a popular effort, of value, benefiting children, families, and the entire nation (Hymes 1975).

Head Start

During the 1960s our nation became increasingly aware of the extensive discrimination existing in its educational system. In an attempt to promote equality of educational opportunity for all children, the Head Start program was initiated. Dewey had long ago suggested that education should not be actively

> used as an instrument to make easier the exploitation of one class by another. School facilities must be secured of such amplitude and efficiency as will in fact and not simply in name discount the effects of economic inequalities, and secure to all the wards of the nation equality of equipment for their future careers. (Dewey 1916, p. 98)

It was not until the 1960s—and the advent of Head Start—that our nation acted on Dewey's wish.

It is important to remember that Project Head Start was the result of social forces as well as advancing theories and ideas about the nature of thinking. The work of Jean Piaget (b. 1896)—a Swiss psychologist who had been studying children's thinking for many years—began to receive recognition in the United States during the 1960s. His ideas support the role of activity and action in the development of intelligence. Piaget considers play essential to cognitive development. His emphases on the early years of a child's life, and on experiences, fit nicely into the concept of Head Start.

Benjamin Bloom, who wrote *Stability and Change in Human Characteristics* (1964), and J. Hunt, author of *Experience and Intelligence* (1961), who revised the nation's ideas of the nature of intelligence and thinking, contributed to the conception of Head Start. Both Bloom and Hunt called for the end of viewing intelligence as a stable, fixed, unalterable trait. Both reviewed the literature and research on the relation between intelligence and experience and reached the conclusion that intelligence is malleable. The research, first on animals, then with children, seemed to support the idea that children's early experiences have a profound effect on later intellectual growth. According to Bloom and Hunt, intelligence is directly influenced by experiences, or lack of experiences, especially during the early years of life. Based on this logic, Project Head Start was designed and implemented. Once again social forces combined with changing theories, leading to the growth and permanent expansion of early childhood education.

Project Head Start was designed to compensate for the detrimental effects of poverty by giving children enriching preschool experiences. It was believed that children who would receive the compensatory program would increase in intellectual functioning and subsequently would achieve successfully in the school setting, be prepared for careers, and hence the cycle of poverty in our country would once and for all be broken.

Calling Head Start a miracle of instant organization and a miracle of welcoming community response, Hymes (1975, p. 31) describes the program as "committed in theory to the development of the whole child and to the well-being of the family from which the child comes and to the development of strength in the community in which that family has its roots."

Conceived during the winter of 1965 and implemented during the summer of 1965, Head Start enrolled 580,000 children from Guam, the Virgin Islands, and Puerto Rico, from Indian and Eskimo villages, from every city, rural community, and state in the nation. Beginning as a summer program, funded under the Office of Economic Opportunity, Head Start (because of the success of the first summer's program), was expanded in 1966 to include full-year programs. Now under the Administration of Children, Youth and Families, Head Start continues to provide comprehensive preschool programs for over 700,000 children.

Although the WPA and Lanham programs ended with solution of the employment crises, Head Start survives and prospers. Today Head Start continues to foster children's total development and support families and communities. In 1977 Head Start received its first major expansion in funding since 1968, permitting an increase in the number of children and families served, and the numbers who benefit from the program.

And benefit they do! The results of evaluations of Head Start show that children who participate in a full-year Head Start program do achieve well in school. Fewer children with the Head Start experience repeat grades as compared to those children of similar backgrounds without the experience; fewer children with Head Start experiences are in special classes, or in institutions as compared to those children without the experience (Lazar 1977).

Is Head Start a success? "Head Start, the most innovative program ever mounted on behalf of America's children, is alive and well . . . in regard to whether Head Start is a success or a failure, I think the issue is beyond debate" (Zigler 1978, p. 5).

Credit for the success of Head Start lies with the early childhood educators who designed and nurtured the program. Unlike the beginning days of early childhood education when the pioneers in the kindergarten and nursery school movement could be counted on one hand, the early childhood educators responsible for Head Start are numerous. In every area of the country, diligent people, imbued with the same spirit of innovative creativity the early pioneers had, worked, sacrificed, and struggled to make Head Start a successful and permanent part of American education.

The educators responsible for making Head Start a success were not only like the early pioneers in spirit, but also in their method of working. Just as Anna Bryan constantly revised her thinking, trying out new ideas, testing, changing, and experimenting, Head Starters continually analyzed their methods, changing and refining both method and rationale. As a result, Planned Variation, Home Start, Health Start, Project Follow Through, parent child centers, and model programs resulted. New methods and ideas, based on research, experimentation, and theory were implemented. Programs changed to respond to changing community needs. Research, experimentation, and change continue to be integral to the Head Start program.

Early Childhood Education Today

When Mrs. Schurz opened her kindergarten on the front porch of her Watertown, Wisconsin home, fewer than a dozen children were involved. The number of children in nursery schools, day care centers, Head Start programs, and kindergartens has multiplied many times. With each burst of activity, schools for children under the age of six became more and more firmly entrenched in America.

Even though the number of children three to five years old in the United States dropped considerably between 1967 and 1976, enrollment in the nation's nursery schools and kindergartens increased sharply (Nursery School and Kindergarten Enrollment 1978). The proportion of children aged three to five enrolled in preschool programs increased from thirty-two percent in 1967 to almost fifty percent in 1976, with the rise especially noteworthy for three and four year olds. In 1967 only fourteen percent of all three and four year olds were enrolled in a preschool. In 1976 the proportion had risen to about thirty-one percent. The enrollment rate of five year olds increased by about one-fourth, from sixty-five percent to eighty-one percent over the same period.

That more mothers sought and accepted employment outside the home seems to account for the increase; yet nonemployed mothers—especially those who completed some college—also enroll children in nursery schools. These mothers believe that the preschool provides worthwhile educational experiences for children. For example, among three and four year olds, twenty-seven percent whose mothers had finished high school were in nursery school, while forty percent of children whose mothers had finished one to three years of college were enrolled, and sixty-three percent of children whose mothers had completed four or more years of college were enrolled in some type of preschool.

As the numbers of children enrolled in preschool programs expand, so do the challenges. Now as in the past, early childhood education is being called on not only to provide educational experiences for young children, but also to strengthen the family unit, unite and improve communities, identify and work with the abused child, (and the abusing parents), and design programs for children with special needs.

In Summary

The pioneers in early childhood education faced many challenges and met them successfully. Based on Froebel's ideas, programs that stressed learning through activity were developed. Later, Anna Bryan—using the theories of G. Stanley Hall and John Dewey—broke with Froebelian tradition and created a program more fully cognizant of the child's interests and needs.

Because early childhood education is now available to so many children, today's early childhood educator has different, yet every bit as challenging, problems to solve. But today's educators have the past to help them as they face the new challenges. Jordan (1973) helps us to see how the past will influence the future.

> To disregard the past would render us impotent to determine where we are going. Rootlessness in the past forces one into a pattern of living entirely in the present, reacting rather than initiating action, always responding on the basis of impulse rather than careful thought. This pattern of living is devoid of a sense of future; it is without long-range goals that provide the perspective needed for wise decision making. . . . Innovations lacking solid roots in the past can hardly serve as a vision for the future. (D.C. Jordan 1973, p. 289)

Early childhood educators do have a rich heritage. An understanding of this heritage provides today's educator with the pride of participating in a profession dominated by innovative, creative, dauntless persons, and this knowledge, when integrated with current research and theories, can serve as a vision for the future.

Resources

One brief chapter cannot fully acquaint you with the fascinating history of early childhood education. Each person should build his or her own understanding of that history. Here are some resources that may be helpful.

HYMES, JAMES L., *Living History Interviews*. Carmel, Ca.: Hacienda Press, 1978.

STEINER, G. Y., *The Children's Cause*. Washington, D.C.: The Brookings Institute, 1978.

SYNDER, AGNES, *Dauntless Women in Early Childhood Education*. Washington, D.C.: Association of Childhood Education International, 1972.

WEBER, EVELYN, *The Kindergarten*. New York: Teachers College Press, 1969.

Projects

1. What is your personal history of early childhood education? Record that history. Did you attend a day care or Head Start program? What do you recall of these experiences? What impressed you the most? What was the teacher like? How did this first experience influence your ideas about school? How did these first experiences affect your later schooling?

2. Review the history of early childhood education in your own community. When was the first school for children under the age of six opened? Who was instrumental in starting this school? How was it funded?

3. If it is possible, interview retired teachers or older persons in your community. Perhaps they can relate their experiences with early childhood education. What do they remember most about their first school experiences? How are their recollections similar and different from yours?

4. Make a point to visit a number of early childhood programs in your community. Keep a record of how they are similar in program, services to children and families, and how they differ. Try to visit at least one Head Start or Home Start program, a day care center and family day care program, a cooperative nursery school, a proprietary nursery school, and a public school prekindergarten or kindergarten program.

5. Select one of these programs (Head Start, day care, kindergarten, etc.) and trace the history of the program in your community. Each program had different reasons for beginning, each has a unique and interesting history.

6. Interview members of your family or a number of persons in your community. Ask these persons if they believe schools for young children should be available in your community, who should pay for these schools and which agency—state, family, or church—should be responsible for these schools.

References

BIBER, B., "Cognition in Early Childhood Education: a Historical Perspective," in *Early Childhood Education: Issues and Insights*, eds. B. Spodek and H.J. Walberg; pp. 41–65. Berkeley, California: McCutchan Publishing Corporation, 1977.

BLOOM, B. S., *Stability and Change in Human Characteristics*. New York: John Wiley & Sons, Inc., 1964.

DEWEY, J., *Democracy and Education*. New York: The Free Press, 1944. First published 1916.

ERIKSON, E., *Identity: Youth and Crisis*. New York: W.W. Norton & Co., Inc., 1968.

GARLAND, J. H., "Elizabeth Palmer Peabody," in *Pioneers of the Kindergarten in America;* ed. International Kindergarten Union: Committee of Nineteen, pp. 19–26. New York: The Century Co., 1924.

GOODYKOONTZ, B., "Recent History and Present Status of Education of Young Children," in *The Forty-Sixth Yearbook of the National Society for the Study of Education:*

Part II Early Childhood Education, pp. 44–69, ed. N.B. Henry. Chicago, Illinois: The University of Chicago Press, 1948.

HARRISON, E., "The Growth of the Kindergarten in the United States," in *Pioneers of the Kindergarten in America,* ed. International Kindergarten Union: Committee of Nineteen, pp. 3–19. New York: The Century Co., 1924.

HILL, P. S., "Anna E. Bryan," in *Pioneers of the Kindergarten in America,* ed. International Kindergarten Union: Committee of Nineteen, pp. 223–231. New York: The Century Co., 1924.

HYMES, J. *Early Childhood Education: an Introduction to the Profession* (2nd. ed.) Washington, D.C.: National Association for the Education of Young Children, 1975.

HYMES, J. *Living History Interviews: Book 2. Care of the Children of Working Mothers.* Carmel, California: Hacienda Press, 1978.

HUNT, J. *Intelligence and Experience.* New York: Ronald Press, 1961.

JORDAN, D. C. and STREET, D. T., "The Anisa Model: A New Basis for Educational Planning." *Young Children,* 28, 5 (1973). pp. 289–307.

LAZAR, I., "The Persistence of Preschool Effects: a Long-term Follow-up of Fourteen Infant and Preschool Experiments." Washington, D.C.: U.S. Government Printing Office, 1977.

NANCE, C. E., "What holds teachers captive?" *Chldhood Education,* 44, 8 (1975), pp. 474–477.

NEIL, H., "William Torrey Harris," in *Pioneers of the Kindergarten in America,* ed. International Kindergarten Union: Committee of Nineteen, pp. 167–184. New York: The Century Co., 1924.

NEWELL, B. B., "Alice Putnam," in *Pioneers of the Kindergarten in America,* ed. International Kindergarten Union: Committee of Nineteen, pp. 204–223. New York: The Century Co., 1924.

Nursery School and Kindergarten Enrollment of Children and Labor Force Participation of Their Mothers: October 1967 to October 1976. Series p-20, No. 318. Washington, D.C.: U.S. Government Printing Office, 1976.

SYNDER, A., *Dauntless Women in Early Childhood Education.* Washington, D.C.: Association for Childhood Education International, 1972.

STEINER, G. Y. *The Children's Cause.* Washington, D.C.: The Brookings Institute, 1976.

TEMPLE, A. and PARKER, S. C., *Unified Kindergarten and First-Grade Teaching.* New York: Ginn and Company, 1925.

WEBER, E., *The Kindergarten: Its Encounter with Educational Thought in America.* New York: Teachers College Press, 1969.

WHEELOCK, L., "A Tribute to Kate Douglas Wiggin," in *Pioneers of the Kindergarten in America,* ed. International Kindergarten Union: Committee of Nineteen, pp. 296–298. New York: The Century Co., 1924.

YONEMURA, M., "Learning What Children Know," *Childhood Education,* 51, 2 (1974), pp. 64–68.

ZIGLER, E., "America's Head Strat Program: an Agenda for Its Second Decade," *Young Children,* 33, 5 (1978), pp. 4–14.

2

Becoming a Teacher
of Young Children

To be relevant to the future you must be pioneers in the present, and pioneers have got to be tough.

W. Bloomberg, Jr., 1967, p. 130.

Today's early childhood educator must be able to capture the intellectual toughness and creative spirit of education pioneers of the past. Although early childhood education is an accepted part of schooling today, the challenges facing teachers are no less than those faced by the early education pioneers. More than ever before, the early childhood educator must be a tough-minded pioneer, able to dare, risk, try, innovate, and experiment.

It may not be easy, but you can develop the kind of intellectual toughness necessary to become a teacher of young children. Teachers of young children must gain the knowledge and expertise that characterizes the true professional. "This may not be easy, however, as I see it, a genuine professionalism is essential for the development and maintenance of effective programs for early education and care" (Almy 1975, p. 32).

Making the Decision

The early childhood education pioneers were double specialists. They took theory and turned it into practice, and they turned practice into theory, as well. Teachers today must recognize that these same skills will be required of

18

them, and many more. Before deciding to become a teacher of young children, you should fully recognize the complexities of the position. Teaching young children is hard. "The younger the child the more difficult it is to teach him and the more pregnant that teaching is with future consequences" (Piaget 1971, p. 127). Hymes puts is more bluntly, "You have to be smart and very well informed to teach young children well, if you work with older children you have the textbook to protect you . . . you have to be on your toes to keep up with young children" (Hymes 1974, p. 68).

Preschool teachers today must be masters of many things. They must be trained in psychology, sociology, health and nutrition, family counseling, and have knowledge of all of the curriculum content areas including: geography, mathematics, science, reading, art, music, and dance. And most of all they must be able to synthesize knowledge, analyze it, and reach new conclusions, constantly revising, reworking their own thinking and practice.

Prospective teachers of young children should know themselves before making the decision. They must fully recognize the difficulty of the job and the skills and knowledge they must gain. It is important to consider the choice of early childhood education as a career carefully, for once the decision is made, it is likely to lead to a long-term commitment.

In teaching there is no guarantee of a quick rise up the career ladder. There is not much of a ladder to begin with, and although teachers are promoted to become supervisors, consultants, or directors of programs, research suggests that the majority of teachers entering the classroom remain there for their entire careers. Nine out of ten teachers in the field say they will stay with children until retirement (National Education Association 1977, p. 49).

The Rewards

As hard as the job is, as intellectually, physically, and emotionally demanding, teaching young children is also a joyous experience. To those who have worked with young children, nothing can equal the satisfaction, excitement, and reward that comes from teaching. First, early childhood teachers have the satisfaction that comes from being in a profession dominated by giants, of taking a place among those who through hard work, understanding of children, and intellectual toughness changed the very nature of American education.

Then, too, as the awareness of the importance of the early years becomes more widely appreciated, the early childhood teacher achieves, little by little, more and more respect. As more highly qualified, sensitive, knowledgeable, and aware persons enter the field, respect for the profession grows.

But most of all there is the pure joy of working with young children. Nothing compares to being with preschoolers. The thrill of being with a child discovering new things and mastering new skills cannot be described. Preschoolers experience life fully, seeing each day as a fresh, wonderful day of waiting adventures. It is difficult not to be caught up in the same anticipation and joy of life when you are with young children.

Teaching is hard work.

Young children do not hold back. There is no hidden agenda when you are with children. When relating to adults there is often the question, "I know what you said, but what did you really mean by that?" With children there is no doubt. Their anger, hostility, joy, sadness, and frustration are expressed freely—sometimes too freely for comfort—but it is an honest, straightforward, no-doubt-about-it way of relating that many teachers find refreshing.

Because children do express their feelings openly, they are often receptive to creative experiences. Children paint, draw, model, dance, sing, build, and play uninhibitedly. "They are experimental, ever trying something that no one else has thought of doing" (Hymes 1974, p. 65). With children being so open and experimental, it is unlikely that a teacher could become bored.

No child, no group of children, no day is ever exactly the same as another. Teachers find they must continue their own learning and growing in order to stay relevant. No matter how long you teach, there is always another skill to master, new technique to learn, or findings from another research study to try out. Always learning, always changing, always experimenting, the teacher faces an exciting challenge.

The Same Yet Different

Teachers of young children must possess the same ability to experiment and create that the leaders of the past had, yet today's teachers are different. Most of the early pioneers in the kindergarten movement were white, wealthy women. They were able to take up causes and devote their lives and fortunes to improving the quality of life for others. Even in the 1950s the core of teachers, although perhaps not wealthy, remained women.

Today's total population of teachers is much more representative of the population at large. Teachers of young children today represent every race, culture, and ethnic group found in the United States. No longer, of course, is the field open only to women.

Because it is beneficial for children to have role models of both sexes, deliberate attempts have been made to encourage men to become preschool and kindergarten teachers. The push to involve men in the lives of young children, however, can lead to discrimination against women.

In 1977 ninety-three percent of all teachers were female, but over ninety-seven percent were supervised by a male. It has been typical for men to receive the first choice of position and to be given the first opportunity for promotion in the field of teaching. While women continue to be in the minority in other professions—medicine, law, business—they are also losing their deserved place in the profession of teaching, a place that historically has been theirs (N.E.A. 1977).

Equality of opportunity for positions in early childhood education, and for advancement in the field, must be possible for both men and women. The time has come to ask some hard questions about equality of opportunity for both men and women. If either men or women are being denied teaching positions, what can be done about it? And if women are not fully represented in positions of leadership within the field of early childhood education, why aren't they? Is it possible that women willingly yield leadership to men, do not prepare themselves for leadership, or is it that women fail to accept the responsibility of leadership when it is offered to them? Or have they been denied the opportunity to lead because of discrimination?

The pioneers might be surprised to see today's teachers.

The pioneers of early childhood education might be surprised at the number of positions available for today's educator. In the past, there were jobs available in either nursery schools or kindergartens. Today there is a wide variety and diversity of career opportunities. Although most positions involve direct contact with children in a classroom or group setting, there are a number of other careers possible that involve working with children at home with the family, in a community agency, or in other organizations.

Public school systems continue to employ persons trained in early childhood education as prekindergarten, kindergarten, or primary school teachers. Increased awareness of the importance of the early years of life has led public schools to sponsor programs for children as young as the age of two. In addition to working directly with children, early childhood educators (under the auspices of the public school), may find employment as supervisors, parent involvement coordinators, home visitors, curriculum developers, or in other leadership positions.

Employment opportunities are also available outside of the public school. Nursery schools; church-related, community-sponsored, or privately run day care centers; Head Start programs; and other federally supported programs, employ a variety of persons trained in early childhood education. Teacher aides, teachers, directors, supervisors, curriculum specialists, and consultants are all needed in non-public school programs.

Increasingly, programs other than those in the public school or child care area are opening up for teachers. Recreation department, licensing agencies, health departments, department of social services—even department stores, hospitals, and state legislatures—often find need for persons who understand the complex issues involved in working with young children and their families. Teachers have been hired to consult with local television stations, in toy or clothing purchasing, or as legislative aides. Table 2–1 offers suggestions for a broad range of programs and positions that might be available in early childhood education.

Know Yourself

Entering teaching without fully examining what loving little children means can lead to disaster. Educators must understand that the same exuberance, inhibition, and freedom of expression that makes one enjoy being with children can also be very demanding and frustrating. Children cannot wait. They are impatient. They make constant demands on the adults around them. Sometimes they throw up, bite, scream, kick, and refuse to cooperate. Sometimes they just sit, stonefaced and determined not to become involved.

Before reaching a decision to teach, it is worthwhile to spend an extended period of time with young children. The volunteer in a neighborhood nursery school or day care center is warmly appreciated and has a good opportunity to become fully acquainted with children. Babysitting, even making a point

TABLE 2–1
Early Childhood Education Categories of Programs and Positions

Program Type	Position
1. School System	Program Director
	Program Supervisor
	Curriculum Specialist
	Principal
	Team Leader
	Teacher Trainer-Consultant
	Teacher
	Model Specialist (Montessori, Piaget, and so on)
2. Child Care Programs	
Multiple Site	Owner-Operator
Single Site	Administrator
Industrial Model	Education Director-
Factory	Coordinator-Specialist
Business	Supervisor
Hospital	Teacher
High School	Parent Educator
University	
Shopping Center	
Flexible Schedule Center	
Campus Based "Drop In"	
Shopping Mall	
Home Based	
3. Head Start—Child Development Programs	
Half Day	Director
Full Day	Education Supervisor
Home Based	Curriculum Coordinator
Special Needs	Parent Educator
	Teacher
4. Nursery School Programs	
Multiple Site	Director-Owner
Single Site	Education Specialist
Parent Cooperative	Teacher
Church Related	
Social Service Agency	
5. Licensing Agencies	
State	Administrator-Director
County	Supervisor
City	Site Visitor
6. Other Type Programs	
Department Store	Toy Consultant-Buyer
	Drop In Care Giver
Media	
Radio	Writer-Creator
Television	Reviewer-Critiquer
Children's Programs	Consultant
Parent Programs	Programmer

TABLE 2–1 *(continued)*

Early Childhood Education Categories of Program and Positions

Program Type	Position
Research	Director
	Writer
	Field Worker
Fine Arts	
Ballet	Teacher of Gifted-Talented
Music	
Art	
Hospital	E.C.E. Educator: Staff-Team
	Teacher of Children
Museum	Writer-Programmer
	Educator
Home Based Programs	Parent Consultant
	Educator of Children with Special Needs
Recreation Programs	Teacher
Community Programs	Teacher of Children
	Parent Educator
	Police Department-Fire Department-Social Service Personnel Consultant
High School Based Child	Director
Development Program	Teacher

Reprinted with permission from Mary Mel O'Dowd, University of Wisconsin-Milwaukee

of observing children when you are shopping or traveling, can help develop realistic expectations of what working with children will entail.

Other people feel safe and secure with very young children. After all, young children cannot correct one's mistakes. They readily accept explanations, and even if they wanted to, they could not challenge a teacher's writing, spelling, or statements.

Then, too, others may be uncertain or insecure about their own ability to relate effectively with adults and will choose to work with children instead. It is important, if this is the case, to recognize that working with children also means working with adults. Teachers must feel comfortable relating to team members, aides, school staff, parents, and other members of the community.

Still other people believe that their own unsatisfied needs for approval and love will be met by working with young children. The unconditional love children give to their teachers is unconsciously sought after. It is true that a person's own needs for attention, love, and acceptance can be met when working with children, but these needs must be fully understood so the children will not be manipulated and damaged by them. In any case, entering the profession of early childhood education to meet unfulfilled needs for love or security or based on false assumptions about the nature of young children can lead to bitter disappointment and an unhappy career.

ACCEPTING ALL CHILDREN

Some of the early education pioneers seemed to have difficulty fully accepting the cultural heritage of all of the children they worked with. Kate Douglas Wiggin, recalling the early kindergarten program in the tar flats of San Francisco, writes, "Many days were spent in learning the unpronounceable names of my flock and in keeping them from murdering one another until Froebel's justly celebrated law of love could be made a working proposition" (Weber 1969, p. 43).

In her book, *The Story of Patsy*, written to raise money for the expansion of the kindergartens in San Francisco, Wiggin further illustrates her desire to inhibit behaviors that did not meet her expectations. In a passage that has Patsy telling the teacher about the activities in his home, the teacher responds, "Please don't talk street words to Miss Kate!" (Weber 1979, p. 44).

Today's teacher must be aware that our nation is multicultural and must accept that within any given classroom, any number of cultures may be represented. Valuing diversity, recognizing the right of individuals to be different, and placing value on the uniqueness of all cultures helps teachers to accept all children.

Acceptance of children's cultural backgrounds doesn't happen automatically or easily. Culture directs the way people behave, act, and the things they value. Culture is a value-ladened concept. It provides the members of a society with the *goods* and the *bads*, the *beautifuls* and the *uglies*, the *shoulds* and the *should nots* (Zais 1976, p. 161). If a person has a preconceived and inflexible idea about what is good to eat, how to eat it, and when, or how to behave in certain situations, he may have trouble accepting all children, especially those who come to school with a different set of goods or bads than he has.

Prospective teachers should ask themselves how they feel about speech patterns, cleanliness, eating habits, manners, ways of doing tasks—why they feel as they do about these things and where they learned to think the way they do about them. Even with a clear understanding of their own value systems, teachers also need to be fully cognizant of the value systems of other ethnic and cultural groups.

Without full understanding of the children's backgrounds and cultural heritages, teachers may, without even knowing it, insult children, making them feel less than they should about themselves, their way of doing things, and the way of life that is acceptable to them. The basic lesson taught to the staff of every decent hotel, "Don't insult the clientele," should be a part of every teacher's basic attitude and behavior (Zais 1976, p. 161).

　It is also important that teachers of young children examine and gain an understanding of their own basic ideas about sex roles. Teachers might ask themselves how they feel about girls who are aggressive, who hit, fight, kick, scream, and get dirty, or boys who put on women's clothing and play with dolls and dishes. Teachers do, subtly and sometimes not so subtly, interact with girls in ways that differ from the ways they interact with boys and actually serve to perpetuate sex role stereotyping (Belotti 1978).

Observing nursery school teachers at work, Belotti (1978) found that boys were valued for what they would be and girls for what they would give. Girls, she suggested, aware of their lower status, tried harder to please, to be attentive and well behaved, while boys were already being rewarded for their potential.

Others (Serbin and O'Leary 1975) have also observed how teachers interact with boys and girls in a nursery school. In this study it was found that teachers rewarded girls for dependent behaviors, repeatedly paying attention to girls who clung to them, stood near them, or waited for directions. At the same time the teachers praised the boys for things they did on their own, for being independent.

Teachers also were found to challenge boys to try harder, to do a task again and achieve mastery over it. Perhaps this is because boys were not neat in their work, nor overly obedient. Girls, on the other hand, were never challenged to greater achievement. This challenge differential may be related to women in our society having achieved far less than men in certain fields of endeavor. Fewer than eighteen percent of all doctorates awarded in our nation go to women (Data Book 1977). Teachers of young children might ask themselves "could it be that women achieve less in society because, as girls, they were rewarded in nursery school for being dependent and obedient, or because no one has ever asked them to try harder or challenged them with tasks that required just a little more effort." (Serbin and O'Leary 1975, p. 40).

Searching Your Values

Froebel, Peabody, Montessori, and Hill succeeded in implementing their ideas. Part of their success, perhaps, was due to the clear idea they had about the nature of children. This idea provided them with a foundation on which to make choices and decisions and afforded a solid base from which to create programs for young children.

Beginning teachers often see little value in examining their personal philosophy or theory of the child. Theory, philosophy, and the social foundations of education do not seem important to them. "Give us ideas, show us how to teach, we'll pick up that theory later!" Teachers without a clear sense of their own values and belief system, and the ways this belief system is translated into practice, do not have a base or foundation on which to make decisions or to interpret events.

Teachers without theory to guide them base decisions on myths, folklore, old tales, what someone else said, or just plain common sense. Sometimes common sense, or doing what someone else said, is good and can work. But far too often making decisions which affect the lives of children without a theoretical base leads to haphazard, less-than-effective teaching.

Successful teachers have a basic idea of what they believe, a vision of where they are going, and an idea of what they believe children can become. The more clearly teachers perceive their own values and understand the theoretical base of teaching, the greater their chances of success. Beginning teachers who would like to reject examination of their own values and theory of teaching need to remember Justice Oliver Wendell Holmes's statement, "A theory is the most practical thing in the world."

CHILDREN ARE GOOD

Froebel knew exactly what he believed the nature of humankind to be. "Man as a child, resembles the flower on the plant, the blossom on the tree; as these are in relation to the tree, so is the child in relation to humanity—a young bud, a fresh blossom; and as such, it bears, includes and proclaims the ceaseless reappearance of new human life" (Froebel 1900, p. 7).

Certain that the child, by nature, was good, Froebel designed a garden for them. Here, in the kindergarten, children could grow freely, relating to one another in harmony with nature. In this garden for children, the child's natural goodness could unfold, as naturally as flowers develop, bud, and bloom.

This assumption about the nature of the child was not new; it was built from the philosophy of Jean Jacques Rousseau. In the book *Emile*, Rousseau stated his ideas that human beings, when living in a state of nature, isolated and without language, were good, but as soon as they begin to live together in society, they become evil. Rousseau argued that if humans were created by God, in God's image, then they came into existence uncorrupted and perfect. If children were not good, then it was the result of them having been exposed to a corrupt and imperfect society.

Believing that children are, by nature, good, leads to very definite conclusions about teaching, curriculum, and programs for young children. Rousseau's ideas are, in fact, used as the basis of many of today's programs.

> Again and again, modern thinking resounds in Rousseau's philosophy. In fact, Rousseau might be called the grandfather of modern psychology. He emphasized physical activity as the curriculum for young children. Children were to learn totally from their own direct experience and exploration of the environment, a point of view expressed earlier by Comenius and reiterated later by Pestalozzi, Froebel, Dewey and Piaget. (J. Frost and J. Kissinger 1976, p. 18)

Based entirely on the concept that children are innately wise and good, A. S. Neill developed the Summerhill school. According to Neill, children, if left to themselves—without adult suggestion of any kind—would develop into all they were capable of becoming. At Summerhill, children were permitted the freedom to be themselves. "We had to renounce all discipline, all direction, all suggestion, all moral training, all religious illustration. We have been called brave, but it did not take courage, all it required was that we had complete belief in the child as a good, not an evil being" (Neill 1960, p. 188).

To a certain extent the British Infant Schools, Bank Street model of planned variation, the nursery school of Harriet Johnson, and many other contemporary nursery schools embrace the idea that children are, by nature, good. Today's schools, however, are guided by more than a mere belief in the goodness of children. Maturational and child growth and development theories added scientific facts to the theory of the natural goodness of the child.

Arnold Gesell (who charted normal patterns of growth and development of children, suggesting that certain stages of development fit with specific ages of children), believed that growth was a more or less automatic unfolding of behavior. Maturation and time were necessary for this unfolding. All in all, the child growth and development theories of Gesell were consistent with those of Rousseau and Froebel.

Teachers today find these theories viable. When teachers accept the idea that children are good, that children proceed through normal stages of growth and development, stages that cannot be speeded up by any outward pressure, teachers act as guides to them. These teachers plan programs for children designed to permit children freedom of movement, expression, and thought. They trust children's natural patterns of growth and development and so do not push children to master tasks and skills believed to be inconsistent with the child's maturational level. Rather, these teachers plan programs and structure experiences that will foster the natural growth and development of children. Rather than imposing laws, rules, and punishments on children, these teachers create an environment that frees children to grow.

When teachers trust children, and their normal development, they plan for children to live within an enriched environment, replete with many choices of materials and opportunities for self-expression. These teachers use children's growth patterns, the ages and stages, as guides to planning activities. They attempt to find activities and experiences for the children that will enable them to use developing skills but never push for attainment of a skill or task before the children are ready. Often called child-centered, these teachers take cues from the children themselves as they plan activities. They look to the child for direction and see the child as the center of the teaching and learning processes.

CHILDREN ARE BAD

There was no doubt about the nature of the child in Colonial America. Under the Puritanical system, children were believed to be evil, born in and filled with Original Sin. The New England Primer begins, "In Adam's fall, we sinned all." It was from this belief in Original Sin that public education in our country began. The Old Deluder Satan Act, passed in 1647, made education compulsory (but not free), for every child in the Bay Colony. The purpose of this education was to teach children to read and to understand the principles of religion in order to be saved from Satan.

If children were bad, evil, soiled, damned, and helpless, it followed that they needed saving. When life is conceived of as a battleground where opposing spirits vie for human souls, souls that without saving will fall to Satan, then the treatment of children is usually punitive. It was believed that one could only attain goodness through suffering and the expiation of wrongdoing (Howard 1975, p. 63).

Unfortunately this ancient and negative view of children, a part of our heritage, is still very much a part of our value system today. We've all heard, at one time or another, a parent say, "Let her cry, it's good for her!" or "After all, she has to learn." "I hit her every time she says No; I won't have a spoiled child." And although the majority of theologians have a more positive view of the nature of children, some Sunday schools continue to teach that children are evil, and that to be saved, their stubborn, evil will must be broken through punishment.

> When we sin, we sometimes get spankings or scoldings or some other kind of punishment. Sometimes spankings and scoldings help us. Someone who loves us may spank or scold us to help us remember to be good next time. But spankings and scoldings still hurt. Satan doesn't like them to help us. But he sure likes them to hurt us a lot! Again and again and again and again. That's one reason he likes us to keep on doing mean things—so we'll get lots of punishment. (Mission Life 1976, p. 3)

Add to this idea the belief that children are born instinctively aggressive, antisocial, and hedonistic, a belief that stemmed from interpretations of the theories of Sigmund Freud, and you have children appearing in need of even more control and direction. Freud believed that humankind was basically antisocial and hostile, with behavior being directed by inner drives to satisfy pleasure seeking. When teachers believe that children are born in sin, and that they will spend the rest of their lives seeking self-gratification, it is easy to see how highly structured, sometimes punitive programs for children can develop.

The nursery school teacher who makes a very active, aggressive boy sit on a bench while the other children are running and playing outdoors, "so he'll learn he can't throw sand," instead of helping the child gain the skills he needs to work off excess energy and aggression, or the kindergarten teacher who refuses to give a child a treat, or special task, "because she's such a showoff and needs to learn she's not so special," may be acting on the belief that children are sinful, driven by needs for self-gratification.

Contrast the view of the child as sinful and hedonistic with that of Harriet Johnson, who in discussing the child's natural curiosity and activity wrote,

> The older theologians had a name for it. They called it "Original Sin" and spelled it with capital letters. It remained for the modern pedagogue to see that it could be capitalized in another way. She calls it the beginnings of scientific inquiry, and gives the young inquirers a laboratory; the classrooms and playgrounds of the newer education—provides materials, tools, space, time, equipment so basic impulses of children can be used. (Harriet Johnson 1936, p. 33)

Even without realizing it, teachers who endorse this view of the child may assign difficult and dull tasks for children to complete, with the idea that the more painful the activity, the better it is for the child. A second grade girl, forced to memorize the spelling of the days of the week, then to spell the months of the year—even though she has no concept of time or seasons—may have a teacher who believes that children's wills must be broken and that they must learn to obey in order to reach salvation.

Many of the trends in today's programs seem to reflect the idea that the more painful and boring a task, the better it is for children. The emphases on learning to read earlier and earlier, curricula that focus on teaching children colors, shapes, and numbers, and the expectation that children memorize meaningless material reflect the idea that children should not enjoy themselves too much, but should be bored and pained in order to reach salvation.

CHILDREN ARE REACTIVE

Some educators believe that children are neither bad nor good, but simply neutral, more or less passive, directed by others and the environment. Those who believe this way find the *behavioristic theory* of learning congruent with their ideas of human nature and children. Behaviorism is not a simple theory. There are many different theories collected under the title behaviorism. The term, however, has been used broadly to describe those theories based on *stimulus-response* or on *conditioning* as the foundation of learning.

The roots of all behavioristic theory can be traced to the original work of Ivan Pavlov, who by putting meat powder in dogs' mouths and tapping a tuning fork at the same time, found the dogs eventually would salivate at the sound of a tuning fork alone. Given the stimulus—the tuning fork—the dogs responded with salivation.

In America, Edward Thorndike called this stimulus-response, S–R bond theory, connectionism. Making the assumption that through conditioning, specific responses come to be linked with specific stimuli, Thorndike believed that the way these connections were formed was through trial and error. In the 1930s John Watson expanded and clarified Thorndike's ideas. Watson believed it was impossible to study thought processes, only behavior. Rather than speculate about learning as a change in mental states, he believed that psychologists should attend only to the objective and scientific study of behavior.

B. F. Skinner further refined and expanded these ideas. Skinner suggested that all human behavior is a product of *reinforcement*. People change others by arranging reinforcing consequences. Skinner uses the reinforcement theory to explain how we learn to walk, talk, read, or learn anything.

Today's behaviorists continue to refine and rethink the theory. Albert Bandura (1963) believes that behavior is influenced by its consequences, but also that it is not the paired experiences which result in learning but the learner's recognition of the relationship. Bandura thus sees the learner's ability to observe and infer as a part of the theory of behaviorism.

Variations of the behaviorists' approach are prevalent. A number of model programs such as Becker-Engleman, Distar, the Bushell model, and curriculum kits such as the Peabody Language Kit, and Sullivan Programmed Readers are based on some variation of the behaviorist theory of learning and the belief that children are indeed passive, reactive beings.

Teachers who accept the idea that children are passive and reactive believe that children are born with repertories of response capabilities and abilities to learn. That is, children can learn when the environmental circumstances are arranged in patterns that permit children to behave in certain ways, when specific consequences are produced. If a girl hangs up her coat, receives a reward—a smile, pat on the back, cookie from the teacher—immediately following the act of hanging up the coat, it is likely that the child will repeat the behavior. Rather than worrying about whether the child has learned the concept of hanging up a coat, it is the behavior that concerns the teacher. The coat is on the hook.

The teaching process begins when the teachers identify the behaviors they want the child to exhibit. The teacher is in control, deciding on the end behavior, leading the child to that behavior through directed tasks, and then observing the child to determine whether or not the child does, in fact, exhibit the desired behavior. To carry this sequence out, teachers write *behavioral objectives*, identifying the end behavior, the conditions under which the behavior will be exhibited, and in some cases, the number of times the behavior will be exhibited by a certain percentage of the children.

When teachers accept this theory, it is the teachers who are active. Children make few choices about what or how they will learn a given behavior or skill. It is the teacher who is in charge, planning, implementing, and evaluating. If children do not exhibit the behavior identified, then the teacher revises the plans and begins again.

CHILDREN ARE INTERACTIVE

Rejecting the idea that children are passive, educators today, like those of the past, believe that children are active beings, who learn only as they interact with the environment and with others. Teachers accepting the fact that children are interactive endorse the *cognitive developmental* theory of learning. These teachers believe that children are action-orientated, searching, seeking, adapting beings. Because children are viewed as active, rather than passive, teachers place stress on children's involvement with their environment. They provide numerous contacts with people, things, and processes within the environment and ask children to draw relationships between their experiences.

Those who see the child as an interactive being are not necessarily concerned with outcome behaviors. More important are the processes the child undergoes rather than the end behavior exhibited. Based on the works of Piaget, the cognitive developmental theory of learning focuses on how children think, and how the thinking process changes as the children grow, mature, experience, and interact with others and the environment.

The most basic assumption of cognitive theory is that human behavior is not determined in any direct way by the immediate situation in which it occurs. Intervening between the situation and behavior is cognition, the category or process of knowing. Children think about what they are doing, they don't simply react like a Pavlovian dog to the sound of a tuning fork. (W. D. Rohwer 1974, p. 109)

As the word *cognitive* implies, the cognitive developmental theory of Piaget is concerned with the thinking of the child. According to Piaget the child is an active participant in his own intellectual development and learning; his cognitive development proceeds through an invariant sequence of stages; progress through the stages is accomplished by *assimilation, accommodation,* and *equilibration;* and the stages of growth are characterized by qualitative differences in *cognitive structures*.

Teachers endorsing this theory believe that children construct their own ways of thinking, and their own ideas about the nature of reality. The child is the doer and learner, constructing an idea of the world around him or her through experiments with the world. Maturation and experience will determine the kinds of experiments children can do at any given time, but they will not learn unless they actually do the experimenting themselves. This idea that children are actively involved in their own intellectual development is the first cornerstone of Piagetian theory.

The second cornerstone is that the child proceeds through a series of *age-specific stages*, which do not change or vary in sequence, but are characterized by increasing objectivity and reality. A third cornerstone is that the progress through the stages is not haphazard, but systematic. The process requires some explanation using Piaget's vocabulary. To begin with, what a child knows is organized into a cognitive structure. The structure is "a general framework or form of thinking . . . a way of processing information" (Rohwer 1974, pp. 128–129). As children react to their environment, they take in information, mentally act upon it according to their current ways of thinking, and fit it into their existing cognitive structure through a process called assimilation.

As children act on this new information to assimilate it, they must also adjust their cognitive structure by a process called accommodation, to encompass this new information. As a result of this learning, the child has a somewhat new way of thinking about the world, as he or she looks for new information to assimilate.

The balance between assimilation and accommodation is called *equilibrium*. Equilibrium is a dynamic state that can always be changed by further assimilation and accommodation. A state of *disequilibrium* exists when children cannot reconcile their current views of reality with what they perceive.

An example from a nursery school teacher helps to clarify these ideas. The teacher tells of John, working at the sink with water, and a large selection of cups, bowls, bottles, pitchers and funnels.

Through a long series of "experiments" that looked like trial and error, John eventually learned the use of a funnel, assimilated that information into his previous knowledge of pouring, changed (accommodated) his pouring behavior so that he reached immediately for a funnel before starting to pour, and confirmed his new knowledge by delightedly pouring, with the aid of various funnels, to and from all sizes and shapes of containers. He had achieved equilibrium at a higher level of behavior than before.

On another day John was again at the sink. This time he was scooping up water with a bowl, pouring it through a funnel into a jar, and then transferring the water to a dishpan on the counter. He did this over and over with evident satisfaction. Then he started scooping up water with a plastic pitcher and pouring directly into the jar, apparently not paying attention to the fact that the pitcher was larger than the bowl he had been using. When the jar was full, he kept right on pouring, and seemed genuinely surprised at the overflow. He kept trying to get all the pitcherful of water into the jar, with growing puzzlement. He was in disequilibrium, according to Piaget's theory, because he could sense the inadequacy of his present structure (Rohwer 1974, p. 179) of cognition. What he saw contradicted with what he knew. I tried to help, but true to the dictum of Piaget that "telling children is not teaching" (Lavetelli 1968, p. 2), he did not understand. Eventually John solved the problem for himself, by his own activity and again achieved equilibrium at a still higher level of understanding about pouring water. (Hanes 1978, pp. 5–6)*

The last cornerstone of Piaget's theory of cognitive growth is that each stage of a child's development has its characteristic cognitive structures, and that these structures differ not only in complexity but also in a qualitative way. That is, when children acquire a new cognitive structure, they think according to a new set of rules, and therefore they are able to know things that they could not know before.

Teachers who endorse this view act differently from those who believe children are either passive or simply good or bad. There is more teacher initiative and intervention when teachers believe that children are interactive. Teachers add props and materials, suggestions for the use of the materials, and verbal labels to ensure that each child gets the most out of his or her explorations and experiences with the environment. For instance, a teacher may control the number, size, and shape of blocks and trucks children are to play with in order to help them develop classification skills. And she may use language in an exacting way, to foster children's thinking. "Which truck is first?" "How many blue blocks do you have?" "John's blocks are the highest now." "Susan is first in line." "Who has the most blocks in his garage?"

In this way the teacher is a provider of material and stimuli as well as a mediator of children's experiences. Beginning with the concrete experience, she draws children to the abstract with language, symbols, and pictures. This teacher looks on every aspect of children's lives as a means of learning and of teaching (Rohwer 1974), and sees herself as a professional who has the knowledge and skill to enable her to teach at the very moment the child is willing and able to learn.

This teacher is very much like those of the 1930s of whom Biber speaks (1977). These teachers, although they did not have the knowledge from Piaget today's teachers have, did believe that teaching consisted of (1) exploiting daily

*Reprinted by permission from Helen Hanes.

encounters—both physical and social, as well as encounters with materials—to stimulate children's thinking processes; (2) helping children in their cognitive search for relationships by providing varied opportunities for children to have direct contact with the environment, people and processes; and (3) using play as the major vehicle for learning and teaching.

In Summary

> The tragedy is that most people do not recognize the life and death nature of teaching, critical decisions of motivation, reinforcement, reward, ego enhancement, and goal direction. Proper professional decisions enhance learning and life; improper decisions send the learner towards incremental death in opennness to experience and inability to learn and contribute to life. (Howsam and others 1976, p. 15)

Today's teachers, like those in the past, will be forced to make many decisions that affect the lives of children and families. More than ever before, teachers today must have a clear understanding of self. They must know why they are doing things and be able to base decisions on knowledge of self, others, and theory.

There is no single value system or learning theory that will enable teachers to make the right decisions, or to decide which action is right or wrong. Nevertheless, an understanding of the various learning theories of Piaget, Thorndike, Skinner, and others is essential. Teachers must challenge both boys and girls of all races and cultures to achieve. Since the teaching process depends on the interaction of the child with the teacher and with the environment, it is important that the teacher provide numerous contacts with people, processes, and things. Furthermore, the teacher should see all aspects of a child's life as a means of instruction.

Recognition of your own values and feelings about the nature of children and teaching will permit objective decisions and actions. With this understanding there is a rationale for making decisions, a purpose for action, and the opportunity to become a thoroughly prepared professional.

Resources

These books may help the serious student gain insight and understanding of themselves and their profession.

ALMY, MILLIE, *The Early Childhood Educator at Work*. New York: McGraw-Hill Book Company, 1975.

BIGGE, L. M., *Learning Theories for Teachers*. New York: Harper & Row, Publishers, 1971.

ROHWER, WILLIAM, Paul Ammon and Phebe Cramer, *Understanding Intellectual Development*. Hinsdale, Ill.: The Dryden Press, 1974.

A part of becoming a professional educator is taking part in the activities of professional organizations. Joining together with others concerned with the welfare and education of young children is a valuable experience. The following are some of the organizations available for teachers of young children. Ask to be placed on their mailing lists to receive information on publications, meeting dates, and free or inexpensive materials.

National Association for the Education of Young Children
1834 Connecticut Avenue, N.W.
Washington, D.C. 20009

Association for Childhood Education International
3615 Wisconsin Avenue, N.W.
Washington, D.C. 20016

Child Study Association of America
50 Madison Avenue
New York, New York 10010

Family Service Association of America
44 East Twenty-Third Street
New York, New York 10010

Children's Defense Fund
1520 New Hampshire Avenue, N.W.
Washington, D.C. 20002

Child Welfare League of America
67 Irving Place
New York, New York 10003

Bank Street College of Education
610 West 112th Street
New York, New York 10025

ERIC Clearinghouse on Early Childhood Education
805 West Pennsylvania Avenue
Urbana, Illinois 61801

Play Schools Association
111 East Fifty-ninth Street
New York, New York 10022

Projects

1. Analyze your own view of the nature of children. Do you think children are born bad, good, or neutral? Where do you think your ideas of children came from? Did your own schooling and experiences contribute to your views? What are the implications of your ideas of children? What kind of teacher will you be?

2. Interview preschool teachers and Sunday school teachers to find out their views of children. Do they think children are good, interactive, learning beings? Can these teachers tell where their ideas came from and how these ideas influence their teaching, selection of materials, and interactions with children?

3. Search yourself and ask yourself the hard questions. How do you really feel about boys and girls. Do you believe that boys and girls are equals or that one sex is superior

to the other? How do you feel about children of cultural or racial backgrounds that differ from yours? Do you view differences as of value or to be avoided?

4. Visit a number of preschool situations and record every time you observe teachers interacting with children in ways that suggest they believe children are not basically good. Can you note other instances in which teachers interact with children and illustrate their belief in the interactive nature of children?

5. Read something written by A. S. Neill, S. Berieter and David Weikart, or Constance Kamii. Can you tell which theories are the bases for the writings of these authors? What of their ideas can you use? With which ideas do you concur? With which do you disagree?

References

ALMY, M., *The Early Childhood Educator at Work*. New York: McGraw-Hill Book Company, 1975.

BANDURA, A. and WALTERS, R. H., *Social Learning and Personality Development*. New York: Holt, Rinehart and Winston, 1963.

BELOTTI, E. G., *What Are Little Girls Made of: the Roots of Feminine Stereotypes*. New York: Schocken Books, 1978.

BIBER, B., "Cognition in Early Childhood Education: a Historical Perspective," in *Early Childhood Education: Issues and Insights*, eds. B. Spodek and H. J. Walberg, pp. 41–65. Berkeley, California: McCutchen Publishing Corporation, 1977.

BLOOMBERG, W., JR., "The Young Child in Cultural Change," *Young Children*, 22, 3 (1967), pp. 130–134.

Data Book. "The Status of Educational Research and Development in the United States." Washington, D.C.: U.S. Government Printing Office, 1977.

FROEBEL, F., *Pedagogics of the Kindergarten*. New York: D. Appleton and Company, 1900.

FROST, J. L. AND KISSINGER, J. B., *The Young Child and the Educative Process*. New York: Holt, Rinehart and Winston, 1976.

HANES, H., "My Understanding of Cognitive Development." Unpublished paper. College Park, Md.: University of Maryland, 1978.

HOWARD, A. E., "When Children Talk Back—Listen!" in *Early Childhood Education: It's an Art! It's a Science!* ed. J. D. Andrews. Washington, D.C.: National Association for the Education of Young Children, 1975.

HOWSAM, R. B., CORRIGAN, D. C., DENEMARK, G. W., and NASH, N. J.: "Educating a Profession." Washington, D.C.: The Bicentenniel Commission for the Profession of Teaching of the American Association of Colleges for Teacher Education, 1976.

HYMES, J., *Teaching the Child under Six* (2nd ed.). Columbus, Ohio: Charles E. Merrill Publishing Co., 1974.

JOHNSON, H., *School Begins at Two*. New York: New Republic, Inc., 1936.

LAVETELLI, C. S. "A Piaget-Derived Model for Compensatory Preschool Education," in *Early Childhood Education Rediscovered*, ed. J. L. FROST. New York: Holt, Rinehart and Winston, 1968.

Mission Life. St. Louis, Missouri: Concordia Publishing Co., 1976.

National Education Association, *The Status of the American Public School Teacher: 1975–1976*. Washington, D.C.: National Education Association, 1977.

NEILL, A. S., *Summerhill: a Radical Approach to Child Rearing*. New York: Hart Publishing Co., 1960.

O'DOWD, M. M., "Categories of Programs and Positions in Early Childhood Education." Milwaukee, Wis.: University of Wisconsin, 1978.

PIAGET, J., *Science of Education and the Psychology of the Child*. New York: Viking Compass Edition, 1971.

ROHWER, W. D., AMMON, P. P., AND CRAMER, P., *Understanding Intellectual Development*. Hinsdale, Ill.: The Dryden Press, 1974.

SERBIN, L. A., AND O'LEARY, K. D., "How Nursery Schools Teach Girls to Shut up," *Psychology Today* (December 1975), pp. 57–63.

WARREN, R. M., "Caring: Supporting Children's Growth." Washington, D.C.: National Association for the Education of Young Children, 1977.

WEBER, E., *The Kindergarten: Its Encounter with Educational Thought in America*. New York: Teachers College Press, 1969.

ZAIS, R. S., *Curriculum: Principles and Foundations*. New York: Thomas Y. Crowell Company, Inc., 1976.

3

Getting to Know the Children

Let the children lead you and you will not go far astray. Study them and let their actions serve as your guide!

Alice Putnam, 1924, p. 281.

Knowledge of young children is certainly not all one needs in order to become an effective teacher of young children. But if you do know children and have a clear understanding of how they learn and what their needs are, you have a point of departure for planning, a solid base on which to make decisions.

No one has the power to predict the future or foresee what new trends will come to early childhood education. We do know, however, that there will be demands, new challenges, and new priorities in the future. Early childhood education, once believed a pleasant way for children to pass their time, has today been given all-powerful qualities (Zimilies 1978). Because early childhood experiences have been called on in the past to break the poverty cycle—through Head Start—to support children and families, and to change communities, it will probably be called on again to help society solve new problems. It is as important as ever for teachers of young children to have a clear understanding of the nature of the child in order to make wise decisions for the future.

The world will change, attitudes toward children and learning will change, but some things will stay the same.

Study the children!

The growth of the child is much the same as it has always been. Attitudes toward children are changing, yet the human organism, especially during the early years of life, is not tremendously different from what it has been all along. . . . All children today, as all children in the past, develop in the same predictable patterned pathways . . . Only the grown ups seem to change and they, happily seem to be changing for the better in their increased concern, their more sympathetic and understanding approach to those children they love. (A. Gesell 1974, p. x)

Alice Putnam was right! If we look to the child as our guide it will be hard to make too many mistakes. Knowledge of children can "give direction to how and why children should be educated at various developmental stages. We need to make this knowledge more explicit and learn to use it if early childhood education is to function effectively during this period of expansion" (Zimilies 1978, n.p.).

Children Are the Same

All children are very much alike. They all grow, and their growth does follow predictable patterns. Development is continuous and organized; it takes a long time for a child to grow and develop, and the child cannot be hurried or pushed through the stages through which all must go.

Physical Development

Even though children of the same age vary in size and physical ability, every child's proportion is the same, and compared to that of an adult, it is all wrong. Children's heads are too large for their bodies, being about one-fourth of their total size. This seems to keep young children off balance. They are clumsy, and the word toddler very accurately describes the young child.

Two and three year olds walk with their legs far apart. They stand with their legs apart, as if to plant themselves against some oncoming breeze that could throw them down. They are uncertain about their bodies; and while two and three year olds do run, jump, climb, and walk, there is always that look of toddling, of not being really sure of their control over large muscles.

Four and five year olds, in contrast, are active and assured as they walk, run, skip, and climb. By four and five, children have even gained control over small muscles, they can use a crayon and paper, cut and paste, and even button coats and tie shoes.

Because young children are in a stage of physical development, they have a need for activity. They need to test out what they can and cannot do with their bodies. Teachers trying to eliminate physical movement from a preschool program are in trouble. The young must move; it is a part of every young child's needs and nature.

It is important for a teacher to realize this fact—for a child's physical activity is related to intellectual, social, and emotional growth. Learning comes only as a child interacts physically with the environment. As the children practice physical skills, and exercise large muscles, they grow in confidence and in knowledge.

Physical skills play an important, critical part, not only in the intellectual development of the child, but also in the child's social and emotional growth. A child who is sure of himself physically, who can run, who can catch a ball, is a child who has confidence in his own abilities, and has achieved mastery over self, and mastery over environment. With this confidence a child can reach out and learn to relate to others, to try new things, to learn.

Social/Emotional Development

Socially and emotionally, too, all young children are alike; they all go through identical stages. Yes, children do differ, but basically all are learning about their own emotions and how to relate to others. It is a difficult time for young children for there is so much to learn. First children must learn to separate from parents, and then, after learning who they are, they must learn to relate to others.

It is not easy to separate from parents. Children are so totally dependent upon adults for all of their needs that it is frightening to say no to, or to leave those same adults. But it is absolutely necessary. All children must learn to move away from the familiar relationships of home and neighborhood. Sometimes the child's entrance into a day care or early childhood program will be the first experience of separating from parents and learning to be an independent person.

This separation is necessary for children to become autonomous beings. At the same time, the preschool children (while developing autonomy) must learn to become a part of a group. They must learn to give up some of their newly developed autonomy and participate in the give and take, the cooperative efforts of living with others.

All young children have a difficult time with social relations because of their egocentric thought. They cannot see another's point of view. Only their own! Snatching a toy away from another child seems all right; the child wants it and cannot see that the other child may want it too. In fact, young children are often bewildered at the accompanying fuss the child whose toy has been taken away makes. As children grow intellectually, they grow socially. When children understand that others have ideas too, and that they will have to adjust their own ideas in order to get along with others, social relationships develop. When children can use language to communicate their own ideas, and understand the ideas of others, social relationships are facilitated.

Intellectual Development

Furthermore all young children are similar in their intellectual growth. Each experiences the same intellectual needs. All children learn through manipulation of the world about them. They learn as they physically move, explore, taste, smell, touch, and push the things in their environment.

Children are active learners. Their thought and actions are more interdependent than they will ever be again. According to Piaget (1969) the first stage of intellectual development is actually physical, and is called *sensori-motor intelligence*. Even when children advance through the first stage of sensori-motor intelligence, their need for activity does not stop as they grow intellectually.

The development of language is especially important for all children. In fact there is a question whether language and thought are the very same thing. There is agreement, however, that language and thought are closely related. Once a child can use words to label things in the environment it is easier to learn, for now the child can use a symbol—the word—to think about something that is not present.

Children Have the Same Needs

Just as all children are similar in their intellectual, physical, and social development, they are similar in their needs. Children today need to find the very same things in a preschool as did the children who met on Mrs. Schurz's front porch in Watertown, Wisconsin, so long ago.

Today's children need to find the same type of dedicated teacher—one who plans carefully to meet their individual needs. Some of these needs are as follows.

Physical Safety

A basic need of all living things is for physical safety. All children need food, shelter, and warmth. These needs remain throughout life. Growing children need a preschool program that provides time for physical exercise and rest, for nourishment, and for physical care. Children also need to begin to learn how their growth and development is related to the care they receive, the food they eat, and their physical activity.

Erikson (1950) believes that meeting the child's physical needs is important for the child to develop trust. A child who has not experienced being fed when hungry, or had other needs for physical care and comfort met by sensitive adults, may never develop a sense of trust. To Erikson, this sense of trust forms the basis of a child's sense of identity. This sense of identity, of knowing who one is, later becomes a feeling of competence to reach out to trust others and the environment.

Throughout the history of the world children have had a great need for security. First they must feel physically secure, and then they must have the security of being with adults who respect them as individuals and accept them as they are. When there are enough adults in a group of children, each child's individual needs can be met. Children can rest when they need to, play when they feel like it, and find nourishment when their bodies dictate it. This individual care contributes to feelings of security.

Security also comes when children find a consistency between their home and school. Even when values conflict between home and school, the child must have a feeling of congruence in order to develop security. This means a strong home-school relationship must be developed.

Freedom

Along with the need for security all children must have freedom. All young children must be free to initiate, plan, and attack their environment. The urge to take the initiative (acting and reacting with the environment and others), is basic to the lives of all young children.

Without this freedom to explore and manipulate, to probe and touch, to find out for themselves, children may never learn. As Froebel planned for children's self-activity, so must today's teachers recognize, and plan for each child's need to develop a sense of initiative by giving children space, materials, and the freedom to try out, to discover for themselves.

Companionship

Human beings are human, in part, because of their basic need to be with others. In a preschool setting, children can find the companionship they need. Here they can feel the satisfaction of becoming a part of a group, of doing and being with others.

Young children are attached to their own family group, and find companionship in their home and neighborhood. In a preschool group, they have the companionship of other children and other adults. Here children can learn to get along with others and have the opportunity to form close friendships and to learn standards for social behavior.

Every child needs to find a challenge, but each child must be challenged as an individual. Hunt (1961) calls this the problem of the match. If children do not perceive the preschool setting as challenging, they will not see any need to learn anything. If a challenge is there, but perceived as too great, then the child does not even dare to risk trying. Learning is simply too dangerous if the challenge is too great, for failure seems easy and is to be avoided.

A preschool program can introduce children to the challenge of the new and unknown, but must begin with things that are familiar to the child. Ever extending the familiar and secure so children will be willing and able to reach for new knowledge, and will dare to take a risk and learn, is a goal of all preschool programs.

Children Are Different

Each child is an individual. Children develop at their own rate and time, and in their own way. Within any group of preschool or primary school children, you are likely to find a wide range of individual differences.

Children will differ physically. Some five year olds are physically mature and are taken for seven year olds. Others have difficulty managing their own bodies and cannot sit still, walk, or run surely, or use crayons and scissors.

Many children are capable of controlling themselves, both physically and socially, so much so that they can gain control of others. Other children have difficulty facing their peers and are shy with strange adults. Many children seem intellectually mature, understanding abstractions and using information to make generalizations of the world about them. On the other hand, some children, of the same age, and in the same group, may just be learning to use words to represent things.

Children differ in the background of experiences they bring to the preschool. To a certain extent this background influences their total development. There is a strong relationship between children's experiences and their intellectual, social, and emotional growth. "We must consider each human individual as unique in the expression of his biocultural heritage—almost a biocultural species in himself" (Cobb 1977, p. 16).

Understanding the individuality of each child permits effective teaching. Teachers must learn all they can about individual children, about their individual needs, abilities, likes, dislikes, and strengths. Teachers can learn about children through direct observation, parent conferences and home visits, as well as through standardized tests.

Getting to Know All Children

"I take a step back and observe children. Children are individuals with different likes, dislikes and abilities. As they grow they surprise us constantly with new changes and challenge us to relate to them in new ways" (Chan 1978, p. 56). One way to learn about children's individuality is to observe them closely.

Learning to observe children is both an art and a science. It is not something that automatically develops as you begin to work with children. Observing takes time, study, and practice to learn and refine. "One needs to be an insider, taking the perspective of the child's environment and experiences, constantly relating to the child in new ways and growing with the child" (Chan 1978, p. 62).

Observing is very important in understanding the young child. You don't get very far when you ask young children to tell about themselves or to explain their behavior. Children's vocabulary is limited as is their understanding of their own feelings. One child repeated over and over, "I was brave when I went to the doctor, very brave, really brave. What does brave mean?"

Even test and personality rating scales or projective instruments, although they provide some help in understanding children, are not as effective with preschoolers as they are with older children. "For the present, our best technique seems to be the careful gathering of evidence via the on the spot record" (Cohen 1968, p. 1).

Piaget learned much about the nature of children through careful observation and record keeping on his own three children. Piaget observed his children in unstructured situations as they played or were being cared for and in structured settings where he recorded the child's response. One observation was made by hiding a baby's rattle under a blanket. The baby did not look for the rattle, and Piaget concluded that the baby was not able to think of something he could not see. Later Piaget repeated the experiment and found that as children grow, they will search for the rattle.

Other obsrevations were made by Piaget with the use of questions. Piaget probed children's thought processes, observed and recorded their responses, and gained insights into their thinking. When Piaget asked a child, "Can clouds feel the wind or not?" and the child answered, "Yes, it drives them"; or "If I pull this button off, will it feel it?" and received the answer "Yes, because the button would break"; he learned that children attribute consciousness to things, just as they do to themselves.

Historically nursery school teachers have used observations of the children as a base for their planning and curriculum. The training of the early kindergarteners called for learning to keep records and noting the children's performance on specific tasks. During the 1930s teachers were trained to observe children, and to objectively record their observations, drawing conclusions about the growth of the child from a number of recorded anecdotes. By collecting observations of particular children throughout a day, week, or even school year, a teacher could identify the ways children learned, interacted— with others and materials—as well as strengths and weaknesses, likes and dislikes.

It takes practice to learn to observe meaningfully. A student teacher completing an observation on a particular child reported that the child was anxious and uncomfortable in the classroom, nervous with other children. The student teacher was not observing, but actually inferring and concluding.

She was asked to repeat the observation on another day, but this time was told to report only the behaviors of the child. The student then reported, "The child's hands shook as she worked the puzzle." "She twitched and wiggled in her chair at snack time, spilling the juice." "As she walked across the room her body seem to twitch with every step she took." This observation described the behavior of the child, a child who had been diagnosed as having a form of brain damage that resulted in uncertain body control and twitching. Rather than the child being nervous with others, uncomfortable with the group, she had a physical problem.

Observations should always focus on the behavior of the child. Calling a child anxious, or emotionally disturbed, does not help the child, teacher, or other professional understand the child. Describing behaviors, however, in a number of different situations over a period of time does provide information about the individual child that can be used to plan the best educational experiences, or support services for the child.

When the focus of the observation is on the behavior of the child, within a given situation, the observation is more accurate and objective. All observations, even when focused on a specific behavior, will nevertheless have a measure of the observer's subjectivity. Just the act of deciding what to observe and what to record permits a person's value system and beliefs to enter into the process; but it is possible to learn to control subjectivity when observing children.

Beginners have often found that working in teams, recording their individual observations of the same child at the same time period, and then comparing the two records for similarities and differences, is useful in building objectivity. Asking an experienced teacher to read and react to one's observations of a child she is familiar with can also aid in learning to focus observations objectively on the behavior of children.

Just as a scientist carefully describes the results of an experiment, using words that are accurate and descriptive, a teacher can use language as a tool in recording objective and meaningful observations of children. Such verbs as stomp, strut, run, walk, and skip describe different ways of moving across the room.

Cohen (1968) suggests that teachers become accustomed to using descriptive language when recording observations. She gives a number of useful synonyms:

happy—jubilant, cheerful, bubbling, bouncy, sparkling, delighted, cheerful, content.

sad—mournful, wistful, depressed, downhearted, gloomy, heavy-hearted, melancholy.

run—stampede, whirl, dash, dart, speed, bolt.

say—whisper, bellow, shout, scream, roar, lisp, whine, demand, tell, murmur.

cry—wail, howl, whimper, fuss, bawl, sob, mourn, weep.

Taking complete observations adds to their meaning. Children do not live in a vacuum, so it is important to record a complete observation, telling something of the situation the child was in, the bit of behavior observed, and something of the setting or situation prior to the observation. Note the time of day and other aspects of the event—any factors that may be important or have contributed to the behavior—and then some record should be made of what followed the observation. This provides a total picture for use in describing the child, rather than just a depiction of an isolated bit of behavior.

GUIDELINES FOR OBSERVING

Some guidelines can be followed for observing children. Teachers will want to focus on every aspect of the child's development, and complete observations in a number of different settings and situations over a period of time.

Focusing on all aspects of the child's development will give a teacher an extensive description of the child. Some observations should focus on children's physical development. A description of physical condition and appearance including build, height, and weight can be useful as a point of departure. Then the teacher can note how children use their bodies in play, with materials and equipment, and with others, what parts of the body are under control; which areas of physical development seem less or more developed; how small and large muscles are used; and what skills need further work. These observations, when compared over time, will pinpoint areas of growth, strength, and need.

Other observations should focus on children's social life and development by describing how children relate to others. Teachers can see what children do when they are alone; how they enter a group, how they initiate contact with others, and what happens when they are interrupted in the midst of an independent activity. Some additional things that might be noted are the types of verbal and nonverbal interactions that take place, the child's expressions and body positions, as well as the other children's reactions. Observations should be made when the child is alone, with small groups of children, and with large groups, as well as when the child is interacting with other adults, or with adults and siblings within the family.

Children's emotional development should also be observed. Teachers can record how children meet frustrations and hostility, how they exhibit attachment behaviors, and how they handle and release aggressive feelings. Problem solving, attention getting, and tension building are other areas of concern. Further cues to emotional development can be found in children's behavior during separation and reunion at the beginning and the end of the day.

Children's intellectual growth should provide focus for other observations. Such skills as the ability to understand and use language—as seen in the type of words and length of sentences used—to make decisions, and solve problems can all be observed and recorded. Other signs of intellectual growth might include the amount and type of curiosity children exhibit, their ability to relate past events to the present, their knowledge of the world as revealed in play, and the types and purposes of questions they ask.

Often the free play time, either indoors or outside, provides the ideal opportunity to conduct observations. During free play children can be observed counting, talking to others, labeling their environment, solving problems, and interacting with others. They will take on roles of adults they know and show their emotions through their play. Teachers are also able to record behaviors during free activity time as they move through the room working with individuals or small groups of children.

Even though it is easy and useful to make observations during free activity time, it is important that observations be conducted over a period of time, in a variety of situations. Cohen (1968) suggests that observations be conducted throughout the day, some in open-ended situations, others during routines, and still others when children are in a more structured group activity. Observations can take place during snack or lunch, rest, nap, and group times. A sample of behaviors in all situations can add up to a meaningful description of the child's total development See Figure 3–1 for sample observations that focus on one brief behavior episode of individual children.

USING THE OBSERVATIONS

"Observations provide a way of becoming acquainted with children's interactions . . . through observations it is possible to identify differences in the ways children learn. Because the planning done in any classroom is de-

FIGURE 3–1

Sample Observations

---

1. Navone—Use of Materials   Tuesday, A.M., September 4
Navone at sand table. Pulls for and grabs every toy or tool in reach. Does not walk around box to get other tools. Piles up containers next to her, shoves all spoons in left hand. Begins using spoons, taking one at a time from left hand, tosses sand with spoon, discards, then uses the next spoon. Navone begins filling containers with sand and then dumping the sand out. Doing this with each container, she then brushes her hands off and runs to dramatic play area. Total time at sand table—three minutes.

2. Robert—Relation to Adults   Monday, A.M., February 10
Robert runs to the school door, leaving his mother far behind. Entering room he tosses coat on hanger and runs to the blocks calling to the other children, "Hey Margaret, Kat, come build the airport." Mother walks over to Robert and says "good-bye." Robert barely looks up from the blocks and says, "See ya later."

3. Susan—Relation to Peers   Wednesday, P.M., March 4
Susan sits at the clay table with Juan, Penny, and Andrea. Modeling clay, tongue depressors, and rolling pins on table. Susan pats clay, looks at Juan without smiling. Penny and Andrea begin sing-song "Patty, watty, fatty clay" and giggle. Susan smiles at them, but doesn't speak, giggle, or enter into song. Juan reaches and grabs her clay stick, she looks at him and letting him have the stick, continues patting her clay.

---

pendent upon an awareness of these factors, a good teacher must use observations daily" (Lindberg and Swedlow 1976, p. 3). To Lindberg, observing and teaching are the same thing. Knowledge of the children is required for planning and teaching as well as for evaluation of children, teacher, and program.

When the teacher's observations of children are objective and systematically completed, they provide a base for more than teaching. State departments of education and local school systems have mandated observations of children in order to identify and diagnose children with special needs. Based on the idea that preschool children with potential learning disabilities can be identified through teacher observations, and that once identified the potential problems can be resolved, early screening and identification programs have been implemented in many states. "The purpose of the system is to evaluate student behavior over a long period of time within the classroom environment and to offer teachers immediate feedback from children. The system is based on a strong and enduring commitment to provide successful learning experiences for children before a pattern of failure is established" (Maryland State Department of Education 1975).

When children are observed under similar circumstances, or completing tasks, over at least a five-day period, Raskin (1975) believes that behaviors that are similar, yet deviate from the norm, can be identified. This identification can then serve as the basis for referring children for further observation, screening, or testing. For children with special needs, a teacher's accurate obser-

Informal testing is one way to learn about children.

vations may serve as the base of discussion when he meets with other professionals working with the child. These observations communicate to others how the child behaves in the classroom, the progress that is being made, or the areas of development in need of help.

Observations of the children will also be useful in meeting with parents. Discussing the child's growth and development with a clear observational record in hand will lead to a productive conference.

There are cautions when recording observations of children. Confidentiality must be respected with recorded observations. When sharing observations with other professionals, perhaps members of a health or social services team, it is understood that the information must be kept confidential. The professional understands and respects the responsibility of passing on every understanding about a child, but also understands that the information will be used in confidence, to benefit child and family.

> Statements about a child should never be made in front of him or other children. It is equally important to refrain from talking about any classroom observations or other school business outside the school, no matter how great the temptation. Talking to a colleague about a child on a bus or in other public places is professionally unethical. (L. Lindberg and R. Swedlow 1975, p. 8)

USING OTHER TYPES OF OBSERVATIONS

There are other types of observations that can be made. Sometimes teachers will use a rating form, or checklist of behaviors for which to look. These forms are available from school systems, or in textbooks on child growth and development. They might include such items as

1. Can select an activity and follow through to completion
2. Uses verbal means of expressing anger rather than physical
3. Shows confidence with others
4. Respects the rights of others
5. Uses equipment with care
6. Dresses self

In addition to informal rating scales, other types of observational instruments can be used. Some of these may be standardized and can be used by an outside observer to record teacher and child behaviors within a classroom.

Standardized Testing

Teacher observations, rating scales, and standardized observations are useful in collecting information that helps teachers understand children, and describe a child's progress in relation to other children in the class. Standardized tests are simply another form of observation of a child's behavior. Such a test, however, differs from teacher observations in that it gives a measure of a sample of behavior, under prescribed conditions, that can be compared with a larger population of children. The standardized score lets a teacher know where a child stands in relation to a given population of children at a regional or national level. It is like a map on which the individual's present position can be located (Anastasi 1976, p. 6).

In an attempt to document the effectiveness of preschool-primary programs, school systems, state departments of education, and programs funded with Federal money, teachers often give standardized tests to children. These scores let the school system or funding agency know how well the children did on a specific task in comparison to children in the rest of the nation. Even when school systems do not mandate the use of standardized tests, some teachers give the tests and find that the test scores are useful as a means of evaluating individual children and teaching programs.

Scores from a standardized test for individual children or from a class can also be used by teachers as a diagnostic tool. Teachers can look at the test scores and determine which children or groups of children need additional time or experiences to master specific skills or materials. Standardized test scores have also been used to help people predict how well a child will do in some future situation. If a preschool child does well on a standardized measure of reading readiness, the teacher has a piece of information that may predict the child's success in the first grade.

There are many different types of standardized instruments. Some are paper and pencil tests that are given to groups of children, others are administered on an individual basis using interview techniques. There are tests of reading readiness, school readiness, achievement, intelligence, self-concept, concept attainment, and physical development, as well as batteries designed to assess social and/or emotional and personality factors.

Because the tests are standardized, they must be given exactly according to the directions in the test manual. Any time a teacher deviates from the directions in the manual when administering or scoring a standardized test, the standardization is destroyed, and the score no longer has meaning. Because of this, teachers must be familiar with the examination procedures before giving the test to children. The teacher should review the test manual and then practice giving the test to another teacher or to a small group of children who will not be taking the test.

Most teachers are anxious to know all they can about a child. The more a teacher knows, the more information he has, the better he is able to plan for children's needs, and the more effective he will be. The standardized test is a useful tool to collect information about children. But it is only that, a tool, and one of many tools at hand.

CAUTIONS

Older children are used to following directions and sitting for long periods of time. They are able to understand verbal instructions and do not pose the same problems younger children do during the administration of standardized tests. Young children, with their egocentric thought, often have their own ideas of how to take a test, and frequently these ideas are not what the test makers had in mind.

Christie Marie reported to her mother, the day the reading readiness tests were administered, that she must have done the best in the class because she finished marking every page of the booklet before the teacher had given all of the children a booklet. Robert proudly told his mother about taking a test given at the end of the preschool program, "I told that lady I did that for her when I came to school and I wouldn't do it again; she was dumb!"

For any number of reasons, some known only to the young egocentric child himself, the taking of a standardized test is foreign. There is nothing you can do to convince a child to answer, respond, or react in the manner the test constructors had in mind.

Then too, if the teacher does not administer the test himself, the child may be shy, negative, or stubborn when confronted by a stranger asking probing questions. Testing preschool children often requires much flexibility on the part of the tester and the ability to turn the testing situation into a game of attracting and holding a young child's attention, though this may not be desirable, or permitted, under the conditions of the standardized test.

The limited attention span of preschoolers is another problem in administering tests. Some children are likely to get up and leave in the middle of a test. If they do consent to sit through an entire test, they might lose interest and answer haphazardly, without thought and motivation.

Even if the testing situation does go smoothly and children seem to enjoy the experience and stick with it, the teacher should remember that the results of a test tell only how well a child did in relation to a given population of children. Assessing something as complex as a child calls for collecting a lot of information, and the score on a standardized test is just one sample of a child's behavior at one point in time.

SELECTING TESTS

Often no one asks a teacher what kind of test she believes is best for the children. School boards, committees, or researchers often make that decision for the teacher; yet, whenever possible, it is important for the teacher to be involved in selecting the tests. A test must be well chosen and appropriate for both the children and the program. The teacher is, perhaps, the one most able to decide the appropriateness of any given test, for it is he who knows the children and the program better than any other person.

When looking over different standardized tests that are available a teacher might ask:

1. Is the test efficient? How long will it take to give the test? How much time will it take from the school day and who will give it? Can an aide or volunteer be trained to give the test to individual children or to assist if the test is to be given to the entire group?

2. How valid is the test? Does the test, in fact, assess what it says it does? Sometimes a test is said to be valid because the scores a child receives on it correspond to the scores on some other tests that claim to measure the same thing. A test can also be said to be valid if it predicts with accuracy. A test of reading readiness that predicts accurately—who will, and who will not, succeed in the first grade— can be called valid. The content of a test should also be valid. Here is where the

classroom teacher should be consulted in test selection. If the content of the test is based on Piagetian tasks, and the goals of a program are not, the test content cannot be called valid for that class. A test whose content focuses on letters and numbers, when the goals of the program are the process skills of thinking and reasoning, cannot be considered valid for that program.

3. Is the test reliable? It is also important to select tests that are reliable and measure the same behavior each time they are given. Children should score consistently on each administration or on different parts of the same test.

4. Has the test been developed on children whose backgrounds are similar to the children to whom it will be given? The concern that many standardized tests have been developed on white, middle-class children is of critical importance. Because many tests were developed on middle-class children, they are not appropriate for children of minority groups or children who are from other cultures and classes. These tests do not take into acount the attitudes, characteristics, or background of experiences minority or lower-class children bring to the testing situation; they have been called culturally biased for they favor one group of children over others. It is probably impossible for any test not to reflect the majority culture in which it was developed, but it is important for a teacher to understand that children from backgrounds that differ from those of middle-class children may score differently on these tests.

Tests that have been developed on middle-class populations cannot tell how well culturally or educationally disadvantaged children might have done had they been reared in a more advantageous environment. Anastasi (1976) believes that rather than develop tests that compensate for cultural deprivation or eliminate the effects of such deprivation from the test scores, tests should reveal the effects of being reared in poverty so that

> . . . appropriate remedial steps can be taken. To conceal the effects of cultural disadvantages by rejecting tests or by trying to devise tests that are insensitive to such effects can only retard progress toward a genuine solution of social problems. Such reactions toward tests are equivalent to breaking a thermomenter because it registers a body temperature of 101°. (A. Anastasi 1976, p. 60)

Test scores can be used constructively, even when the test was designed for a specific population. These scores, if the teacher recognizes that they do not fully describe a child's progress, can be used to (1) adjust instruction to individual needs; (2) help a teacher recognize individual differences, and (3) achieve a better match between the child's home and school background. The scores, however, can never be used to label children, to discriminate against them, or to group them into segregated classes.

5. How will children with special needs take the test? When children who are speech, hearing, or visually impaired are in the classroom, how can the test be administered to these children? What adjustments can be made to permit all children, even those with handicaps or special needs, to manage the procedure of taking the test?

USING TYPES OF TESTS

There are tests of achievement, intelligence, psychomotor skills, creativity, and social-emotional characteristics. The Buros *Mental Measurements Yearbook* (1972) reviews available tests in use today.

Achievement Tests. People are interested in what a child has achieved or learned in a preschool setting. Most achievement tests will assess what a child has learned in school. They are designed to measure the extent to which children have acquired specific objectives of the school or have benefited from school instruction. The Caldwell *Cooperative Preschool Inventory* is one achievement test designed to measure what a child has achieved in a preschool. The *Cooperative Preschool Inventory* is easily administered to individual children. It gives a teacher some indication of a child's social knowledge, concepts—both verbal and numerical—and perceptual motor knowledge. It only takes about ten–fifteen minutes to administer, and because it actively involves the child in a number of interesting tasks, it is both easy and enjoyable to give.

Readiness tests are another form of achievement tests. These tests, however, are purported to predict a child's readiness for learning, or a child's attainment of prerequisite skills, knowledge, attitudes, motivation, and other traits that should permit success in school. The *Metropolitan Readiness Test* is one example of a widely used readiness test. It has a verbal, number recognition, listening, comprehension, and letter recognition subtest. It is given to a group, usually by the classroom teacher. It is administered orally, and children mark in booklets. The test does seem to be a good predictor of success in school.

Intelligence Tests. Intelligence tests, as compared to achievement tests, are supposed to assess a child's aptitude or general ability. The *Stanford Binet* is the most widely known intelligence scale, but it requires a trained psychologist to administer it. Other intelligence tests gain validity by comparing the scores a child makes on them with the score the child makes on the *Binet*.

Alfred Binet was commissioned by the French government in the early 1900s to devise a method of selecting feebleminded children from the population of school children so these children could be placed in special classes. Binet, collaborating with Théodore Simon, devised a number of tasks that were graded in difficulty according to the proportion of children who could pass them. The tasks were based on common sense, adaptability, and judgment.

Piaget also worked with Simon and Binet on the development of these tasks. He became so intrigued with the wrong answers children gave to some of the items that he gave up the study of biology to study the mental thought processes of children.

The *Binet* test received wide acceptance in America during the early 1900s. The test gradually became known as the "granddaddy of all intelligence tests." It has been used to assess the effectiveness of preschool programs and to diagnose educational needs of children and adults; clinical psychologists use it as a screening device.

Because the *Binet* does require a trained psychologist to administer it, other intelligence tests are usually used by preschool teachers. Among the many scales available, the *Peabody Picture Vocabulary Test* is widely known. All this test requires is that a child point to the picture the examiner verbally describes. The *Peabody* has been widely used to assess the effectiveness of preschool programs. It is easy to administer, quick, and usually of interest to children.

Social Emotional Tests. It is also of interest for educators to assess characteristics of children other than intelligence and achievement. Knowledge of the child's self-concept, emotional adjustment, attitudes toward school, and other emotional variables provides a preschool teacher with useful information for diagnostic and evaluative purposes. Some social-emotional tests ask children to tell about themselves, to make self-reports, and others ask the teacher to infer, based on observations, children's emotional or social adjustment.

Creativity. Other tests assess the child's level of creativity. Unlike an intelligence or achievement test, a test of creativity assesses *divergent thought*. The intelligence and achievement tests demand the one correct answer while the creativity test accepts many divergent answers. The creativity tests are scored on the basis of the quality and quantity of divergent responses the child gives. The *Torrance Tests of Creative Thinking* are available for use with children as young as five years of age. The tests ask children to draw pictures, or to complete pictures or stories; they are scored on the basis of the originality, flexibility, elaboration, and fluency of the child's responses.

Psychomotor Tests. There are a variety of standardized instruments assessing the child's psychomotor capability. The *Developmental Test of Visual Motor Integration*, for children between the ages of two and eight, can be administered by a classroom teacher. Other tests of psychomotor skills include the *Marianne Frostig Developmental Test of Visual Perception* and the *Purdue Perceptual Motor Survey*.

USING TEST RESULTS

There is much concern about the use of standardized test scores with young children. When the test score is the only item of information available on a child, and decisions are made on the basis of this one score, the concern is valid. It is certainly impossible to believe that a score on one test tells very much about the multidimensional nature of the young child.

Preschool educators are offended when children are grouped on the basis of a test score. Labeling and grouping preschool children as slow, average, or fast because of one score on a standardized test is dangerous, discriminatory, and erroneous. Children, once labeled and grouped, often remain in the same group throughout their school life and are denied the opportunities to achieve their full potential. Then too, grouping children on the basis of a score discriminates against each child for it negates interactions between children who possess different characteristics.

The error in labeling and grouping children on the basis of a test score is that teachers may believe that all of the children in the group have identical needs. It is known that within any group of children, the differences between the children are great. When a group is constructed on the basis of likeness of test scores, a teacher may present activities and instruction inappropriate for many in the group.

Teachers must develop a common sense approach to the use of standardized testing. Tests do provide useful information to a teacher and a school system. But as Skinner (1968) states, a test score is just one piece of information and gives little assurance that the child will make use of what he knows . . . the ability to mark answers on a test booklet or standardized test is, after all, a relatively rare form of behavior.

REPORTING TEST RESULTS TO PARENTS

Parents have a legal right to know when their children are being tested, for what purpose, and how their child has done on the test. Any time a school system, teacher, or researcher tests a child, there is an obligation to communicate the test results to the child's parents in a way that is understood by the parents. The teacher may choose to have a conference with the parent or to report the results of the test in writing, but whatever method is selected, the information given to the parent must be accurate.

First, know the child and the parents. Think about what previous knowledge the family has of standardized testing. Have they, for instance, taken tests themselves when they graduated from grade or high school? How were these test results reported at the time? It may be that a teacher can use the parent's background of experiences as a base on which to present the child's testing information.

Next, the teacher should be familiar with the test and the meaning of the test results. You can look carefully at the content of the test so you can explain the various items of the test to the parents and tell what kinds of skills and qualities the items are measuring. You can also tell the parents how the child stands in relation to others of similar backgrounds across the country. If you are unsure, then you must ask for help from the school system, principal, or test administrator.

It is also important not to focus only on the test results. There are other types of information to share with parents based on your objective observations of the child working with others on a daily basis. The kind of work the child has done in the class, other test scores, and rating scales can all be used when reporting test results to parents, and help to place the one score on a standardized test in perspective.

In Summary

If you want to become one of those teachers who really care, who can really make a difference, you will have to get to know children. Getting to know children requires some work. Children are complex individuals, in many ways they're alike, yet each is so very different. Learning to observe objectively and carefully, and learning to use observations, are two big steps in getting to know children. Through observations, the teacher can note and record childrens' physical development, social and emotional growth, and intellectual progress in order to meet individual needs and to strengthen or promote individual abilities. Observations may be shared with other professionals and parents.

Standardized tests can be criticized, but the results can be informative. Although these tests may have built-in biases, they provide a useful basis for comparing individual children and groups with children across the nation. Standardized tests are designed to examine achievement, intelligence, social and emotional development, creativity, and psychomotor skills. The results must be shared with parents, but such sharing should include other dimensions of the child's experiences in school. Intelligent understanding of the results of tests can lead to a greater understanding of individual children.

Resources

There are a number of resources to help teachers develop the skills of observation.

COHEN, DOROTHY, and V. STERN, *Observing and Recording the Behavior of Young Children*. New York: Teachers College Press, 1968.

GESELL, ARNOLD, FRANCES ILG, and LOUISE BATES AMES, *Infant and Child in the Culture of Today*. New York: Harper & Row, Publishers, 1974.

LINDBERG, LUCILLE, and RITA SWEDLOW, *Early Childhood Education: A Guide for Observation and Participation*. New York: Allyn & Bacon, Inc., 1976.

Projects

1. Sharpen your skills of observation. Spend at least one hour observing a specific child in a preschool. How does the child relate with others, handle routines and frustration? Note how the child investigates the world. What senses does she use? Record the language the child uses. What questions does she ask, what vocabulary does she use?

2. At another time observe four children of the same sex and age. Try to find ways these children are similar and ways they are different.

3. From a university library, curriculum laboratory, or testing center, obtain sample tests used to assess preschool children. Examine these tests and note the types of information different ones would yield. If you can, interview a teacher of young children to find out what tests she uses and how she uses the results of these tests to better understand children.

References

ANASTASI, A., *Psychological Testing* (4th ed.) New York: Macmillan, Inc., 1976.

BUROS, O.K., *The Seventh Mental Measurements Yearbook*. Highland Park, N.J.: The Gryphon Press, 1972.

CHAN, I., "Observing Young Children, a Science, Working with Them an Art," *Young Children*, 33, 2 (1978), 54–64.

COBB, E., *The Ecology of Imagination in Childhood*. New York: Columbia University Press, 1977.

COHEN, D.H. and STERN, V., *Observing and Recording the Behavior of Young Children*. New York: Teachers College Press. Columbia University, 1968.

ERIKSON, E., *Childhood and Society*. New York: W.W. Norton & Co., Inc., 1950.

GESELL, A.; ILG, F.L.; and AMES, L.B.; *Infant and Child in the Culture of Today* (rev. ed.) New York: Harper & Row, Publishers, 1974.

HUNT, J. McV., *Intelligence and Experience*. New York: The Ronald Press, 1961.

LINDBERG, L., and SWEDLOW, R., *Early Childhood Education: A Guide for Observation and Participation*. Boston: Allyn & Bacon, Inc., 1976.

Maryland State Department of Education. Maryland Systematic Observation Instrument. 1975. Baltimore, Md.: Maryland State Department of Education.

PIAGET, J., and INHELDER, B., *The Psychology of the Child*. New York: Basic Books, Inc., Publishers, 1969.

PUTNAM, A., In *Pioneers of the Kindergarten in America*. New York: The Century Co., 1924, 204–233.

RASKIN, L.W.; TAYLOR, W.J.; and KERCKHOFF, F.G.; "The Teacher as Observer for Assessment: A Guideline," *Young Children*, 30, (1975), 339–345.

SKINNER, B.F., *The Technology of Teaching*. Englewood Cliffs, N.J.: Prentice-Hall, Inc., 1968.

ZIMILIES, H., "Early Childhood Education: A Selected Overview of Current Issues and Trends," *Teachers College Record*, 79, 3 (1978).

4

Learning about Children with Special Needs

All children have needs, but some children's needs are more extensive than others.

Day Care: Serving Children With Special Needs, 1972, p. 8.

Some children do need more than others. Children who are handicapped, abused, or particularly talented do have special needs that must be met in a preschool. Today there is great concern that all schools meet the needs of each child without labeling, isolating, or segregating any child. Because of this concern for the rights of all children to develop their full potential, special focus has been given the abused, gifted, or handicapped child.

Children with special needs have not always been considered in our school system. Although there are reports of schools for retarded children established during the 1800s, it really was not until the turn of the century that even scattered attempts were made to provide educational experiences for children with handicaps or special needs.

In 1922 the Council for Exceptional Children was formed and began to advocate on behalf of children with unique or special needs. During the 1940s and 1950s federal funds were allocated to provide education in the form of separate schools, classes, or home tutoring for children with special needs. These programs, however, segregated the child with special needs from others. An awakening concern for the rights of all persons fostered by the Civil Rights

58

movement of the 1960s focused the nation's attention on the rights of all people, especially those who needed more than others.

The Least Restrictive Environment

All children should have the opportunity to be with others and to develop their full potential in a nonrestrictive environment. Children with handicaps and special needs were being denied the opportunity to learn to live and relate within a normal world. A father seeking a regular preschool program for his cerebral palsied daughter explained, "she will go to a hospital one day a week for physical and speech therapy and continue to attend the special education program two days a week, but for two days I want her to be just a child, to play and to learn to live in a nonhandicapped world." This statement sums up the essence of the recent attempts to provide all children with appropriate educational programs (Cohen 1975).

> Segregated programs did nothing to help the handicapped child get along in the world of the nonhandicapped. Without experiences relating to children and adults who were not handicapped, the child with special needs didn't learn the social skills of relating to others. Enrolled in an integrated group during the early years the handicapped child can learn the ways of the world and some of the problems to be faced . . . as a result of these experiences the child will begin to feel able to function among other people in spite of the disability—that the child has control of his or her life. (Klein 1975, p. 319)

Through integrated programs, playing with one another, children with and without handicaps will learn to relate with one another without embar-

All children have needs.

rassment, fear, or intolerance. Children without handicaps will learn to see the disabled as peers with gifts, inabilities, and abilities. In this way all of society can benefit.

Because children are believed to be most pliable, in terms of basic attitude and value formation, during their early years, integration of handicapped children into regular classrooms has been mandated to begin during the preschool experience. In 1972 Head Start mandated that a certain percentage of the total enrollment consist of children with special needs. In May of 1975 Congress passed Public Law 94–142, the *Education of All Handicapped Children Act,* which gave aid to states for assisting in developing programs for handicapped children. This law mandated that states provide educational environments appropriate for children with special needs from ages three to twenty-one.

Early childhood programs may be most likely to provide an enabling environment for all children. All early childhood programs have included children from heterogeneous backgrounds with different needs and strengths. The programs designed to enable the immigrants to learn the ways of the New World—even though modeled after Peabody's programs, which seem so rigid today—were based on the philosophy that children should be permitted to grow, mature, and achieve at their own pace, with provision made for each child's special needs. The openness, flexibility, and individualization of most early childhood programs provide a natural environment, encouraging all children, including those with special needs, to achieve and find success.

Head Start, for instance, has since 1965, not only accepted children with special needs, but has made every effort to recruit the most disadvantaged children, those with the greatest needs. Other early childhood programs, private, cooperative, day care centers, have consistently served children with handicaps. Because these programs did not have to deal with regulations governing a public school or the government, they were able to readily adjust schedules and programs to the needs of any child. In addition, the comprehensive nature of most preschool programs—which include the components of parental involvement, community organization, health, nutrition, and psychological services—may have also contributed to the idea that mainstreaming should begin in early childhood education.

Teacher Readiness

Won't a child with handicaps make the other children sad or frightened? How will I handle one more child, and a child who can't hear? Am I really prepared to take in handicapped children?

It is normal for a teacher to have these questions, but they are not unanswerable. Most children are very much alike, in fact preschool teachers often report that the handicapped children are so like the other children in their basic needs, that they have long since forgotten how anxious they were when first asked to mainstream. Handicapped children are nice, sometimes awkward, sometimes aggressive, kind or shy, and sometimes they're mean.

The fact is the child with a handicap is an individual, and just like any other individual, has special needs, moods, and a unique personality.

Teachers can and do develop the skills necessary to provide the most enabling environment for all children. It may be helpful for a teacher to think of the basic assumptions of all early childhood programs as he plans to integrate handicapped children. These assumptions can reassure you about your ability to provide for all children, even those with special needs. Remember that:

1. All children are individuals.
2. A child with a handicap is first of all a child, and like all children, regardless of background, physical characteristics or abilities, has the same basic needs for food, shelter, warmth, nurturance, competence, and love.
3. Every child needs to be in the least restrictive environment; an environment that enables each to foster his optimal physical, emotional, and intellectual development.
4. All children do learn, although each may learn at a different rate or in a different way.

On the other hand, it is a serious step to take a child with handicaps into a classroom. It is easy to get carried away with good intentions and idealism, but a lot more than love and good intentions will be required. If mainstreaming is not done with careful preparation and assistance to the teacher, it may not be successful. Without help, some children with handicaps, when mainstreamed into regular classes, experienced peer rejection (Gottlieb 1977), or failed to take as many risks, or try new things as compared to when they were in a special class (Goldstein 1964).

Without special help, no one may benefit.

> In a class of 35 children I taught last year, one was totally deaf. By law, I had to make special lesson plans for him. Reality required that he be able to see my lips at all times. Class discussions were crippled by the need to proceed at a pace that allowed him to lip read every speaker. I sympathize with the goals of mainstreaming the handicapped, but deplore the results of the main stream. (C. Warlick, *Time* 1977, Letter to the Editor)

If this teacher had been given assistance, perhaps training in cued speech, or if the other children had been taught about communicating with the deaf, mainstreaming may not have seemed so negative and overwhelming. If special consultants and assistance is not available, teachers who are asked to mainstream have the right to demand such assistance before accepting any child with special needs.

Volunteers trained to work with children with specific needs should be requested. Perhaps a volunteer who knows braille or who has had experience with the deaf or retarded can spend part of each day in the classroom.

Reduction in class size is another possible help for teachers who are mainstreaming. Recognizing that the needs of some children may require more time, skill, or energy, teacher unions are now negotiating contracts in terms of class composition, instead of class size.

And then there's the help a teacher needs to understand her own attitudes and values. Most of us have been segregated from the handicapped and are uncertain about our own feelings and attitudes toward children with special needs. In-service training sessions, designed to help teachers examine and understand their own attitudes toward children with handicaps and to develop positive attitudes toward children with special needs, can be useful. In order to facilitate positive peer interactions and motivate all children to success, a teacher must convey positive, realistic attitudes toward all children.

The Handicapped Children

Children with a number of different types of handicaps and conditions can be mainstreamed into the regular classroom under Public Law 94–142. Children with hearing problems, the visually impaired, or children with other crippling conditions can successfully find the regular classroom the least restrictive environment. Other children with emotional or behavioral problems, learning disabilities, delayed speech, or slight retardation, may also be integrated into regular classrooms.

VISUALLY IMPAIRED CHILDREN

Mary has some sight in one eye. She is not completely blind. Now four years old, she enjoys being in school, but when she first entered the nursery school, she rocked back and forth and sat alone on the floor making funny noises, moving her hands in front of her face. In addition to attending nursery school, Mary goes to a special class several mornings a week where she is taught mobility training, and as she grows, she will be taught braille and the use of typewriters and recording machines.

Mary's teacher also receives training. One afternoon a week she attends a class on teaching blind children. She has already learned how to help Mary find her way around the class by placing different wind chimes over the bathroom door, the drinking fountain, and the door to the play yard. Carpet squares of different textures are on the floor in paths that lead Mary to the different areas of the room.

The teacher has also learned that she must touch, hug, or pat Mary instead of smiling or using nonverbal signals when communicating. And she has taught the other children how to communicate with Mary. Mary seems to like being in the class; she participates fully in listening to stories, at music times, and during art activities, especially when using modeling materials. Once Mary became involved in the class, she no longer sat and rocked by herself.

Mary's teacher also remembers that Mary needs a little extra help in starting an activity and must depend on others to locate toys before she can participate. She has required extra help in learning to form one-to-one relationships with others.

For the blind child to be successful in a regular classroom, no more than fifteen other children should be present. If there are too many other children the blind child will not be able to get to know them through voice, touch, and other cues. Too many children, in a room that's too large, only serves to confuse the child who is blind or partially seeing.

HEARING IMPAIRED OR DEAF CHILDREN

Bretano is hearing impaired. He seems to function well in a regular Head Start program; so well in fact, that his hearing impairment was not discovered until he had been in the program for several months. Now he wears a hearing aid and is learning to read lips, use cued speech, and speak at the speech clinic. In addition, the speech therapist spends time with Bretano's teacher, who has also learned cued speech and has taught it to some of the children.

Before Bretano's hearing impairment was noticed, he did not participate in music, story, or singing time. The speech therapist made it clear that it was desirable for him to participate in all parts of the program, so the teacher has increased the use of visual aids—such as flannel boards, pictures, puppets, drawing stick figures—when telling stories, singing, giving directions, or sharing information.

Because the hearing impaired children do make a fine adjustment in the regular classroom, they are often the first to be mainstreamed. Teachers may need to spend extra time with these children when they first enter the group to make them feel at home. Conferences with the parents will help identify the things the children enjoy doing, words they do understand, and the best ways to communicate. With the exception of always being certain the child can see the teacher speaking, and the use of concise, clear speech, the hearing impaired child usually interacts normally with the teacher and other children.

SPEECH OR LANGUAGE DELAYED CHILDREN

Roberta is four, but her speech is more like that of a one year old. No one seems to know just why Roberta speaks only in single words or in sentences never more than two words long. She plays well with other children, using physical force to communicate and make her wants known, and, in general, participates in all phases of the program for four year olds. After she was in the program for about one month, she proudly marched around the room and named all of the things in it, pointing to the objects as she named them.

Speech delay or impairment may be caused by many things. It may be the result of meningitis or some other form of brain damage. In other cases, environmental deficits may be the cause of delayed speech. Preschool programs provide many advantages for children with speech problems; the rich environment, verbal interactions with peers and teachers, and language activities can all benefit a child with speech problems. Nevertheless, it is still important for the teacher to have special help and for the child to receive special assistance.

PHYSICALLY DISABLED CHILDREN

Vanitia is physically disabled. She was born with a deformed leg and wears a leg brace and special shoe. She is able to get around the nursery school without any difficulty as long as she takes her time and does not get excited.

Some children have special needs.

She seems well adjusted and even takes part in music and dance activities. Vanitia has learned to care for herself. Sometimes in the sand box, or when playing in the water, she will take off her leg brace herself. The teacher was concerned, at first, that Vanitia would hurt herself because she entered into so many of the activities so enthusiastically, but the pediatrician helped the teacher realize that Vanitia could set limits for herself.

Children with physical handicaps—cerebral palsy, loss of limbs, deformed limbs, accident victims, and children who are either nonambulatory or ambulate with difficulty and require specialized equipment—are likely candidates for placement in a regular preschool program. There are many orthopedic-physical disabilities. When a child with a physical handicap enters the class, the teacher will want to find out all he can about the disability, and consult with the child's parents, physical therapist, or doctor.

Training in how to accommodate to the special equipment the child has, or in how to help the child adjust the equipment, or in changing the room to accommodate the equipment, might be useful. A physical therapist might also recommend special exercises to help the child or offer other suggestions for activities in which the child and the other classmates can participate. Children with physical handicaps do benefit from the regular activities of the preschool. All of the experiences in large and fine muscle control, in socialization, and the language and art activities are beneficial.

MENTALLY RETARDED CHILDREN

Maria is called mentally retarded and has been retarded since birth. Like many retarded children of five, she has trouble following multistep directions and in selecting her own activities. She imitates, rather than initiates, and has trouble attending to tasks for any length of time. Maria has difficulty picking out things that are alike from a group of objects.

She is in a group of four year olds, and finds that the flexibility and small class size suit her. When she does not find a group activity of interest, she wanders away to play with something by herself. She loves all of the art activities and enjoys moving to music. Because she is so interested in school, loves her teacher, and is so affectionate and willing, it is hard for the teacher to believe that Maria won't catch up someday.

Maria's teacher is working with the special education consultant in planning special activities for Maria. The special education teacher has stressed the importance of Maria learning self-care and survival skills. The teacher has also learned to break down tasks for Maria into sequences of simplified short steps and to use more structure and direction than with the other children.

The preschool curriculum, flexible, geared to individual needs, is a comfortable one for the mildly retarded. As with children with other handicaps, teachers must know the child's level of functioning, and may require help in working with the child. A special education consultant can provide that help.

EMOTIONALLY DISTURBED CHILDREN AND CHILDREN WITH BEHAVIOR DISORDERS

Jamie, at six, has trouble controlling himself. He lashes out, hits, and just when the teacher believes everything is going well, he will destroy another child's painting or block building. Jamie is typical of children with normal intelligence who have emotional problems that manifest themselves in behaviors that disrupt and disturb others.

Children with many different types of behavior problems may be mainstreamed into the preschool class. In fact, many such children are enrolled in Head Start and other preschool programs without special assistance. Children who are hyperactive, who are shy or withdrawn, who refuse to participate in the program, or who have many fears and worries that hinder them in a normal setting, may be in any group of children.

Consultation with a school counselor, psychologist, or other expert may be helpful. Teachers often find the techniques of behavior modification—ignoring the inappropriate response of the child, while being certain to reward responses or behaviors that are fitting—helpful. Rearranging the classroom space for time alone, or finding some space within the room, or the school gym, for instance, where pent up energies or emotions can be released may also be helpful for children with behavioral problems.

Beginning

Teachers who have mainstreamed and worked with children with special needs have found the following guidelines useful.

It is good to take the time to relax and observe the child who is being mainstreamed before barging in with plans for special activities or programs. Baum (1978) suggests that a period of observation can be most valuable in learning more about the child, his capabilities, likes, and dislikes, how he relates and interacts with others, and how others relate and interact with him. This baseline of information is valuable in planning a program for the child and deciding where to begin. Observing carefully also provides the teacher with objective information to relay to consultants and to obtain needed help and assistance.

Work with the Parents

Parental involvement is absolutely essential when working with children with special needs. After all, the parents know their children best and can offer valuable suggestions on how to best work with their children. The parents may also be asked to volunteer in the classroom, explain the child's special needs to the other children, or provide training for the teacher.

Use Consultants

Using consultants is also essential. Before meeting with a consultant, it is important for the teacher to be able to clearly describe the child, and the help needed. Before meeting with the consultant, the teacher will want to know whether she needs help in the classroom with all of the children or only the child with special needs; whether the consultant should be available on a special basis as needs arise, or on a continuing basis. Also a teacher should be able to state and define his goals clearly to the consultant, which will help to create a basis for a good working relationship.

Involve Other Children

At times the other children in the group will be of great help. It doesn't automatically happen that preschool children can work together, and it won't happen automatically just because there's a child in the room with special needs. Teachers may be able to teach the other children how to help or assist the child with special needs and encourage all to work together. It may be that simple circle games, building a fort, painting paper boxes, activities that require more than one to complete, can be developed to involve all children successfully.

Focus on Strengths

Having taken the time to observe the child, a teacher has insights into the capabilities of the child. Take advantage of these insights and strengths. Give the child things that can be done successfully. It is also good to take it easy with children with special needs, remembering that you do not have to teach everything at once, that progress will be made one step at a time.

Each day, set aside some time for observing the child and recording bits of behavior and anecdotes. When these observations are put together at the end of a month, or year, they can provide exact records of the child's progress. Videotapes of the class taken over a period of time will let a teacher, as well as consultants, see exactly how the child is fitting in, what strengths are being fostered, where weaknesses still exist.

USE DIFFERENT STRATEGIES

Preschool teachers, used to acting as guides, may find it difficult to structure tasks for children. Yet children with special needs often must know exactly what is expected of them, what they can and cannot do, and have clear, consistent limits well established. Some children with special needs cannot discover for themselves how to use a swing, scissors, or the crayons and need specific tasks designed to enable them to make sense of their world and gain mastery over self.

Building the least restrictive environment for all children is not an easy task. Head Start teachers who have been mainstreaming handicapped children into their programs on a formal basis since 1972 know that it is hard work. But they also know that it works.

In general, Head Start teachers who have worked with handicapped children firmly believe in the concept of mainstreaming and can testify to the value of such a program for all children. Parents also favor the concept and believe it has a positive impact on their lives and the lives of their children.

> These observations reinforce the belief that the handicapped child should not be isolated. Mainstreaming is difficult, but its impact can reach far beyond the child and the immediate situation. If handicapped persons have the right to share the world of the normal, we as educators have a responsibility. We are obligated to try to help children develop the outlook and skills which may enable them to function effectively in spite of a handicap. What better place to start than in a preschool group. (Klein 1975, p. 326)

Recognizing and Reporting Child Abuse

Laws have also mandated that teachers report and work with children who have suffered from abuse and neglect. Child abuse is not new but the mandate that teachers become involved in reporting suspected cases of abuse is new, and teachers must now understand their role when confronted with child abuse.

Child abuse is a part of our heritage. Public whippings of children were condoned by law in the first colonies of the United States, and laws throughout history permitted parents to physically abuse—or even put to death—disobedient children. Even today, there is widespread belief in our nation that parents and other adults should use physical force to control or discipline children.

The 1977 Supreme Court ruling stating that corporal punishment is indeed a legitimate form of discipline within a school setting is just one manifestation of this belief. Then too, as recently as 1976, parents who had blinded or paralyzed preschool children were acquitted and given custody of their children on the grounds that physical force was often necessary in the socialization and disciplining of young children.

It may be that many in our nation actually do endorse the belief that children are born in sin and, like all humankind, are, by nature, evil. If people do accept this doctrine, then corporal punishment—to break the evil spirit—is one part of the belief system. Gil (1970) however, sees violence against children as an integral part of the culture of our country, rather than as a consequence of the doctrine of original sin. The highly competitive nature of our society, along with the violence present in every segment of society, leads to child abuse. Child abuse is only one symptom of the violence that runs rampant in our country.

Bronfenbrenner points out how children in Russia and the United States experience different types of socialization. In Russia adults strive to teach children to cooperate, to care for one another, and to share responsibility. Parents in the United States, on the other hand, teach children to compete and often emphasize the importance of rugged individualism and alienation. To Bronfenbrenner (p. 117, 1970) this type of child rearing leads to "increased alienation, indifference, antagonism and violence" with child abuse being just one form of violence.

Recognizing that there is a problem of violence and abuse of children in our nation, Congress passed the Child Abuse Prevention and Treatment Act. As a result forty-nine states have mandated that teachers, as well as other professionals working with children and families, take an active role in recognizing and reporting the abused child. Virtually every state offers immunity from legal action for those making a child abuse report. Because preschool teachers are the first teachers to come in contact with children, they are in a strategic position to identify and report suspected cases.

Reporting a suspected case of child abuse is not easy. What if a mistake is made? The psychological damage that could result to the child and family if a teacher's suspicions are unfounded should not be underestimated. What if the teacher's suspicions are accurate, but the parents, knowing they are being reported, become more frightened and angry and increase their attacks on the child? Yet not reporting a suspected case of child abuse is just as dangerous, for the data suggest that a child who has been abused or neglected is at great risk of being reinjured and abused.

Teachers must assume their responsibility and be professional in protecting children and families. If a teacher is uncertain of her perceptions, she might seek the advice and support of a school counselor, principal, or director. Perhaps she could consult with other teachers who know the child. The school nurse or other medical personnel connected with the school might also be able to assist. Together they could examine the child's scars or injuries and make a decision whether these could have been accidental or inflicted.

It may be helpful for the beginning teacher to realize that the abusing parents often seek help themselves, or that someone within the family will initiate a request for assistance. It is not unusual for several different persons to report the same case at the same time. The teacher may be just one of several who have noticed that something is wrong with the child.

Each state and every school system will have its own requirements and methods to follow in reporting suspected cases of child abuse. If these are not clarified when you are hired, it is important to ask for guidelines and familiarize yourself with them. In general, once a teacher reports a suspected case, a social service agency or the school system will investigate and decide what steps should be taken.

Defining Child Abuse

Definitions of child abuse and neglect are plentiful. There is no ready consensus as to what constitutes abuse. Some states include sexual assaults, others do not. Usually child abuse and neglect refer to the maltreatment of children which can include physical injury or injuries inflicted by other than accidental means, as well as failure to provide sustenance, clothing, shelter, medical attention, or other care necessary for a child's well being.

Physical abuse is most likely to be noticed by a teacher. A child with blackened eyes, scars, or broken bones is not easily ignored. Other types of abuse: nutritional deprivation, the need for medical care—eyeglasses, immunizations, dental care—are not always as readily apparent. Nor are the effects of emotional abuse.

Often the abused child will tell the teacher exactly what happened to her. At other times she will tell several different stories, or she will remain quiet for fear of further beatings, or for some other reason, she will not be able to describe what happened. In trying to identify abused children, teachers can remember that, in general, children who have been abused or neglected

- cry for no apparent reason, frequently and repeatedly.
- are afraid of everyone and everything and are not willing to take the normal risks that others do.
- have unexplained lacerations and bruises, repeated, bizarre injuries.
- do not want to go home after school.
- are ill cared for, inadequately, inappropriately dressed.
- are unclean, smelling of urine or stools.
- withdraw from adult contact, are distrustful.
- exhibit destructive behavior.
- smell of alcohol.
- are below normal height and weight.
- are afraid of their parents, fear other adults.
- withdraw from peer interaction, seem extremely introverted, passive, inhibited.
- may be hyperactive or aggressive, start fights easily, lashing out physically at other children.
- are sick and absent from school more frequently and for longer periods of time than are other children.

• may have short attention spans, lack interest in problem solving, be unresponsive to praise, lack motivation, appear apathetic in comparison to others.
• exhibit sudden and dramatic changes in behavior, are given to emotional outbursts.
• are tired and often fall asleep in class. (Gil 1970)

Doing Something about It

Once a teacher reports a suspected case of child abuse, her work is considered complete. But the child is still in the classroom with unmet needs. The abused child—frightened, withdrawn, or physically hostile—is in great need of comfort, consistency, and continuing reassurance that at school she will not be hurt. The abused child who acts out, lashing aggressively at others, hitting and fighting, needs the same type of reassurance as the withdrawn, passive, inhibited child. When an abused child is in the classroom teachers might

1. Take time to observe the child, noting when she acts out or withdraws, what seems to please her, how she meets the attempts of other children to reach her, and how she handles frustration and praise. Take the same time to become familiar with the child's records, consulting with the physician, school nurse, counselor, social worker, and parents in order to learn all you can about the child.
2. Try asking a volunteer to spend full time with the abused child. A sensitive volunteer, who is given primary responsibility for assuring the abused child that she is safe and secure in the classroom, might be helpful in giving the child the support she needs to begin to learn to trust herself, others, and the environment. For the overtly aggressive child, a volunteer offers help in learning to control strong feelings, redirecting behavior, or offering a safe alternative.
3. Use caution in making advances. The child who has been hurt fears and distrusts adults. The teacher might move slowly to establish trust. Taking every opportunity to subtly and not so subtly offer support, affection, and love. A compliment, smile, a wink, might precede actual physical affection. A hug, an arm around the shoulder, could frighten an insecure child who has only known adult arms that hit and hurt.
4. Find safe and acceptable ways for the child to release aggressive feelings. The child might be encouraged to run, climb outside, ride a trike as fast as she can or pound the clay, wood, or punching bag just as hard as can be. The use of dolls and figures representing parents and children offers another type of outlet for feelings. Painting, singing, drawing, and the arts provide additional release.
5. Give the child tasks that provide challenges and can be completed successfully. It may be that these tasks should be more tightly structured than those given to other children, depending on the child. Instead of presenting an array of puzzles to select from, the teacher might select puzzles for the child, picking those that provide a greater amount of built in success. Success in school, whether in learning to feed the rabbit, taking care of paint brushes, or looking at pictures in a book, will lead to desperately needed feelings of self-confidence.
6. Use the other children to help the child build feelings of self-confidence. Young children can be taught the social skills of including the abused child in their play groups and can be reminded to invite her to join them or to select her to do some special task.
7. Help the child learn to establish controls. Little by little the overly aggressive

child may learn to control hostile feelings. By accepting the child's anger (I know how very angry you are) and redirecting it (I cannot let you bite me or the other children, but you may hit this), you can help children begin to learn to control their rage. Some children can get themselves into control if they are able to leave the group and be by themselves for a few minutes.

Working with the Parents

When you have an abused child in your class, you have the responsibility to provide that child with a supportive, secure, and safe environment at school, but you also have a responsibility to the child's family. The idea of the teacher of young children becoming involved with the child's home life is not new to early childhood education. In the 1880s Susan Blow pointed out that the child's life in the kindergarten could not be divorced from his life at home. Blow established the idea of home visitations and held mothers' meetings at the Des Peres school in St. Louis which housed the first public school kindergarten program.

Like the kindergarten teacher of long ago, today's teachers can attempt to involve the parents in the child's activities at school. Some activities are a regular part of the school program such as work in the classroom, observations and visits. When working with the abusive parent, there may be things that must occur prior to asking the parent to participate in the regular activities of the school.

In the case of the abusive parent, the teacher may first need to establish a feeling of trust and caring before either visiting in the home or inviting the parents to visit and spend time in the school. Consultation with social service agencies or prior contact with the parent, at arrival and departure times, may be the place to begin building trust.

It's generally accepted that the tension and pressures of today's life, sometimes arising from poverty, can lead to child abuse. A teacher who knows the parents may be able to help them find ways of reducing tensions and pressures. Teachers, along with the social services team, may help parents identify and use local recreational, medical, nutritional, or other community services. Sometimes, with a teacher as a friend to go with you to the library, or health clinic, it may be easier to use community services. In other cases, just the fact that the teacher is interested, and brings to the home good reports of the child's progress, books, or toys for the child to use at home can help the parents through stressful times.

Once teachers have established that they are nonjudgmental, but concerned about the child and the family, they might begin to help parents understand normal child behaviors. As involvement between teacher and parent builds, parents might be helped to understand that all children say "no" or that there are alternative, nonviolent ways of disciplining children.

If parents have been able to volunteer or observe in school, they will have seen for themselves the normal range of children's behaviors and effective ways of directing children. Gil (1970) believes that if parents could learn to discipline children without the use of physical violence, a major step in the prevention of child abuse would be taken. Parents must know that physical attack is not a sign of strength and that it rarely is as successful as firmness, consistency, love, patience, and rational authority (Gil, 1970).

Teachers may also be able to give parents a measure of strength and stability needed for them to function effectively. Remembering that the parents are themselves in need of love, security, and friendship helps the teacher to be nonjudgmental and to begin to work with the parent.

There is no easy answer to the complicated problems of child abuse in our country. There is the recognition of the problem, and the mandate that teachers, suspecting child abuse, report it to the authorities. Yet there are few tried guidelines for teachers to follow, and few sure answers to their questions. School systems are now including in-service training programs in recognizing and reporting child abuse and helping to handle children who have been abused as well as working with their parents.

The Gifted Child

"All children have gifts. The task of the teacher is to identify and to provide a suitable climate for their growth" (Leeper, 1974, p. 443). Preschool teachers, throughout the history of early childhood education, have recognized and respected the individuality of all children. Young children are so individualistic, so uninhibited, and so diverse that in a way their individual gifts cannot be ignored. But today there is a renewed push to provide for children with special gifts.

The gifted child movement, according to Gowan (1977) has been fostered by a belief in humanism and has the following characteristics:

1. A sense of the innate dignity, uniqueness, and worth of human individuality which is seen as something transcending social groups, laws, restrictions, and generalities. Human beings are not merely reactive creatures, but are ends in themselves.
2. A sense of development, of process, of growth or change, and of becoming or unfoldment. Evolution and human life are seen as twin aspects of the debut of new powers, an expanding concept of intellect.
3. Concern for the unusual, in persons, things, and events, particularly for understanding, appreciating, and valuing the unusual because of the possibility that it is through examining the unusual that we have the best chance of gaining greater knowledge about things, events, and ourselves.

Given the framework of humanism, it is fitting that our nation should begin to focus on providing equality of opportunity for children with special talents. It is estimated that fewer than four percent of all of our nation's gifted and talented youth have received services commensurate with their needs. In 1971 only ten states had a full-time person in their state departments of education working in behalf of the gifted and talented, and only twelve institutions of higher education provided graduate level programs for teachers specializing in the education of the gifted (Gowan, 1977).

At the same time that funds, training programs, and special enrichment and intervention projects were being implemented for children from economically disadvantaged backgrounds, a kind of reverse discrimination existed for the gifted child. Gifted children, some 2.5 million youth, have been a neglected natural resource. There is also the erroneous belief that the gifted and talented child is from an upper-middle-class background, when in fact, there are "potentially the same proportion of gifted and talented from the ghettos, the Indian reservations and the barrios of this country" (Lyon 1976, p. 34).

Legislation has now been passed calling for all school systems to identify gifted and talented children and to provide programs that will enable these children to develop their full potential. As basic attitudes, values, and skills are believed to develop during the early years of life, teachers of young children are particularly involved.

Identifying the Gifted and Talented

Historically the term *gifted* has included only those children who scored above 120 on an intelligence test or were in the top 2 percent of their group. In 1931 the White House Conference on the Gifted stated that the term gifted was to refer only to those children who had exceptional intelligence and was not to inappropriately include those children with special talents in music, arts, poetry, or other areas (Getzels, 1973).

Today, however, legislation has provided for a broadened concept and definition of giftedness. The definition varies from state to state, yet all definitions are more inclusive than intelligence test scores. While some state departments of education have asked teachers to identify all those children who do score above a certain point on an intelligence test, most have added to this requirement identification of those children believed to have potential for outstanding performance in mechanical or manipulative skills; the art of expressing ideas, either orally or in writing; or skills in music, art, human relations; or any other worthwhile human achievement.

Because the definition of the gifted is broad, a number of different methods are being used to locate those children with special talents. The intelligence test or test of creative thinking is usually supplemented with teacher judgments based on observations of children in various settings and situations.

It may be easy to identify some children who have special talents. The three year old who sits at a piano and begins to play music or the four year old who is reading fluently can hardly be ignored. But in many cases, young children's gifts are not nearly so apparent, and may go unnoticed. Long ago Harriet Johnson wrote that the growth of very young children is uneven, and that early maturation may be a sign of giftedness, but it might also be a sign of environmental enrichment. A child who appears unique at age two or three may be quite different when she reaches the age of four or five. It is difficult to know which traits of young children will persist and which will not (1928).

We do know, however, from the work of Terman—who is called the father of the gifted child movement (Gowan, 1977)—that the gifted are a diverse group, not easily identified by the same characteristics. Terman's gifted children were identified using scores on an intelligence test, but even using this single measure, Terman found that the gifted are

- not homogenous, but differ among themselves in many ways, with only stability of intelligence in common;
- not puny, asocial, or psychotic. In no way are children who are talented or gifted unstable emotionally or socially;
- able to benefit from acceleration at all levels of schooling;
- able to maintain their superiority in intelligence and even increase in intelligence through middle life.

Not only is it difficult to identify young gifted children, it's also hard to know what program is best for them. Since the time of Hollingworth (1926) different approaches to meeting their needs have been tried. Segregating the gifted into special classes, accelerating them by placing them with older children, or giving work of increased difficulty and providing enriching experiences have all been tried.

Some research supports the idea of segregating gifted children into special classes (Passow, 1958). Yet there is the philosophical problem of placing any child into a special class or group. Segregation by race, sex, or intelligence is not acceptable. While some insist that the gifted child will be bored by classmates of average abilities, others believe that segregating the gifted into special classes will create an intellectual elite, an elite who will be unable to learn from others who are not gifted, or to relate with others effectively.

Acceleration of the gifted is also controversial. Skipping kindergarten or a grade or working with children who are older could affect a child's social and emotional growth. Acceleration, when it does consider the child's social and emotional needs has been found to be beneficial (Marland, 1971).

Enrichment is another way schools have met the needs of the talented or gifted. Enrichment was first popular during the 1930s as programs used Hollingworth's ideas. Hollingworth believed that keeping a child with her social and age group was better than segregation or acceleration (Getzels, 1973). Research is favorable toward enrichment programs (Carter, 1960), and the judgment of teachers, parents, and children are all favorable.

Perhaps the way to meet the needs of the gifted is to provide "a good school for young children that will provide adequate challenge for the superior child without 'special' consideration and at the same time use these provisions for the enrichment of the educational experiences of the other children" (Leeper, 1974, p. 444). Teachers of young children, knowledgeable of each individual, firm in their conviction for the need for open-ended, individualized activities, can and do provide for the gifted child.

When programs are based on play, freedom of choice, activity, and on the concept of the child as an active, self-initiated learner, all children—the gifted, average, or slow—can move at their own pace. In this type of program all children can find the challenge, enrichment, or acceleration necessary to develop their full potential.

In Summary

"Many teachers of handicapped children have observed that once they come to feel at ease, and capable of meeting the special needs related to a particular condition, they view children with disabilities differently: it becomes apparent that the handicapped child's basic needs are the same, except in degree, as those of all children." (Responding to Individual Needs 1976, p. 1)

It may seem overwhelming when you first think about meeting the needs of children who are gifted, handicapped, or abused. Yet teachers have found that children are more alike than different and that all children do have the same basic needs.

Working with children who are gifted, abused, or handicapped does, however, require careful planning. First you should be able to assess each individual child, using skills of observation and results of standardized testing. Next you can work with specialists or other staff members to help plan the best classroom spaces, management, and program to meet the needs of all children. Consultation with parents, physicians, social service agencies, and other members of the community should provide further support where needed. Federal and state laws mandate mainstreaming the handicapped, the abused, and the gifted. Implementing those programs creatively and intelligently offers exiciting and challenging opportunities for both teachers and children.

Resources

The following books may be helpful in learning more about children who have special needs.

BAUM, S. J., and M. G. LASHER, *Are You Ready to Mainstream?* Columbus, Ohio: Charles E. Merrill Publishing Company, 1976.

McLOUGHLIN, JAMES A., and SUSAN M. KERSMAN, "Mainstreaming in Early Childhood: Strategies and Resources." *Young Children*. 34, 4 (1979), 54–66.

PAYNE, JAMES S., and others, *Exceptional Children in Focus*. (2nd ed.) Columbus, Ohio: Charles E. Merrill Publishing Company. 1979.

The Administration for Children, Youth and Families, Box 1182, Washington, D.C., 20013, can be contacted for free or inexpensive materials on children with special needs. The booklet, *Responding to Individual Needs in Head Start*, is just one of many available to help teachers understand children with special needs.

Materials on child abuse are also available through the Administration for Children,

Youth and Families. In addition, The National Center on Child Abuse and Neglect, HEW, Washington, D.C. 20201, can be contacted for additional help in recognizing and combatting child abuse.

Julian Stanley, ed., *The Gifted and Creative: A Fifty Year Perspective*, Baltimore, Md.: Johns Hopkins University Press, 1977.

Projects

1. Visit in a classroom designed to meet the needs of children with handicaps. See if you can determine what the teacher does to meet the needs of individual children. Look for room arrangement and special equipment designed or provided for individual children. Does the teacher utilize volunteers or aides?

2. While visiting in a classroom designed for children with handicaps focus some of your observations on the children. How do these children relate with others? How do they manage physical needs? Materials? How do they relate to adults?

3. Examine your feelings about children with special needs. With a group of classmates discuss your feelings about the gifted and the handicapped. Do you believe children with special needs should be segregated in a special school? Should they be placed with other children in a regular classroom? What would you do as a teacher with a gifted child in your class? A child who is partially deaf? One who has been abused?

References

BAUM, S. J., and LASHER, M. G., *Are You Ready to Mainstream?* Columbus, Ohio: Charles E. Merrill Publishing Company, 1978.

BRONFENBRENNER, U., *Two Worlds of Childhood: United States and United States of Soviet Russia*. New York: Russell Sage Foundation, 1970.

CARTER, H. P., "Gifted Children," in *Encyclopedia of Education Research*, pp. 583–593, ed. C. W. Harris. New York: Macmillan, Inc., 1960.

COHEN, S., "Integrating Children with Handicaps into Early Childhood Education Programs," *Children Today*, 4, 1 (1975), 15–17.

Day Care: Serving Children with Special Needs. Washington, D.C.: Department of Health, Education and Welfare, 1972.

GETZELS, J. W., and DILLON, J. T., "Giftedness and the Education of the Gifted," in *Second Handbook of Research on Teaching*, pp. 689–732, ed. R. M. W. Travers. Chicago: Rand McNally & Company, 1973.

GIL, D. G., *Violence Against Children: Physical Child Abuse in the United States*. Cambridge, Mass.: Harvard University Press, 1970.

GOLDSTEIN, H., MOSS, J., and JORDAN, L., *The Efficacy of Special Class Training on the Development of Mentally Retarded Children*. Champaign, Ill.: Institute for Research on Exceptional Children. University of Illinois, 1964.

GOTTLIEB, J., and GOTTLIEB, B. W., "Stereotypic Attitudes and Behavioral Intentions Toward Handicapped Children, *American Journal of Mental Deficiency*, 82, 1 (1977), 65–71.

GOWAN, J. C., "Background and History of the Gifted Child Movement," in *The Gifted and the Creative: A Fifty Year Perspective*, pp. 5–28, eds. J. C. Stanley; W. C. George; C. H. Solano. Baltimore, Md.: The Johns Hopkins University Press, 1977.

HOLLINGWORTH, L. S., *Gifted Children: Their Nature and Nurture*. New York: Macmillan, Inc., 1926.

JOHNSON, H. M., *Children in the Nursery School*. New York: Agathon Press, 1972. First published 1928.

KLEIN, J. W., "Mainstreaming the Preschooler," *Young Children*, 30, 5 (1975), 317–326.

LEEPER, S. H.; and others, *Good Schools for Young Children* (4th ed.) New York: Macmillan, Inc., 1974.

LYON, H. C., " A New Federal Priority," *Today's Education*, 65, 1 (1976), 33–35.

MARLAND, S. P., JR., *Education of the Gifted and Talented. Volume I: Report to the Congress of the United States by the United States Commissioner of Education*. Washington, D.C.: U.S. Government Printing Office, 1971.

PASSOW, A. H., "Enrichment of Education for the Gifted," in *Education for the Gifted: The Fifty-Seventh Yearbook of the National Society for the Study of Education, Part II*, pp. 193–221, ed. N. B. Henry. Chicago, Ill.: National Society for the Study of Education, 1958.

Responding to Children with Special Needs: A Head Start Series on Needs Assessment. Washington, D.C.: U.S. Department of HEW, 1974.

WARLICK, C., "Letters to the Editor," *Time*, 111, 16 (1977), 5.

Strategies for Teaching

Part II

Knowledge and understanding of the strategies of teaching are necessary if you are to become a truly effective teacher of young children. You will want to learn how to plan, organize the environment, use specific teaching strategies, and communicate effectively.

"Planning and Evaluating," chapter 5, offers an opportunity to examine different goals for early childhood education. Examples of daily and long-range plans are given. Strategies for evaluating children, the program, as well as yourself, are suggested.

The environment is believed to have a powerful influence on the behaviors of children and adults. The ability to organize the environment for learning is seen as critical. Methods for structuring the classroom and play yard, and for understanding the child's total environment are offered in chapter 6.

Chapter 7 introduces you to some of the specific strategies teachers can use when working with young children. An introduction to the use of questioning, reinforcement, feedback, nurturing, and working with groups is given.

The last chapter, "Communicating," discusses the process of communicating with children, parents, and fellow staff members. Both verbal and nonverbal methods can be used by teachers in establishing effective communication with children and adults.

5

Planning and Evaluating

Despite the apparent informality and lack of regimentation, a great deal of planning and organizing takes place before, after and even during the school day.

V. Hildebrand, 1971, p. 28.

Children—active, curious, spontaneous—need teachers who know how to select opportunities for their learning, but they also need teachers who can modify and adjust the plans they make. Teachers must know exactly what they are about; yet they must be able to change in midstream, capitalizing on every encounter children have as a means of fulfilling goals and objectives. Being flexible, being able to toss out plans or change them on a moment's notice, does not mean that you do not plan. In fact it means that you must plan all the time, before school begins, during school, and after school is over.

Before

One of the first things you must do is decide on general goals for your program and for individual children. You internalize these goals and then use them to direct your actions. With a clear idea of the goals for each child, as well as for the program and group, it is possible to take a child's fleeting interest in a subject and build on it. Once you decide on general and individual goals, you

81

Teachers plan for children's learning.

hold these for yourself, remember them, and use them to guide you as you work with the children.

Teachers select goals to fit the children, their program, and their own values. There is no shortage of goals and objectives from which to select. State departments of education, programs such as Home or Head Start, day care or nursery schools, all have established goals and objectives. Figure 3 is an example of goals and objectives one state department of education has suggested for preschool programs.

Teachers can use goal statements like these to direct their planning, or they can decide on goals to meet the specific focus of their programs. The pioneers of early education set goals designed to help immigrant children and their families become assimilated into the culture of America. Head Start teachers select goals to enable children to succeed in later schooling (The Persistence of Preschool Effects 1978). Teachers working in a day care center might have different goals than their counterparts in a church-sponsored nursery school or a parent cooperative.

When selecting goals it is also important to look to the children. Knowledge of children will help you decide which goals are obtainable and realistic. If you know children, you know that certain things will be in reach of the children and other things, given the children's stage of growth and development, will simply not be possible. If you are working with children who have

FIGURE 3

Objectives

The objectives of a good program for children under six are:

To help each child experience intellectual growth and educational stimulation by:

- developing a positive attitude toward learning
- making discoveries, developing problem-solving ability.
- sharpening sensory awareness, learning about his environment by exploring, observing, listening, touching, tasting, smelling, and balancing.
- expressing himself verbally, communicating with others, increasing his vocabulary, gaining skill in enunciation and pronunciation, developing auditory discrimination.
- listening to and appreciating stories, poetry, music, and rhythms.
- developing concepts and understandings about the world around him.
- participating in dramatic play, dramatizing stories, telling experiences in sequence, reporting on trips, helping to plan group experiences.
- acquiring an understanding of concepts in mathematics, science, social sciences, language arts, and other curriculum areas.
- experimenting with tools, materials, and equipment designed to lay basic foundations for future learnings.

To help each child become emotionally sound by:

- building a positive self-concept; valuing himself as a unique individual.
- developing confidence in himself and his abilities; becoming independent and self-reliant.
- developing confidence in others: children, parents, teachers, and other adults in his immediate environment.
- persisting in his efforts; experiencing success.
- accepting and adjusting to opposition or lack of success.
- expressing his emotions of affection, pleasure, boredom, sympathy, compassion, humor, laughter, fear, anxiety, anger, frustration, hostility, jealousy, and learning how to channel them constructively.
- building empathy for the feelings and emotions of others.

To help each child become socially well adjusted by:

- building positive relationships within his family, with his peers, with adults outside his home.
- experiencing a recognition of his own rights as a human being in a democratic society.
- learning to respect the rights of others.
- learning to cooperate with others and to respect those in authority.
- learning to participate as a leader and a follower.
- learning through experience to share possessions and to take turns.
- assuming responsibility for his own acts.
- learning to give and to accept helpful criticism.
- learning to respond to directions and to accept the limits involved in living in a democratic society.
- accepting the responsibility of caring for his own possessions and for the property of others.

To help each child acquire physical well-being by:

- developing muscular control and coordination.
- establishing desirable health habits such as toilet routines, hand-washing, relaxation during rest period, suitable clothing for weather conditions, positive attitudes toward nourishing foods.
- developing wholesome attitudes toward body and bodily functions.
- practicing good posture for walking, running sitting, standing and lying down.
- accepting casually and without embarrassment the physical differences between boys and girls.
- practicing safety procedures in the use of tools and equipment.

- developing security through confidence in safety practices.
- experiencing a balanced program of activity, relaxation and rest.
- accepting and understanding disabilities in himself and others.
- developing positive attitudes toward the physician, nurse, dentist and community health authorities.
- engaging in a variety of motor activities such as running, skipping, jumping, hopping, climbing, pushing, lifting, pulling, sliding, falling, and rolling.
- gaining skill in throwing, catching, bouncing and rolling a ball, walking and balancing on boards, suspending his weight from horizontal bars and ladders, turning somersaults and climbing on apparatus.
- recognizing safety hazards such as deep water, strange animals, broken glass, wire, sharp edges, splinters, etc.
- refusing to accept rides and gifts from strangers.

To help each child develop aesthetic growth through:

- exercising all his senses.
- awareness of beauty in the world around him.
- expressing feelings as well as ideas.
- appreciation of the contributions of various cultures in music, art, language, dance, and other forms of creative expresssion.
- enjoyment of good literature, poetry, story-telling, and dramatization.
- expressing himself creatively through language, movement, music, art, construction, and other activities.
- experiencing the joy of creating and interpreting his own work.
- appreciating the productions and aesthetic expressions of others.
- enjoyment of the contributions of musicians, artists, dancers, writers, poets, and artisans in the community.

Reprinted with permission from The Florida State Department of Education.
Bulletin 76. A Guide: Early Childhood Education in Florida Schools.
State Department of Education,
Tallahassee, Florida, pp. 17–18, 1969.

special needs or talents, you will also want to consider these when selecting goals.

Your own values will also direct some goals. Your own views of the nature of the child, what you believe children can become, will affect your selection of goals. The questions you must ask are What kind of person do we want to develop? What kind of person is needed to live successfully within a democracy?

The fact that we do live in a democratic society is important. In a democracy children must grow to become thinking, creating people, competent to do, to make decisions for themselves. This means that the goals of preschool should focus on those things that will enable children to become effective members of a democratic society. All children need to be

1. Competent

In order to gain the competence necessary for life in a democratic society, children must have knowledge of many things, of how systems work, and how to think for themselves. They will need to be skilled in communicating, able to speak, listen, and later read and write effectively. They will need to be able to reason, think, and value. Specific goals for children might include such things as

- having many opportunities for experiences which arouse curiosity and enthusiasm.
- trying new things, to experiment, test, and discover.
- planning, thinking, and making decisions.

- solving problems, questioning, organizing, and classifying information.
- developing an interest in books and other printed material.
- clarifying word concepts.
- enlarging vocabulary.
- increasing understanding of the mathematical world, size, shape, space, simple quantity and time relationships.
- communicating ideas of number and quantity.

2. Cooperative

A democracy cannot survive unless its members can cooperate and work together. Preschool experiences can be planned to permit children to learn to work together and form a community. Some examples of goals for the child are

- respect for others, both children and adults.
- tolerance for others.
- learning to help others, and develop feelings of empathy for others.
- working and playing with others.

3. Autonomous

It may sometimes be uncomfortable working with children who make their own decisions. After all, when you ask children to make decisions you are saying that you are willing to accept these decisions. Permitting children the autonomy of making, and then living with, their own decisions calls for teachers who are able to handle a certain amount of ambiguity. Teachers believing in democracy accept this ambiguity, for they know that it takes a lot of practice making decisions before children will be autonomous. Some examples of goals to foster the child's autonomy are

- developing independence by making choices and decisions.
- recognizing her own feelings and beginning to develop self-control over these feelings.
- developing feelings of adequacy and self-respect.

4. Creative

In order for our society to continue we need people who are capable of seeing new solutions to old problems. Children can gain experiences in preschool that will permit them to see relationships between experiences and then come up with new ideas, creative solutions to problems, and new and different ways of thinking and doing things. Examples of specific goals for fostering children's creativity might include

- using material in new and different ways.
- solving problems.
- developing ideas.
- using imagination.
- developing humor and joy.

The Lesson Plan

Once goals and objectives have been determined, teachers have a basis for making plans. "But do we have to write it all out? After all, with young children you simply can't do all that planning!" The experienced teacher recognizes the changing nature of lesson plans, but he also recognizes the need for careful planning. Careful planning means writing lesson plans. The very act of writing a plan, of specifying goals and objectives, and determining how these objectives will be obtained, helps you to clarify your own thinking and internalize your goals. There is evidence that suggests the more carefully a teacher plans, the more progress children make (Weikart 1971). Teachers who know what it is they wish to accomplish and how they will do it are much more successful than those who have only a vague idea of what they wish to do and why.

The first step in planning is to indicate the changes in children's behavior that are desired. A goal statement, telling what it is the children, or the child, will learn, is necessary. A behaviorist might maintain that this statement includes a description of what changes in the child's behavior will constitute the obtainment of objectives. According to a behaviorist, the objectives should be stated in terms of what the child can do, and the statement must be specific. For example, an objective for preschool children to "know their colors" would be considered inadequate. This objective should be stated, according to a behaviorist, in the following way

1. Given a box of crayons, the child will correctly identify nine colors by name (three primary, three secondary, plus black, brown, and white).
2. The child will correctly name an object in her surroundings or from memory that is the color of each of the named crayons.
3. The child will use correctly, in relation to color, the words light and dark and will be able to point out examples of each on the "Butterfly Lotto" game cards.

A teacher who endorses the cognitive developmental theory will state goals differently. A cognitive teacher describes the goals of education as "a particular way of thinking about particular kinds of content. The attainment of such goals is inferred from different kinds of behavior in a variety of situations, not from a restricted set of specific performances" (Rohwer, W. D., Ammon, P. R., and Cramer, P. 1974, p. 245).

Weikart (1971) suggests that a goal statement in a cognitively oriented curriculum only requires that the teacher answer two questions: (1) Where are the children right now in terms of their own mental abilities? and (2) Where is it that I want to take them; in what ways do I want them to grow mentally?" (p. 13). After the teacher has decided on the goals by answering these two questions, she then considers how to help the children move from where they are toward these predetermined goals.

The second stage of lesson planning is deciding on the things you and the children will do to obtain your goals. You must decide on activities that will foster your goals, how to sequence the activities, as well as how to match these to children's level of development.

The final stage in planning is deciding whether or not the children, or the child, has in fact achieved the desired goals. A teacher who states the goals in behavioral terms has already built evaluation into the lesson plans. When you state the goals of your lesson as "The child will be able to name three colors when presented with a box of nine crayons," all you have to do to evaluate the lesson is to see if the child can do this.

To the cognitively oriented teacher, evaluation also means observing children to see whether or not the goals have been reached. Rather than just observing in one situation, however, this teacher observes children in a variety of situations over time. If your goal was to teach children concepts of in and out, you might observe them to see if they can follow directions when playing with a cardboard box. "Go in the box, walk out of the box." Or you might see if children can use the words correctly when observing their rabbits. "The rabbits are in the hutch. No, they just came out!" You might, at another time, observe children using the words in and out as they refer to a picture in a book. Having observed children using the concepts of in and out in a variety of situations, the teacher would then conclude that they have obtained an understanding of in and out.

Daily Plans

Each day has its own rhythm and unity, and through planning, its own purpose. The very nature of the rhythm and pattern of the day—the beginning, midpoint, and the ending, and the natural rhythms of the children, with needs for activity, rest, and nourishment direct daily plans.

The rhythms of the children and the patterns of the day serve as guideposts and natural divisions. In the freshness of the morning, when children themselves are fresh, the program provides for active, challenging experiences. The beginning of the day is usually reserved for a large block of activity time in which the children become involved in play. Following this children naturally require a period of rest and quiet.

Rest may consist of a quiet activity—story, song, listening to a record— followed by juice or some type of refreshment. This change of pace is followed by another active period. Then it is time for midday lunch and a longer rest period, with young children usually napping for an hour or so. The final period of the day is reserved for play and activity, but often this time is more subdued than the other previous active periods, for the children and the day are running down.

These guideposts—activity, rest, lunch, nap, and play—serve several functions. They help the children develop concepts of time and predictability. "The routine for the class day usually does not vary and is followed throughout the school year, with the result that the children come to anticipate time periods and to mentally reconstruct past events. This invariance contributes a certain predictability to class days . . ." (Weikart 1971, p. 52). When things happen in a given, predictable order, children have a measure of emotional security. They can feel safe at school; they know what will happen next; they can depend on a certain order of events.

For any given day there is a set schedule of activities. There are times established by the school for arrival of the children, lunch, dismissal, and perhaps even outdoor play if the yard must be shared by several groups of children. Within this schedule of events, you plan for

• a balance during the day. There should be a balance between active and quiet activities, group and individual experiences, manipulative, concrete activities and symbolic, abstract experiences.

• flexibility. Even though there is an established routine to each day that is predictable, there should be enough flexibility to meet the needs of the group and the individuals within the group. If the plans call for a rest time, but the children are still highly involved in some activity, there should be freedom enough for the children to continue. Or if the daily plans call for a period of quiet, but the children are bursting with unspent energy, the teacher should be free to call for a marching band, or other large-muscle, active experience.

•   each individual child. Each child, those with special needs included, should be able to establish his own rhythm during any day. The child who wants to finish lunch quickly and get on with resting should be able to do so. The child who does not nap should be able to find a satisfying activity to engage in once the others are asleep, instead of tossing restlessly on a cot simply because it is time for nap.

• transitions. Between each activity there is a transition time. These times, preceded by directions that let children know what will come next, and what they are to do to prepare for the next activity, will be a part of every daily plan. In planning for transitions teachers can ask, How will children move from one activity, or space, to another? What can I do to make this time of interest to the children or to increase the learning potential of the time? Sometimes teachers find that singing a song, finger play, or playing a game will both increase the value of and ease this time of transition.

• program goals. Each day should be planned to further the goals of the program and the objectives for each child.

• evaluation. Each day should be evaluated. Often children can be involved in the evaluation; they can be asked to recall the events of the day, discuss them, and evaluate them. Questions such as, What parts of the day did you like? Why? What should we do again? How could we solve that problem? could lead children to taking part in evaluating the day. In addition, teachers can evaluate their own performance at the end of the day as well as the performance of children.

There are many different forms of daily plans. Teachers in each program will want to decide on plans for their day. Figures 4 and 5 give examples of daily plans for children of different ages in programs that are full- and half-day.

FIGURE 4

In the Daily Schedule

3-, 4-, 5-, 6-Year Olds . . .	Need Time for	. . .5-, 6-, 7-, 8-Year Olds .
Arrival	—time to receive individual attention from the staff and be helped with coats, boots, etc. if necessary	

		—time to talk with staff and with friends —time to get help in starting an activity	
Planning	—time to become informed about the plans for the day (very young children) —time to help staff to plan their day		—time to receive guidance in planning their day —time to receive guidance in developing individual plans for projects and independent activities
Caring for their own needs		—time to use the bathroom —time to use the drinking fountain —time for snacks —time to take off or put on coats, boots, sweaters, etc. —time to rest when tired	
Indoor activities		—learning experiences related to various content and skill development areas; large blocks of time to pursue interest areas and needs: painting, reading, house corner, blocks, work bench, water table, puzzles, games, science table, live animals	
Outdoor activities		—Large blocks of time to use playground equipment (climbing apparatus, tree stumps, inner tubes, tricycles, wagons, bikes, skates, etc.); take walks; plant gardens; play with sand and water; engage in games appropriate to their age	
Quiet		—time to enjoy books (look at books, read to themselves, have stories read to them) —time to listen to music (records, tapes, visiting musicians)	

89

FIGURE 4 (*continued*)
In the Daily Schedule

3-, 4-, 5-, 6-Year Olds . . .		Need Time for	. . . 5-, 6-, 7-, 8- Year Olds
		—time to see slides, filmstrips, movies	
		—time to play quiet games	
		—time to rest on individual mats, towels, beds if necessary	
		—time for conversation with friends	
		—time to enjoy being alone	
Meals as determined by length of school day and community needs	—in the classroom	—time for family-style meals	—in the cafeteria
		—time to wash hands before meals	
		—time to cleanup after meals	
Trips and visits by resource persons		—time to walk or ride to places of interest	
		—short periods of time to listen to interesting adults and older children (policemen, artists, farmers, boy scouts, 4-H'ers)	
Cleanup		—time to put away materials and toys with the help of adults	
Evaluation		—time to discuss the day's learning with guidance of adults (share a painting, relate school and home experiences)	
		—time to discuss any concerns (playground problems, meal time, etc.)	
		—time to plan for tomorrow	

Guidelines for Early Childhood Education: Vol. XLVIII, Number 4, 1972 pp. 39–41.
Maryland State Department of Education
P.O. Box 8717
Friendship International Airport
Baltimore, Maryland 21240
Reprinted with permission.

FIGURE 5
Typical Schedules

3 Year Olds ½ Day	Full Day	4 Year Olds ½ Day
9:00–9:45 Activity period Dramatic play—home center Dramatic play—store center Blockbuilding Easel and finger painting Science—feeding fish, turtles, etc. Puppets—stories Singing **9:45–9:50** Clean-up **9:50–10:00** Handwashing, toileting **10:00–10:15** Snack or juice **10:15–10:40** Rest on mats **10:40–11:00** Put away mats Story Singing Rhythm **11:00–12:00** Outside play Short trips	**7:30–9:00** Arrival and health inspection, if required Outdoor play, if weather permits: jungle gym, bars, slides, swings, balls, sand, water play, wheel toys **9:00–9:15** Toilet routine **9:15–9:30** Juice or snack **9:30–10:00** Conversation, story, poetry **10:00** Creative activity: clay, paints, collage, blocks, woodwork tools, finger paints, dramatic play in housekeeping area **11:00** Clean-up **11:20** Quiet rest on cots **11:30** Lunch **12:00** Clean-up, toileting, preparation for rest **12:15** Naps on cots **2:00–2:30** Wake-up, toilet routine, dress **2:30** Quiet play at tables until all are awake Snack, milk, or juice **3:00** Outdoor play, walk or short trip in neighborhood **3:45** Toileting, water **4:00** Music, rhythms, dances **4:30** Getting ready to go home, toileting (for those who leave at 5:00) **5:00** Dismissal for some	**8:30–9:00** Arrival Supervised free play **9:00** Conversation, planning, checking attendance **9:15** Outdoor play: climbing, swinging, ball play, rope-jumping, simple games, sand or water play, short trips **10:00** Washing, toileting, setting table for snack **10:15** Juice or snack **10:30** Story, puppets, poetry Choosing activity for work period **11:00** Activity or work period Housekeeping: dish washing, washing doll clothes, marketing, telephoning, sweeping, mopping, dusting, etc., block building (hollow, unit or small blocks); painting; finger-painting: clay modeling: constructing with wood; working puzzles; taking care of pets, plants; cooking experiences Clean-up **11:45** Music, singing, playing instruments, listening to records, dancing, rhythmic activities **12:00 or 12:30** Dismissal

FIGURE 5 *(continued)*
Typical Schdules

3 Year Olds ½ Day	Full Day	4 Year Olds ½ Day
	5:15 Apple, carrot sticks or light snack for those who stay until 6 or later **5:30** Quiet play at tables, stories **6:00** Home	

	5 Year Olds	
Full Day	½ Day	Full Day

Full Day	½ Day	Full Day
7:30–8:30 Arrival, health inspection, outdoor play if weather permits until all arrive **8:30 or 9:00** Simple opening routine, plans for the day Activity period (see above for 4's) **10:00** Clean-up, toileting, washing, preparing table for snack or juice **10:15** Snack or juice **10:30** Outdoor activities (see 4's above) (In Florida during the hottest part of the season outdoor play may be shortened or schedule rearranged) Trips or nature walks **11:30** Washing for lunch, toileting, setting table Quiet time with books or in cots, if children are over-stimulated **12:00** Lunch, children serving themselves and cleaning tables **12:30** Preparation for rest Rest on cots	**8:30** Arrival, individual greeting Opening exercises (on public address system in some public schools), salute to flag, patriotic song Roll call (similarities in beginning letters of names, rhyming names, etc., may be part of roll call, later in year cards with names may be used for sight recognition during roll call, etc., finding out how many are present, how many are absent, girls, boys, etc.) Checking the calendar and day's weather Newstime with child as chairman and children reporting on special personal event, news from newspaper, T.V. or radio of interest to group **9:00** Music, rhythms, physical exercises to music, playing musical instruments **9:20** Planning for work activities Children choose from such activities as: making picture scrapbook, making collages, finger-painting, tempera painting, clay-work, block-building, housekeeping play, woodwork, etc. Clean-up activity	**8:30** Arrival, free play outdoors Opening exercises (see 5's above) **9:00** Activity or work period (see 5's above) **10:00** Clean-up, handwashing, setting table for juice Juice and crackers or cookies **10:30** Outdoor play (see 5's above) **11:15** Bathroom, wash-up for lunch, set tables, put down cots **11:30** Library and story-time, poetry appreciation, choral reading **12:00** Lunch with children serving themselves, one child serving as host or hostess at each table, teachers alternating tables from day to day Clearing and cleaning up tables **12:30** Rest on cots **1:30** Dressing, putting away cots **1:45** Outdoor play, organized games Trips in cars or buses to places of interest Special events such as visitor

92

2:00

Toileting, dressing, looking at books, playing with puzzles, quiet activities until all resters are awake, children put away cots

2:30

Afternoon snack

Table conversation, clean-up

2:50

Music, rhythms, singing, playing instruments, dancing, listening to records

3:20

Outdoor play or special activity such as making instant pudding, baking cookies, popping corn, digging and planting gardens; experimentation with science aspects of the environment

4:20

Story, film-strips, movies, slides

Quiet games, review of the day, plans for the next day

5:00

Dismissal for some

5:15

Light evening snack

Quiet games, songs, individual time with teacher until picked up to go home

10:00

Children spread mats for rest time and then go out to play; free choice of outdoor equipment, organized games, rope jumping, water play, short trips

10:30

Children come in from outdoor play and lie down on mats already spread

Quiet music during rest

10:50

Put away mats

Self-service juice and cookies at tables

11:00

Stories, poems, dramatization of stories, discussion

11:30 or 12:00

Children go home

to play an instrument, tell children about various occupations such as policeman, postman, etc., show slides, movies

Cooking experiences, making butter

Science experiments, gardening, etc.

Dramatization of simple stories

Construction activities such as building grocery corner in room

3:00

Clean-up and arrange room for following day

Wash-up and prepare for light snack

Snack or milk

3:30

Music, rhythms, dance, instruments, etc.

Quiet play until time to go home

Dismissal for those who accompany older brothers and sisters home from school

4:00

Summary of day and plans for next day

Reprinted with permission.
Bulletin 76, 1969. A Guide: Early Childhood Education in Florida Schools.
State Department of Education, Tallahassee, Florida, p. 17–18.

Long-Range Planning

Just as there is a focus and balance to every day, there is a focus and balance to each week, month, and school year. Goodlad (1973) reports that few of the teachers he observed had any clear sense of direction for the year, "We found scarcely any instances where teachers of young children were proceeding with a rather precise, sequenced curriculum designed to develop specific behaviors clearly envisioned by these teachers" (p. 137).

Teachers, even though it is difficult, must be able to visualize their program over a year. Thinking about where the children will be at the end of a week, month, or year will help in long-range planning. The ability to visualize where the children will be at the end of a longer period of time is necessary to provide a sense of direction for the total program.

Once you can visualize children over time, you can plan experiences and activities in sequence over a period of time. Familiar with the developmental levels of children and the types of experiences needed to reach the next developmental level, you can decide on materials for the beginning of a year and how to rearrange these materials to meet another level of maturity.

During

"In teaching, planning and doing are inextricably woven together. Planning is the selection of opportunities for learning experiences. Doing is creating experiences in the classroom, working from, but continuously modifying and adjusting the plans that are made prior to interacting with the students" (Joyce 1978, p. 1). Especially when working with young children, teaching and planning go hand in hand.

When working with young children, you must be ready to change plans and follow the interests of the children. It takes a little practice, as well as a philosophy that values children as learning, active beings. In a good school for young children, teachers give children large blocks of time for play. During these activity or work times, children are free to select their own learning materials, friends to work with, and activities to initiate or complete. It is at this time when the most teaching and learning takes place.

It is during these times that you change plans and make new ones. You constantly challenge yourself (but keep yourself in control), in an attempt to give children the opportunity to follow their own interests (Johnson 1928). "If a restricted domestic play with dolls absorbs him, one will give him added facilities for carrying it on as the occasion arises rather than introducing unrelated materials. One would not supplement his drive toward boat building and boat play with a trip to the circus or zoo" (Johnson 1936).

During the day you should constantly check yourself and your plans to be certain children are following their own interests. But there are other times that you structure spontaneous encouners to foster specific learning. Sometimes you might structure the environment in a way that presents children with problems to solve. The paste jar lids are deliberately left the way the children put them and the paste dries out. The next time the children go to paste, they can't. "Why did the paste dry out? What should we do?" Heavy blocks are added in the building area so more than one child must help in building. Or only one hole punch is provided, and children have to figure out how to share it.

Then too, you can arrange materials so children will have the opportunity to learn, practice, and reinforce concepts that you have previously identified as important for obtaining goals and objectives. The attribute blocks may be placed on a table and children asked to tell which is largest, smallest, green, or red as they play. Or place plastic bottles of various sizes and shapes at the water table, and as children play, use words to describe them.

There are other spontaneous events you actually plan for ahead of time.

94

These are the things you know will happen, sometime or other during the year. Thinking ahead you can make specific plans to capitalize on the first snowy day, a pair of new shoes, a loose tooth, or a birthday. These are things that you know will happen, and you can always keep plans and materials ready.

Plan ahead for

- seasonal changes—come spring, an apple tree will bloom, grasshoppers will be in abundance, or monarch butterfles will visit.
- conflicts—in any preschool classroom there will be opportunities to introduce ideas of sharing as children learn to cooperate.
- number and mathematics ideas—children must count and experience math concepts in setting tables, deciding if there are enough crackers or blocks.
- things of interest to children—you know young children and you know that certain things hold their interest—living things, insects, growing plants; mechanical things—tools of repairmen, automobiles, airplanes.

Although you will have plans in readiness, these things capture children's attention and interest. Because of the seemingly spontaneous nature of these events, children become intensely involved and highly motivated to learn.

After

Planning continues after children leave class. As teachers evaluate their day, week, or month, they adjust their plans. Evaluation can take several forms. It is natural to discuss the events of a day with friends or family. "Do you know what David did today?" or "We really must do something about those bathrooms!" and "So many of the children were interested in building with the blocks, it was really fascinating to see them." Sometimes comments are made about the day in general, "It was a fine day," or "I sure hope I won't have to face a day like today again."

This evaluation is informal, on a feeling level, and because it is, it is not sufficient in and of itself to serve as the only way of evaluating the teaching-learning process. Being able to express feelings and vent frustrations is important, for it helps you to clarify your thoughts and feelings and can even serve to pinpoint problem areas. Yet a more systematic and formal evaluation is necessary.

Information for formal evaluations can be gleaned from a number of sources. Observations of the children, standardized tests, parent-teacher conferences, home visits, and samples of children's work, all provide the basis for formal evaluations.

Evaluating Children

Everyone wants children to do well, to learn and succeed in school. The focus of a part of the formal evaluation of any preschool or primary program will be the child. This evaluation is often ongoing. It takes place as teachers

Everyone wants children to do well.

and others look at evidence of the child's progress, through observations, interviews, tests, and other sources of information. This information about individual children should enable a teacher to modify, change, adapt, or decide on goals and objectives. Because this continuous evaluation often forms the program, it is called *formative*. Looking at the progress of individual children, teachers make changes in the environment, in the types of experiences and activities they will present, forming the total program as they go.

The progress of the group will also be evaluated. When children are given a standardized test the group's progress may serve to sum up the success of the program. This evaluation is often called *summative*, for it gives a sum of the program. Summative evaluations of children's progress should come at the end of the experience and give an indication of the success of the total program.

Evaluating the Program

Evidence of the success of a program may come from summative evaluations completed on children. It is common practice for a school system or other agency to use a standardized test to evaluate the total program. The results of this type of evaluation offer teachers feedback on how successful they were in fulfilling goals and objectives.

The evaluation process should include everyone who is a member of the teaching-learning team. The aides, volunteers, principal, and parents should be involved. Perhaps members of the community will also be asked to participate in deciding on the success of a total program.

Beginning teachers often do not give much thought to evaluating themselves. Katz (1977) reports that beginners are concerned with survival, just making it from one day to the next. New teachers are worried about discipline, if they will be liked, and if they will succeed. Once this initial phase is over, however, you will begin to think about how you are doing and how you can improve your teaching.

Some teachers can use videotapes of themselves as a base for self-evaluation. Tapes made during the day can later be analyzed.

If supervised by a principal or director, you can ask your supervisor to observe you and help you evaluate your work. Before you ask someone in to evaluate you, you should both discuss your goals and objectives. If the supervisor does not know what to look for, or understand what you are trying to do, the observation will not be fruitful. A teacher might ask an outsider to observe how she is progressing in using new vocabulary, handling routines, or giving feedback to individuals.

In Summary

Teachers select and plan for children's learning. They base the selection of activities on their own values, the goals of the program, and on the needs of all of the children. They prepare children to be effective members of a democratic society. In planning, whether for short-term daily plans or for long-range plans, you should be able to identify how children will change as a result of their experience.

There are many variations for daily and long-term plans. Behaviorists and cognitive developmental theorists have different approaches to planning. It is important, however, to plan for balance based on the rhythm of the children and the day or the season. Flexibility and adaptability can be incorporated into the plans. Teachers seek neither rigidity nor total spontaneity; they must accomodate both direction and change.

Evaluation is an essential part of planning. Information for evaluating a program can be found in observations of individual children, standardized tests, conferences with parents, or informal rating scales. Some standards of evaluation are even built into lesson plans. Evaluation includes focus on children, the total program, and yourself.

Resources

Most state departments of education and local county school systems will have developed goals and objectives for programs in early childhood education, as well as possible daily plans and long-range plans. Contact your local school system for copies of their curriculum guides, and write to your state department of education requesting a copy of their early childhood education curriculum guides. The following guidelines are excellent:

Guidelines for Early Childhood Education
Maryland School Bulletin, Vol. XLVIII, Number 4, 1972
Maryland State Department of Education
P.O. Box 8717
Friendship International Airport
Baltimore, Maryland 21240

A Guide: Early Childhood Education in Florida Schools
Bulletin, 76, 1969.
State Department of Education
Tallahassee, Florida

Kindergarten, 1966
Ontario Department of Education
Ontario, Canada

Projects

1. Ask a preschool teacher if you can review her plans. How did she determine her goals and objectives? How does she plan to meet these goals? How do her plans reflect concern for individual children as well as for the total group of children?

2. What goals and objectives would you select for a school for young children? Make a list of all of the things you think important for children to learn. Which of these are similar to the general goal statements listed in Figure 3? Which are not? How many of the goals do you think can be achieved within the preschool?

3. Obtain goal statements from a Head or Home Start program, a day care center, and a cooperative nursery school. Compare these goals and objectives. Are they similar? Different? Which of the goal statements do you endorse?

4. Try your hand at writing a lesson plan for a group of four-year-old children. Pick any topic, or take the idea of fostering children's exploration of texture in their environment. How will you introduce the lesson? What activities will you do, and which will the children do, and how will you evaluate the lesson? Be certain to identify your exact goal.

5. Observe in a preschool setting and note each time children encounter a learning situation that was not preplanned. How did the teacher use these encounters to foster learning?

6. Once you are teaching you will become very busy with day-to-day activities. Before you actually enter teaching, take time to think about plans for spontaneous encounters you know will happen. Write a lesson plan and collect materials for lessons on changing weather, birthdays, conservation of materials, and accidents that could occur on the play yard.

References

GOODLAD, J.I.; KLEIN, M.F.; NOVOTNEY, J.M.; *Early Schooling in the United States*. New York: McGraw-Hill Book Company, 1973.

HILDEBRAND, V., *Introduction to Early Childhood Education*. New York: Macmillan, Inc., 1971.

JOHNSON, H., *Children in "the Nursery School."* New York: Agathon Press, Inc., 1972. First published 1928.

————, *School Begins at Two*. New York: New Republic, Inc., 1936.

JOYCE, B.R., *Selecting Learning Experiences: Linking Theory and Practice*. Washington, D.C.: Association for Supervision and Curriculum Development, 1978.

KATZ, L.G., *Talks with Teachers*. Washington, D.C.: National Association for the Education of Young Children, 1977.

The Persistence of Preschool Effects. Washington, D.C.: U.S. Government Printing Office, 1977.

ROHWER, W.D.; AMMON, P.R.; and CRAMER, P.; *Understanding Intellectual Development*. Hinsdale, Ill.: The Dryden Press, 1974.

WEIKART, D.P. and others; *The Cognitively Oriented Curriculum: A Framework for Preschool Teachers*. Urbana, Ill.: The University of Illinois. ERIC and the National Association for the Education of Young Children, 1971.

6

Organizing the Environment for Learning

The only way adults consciously control the kind of education which the immature get is by controlling the environment in which they act, and hence think and feel. We never educate directly, but indirectly, by means of the environment.

John Dewey 1916, p. 18.

The physical environment alone does not make an early childhood program. If children are to grow to become productive members of a democracy, they have more to learn than any room or physical environment can teach. It is the teacher, interacting with the children within a planned environment, who actually creates a program for young children. Yet the environment undeniably controls, either directly or indirectly, many of the teacher's and children's behaviors, actions, and interactions.

There is an undeniable and essential *fittingness* between the environment and the behavior of its inhabitants (Prescott 1977, p. 118). Think of your own home. What is done in the kitchen is uniquely different from the behaviors that take place in the living room or bedroom. The arrangement of the physical environment in a kitchen, bedroom, or bathroom dictates what types of activities, behaviors, and interactions will take place in that space.

Just as the physical arrangement of a home directs behaviors and interactions of the family members, the environment of a child care center, nursery school, or kindergarten will influence the behaviors of both children and teacher. The idea that the physical environment is a potent influencer of behavior is not new. To Rousseau the environment—if pure and unadulterated

100

Activities fit the environment.

by man's perversions—was sufficient in and of itself to educate the child. Froebel too believed fully in the power of a prepared environment, likening the kindergarten to a garden for children, where they could grow as naturally as the flowers in a well-tended garden.

Continuing throughout the history of early childhood education, the environment received the attention of educators. Montessori's entire program centered around preparing an ordered environment, and Patty Smith Hill wrote that the McMillan sisters of England "presented a most convincing study of the power of early environment which provides for health of body and refinements of beauty saturated with all those human values which make for morality and mental and emotional health" (Hill 1921, p. v.). Johnson (1928, p. 65) stated, "Our environment must be one in which the processes for growth go on fully and at an adequate rate."

The Teacher's Values

Does the environment shape the teacher's behavior or does the teacher shape the environment? Churchill said, "We shape our buildings and afterwards our buildings shape us" (Getzels 1974, p. 220). The fact of the physical environment is clear. The walls are there, the shape of the building is fixed; a teacher cannot change it. On the other hand, how the teacher uses the environment and how she arranges things within the set physical structure depends on that teacher. As in all teaching, the vision the teacher has of the child, what

101

she believes the nature of children to be, and her own values and belief systems will determine how she will use the environment.

A classroom designed by a teacher who sees the child as a reactive being, who endorses the behaviorist theory of learning, may be quite different than a classroom prepared by a teacher who views the child as Rousseau or Froebel did. The behaviorist would use specific equipment to teach specific skills and tasks. Programmed materials might be available; play equipment would be selected by the teacher and given to the children to foster specific goals. Open-ended materials—such as sand, mud, wood, clay, dress-up clothing— might not receive prominence. In fact these might even be limited in order to provide room for tables and chairs for each of the children and for teacher-directed activities.

A room designed by a teacher who embraces the theories of Rousseau and Froebel would be very different. Whatever would lead the children to self-activity would be favored. This teacher might equip the room with many open-ended materials—clay, paints, paper, crayons, dolls, clothing to dress up in, books, dishes, blocks, mud, sand, and water. And all of the materials would be arranged in such a way that the children could use them without teacher direction or interference.

A teacher who views children as organisms driven by the need to satisfy curiosity as much as by the need to satisfy hunger, as do Piaget, Hunt, and others, believe that the

> central fact in the growth and development of children is not hunger sat-
> isfaction or thirst satisfaction, or some other so called primary drive sat-
> isfaction, but the opportunity for effective interaction with the environment
> as manifested in the child's curiosity and explorative activity. (J.W. Getzels
> 1975, p. 9)

Teachers who see children as interactive, cognitive individuals provide novelty, sensory variation, and challenge in the environment. They select materials that provide for the individual's interests, rate of learning, and learning style. A programmed text or material might be available for the child who finds this type of experience of interest or value, open-ended materials would be present, and even Montessori materials.

There would be a subtle, but important difference in the arrangement of this environment and one arranged by a teacher who sees children as Rousseau did. This environment would be arranged in such a way that the children would have to identify and solve problems. Materials would be arranged together in groups, permitting children to classify and categorize their environment. There would be order and sequence in the arrangement of the materials. Not that this order and sequence would by itself guarantee the purposeful use of the materials, but it would facilitate the child's activities.

As children grow, change, and develop, the environment would also change. Progressively more complex materials would be added giving children the possibility for seeing new relationships between objects and things. This environment would be built on the vision of children as growing, thinking, intelligent, active beings.

INDOOR ENVIRONMENTS FOR LEARNERS

Dewey, who had a vision of the child as a learning, thinking, interactive being, tells the story of trying to find school furniture especially suited for children. All the school supply stores carried were desks and chairs. Finally one furniture dealer said to the disappointed Dewey, "I am afraid we have not what you want. You want something at which the children may work; these are all for listening" (Dewey 1900, p. 48).

Furniture alone does not reflect the vision of a child as a learner; the entire environment must be arranged for a physically, intellectually, and socially active child. In planning an environment for children as learners, teachers can consider (1) the reality of the physical environment; (2) child growth and development as well as the goals and purposes of the program.

A Realistic Appraisal of Learning Environments

Perhaps in some future time and place, spaces will be designed and built for children. There would be clean, open spaces, inside and out. Bathrooms and sinks with hot and cold running water would be in each room; there would be a room just for teachers, and another for parents; and each room would open onto a patio covered with an overhang. The outside spaces would be plentiful and varied. For the time being, however, many teachers must make the best of a less-than-ideal physical environment as Dewey did.

There are, in fact, many high-quality programs for children operating in buildings and physical plants that were not designed just for children. Head Start programs operate out of church basements, storefronts, and old homes. Other programs for young children are housed in school gymnasiums, shopping malls, factories, and office buildings.

Teachers with an understanding of the child as a learning, active being can and do turn even the most unpromising physical environment into one that fosters children's total growth. It has been done. The most ready examples are in the Head Start program. During the first summer and year of Head Start, few environments were specifically designed for use by children. But with careful planning teachers covered dark, dreary basement walls with children's paintings, strategically placed spotlights in dark stairwells highlighting an arrangement of flowers or plants, and turned dismal places into gardens where children could grow. Murphy (1977, p. 7), recalling these centers, states,

103

"When a child care center has successfully fixed up a tumbledown place, it stands out like a shining example in a drab neighborhood."

When spaces for children are less than ideal, teachers must make some hard decisions about their use. The ideas of Cornelia Goldsmith (1972), who helped day care operators in New York City make the most of whatever situation they were in, can be of use to preschool teachers today. When operators applied to the city for a license, they were asked to bring to the agency, in writing, a (1) detailed floor plan of indoor and outdoor spaces; (2) written statement of the goals, objectives, and purpose of the program; (3) information about the nature of the children served; and (4) budget information. With these realities clearly in view the day care operators were helped to plan effective environments for children's learning.

Only after teachers clearly see the reality of the situation can they ask themselves:

1. Can separate rooms be closed off, or opened up? Could one room in a home be used as a block building room? Could another room be cleared of all furniture and used only for physical activity?
2. Will wide-open spaces in a room lead to discipline problems? How can these spaces be divided so the teacher has control over all children? Can the spaces be divided and organized to direct children in subtle ways? What screens can be built to provide smaller spaces for individual or small group work and play?
3. When space is limited, is there some way to create spaces where children can work undisturbed and protected, with distractions reduced so children can concentrate?
4. How can adult traffic be rerouted so children are not interrupted while at work or play?
5. How can storage spaces be provided?
6. What can be done to decorate the room, to brighten and create aesthetically appealing places?
7. How prepared am I to rearrange furniture as necessary? Who can help during the day if we want the tables moved to the side of the room for music activities?
8. What provisions can be made for children with special needs? Can all children including those in wheelchairs, or with braces, with hearing or visual impairment, function in the room?

Every teacher, when planning the environment, must ask herself these questions; however, when the physical plant is less than ideal, the questions become more critical. Will a swing take up valuable playground space that could be better utilized with some piece of equipment that can be stored when the children's interests change? How will children have safe, but ready, access to the bathrooms when playing outdoors? Considering the nature and needs of the young child helps the teacher answer these questions.

Child Growth and Development

Children who are physically, intellectually, socially, and emotionally active require space. The Federal Interagency Day Care Requirements (1968) suggest that there be at least thirty-five square feet of indoor space per child, not counting bathrooms, halls, or kitchens; others (Hymes, 1974) believe that between forty and fifty square feet of space per child is more ideal. At least seventy-five square feet of space per child outdoors is suggested. When there is less space inside, it may be that the outdoor spaces can be used for more of the day. The amount of empty space seems as important as amount of total space. When large numbers of children are present in one group, it appears as if a larger total square footage of space is beneficial, and a larger amount of empty space is required to help children move through the room.

When planning for active children, consider not only the amount of space, but also the things in the space and the way they are arranged. The quality of the space—giving children materials and equipment they can push, shove, stack, climb into and out of, around and under, without knocking into each other or equipment—is of utmost importance.

PLANNING FOR INTELLECTUAL AND PHYSICAL ACTIVITY

Young children are both physically and intellectually active. Piaget points out that for the first years of life a child's intellectual activity is actually physical activity (Piaget 1969). The sensorimotor stage of intelligence as described by Piaget dictates that space be organized in ways that permit children's intellectual development.

Establishing centers of interest, with all dramatic play materials in one area of the room, blocks in another, and quiet table games together in another corner of the room gives children a sense of purpose for the materials as well as clearly defined areas for specific types of activities. This ordering helps children see relationships and fosters their intellectual growth.

Planning for traffic patterns through the space also is related to children's thinking and learning (Le Laurin and Risley 1972). When traffic patterns were clearly defined and part of the room arrangement plan, there was less aimless activity or wandering about on the part of the children, and there was more time spent by the children in constructive activities, either with others or with materials.

One way to plan for traffic patterns is to make a floor plan of the room. What will happen if the easels are placed near the windows? Will children have access to the sink or the drying rack? How will children get to the library area? Can the teacher or other adult have easy access to any area of the room? What about the children with handicaps, can they manage to get from place to place without difficulty?

Even when teachers plan and think ahead, they still need to adjust the arrangement of things within space as the children, or each group of children, use the space. It takes a period of experimentation. Trying the room arranged one way, changing it to accommodate differences in children, and moving the equipment around may be necessary before the ideal room arrangement is reached.

Another way to foster children's intellectual growth through room arrangement is to select toys that have no predetermined use, that are not detailed or complex, but permit children to develop their own genuine play interests. Boxes, boards, planks, and pieces of hoses motivate children to seek solutions, to imagine that one thing is another, in effect to use symbols. The block becomes a barber's razor, a knotted rag, a doll. Sand, rocks, blocks, unstructured materials like clay, paints, paper, and crayons can be used by the children in many different ways.

"In our choice of equipment we have tried to provide materials which would not only develop the bodies of children, but also have genuine play content and follow the lines of genuine play interests of the children" (Johnson 1928, p. 68). Toys that permit children to repeat activities and actions are also preferred by young children (Millar 1968, p. 210), but a certain degree of novelty and variety should also be present.

Intellectually, children need to see, feel, and experience the relationships between different materials and things within the environment. They need to see, feel, and actually experience for themselves the differences between a large, hollow, light block and a smaller, but solid wood, heavier block, or to find out that the tall, narrow container holds the same amount of sand and water as the square, short container. Any equipment or material that permits children to compare and contrast sizes, shapes, colors, textures, weights, to see likenesses and differences, or relationships between objects and things, facilitates children's intellectual development.

PLANNING FOR SOCIAL ACTIVITY

"It is essential to our plan that the social organization should be so fluid that escape may be easy for any individual at any time" (Johnson 1928, p. 86). Planning spaces for play must consider the social needs and development of the young child as well as the intellectual needs. There must be a place for children to work together and materials deliberately arranged for group activity, but there must also be places for children to be alone, and things for them to work with while alone.

When there is a lack of space and too many children within any one space, fewer pro-social behaviors and more aggressive acts occur (Cannon 1966). This seems true both inside and outside. Children engaged in many more aggressive activities outdoors when playground spaces were limited (Ginsburg and Pollman 1975).

The number of play materials available also seems to influence the social behaviors of children. When few toys are available, more destructive play and aggressive behavior occurs (Rohe, Patterson, and Altman 1975). If aggressive behavior is not desired, then teachers should provide adequate equipment for the number of children within any group. Large, movable play apparatus, climbing units that can be taken apart and rebuilt, large blocks, wood planks, and boxes have also been found to be more conducive to creative, social play than very small items of equipment (Smith 1974). It seems as if the larger materials require several children, together, to create an item for play, while the smaller pieces of equipment can be used alone.

Planning for children's social learning must also take into consideration the child's total background. Each school environment should reflect the child's social background. "The learning in school should be continuous with that out of school. There should be free interplay between the two. This is possible only where there are numerous points of contact between the social interests of the one and the other" (Dewey 1900, p. 358). The school environment of children of migrant workers should somehow differ from that of children in the inner city of Chicago, or from that provided for children of Native American heritage.

With young children's needs being so similar, no matter what their background or heritage, it is true that preschool environments across the nation will also be similar. Yet teachers must be sensitive to the cultural heritage of each group of children as they plan for children's social growth. As Dewey suggested, the more contacts teachers have with the parents and with the child's home, the better they will be able to make the school environment congruent with the home. When the teacher knows the parents and the cultural heritage of the family, she will be able to select different types of cooking equipment, tools, dress-up clothing, books, and other materials that will permit the children to reenact their social life at home and find a familiar base for work and play at school.

PLANNING FOR EMOTIONAL ACTIVITY

Environments for young children must also consider the emotional activity of the young. Children are egocentric, they care about themselves. With children it is the big *I* and the little *you*. Since it is the nature of the child to be egocentric, children are quick to express their emotions. They will fly off in a rage, kicking and lashing out, or quickly withdraw into themselves, sulking at any invitation to join the group. And they are just as quick to express joy or happiness, burst into giggles, or dance and sing with glee.

Because children's emotions are so close to the surface, space should be available for the safe expression of emotions. Clearly defining areas for various types of equipment, providing enough materials, and planning traffic patterns help meet children's emotional needs. They also need materials and equipment that will permit safe, healthy expression and release of emotions. A climbing unit that is just high enough to challenge, yet not so high as to frighten, or boxes that can be shoved and stacked (but not so easily as to negate children's feeling a sense of accomplishment) are examples of equipment that give children feelings of mastery.

Emotional security also stems from the familiar. Children, just like the motel guest in advertisements, need to know there will be no major surprises within the physical environment. There is a sense of emotional security and mastery when you know that the paste, scissors, and paper will always be in the same place, or that the blocks are always waiting on the open shelves.

Emotional strength grows as children are able to care for the things in the environment without adult help. There are clear places for equipment, and material is accessible to the children. Materials are arranged in a way that communicates their use, as well as storage. Symbols on shelves, a picture of a pair of scissors, or egg cartons turned upside down with holes to place and store the scissors in, clearly let children know how to care for things.

Sameness of the environment, however, does not mean a monotonous, unchanging room. Too much sameness leads children to discomfort and even boredom (Millar 1969, p. 114). The environment does change, but the children are involved in changing it. Wheel toys, and toy people are added to the block area when children's experiences or interests dictate, tools for working with clay or different paints and brushes added to the easel when children have achieved mastery over the previous materials. The decorations of the room change as children create new artwork and their interests change. Children can also be involved in major room changes. They can be asked to give suggestions on storing the records or puzzles, where to place the piano, or how to solve room arrangement problems. "We're having trouble with the blocks, people keep knocking down buildings as they go to wash their hands at the sink, what can we do about this?" gives children the opportunity to offer suggestions for room arrangement.

Toys and materials also reflect the changing interests of the children. Having played store over and over, children gradually find the area dull. So the store is removed, perhaps gradually, until it can be replaced with a new area of interest, perhaps a gas station, airplane, or whatever reflects children's new experiences and interests.

Arranging Inside Spaces

There is no right or wrong way to arrange inside spaces for children's play. Centers of interest, however, are a rational way for adults to "put things in space for children to play with but where things are put seems related to rationale rather than happenstance" (Kritchevsky 1969, p. 40). Areas, or centers of interest, give children the opportunity they need for physical, intellectual, social, and emotional development. The number and type of centers of interest in any one room depends on the size of the space, the number of children in the group, and the needs, ages, and interests of the children. At the very least, however, there should be provision for a dramatic play area; a place for block building; a library corner; manipulative game area; and science, math, art, woodworking, music, and audio-visual centers.

Dramatic Play Areas

This is the traditional play area of the kindergarten. Once called the doll corner, or housekeeping area, it is now called the dramatic play area. This is the place where children have the opportunity to react to the things they experience in their homes, neighborhoods and communities. Here they play, sorting out their world, making sense of the social roles they encounter in real life.

With over one-half of all mothers of children under the age of six in the work force and the breakdown of sex-role stereotyping, the nature of the area and the play that takes place in the area has changed. No longer do children find only replications of their homes, with kitchen equipment, armchairs, and doll babies. No longer do the mommies care for the house and babies, and the daddies go happily off to work. Now children, both boys and girls, care for the home, the children, and play going to work.

Yet in some respects the dramatic play area is the same as it has always been, for here children do find equipment which represents the familiar to them. The objects in the area, or models of objects, are taken from the child's home and neighborhood environment. These provide the child with a safe experiential baseline. "From this baseline, the child can make forays into the unknown under the drive for stimulus variation and can return to this baseline when he finds too much incongruity between what he already knows and the novelty he encounters" (Curry 1974, p. 66).

Usually small groups of five or six children congregate in the dramatic play area at a time. Here they take on the roles they have experienced or observed in life and reach the highest level of social interchange (Shure 1963, p. 102), as "they cooperate to form a family unit, or to act out patient/doctor roles, bus driver, passenger, office worker, and administrator."

A variety of equipment and materials is found in the area. Hartley (1952) believes that teachers have never fully exploited the power of materials in the dramatic play area to influence the growth of children. She relates how highly aggressive boys from tough neighborhoods, where physical prowess was highly valued, spent time in nurturing activities, washing, drying, feeding, and changing baby dolls, when the dress-up dolls were removed and baby dolls were added.

Clothing to dress up in is an essential part of the area. Not everything is available at the same time. Nor is the entire item of clothing or outfit necessary to stimulate dramatic play. Often a mere suggestion of a piece of clothing, such as a piece of lace or discarded curtain, is enough to stimulate children's thinking and direct them to take on a variety of roles. At any one time the dramatic play area might include any of the following items:

Hats—cowboy, police, hard hats, feathered and flowered, fishing, baseball, beret.
Clothes—suit coats, dresses, blouses, shirts, stoles, shawls, half slips with lace trim on the bottom, pieces of lace.
Trimmings—gloves, feathers, flowers, jewelry, ribbons, bows, ties, badges, belts, mufflers, mittens, dress gloves.
Shoes—men's and women's dress-up shoes, work shoes, galoshes, slippers.
Carrying Cases—purses, wallets (with money), tool kits, briefcases, lunch boxes or buckets, tool belts.

Furniture, or suggestions of furniture, are present. Discarded boxes, painted with suggestions of knobs to turn can represent a stove; another box, or wooden crate, becomes a refrigerator. Usually stove, sink, kitchen cupboard, refrigerator, table, and chairs are present in one form or another. But sofas, chairs, and beds can be added. The local thrift shop or church rummage sale is a good place to find the types of equipment that will stimulate children's dramatic play.

Things that are real have special appeal to children. Any electrical or mechanical appliance can be safety proofed and used in the dramatic play area when no longer useful to adults. These items—toasters, irons, radios which can no longer be repaired, must not have plugs, wires, breakable tubes, or electrical or sharp parts. If you need help in fixing items, the shop teacher, or other consultant, might be willing to give assistance.

Teachers usually find that they can furnish the dramatic play area without a great deal of expense by eliciting help from parents, the PTA, or a local church group. Within any dramatic play area, the following items might be found:

Reading Materials—newspapers, telephone books, receipt books, discarded checkbooks, calendars, pad and pencils, old stamps, trading stamps, stationery, cookbooks, advertising circulars, envelopes.

Kitchen Equipment—boxes to represent sink and stove, iron, toaster, egg beater, spoons, pots, pans, cups, dish drainer, towels, sponges, containers for water and soap, muffin tins, empty and safety-proofed cans of food, cans with food still in them, empty boxes of cereal, and cereal boxes filled with pegs or Styrofoam packing bits.

Baby Equipment—dolls, clothes, beds, lotion bottles, baby powder, tubs, high chairs.

Repair Items—tools, pipes, oil cans, hoses, ladders.

Health Aids—Band-Aids, bandages, cotton, stethoscope.

Other Items—bathroom scale, kitchen scale, road maps, suitcases, telephones, gardening equipment, plants.

While the dramatic play area representing the home environment is a permanent part of any school for young children, other dramatic play areas can be established because children's interests are constantly changing.

Prop boxes (Bender 1971) are one way to provide for children's changing play interests when space is a problem. Large, sturdy boxes—beer cases are excellent—are painted, and props suggesting a specific career, activity, or community area are placed in the box. One box might have a mirror, wig, plastic cap, capes, hair rollers, and other items suggesting beauty or barbershop play. Still another box could have bits of hoses, helmets, tools, gloves, and boots, suggesting astronaut play. The boxes, clearly labeled with a picture representing the items in the box, are stacked against a wall or in a corner of the room, and children are free to select the box of props that meets their immediate play interests and needs.

At other times, two chairs with a board across them are all the children need to build a store, post office, or gasoline station. For a store, a cash register, empty food cartons, paper bags, pencils and paper for adding up the bill, play money, wallets, and purses are added. A post office is just as easy to simulate, using the board across two chairs as the window. Stamps, junk mail, rubber stamps, pencils, paper, envelopes, and bags in which to carry the mail make a fine post office.

A dentist or doctor's office is just as easily established. Children need only a suggestion of equipment or items used in these offices to take on the role of patient and doctor. A white coat, chair, tongue depressors, stethoscope, and flashlight should be sufficient to motivate children's dramatic play.

An office corner, with a discarded but working typewriter, rubber stamps, calendars, telephones, paper, pencils, carbon paper, and discarded receipt books encourages children to act out office roles. The same two chairs with a board across them and a sign labeled "Office," "Post Office," or "Doctor" are all that is required.

Some of these dramatic play areas may last a day or two, and then children will move on to another type of play. Others may extend for longer periods of time and become more permanent areas of the room. The purpose of these changing areas is simply to meet children's interests, to facilitate their taking on the roles of others, to allow them to play out their experiences. When these needs are fulfilled, the area can be dismantled or replaced with a different area of interest.

Blocks

An original gift of Froebel, blocks are a tradition in schools for young children. The usefulness of blocks has long been accepted by early childhood educators, but "what is more, blocks have the clear stamp of approval of the children themselves" (Hartley 1952, p. 99). Wherever the blocks are located, children will congregate.

The youngest nursery school child carries the blocks about, handling, shifting them from one place to another. Then she tries stacking them in a mass, without any form or function and with no purpose in mind other than the sensory enjoyment and pleasure of sheer manipulation. Three and four year olds will begin to stack the blocks into structures that they will name. Five year olds can plan ahead, designing and building complex, elaborate structures—airports, castles, farms, or moon houses—which they will want to keep up, add to, and change, continuing the theme of their play over several days, even weeks, if permitted to let the structure stand.

Boys do seem to gravitate to the blocks (Shure 1963; Hartley 1952), and at times teachers may need to encourage girls to elect to build with the blocks or encourage them in some other way to aggressively break down the sexual stereotype that boys are constructors and builders, and girls are helpers.

Social interaction seems high in the block area, and there is often a great deal of cooperative effort and play (Shure 1963; Hartley, 1952). On the other hand, the block area has been found to be the area where the most destructive and aggressive behavior occurs (Houseman 1972; Hartley 1952). Because of this, the block area should be located where teachers can observe the children and be ready with supervision and guidance if necessary. It is also helpful,

A place for blocks.

because the area is a noisy one, to locate it away from quiet activities requiring children's concentration, and out of traffic paths so buildings will not be accidentally destroyed as children move through the room.

Froebel's original blocks were small, and designed to bring the child to God through unity. The blocks were called unit blocks, because two single blocks would make one double, with each block fitting into another to form a whole or unit. Froebel had specific activities for children to complete with these blocks, under the direction of the teacher. Today the blocks still form a whole, but they are larger and are used freely by the children, without teacher control or interference.

A variety of blocks is recommended. The smooth, wooden, solid unit blocks, with arches, semicircles, triangles, double arches; a set of large, hollow blocks to push around; as well as sets of parquet blocks of various shapes, colors, and size give children opportunities to fulfill creative urges.

Although the original investment in a set of wooden blocks is expensive, it is worthwhile. The blocks will last forever, are usable and enjoyed by children of any age, and because there is no predetermined end in mind, are continually attractive to the children.

To facilitate children's use of the blocks, storage on open shelves is best. The blocks can be sorted and categorized on shelves according to size and shape. This way children can see all of the blocks available and can hypothesize about the possibilities for building.

As children create with the blocks, additional materials are added to the area. Lucy Sprague Mitchell (1936) used large brown strips of paper to represent streets and large blue pieces of paper for rivers and lakes. Farm animals, people, wheel toys, all extend children's block play. The use of natural materials, rocks, sticks, pieces of wood, even sand, adds reality to the area. Eventually children will acquire the need to label their buildings, the streets, or parts of the city.

Reading

Every room needs a quiet area for books, a place to be with others, or by oneself, to contemplate, to look at pictures in a book; a place to listen to a record of someone reading a book, or to find a measure of peace and escape from the active areas of the room. A table, small chairs, and shelves for books are all that is necessary. Cushions or carpet squares that the children can carry outside or to any other area in the room are fun. A stuffed arm chair or a rocking chair is comfortable, inviting children to sit and read.

Current magazines, especially those with pictures, can be enjoyed by children. Parts of the newspaper—the magazine section, a sports page, or picture pages—are also valuable in the library.

Reference materials should be a part of the library. Encyclopedias, not necessarily an entire set, but perhaps selected volumes that include topics the children are interested in, picture dictionaries, a teacher's dictionary, and other reference materials foster the habit of seeking information through books.

Catalogues of any kind—toy, clothing, appliance—are real treasures. Children pore over these, just enjoying naming items or dreaming about things they wish they had. If two of the same catalogue are available, children can dream together. Old worn-out books can be cut apart, with pictures mounted on heavy paper and added to the library table. These are used by the children to retell a story, to sequence a story, or just to carry around with them. Scrapbooks, made by the children themselves, and books of children's artwork are favorites; a photo album of pictures of the children on a fieldtrip, the first day of school, using a new piece of playground equipment, or just working and playing, is a best-loved book.

Some teachers like to add materials that encourage children's activity in the library corner. A flannel board, complete with cutouts of a favorite story or two, a chalkboard with chalk for creating chalk talks, puppets, and other props extend children's interest in reading.

Manipulative Games and Table Toys

Another quiet area of the room should be set aside for manipulative toys. Small blocks, things to sort and classify such as bottle caps, buttons, seeds, paint chips—card games, table games, bingo and lotto games, puzzles, pegboards, parquet blocks, Lego blocks, and any other small games can be considered manipulative toys. The games, toys, and materials are stored on open shelves, near a table and set of chairs. Children have access to the materials and select certain ones to take to the table to work with. At other times the teacher may put a puzzle or game on the table as a suggestion to the children.

This area—calling for children to concentrate on a given task, to follow the rules of a game, to sort, classify, and categorize materials, to concentrate on solving a puzzle—should be sheltered from the more active areas of the room. This is clearly a place for children to work, uninterrupted by children pushing trucks or acting out roles of mother and father.

Science

There is really no one place for all of the materials and objects related to science. Growing plants, fish, living animals, insects, indoor and outdoor thermometers are all around the room. Yet, there is still a need for a specific area for the active pursuit of science activities.

Whatever interests the children and fosters the goals of the program can be built on and extended with a science area. Children fascinated with growing things could plant seeds. Some of the seeds could be placed in cups of dirt, others on dampened paper towels or sponges, and children's attention could be focused on the changes that ocur. A prism, different colored plastic squares, and a flashlight allow children to observe the properties of light. A magnifying glass lets the children learn still more about their world by allowing them to see the beauty, simplicity, and complexity of insect wings, leaves, and other things.

Water and sand play can be considered components of the science area. If children are not given the opportunity to explore water under conditions established by the teacher, they will find their own way of playing with water, sneaking it into the dramatic play area or the library. It is so much easier, especially on the teacher, to include water play as an integral part of the program. When the teacher plans to include water, she is fully in control, minimizing unwanted, out-of-control experiments.

It is not necessary to have large, free-standing water tables. These are expensive and take up a lot of space. A dishpan, set on the floor or table top, is really all the children need for water play. They also need things to use with the water—plastic containers of all sorts and types, hoses, strainers, funnels, spoons, cups—anything that will not break and will let children find out about the nature of water.

Things to wash—dolls and doll clothes, windows, tables, or other furniture in the room—give the children another use for water. As with other materials, the use of water and the items added to the water should increase in complexity as the children gain knowledge and mastery over the medium. When the children tire of plain water, soap can be added, and when they tire of blowing bubbles and washing, a drop of food coloring can be added, and when they tire of that, a tray of ice cubes, or block of ice can remotivate and stimulate their interest and promote a different kind of play.

Sand play offers much the same type of science and math experiences as water. Children can determine how much sand fills one container and compare that amount with the sand or water in another container. They might even weigh the sand or water if a scale is handy. A sandbox can be created from any shallow cardboard box or container. The container, whatever it is, can be placed on the floor, on a table or chair. As children experiment with the sand, other materials are added. Water, in plastic squirt bottles, permits the children to dampen the sand so they can create buildings, roads, and cities. Pebbles, sticks, play people, animals, cars, marbles—anything that serves to extend children's play with the sand—are useful.

Art

Art, like science, takes place all over the room. Rather than one center or area for art, there are many. Children need to find clay, boards to work on, and other clay tools stored on one shelf, always waiting for them. This clay, with the boards, can be taken anywhere in the room or can be used on a special table for children who want to work together. Other modeling materials—play and salt dough, plasticine, cornstarch dough, even bread dough—might take the place of clay for specific activities.

Paints can be found at the easels, as well as in other areas of the room. Water colors, brushes, and containers for water and paper might be placed on a shelf; tempera paint can be stored in covered containers, in a six-pack container that can be carried anywhere.

Things to draw with should be handy for the children. Crayons of all types, sizes, and shapes, many kinds of paper, magic markers, pens, pencils, and chalk should be available to the children every day. Paste, scissors, collage materials, and scrap paper, located together, permit children to select the tools and materials they need for any project they have in mind.

Woodworking

No room for young children is complete without some place for wood. An elaborate woodworking bench is not necessary, but children do need to have tools that actually work, soft wood, nails, and a C-clamp to hold a piece of wood to the table while they work. The woodworking center does require supervision, but most importantly it requires direct teaching. It is simply not reasonable to believe that young children will discover for themselves how to use a saw, hammer, and nails to join wood together and build.

It may be necessary to introduce children to one tool at a time. Giving children a hammer, nails, and soft wood or a tree trunk to pound nails into is the first step. Children enjoy pounding nail after nail into the soft wood, removing the nails with the claw end of the hammer and beginning again, until they have firmly mastered themselves, the wood, and hammer. Next, saws can be introduced. The children need to know how to begin making a cut in the wood, how to attach the wood with the C-clamp to the table, and where to place their hands.

Tools can be hung from a pegboard placed above the working table or bench. This gives children easy access to the tools they know how to use. If an outline of the tool is traced with paint or magic marker on the board, children have the added experience of recognizing the configurations of the tools and an aid in keeping tools in their proper places.

If there is space for the woodworking table to become a permanent part of the center, children will have the opportunity to gain the skills necessary to actually construct objects. They begin by joining two pieces of wood together, simply exploring the properties of the materials. Later these joinings make them think of some item—an airplane, car, train—and still later children will plan ahead before they start to build.

The beauty of wood—clean, aromatic, solid, with weight—appeals to children. There is nothing you really need to do a good job with wood besides wood scraps, nails, hammers, and saws, but many teachers have found that locks, hinges, hooks and eyes, pieces of screening, drawer knobs and pulls, and other bits of scrap hardware are treasured by the children and stimulate even more creative building. Other teachers add strong glue to the area, along with carpet scraps, leather, plastics, and other materials that can be affixed to the wood.

Music

Some area in the room can also be set aside for a music center. A small table, perhaps holding a record player, with a selection of records, one or two musical instruments to experiment with, or a selection of other sound makers can offer children the opportunity to listen to, as well as to make, music.

Not all musical instruments need be available all of the time. The teacher can select one or two or a group of instuments to place in the area. She might give the children prior experience with the instruments, introducing them at a music session, but in the area, children can reproduce the sounds they hear and create music at their own pace.

Most young children, with a few simple directions, can use a record player without adult assistance. A variety of records, selected by the teacher, may be placed by the player. The teacher will probably have to limit the volume when children play music during regular playtime. Usually children enjoy the privilege of playing records for themselves, and they do not abuse this privilege.

Audio-Visual Center

Audio-visual materials are a real, and important part of children's lives. Most children spend a great deal of time viewing television, up to forty hours per week, and many have had their own record players since they were toddlers. As a parallel to children's interest and knowledge of audio-visual equipment, a center can be set aside for audio-visual experiences.

Slides of children taken while on a field trip, when the police officer visited the school, or at work and play are of interest to the children when they can show the slides themselves. At other times, a filmstrip, or movie version of a story, or another item of interest can be provided in the center.

Direct teaching of the use of the slide projector or filmstrip projector should take place prior to asking children to use these independently. Perhaps the teacher might even check each child's ability to use each piece of equipment she presents before permitting all children to use the equipment. Supervision will be required to ensure that the equipment will be used properly and enjoyed by all.

In addition to visual aids, a number of listening activities can take place in the audio-visual center. Listening jacks, tape recordings, and record players might be a part of the center. Again, children enjoy listening to their own voices or to the teacher or another adult reading a favorite story, but they also like commercial materials.

Perhaps this center would not be a permanent part of the environment. It is not always feasible to have audio-visual materials for continual use, especially if a school shares the equipment, or equipment is borrowed from the local library. Nor are children always interested in using the same materials over and over.

It is much more appropriate to introduce children to the use of one piece of equipment at a time, letting them use the slide projector to show slides of themselves, or of a story; once the interest is satisfied, remove the projector. The projector can be replaced with a different item of equipment, or the center can be taken down until the next time something of special interest would be appropriate.

It is easy to set up an audio-visual center. Any quiet corner will do. A tri-part screen, set on a table, surrounded by a few chairs, is all that is necessary. Sometimes, depending on the room, a curtain of paper can be taped across a window or some other screen set up to darken this corner enough to permit the children to view the films, slides, or filmstrips.

Evaluation of the Centers

Learning centers do not stay the same all of the time. Depending on the growth of the children and their interests, as well as program goals, the centers change, both in materials available in each center and in the number and type of centers present at any given time. Centers can be introduced by the teacher to focus children's interests, to provide a new experience for the children, to help reinforce the children's interest in a topic or to reinforce concepts children are in the process of developing.

All centers, however, do reflect the child's experiential life at home, in the community, and in the school. There should be some relationship between the centers present, either relating to past experiences or to one another, as children develop a theme in their play.

After the centers have been established, teachers can evaluate the effectiveness of the arrangement. You might ask yourself:

1. What does the room arrangement say about my own philosophy of children? Have I brought my own unique experiences to the centers? If, for example, you enjoy raising tropical fish, do you have an aquarium in the room? If your hobby is growing cacti, do you have desert terrariums in the class?

2. Are the centers placed in the room to permit the children to make clear choices between the centers and within the centers? Are the materials organized so that children can see the relationships between them?

3. What provisions have I made for children with special needs? Are there centers and materials for the gifted (perhaps books on astronomy for the child interested in stars, or a microscope for another child), and for children with handicaps (room for a wheelchair in the centers and ramps to permit access to all areas?

4. Can the equipment be used by children of different ages, with different interests, and different developmental levels? Are there blocks, unstructured art materials, multilevel books, dramatic play equipment that can be used in different ways by children of differing abilities and maturity?

5. Are storage areas clearly defined? Can children use the equipment and then return it to the storage place without adult help?

6. Is there a balance between the highly active, noisy centers and quiet areas? Are these areas separated? Is the library area clearly away from the block area? Are other areas separated with low screens or some other barrier?

7. Are traffic patterns clearly defined so children are not running into one another as they move from center to center? Look at the room—can you see distinct pathways in the room leading to and from each center?

8. Is there a place for beauty—pictures, prints on the walls, or a table set aside to display items with aesthetic qualities? In England teachers drape beautiful pieces of cloth as backdrops for displaying dried flowers, ceramic pieces, and other items.

9. Are there centers for children to play and work in by themselves and other centers for groups of children to work together? Is there a balance between these centers? Are there pillows for the individual children to take to a quiet area to be by themselves? Grouping chairs around a table encourages children to congregate.

10. Is the equipment in the centers complex enough to offer children a challenge, yet simple enough to offer them success? How can you increase the complexity of the centers and the material within the centers as the children grow and develop? Adding pencils and pads of paper to the store area or telephone books and receipt books in the dramatic play area might be an example of increasing the possibility for more complex play.

11. Do the centers reflect and foster the goals of the program, and the goals and objectives you have set for individual children? Check back to your goals. Do the centers include symbols and printed labels to increase children's awareness of the relationship between the spoken and printed word?

OUTDOOR ENVIRONMENTS FOR LEARNERS

"One myth of contemporary education is that most learning takes place in a classroom. . ." (Sommer 1975). The outside environment is every bit as important for children's learning as the inside. The time children spend outside and the learning that takes place is every bit as critical as the time indoors. So often preschool teachers focus on ordering and arranging the indoor environment for learning that they forget the necessity of a carefully planned outdoor learning environment (Goodlad 1973).

Planning for learning outdoors includes the same care, thought, and creativity that planning the inside environment requires. The age, number of children, and the number of groups of children who will use the same play space must all be considered. Of most importance is the size and nature of the space available.

The fencing that closes in spaces, the surfaces that cover the space—whether blacktop, grass, or sand—the number of trees, and access to water often cannot be changed. In addition, the safety features of the space and the equipment within the space must be carefully assessed. In planning for the arrangement of space outdoors, consider that its major purpose is to permit physical activity.

A Realistic Assessment
of Outside Space

The Federal Interagency Day Care Requirements (1968) suggest that seventy-five square feet of space per child is an adequate area for children's outdoor learning. Other sources (Hymes 1974) believe that 100 to 150 square feet of outside space is required for children who are going to be running, jumping, climbing, and exercising their developing large muscles.

Just like inside, lack of space—or too much space—outdoors can present problems. An extremely small play yard negates running and sprinting about, but a space that is too large, too open, and too spread out, splinters groups, and makes it difficult for the children to engage in cooperative play. When space is large, children cannot even see the choices that are possible. Supervision is also more difficult. A teacher simply cannot simultaneously help a child onto a piece of climbing equipment at one end of the yard and offer guidance to children in the sandbox at the other end of the yard.

Harriet Johnson (1928) was not that concerned about the actual number of square feet in her nursery school. Rather, she was concerned about the arrangement of things within the available space and with providing "an environment with which the child's developmental needs are met, whether it be under green trees or in a city back yard" (p. 75).

Johnson (1928, p. 75) actually preferred the city-roof play space to a yard or park, "It can usually be placed so that it receives sun for most of the day and consequently the snow and wet clear from it rapidly."

Space is, nevertheless, the first thing to consider when planning for outdoor play. If space is limited, more decisions will have to be made about the organization of the yard, the type of equipment to provide, and how to provide for large-muscle activities. Johnson (1928) believed that when space was limited, it was important that whatever space was available be used for wheel toys, digging, and other large-muscle activities that could not take place indoors (p. 41).

Another consideration is the type of surface of the play space. If a yard is completely covered with blacktop or concrete, it might be possible for the teacher to arrange to have some of this surfacing removed to permit children spaces to dig, play in mud, or plant seeds. On the other hand, a surface that is all grass or sand may be made more interesting by the addition of some concrete or blacktop, which will permit children to ride wheel toys. Covering an area of hardtop with wood chips, sand, or creating a large sand area are other ways of giving children a variety of textured surfaces to explore outdoors.

Once the size of the space is understood and surfacing considered, the permanent pieces of equipment within the space should be taken up. Teachers might ask what pieces of equipment can and cannot be removed, or how these pieces could be more profitably used by young children. A large climbing unit, designed for older children, might be covered with blankets to create a house, fort, or hiding place. Other items of equipment, perhaps a swing set, could be removed to make room for equipment that is more flexible, which can be taken apart and stored, or used in many different ways.

When children of several different ages must use the same yard, the equipment must be carefully chosen. What may be safe for a five or seven year old may not be safe for a two or three year old. Some teachers have placed ropes around climbing units or other types of permanent equipment clearly not safe for very young children and declared these items "off limits." Equipment designed for the youngest children, which could be damaged by older children, could be declared off limits to the older children.

Making a floor plan or map of the outdoor area may help a teacher decide how to arrange the space, which equipment to take away, which to add, and how to get the most use out of the space. Teachers might ask themselves:

1. Can children find opportunities in the play yard to be by themselves, with another child, or with a group of children?
2. What are the present interests of the children? How can these interests be provided for outdoors? What goals of the program can be fostered outdoors?
3. What is the developmental level of the children? How tall are they, how much weight will it take to push, pull, or play with the equipment? What are the children's specific capabilities and needs in the area of climbing, running, pulling, and pushing?
4. At what times of the day will areas of the yard be in full sun? Shaded? What activities can be planned for open sun or shade?
5. How will children get from one area of the yard to another? How can traffic patterns for running, bicycle and tricycle riding, or for children and adults walking from one area to another be created?
6. Is everything safe for children? Are pieces of glass, stones, and broken equipment removed? Are all objects removed from under climbing equipment? Are sharp edges, nails, bolts, and nuts removed from playthings? As surfacing plays a role in three-quarters of all playground accidents, are surfaces under climbing equipment covered with sand, wood chips, or some other safe, soft surface?
7. What adjustments can be made to permit children with special needs to experience a full range of activity outdoors?

In the United States, play spaces for children are apparently sparsely furnished (Goodlad 1973). Only fifty percent of all playgrounds observed by Goodlad had some type of climbing apparatus, and there was not one single item that was present in at least seventy-five percent of these play spaces. "This offers a rather bleak picture of playgrounds which do little more than allow children to stretch and run. We could find little evidence that the outdoor area, if the school had one at all, was viewed as a place in which the school's program could be continued and extended" (Goodlad 1973, p. 108).

FOR LARGE-MUSCLE ACTIVITY

Priority should be given to equipment that permits children to exercise their large muscles. Children need to be active outdoors, to find things that they can explore with their entire bodies. Sturdy cardboard boxes, always free for the taking at grocery or appliance stores, are well suited to this kind of exploration.

In some areas, heavy wooden crates can still be obtained. Unlike cardboard boxes, wooden boxes have the advantage of weight and durability. If wooden boxes are unavailable free or for a small fee from local stores or factories, they can be built, or purchased from school supply houses.

Slotted boxes are excellent for children's use. These, with plain planks that fit through the slots, are moved by the children, stacked, and used to create things like space ships, trucks, airplanes, houses, or castles. When the children tire of these, the boxes and planks can be separated, rebuilt, and fashioned into something else. The pushing, pulling, and working together that the planks and slotted boxes offer is ideal exercise for children's physical development as well as for the development of social skills in cooperation and cognitive skills of problem solving and planning ahead to construct a specific item.

Cleated planks are an excellent addition to outdoor play. These can also be purchased or constructed by teachers. A cleat, or wooden block, is attached to both ends of a board. The cleat permits children to prop the board on a box, some climbing equipment, or other stationary play yard item and create all types of sliding or climbing play pieces.

Teachers might also purchase long wooden ladders from hardware stores. These ladders can be cut into several parts, giving children short pieces of ladders that can be carried around and used in any number of ways. When placed flat on the ground, they provide an obstacle course to jump through. When cleats are attached to the end of a ladder, the ladder can then be securely attached to a box or climbing unit, and children can safely climb the few steps. The boards, ladders, and boxes provide children with endless opportunities for building and serve any purpose the children's imaginations can dream up.

Cable tables, wooden barrels, climbing equipment, either wooden or metal, and ladders and stands that can be taken apart and put together in a variety of ways offer children the opportunity to work and rework their environment. Steps to climb and jump off of, sawhorses, box seats, anything without a predetermined use, is valuable. Tires and tractor inner tubes of any size can be rolled, pushed, and stacked, or placed on a level surface and used to run, jump, or hop through, in, and around. Other tires might be planted into the ground affording children a safe retreat in which to rest. Large tires have also been used as sand pits, or as seats for children under a tree or in the shade.

Logs and tree trunks can be planted in the ground at different levels, giving the children something to climb up and down. Other tree trunks can be placed in the yard and anchored for a climbing or dramatic play unit. Smaller logs can be carried by the children and used in their constructions.

It may be helpful to think in terms of planning for a combination of equipment that offers children simple, complex, and super-complex play opportunities (Kritchevsky and Prescott 1969).

A simple unit offers children one type of activity and can be used for one purpose. Examples of a simple unit include a rocking horse, swings, tricycle, and jungle gym. These have an obvious use, without subparts, and are typically used by the children in a standard way. A complex unit, however, has parts and suggests more complex play to the children. Examples of a complex unit are a sand table with digging equipment and a play house with supplies. The equipment can be used for many things, in many different ways. Boards, boxes, and planks; a sandbox with play materials and water; a dough table with tools; a tunnel; movable climbing boards and boxes are categorized as super-complex units. These units, with more than three parts, offer children still more complexity and possibilities for play.

A super unit has been

> likened to a large sponge which soaks up a lot of water; it accommodates the children at one time and holds their interest longest. A complex unit is like a smaller sponge and ranks second in degree of interest and number of children it is likely to accommodate at one time. A simple unit is like a paper towel, indispensable but short lived, and ranks third." (Kritchevsky and Prescott 1969, p. 11)

Children need experience with each type of equipment. It might be well for teachers to decide how many simple, complex, and super-complex units are available as a guide to planning. Placement of the units is as important as having a balance between types of equipment. If the play area is very large, it is important not to place play units too far away from one another, in effect, cutting children off from one another. If the units are at least visible from all parts of the play yard, children can see others and the possibility of cooperative play.

If on the other hand the yard is very small, and there is too much equipment in the yard, children may run into each other. If children need the space around an item of equipment in order to move through the yard, there are going to be conflicts and interruptions of their play.

No matter what kind of equipment is present, there should be some empty space in every play yard. Some of the empty space should be planned as pathways between and to the play units, other space left empty, there for children's running, jumping, and free play.

FOR OTHER ACTIVITIES

Although the playground is ideally designed to offer children lots of large-muscle activity, it should also provide for dramatic play, science, mathematics, language, music, and art activities, as well as for manipulative and sensory play. "It should entice children to behave like scientists, artists or engineers. There should be a place where children can plant and care for animals, paint, dress up, make music, play with water, work with tools and grow in creativity and know how—all out of doors" (Stone 1970, p. 20).

Dramatic play can be fostered by adding bits of junk to the outside space. Pieces of hoses, the wooden ladders, a hat—and the children can become fire fighters. Road maps placed with the wheel toys stimulate children's planning for a trip. A few dress-up items—those that would not cause any safety hazards—can be reserved for outdoors. Things like purses, hats, badges, tools, tool kits, pieces of luggage, and kitchen equipment can be taken outside to enhance or extend the play interest of children. These items cannot get caught on climbing equipment, in a swing, or in a tricycle, nor do they stay outdoors. These are props that are taken outdoors to stimulate children's play, or to build on some ongoing interest.

A rubbish heap was found by McMillan (1919) to be the perfect addition to the play area. "A nursery garden must have a free and rich place, a great rubbish heap, stones, flints, bits of can, and old iron and pots. Here every healthy child will want to go, taking out things of his own choosing to build with" (p. 47). Junk, just plain junk, which has been carefully scrutinized to eliminate potential hazards, with jagged edges removed, sharp parts filed down, or easily broken parts removed, fosters children's imagination and promotes a great amount of dramatic play.

In England today, the adventure playgrounds take the place of McMillan's junk heap. In the adventure playgrounds children find all types of junk, wood, mud, sand, water, rocks, and other natural and junk materials for their use. Without adult supervision, the children use the materials to build, create, and construct as they take on different roles in dramatic play.

Many science activities are meant to take place outdoors. Children can blow bubbles with cups of soapy water and straws or a bubble maker created from a pipe cleaner bent into a loop at one end. They can fly a kite or experiment with windmills. They can dry doll clothes on a windy day, paint with water in the sun and shade, and discover more of their world. Tracing shadows outside, at different times of the day, gives children an experience that can be used later to build on their concepts of the earth's rotation around the sun.

A garden plot can be dug, planted, and tended. Hardy plants—collards, green beans, spinach, tomatoes and peas—offer children quick rewards without requiring special attention. Flowers can be planted, marigolds, four o'clocks,

Learning takes place out-of-doors.

or morning glories also grow quickly, flower, and produce without much effort on your part.

Pets can be kept outdoors. Birds, rabbits, ducks, or other pets that stay outdoors allow children to take responsibility for other living beings. But other life on the playground is available, even if pets are not.

Turning over a rock may reveal an entire world of slugs, larvae, or insects. Ants can be observed, counted, and looked at under a magnifying glass. Children can hold a birdwatch to identify all the birds that either land or fly over the play space. Depending on the area, other wildlife can be studied without caging animals or insects. Squirrels, chipmunks, moles, lizards, salamanders, frogs, or turtles might provide the alert teacher with a departure point for observing and studying nature.

Art belongs outdoors too. Not every day perhaps, but on days that are especially hot, or when children have tired of running and jumping about, art materials are welcome. Clipboards, with paper and small boxes of crayons, are fun for the child to carry with her to begin drawing wherever she wishes. A large sheet of brown wrapping paper can be placed on a patio floor, with boxes of crayon scraps at each corner, for children to work together on a mural or just to take a turn at drawing.

A six-pack of paints can also be taken outside and used to paint a picture on paper clipped to the play yard fence, spread on a patio floor, or on easels taken outside. Clay and clay boards, or a table set aside under a tree, or in the shade with some pieces of salt dough, give children a quiet place for modeling activities.

There is really something special about being able to draw with chalk outdoors—if the playground is hardtop or concrete. Large, free, and imaginative chalk drawings can result. Children might also be able to draw on sidewalks, or even the building if everyone understands that the chalk will wash off with the next hard rain.

Woodworking outdoors is ideal. The noise and mess do not matter, and children can work freely, constructing large or small objects.

Sand is a staple of outside play. "With sand, youngsters need little technical know how to make beautiful exacting forms and designs" (Stone 1970), p. 42). Watching children flock to construction sites, where mud and sand piles are left by work crews, one believes there is an instinct driving children to play with sand. Their need to find out about the raw material making up the earth, to explore what they can do, to achieve mastery seems primary.

In some areas it may be unnecessary to actually have a sandbox or pile. The entire yard may be sandy for children's digging, exploration, and construction. However, even when this is the case, a pile of fine building sand is still welcome. The container for the sand need not be elaborate. Some teachers fill the middle of a tractor tire with sand; others set up large logs and fill that area with sand. A discarded wading pool, or any other large container, can be used for sand play, or elaborate sandboxes, complete with wooden seats, can either be purchased or built.

There may be health and safety regulations connected with the sand pile. Many areas of the nation require that any sand pile in use by the children must be covered when the children are not at play. Old plastic shower curtains, pieces of discarded plastic, or canvas tents, anything that is semiwater-proof and will keep animals from defecating in the sand can be used.

Water is absolutely necessary if children are to get the full benefit from sand play. The same plastic squirt bottles filled with water can be used outside and inside, but outside it is easier to provide children with a hose for the sand pile or with large buckets of water for their use. Without water it is difficult for them to create villages, roads, or anything else.

Water play is also natural for outside. The play can begin with an old discarded wading pool, any large container that holds water for even a short period of time, and all types of plastic containers and tools. "A hot day without water is misery" (Stone 1970, p. 42), and during the hot days of late spring, summer, and early fall, it may be possible to permit children to play in sprinklers or hoses.

> The most fascinating and satisfying play material of all is water. We all know that with water children play at their best. The endless wonder that prods children's minds as they work with water and the many ways they appreciate its natural beauty impel youngsters to spend long periods of time utterly engrossed in it. (Stone 1970, p. 43)

It may be that the same need to find out about the nature of the world drives children to continually seek out and enjoy water play.

Even music belongs outside. At times a drum, bells, tambourine, or other musical instrument can be taken outside for the children to use. They may simply enjoy creating sounds where there is no one else to disturb, or they might form marching bands or dance groups.

Books also find a place outdoors. A blanket spread on a grassy part of the yard, under a tree, or in the shade of the building, with a few selected books, suggests to children that they can take a break from their active play and find respite in reading a book.

There is support in the history of early childhood education for the use of natural materials on play yards. Children seem to need to bring mastery to their environment and to work and rework natural materials. Dewey (1916) believed that natural materials, the mud, sand, water, boxes, and boards, brought the child's intelligence into play. Children need to see an end, and decide how to reach it. Materials designed by the adult, on the other hand, with a preconceived end in mind, tend to deny children's true intellectual development. Early childhood educators prefer natural play yards; perhaps their preference stems from Froebel's free communication with nature.

> When they can, children do show you that the best playground apparatus in the world pales by comparison with weeds and grass, hills and flat sandy stretches, wild flowers, sky and clouds and animals and birds. Adults may say, and some unfortunately do say, that in a famous nature park which extends right into the heart of a large city, "but there's nothing to do but feed the ducks", but the children know what to do. (Stone 1970, p. 40)

On the other hand, Prescott (1972), after observing many play spaces for children, advises that some man-made things in the play yard are necessary. "An increase in man-made things will increase teacher satisfaction and child involvement and interest. However, children also need experience with the natural order of the world" (p. 41). Perhaps the best play space is one that offers children a balance between man-made materials and equipment and natural materials; between simple, complex, and super-complex units; active and quiet activities; places to be alone and with others, and a difference of textures, heights, and surfaces.

Whatever the material and play space, the teacher must understand the possibilities of the space and the materials and how to encourage children's exploration of the space. The teacher, simply by pulling a table and chair outdoors, may invite children to be alone. Or she may, by the addition of a homemade scale in the sandbox, invite children to experiment with weight. The timid child may be reassured by the teacher's presence when climbing or helped to see the possibilities of materials. "Put one foot here, and hold on with your hand," or "Hook this ladder here," might be all children need to feel secure. Stone (1970 p. 47) believes that it is the nature of the adult-child interactions that make a play space as much as the size or materials within the space. "The use and scope of playgrounds and parks depends almost entirely

Teachers encourage children's exploration of space.

upon the quality of the human beings supervising them."

Play spaces outdoors, like inside spaces, change. They change naturally with the seasons as snow, wind, sun, or rain dictate different types of activities. But the teacher does the selecting of the materials to add to the play yard as children's interests and needs change, as they grow and develop, or as program goals and objectives are introduced.

THE CHILD'S TOTAL ENVIRONMENT

The child's life space, where she lives, the kind of housing she lives in, clearly is not under the control of the teacher. Yet no planning for the physical environment of a school is complete without knowledge of the child's total environment. An understanding of the relationship between the physical environment of the school and that of the child's total life enables a teacher to better plan and meet individual needs. Knowledge of the child's environment enables teachers to identify resources for learning. Places within walking distance of the school could be identified for interesting field trips, as well as museums, parks, libraries, health, recreation centers, and other resources. Some resources in the area may be of help to children with special needs.

It is clearly understood that teachers, alone, cannot take the responsibility to change a child's environment. Yet it has been predicted that today's educator

will be dedicated to improving the quantity and quality of human services, both in and out of the classrooms . . . educators will be flexible, highly skilled professionals, able to respond to the demands for life-enhancing services by the economically impoverished, the unfulfilled well-to-do, the idealistic yet disinfatuated young. (Nash and Ducharme 1976, p. 447)

Today's teachers must assume the sense of political responsibility implicit in and required of all helping professionals.

Theories of Environmental Influence

"It has long been recognized that the psychological influence of environment on the behavior and development of the child is extremely important" (Musinger 1975, p. 383). Kurt Lewin (1935) first advanced the idea that the environment exerts a powerful force on a child's life. Lewin believed that study of a child's interaction with the total environment would enable a teacher to identify significant forces in the child's life. These understandings would be helpful to the teacher as she planned learning activities and made decisions about the experiences the child would have in the classroom.

Lewin defines the child's life space as all the facts that determine a child's behavior at a given time. In defining the life space, Lewin used the concept of needs. The need for hunger, safety, and so on, became a part of his theory. Lewin assumed that when a child wants to, he establishes a need or intention in his life space and then tries to satisfy the need whenever he has the opportunity. Lewin believed that with maturity, the child produces more varied behavior; despite this greater variety, older children are better organized. The life space of a child expands in area and time with age; as a child matures, life regions become reorganized into a hierarchy; with maturity the child becomes better able to distinguish between reality and fantasy (Musinger 1975, p. 388).

Piaget (1948) has also attempted to explain the relationship between child and environment through his studies of children's conceptions of space. The child's awareness of proximity, closeness, enclosures, and boundaries form the beginnings of the child's understanding of spatial relationships. According to Piaget, the environment acquires significance for the child in stages of learning and development. The child's awareness of life space grows in complexity from the phase in which specific objects have little meaning until the child can gain meaning from symbols.

Freudian theory offers a different explanation of how children learn about and perceive their total environment. According to Freud (1938), the child learns to perceive stimuli from the total environment through sense organs, but sensations that are associated with pain and certain stimuli are avoided. An individual can avoid admitting these perceptions to consciousness, but the feelings remain in the *subconscious* and continue to influence behavior. As a child comes to perceive environment as the result of pleasant or unpleasant encounters with it, she may learn to exclude the parts of it that brought pain in the past. What is admitted to consciousness is that which the child believes to be safe, pleasant, or rewarding. As the child grows, her ideas become more controlled by reality and logic. Baldwin (1967) believes that the child actually determines the environment using these defense mechanisms.

A behaviorist believes that the environment determines behavior. A child is reinforced and conditioned by the environment. Children learn that a response associated with one stimulus brings reward, and later, that a response associated with one stimulus tends also to occur in association with other stimuli similar to the original one. Skinner (1971) believed that the environment modifies and shapes the behavior of the individual.

Environment and Development

While theories offer explanations of the power of the environment to influence children's lives, research documents the relationship between environment and development. The nature of the community, type of housing, and design of the housing have each been related to children's behavior, growth, and development.

THE COMMUNITY

Researchers find it difficult to determine just what parts of community life permit healthy growth and development, but they have concluded that children are indeed very much affected by the community that surrounds them (Barker and Wright 1955). The type of community the child lives in; how the homes, apartments, or high-rise dwellings are placed in relation to each other; the location of streets and the type of traffic; spaces between housing and spaces for parks, play, and other recreational activities do seem to be related to children's health and development (Gump 1975).

The health, hospital admissions of children, and even children's death rates have been related to the way a community is organized. Communities described as high-density and overcrowded, have greater illness and death rates among the child population (Wilner 1962).

How children move through the community also seems to be related to growth. If children can move freely throughout the community, they have opportunities to play with other children, to observe people at work, to participate in community events—things as simple as the birth of kittens or as complex as a traffic accident or the construction of a new building—and can use these experiences as a base for growth and learning (Barker and Wright 1955).

Children who live in rural, isolated areas may not have had the same type of opportunities for learning as children who are from more populated areas. One mother said, "Of course I can't let her leave the farm! Where would she go? The nearest neighbor is three miles away and there's a lot of copperheads in those three miles of field."

Other children, those living in high-density apartments or heavily populated urban areas, are equally deprived of opportunities to observe and participate in community life. Some areas of a city are unsafe for young children. Traffic, street gangs, and other hazards may restrict children's exploration of the environment and hence their learning (Silverstein and Krate 1975).

Children who have had limited opportunities to explore their immediate environment at will may need opportunities in the preschool to

1. Explore their community through field trips and excursions from the school in order to observe people at work and the social systems of the community under the safe supervision of an adult.
2. Develop their curiosity, playfulness, outgoingness. When children must survive living in communities that are not safe, they "grow up fast" (Silverstein and Krate 1975), but they are inhibited from being too curious or outgoing. To foster exploratory behavior in children living in an inner city, high crime area may be hazardous to children. Children growing up under these conditions may appear timid or even reluctant to handle simple play materials or be unable to experiment with or explore toys or puzzles. For these children, a teacher would want to introduce play materials slowly and safely, assuring children that it is all right to experiment and reach out. In some cases a teacher will want to model for the children how the toy or equipment is used or tell them how to use it. It is important to recognize that when children live in unsafe environments, they may have learned to inhibit exploratory behaviors and might need extra help and time in order to understand that it is safe to explore at school.
3. Mess around with their environment. When children are not free to build a house, dig in the mud, mess with sand, dig caves, or build tree houses, they need opportunities to do these things at school. Teachers may want to be certain that all children have the chance to mess with mud and dirt and find out about their world, as well as have the opportunity to build forts and other secret places of childhood with boxes or tents.
4. Play. It may be that children raised in rural, isolated areas, or inner cities without play opportunities will need larger periods of time for free-play activities in order to develop skill in playing with others and in learning to use their imagination and their bodies in physical play.

THE HOUSING

Housing types also seem to influence children's development. To a certain extent, how much space is available in a home will determine how much freedom a child has to explore and experiment with the environment. Most people in our culture prefer to live in single-family dwellings (Steward 1970) that give residents opportunities for freedom and exploration. In single-family housing, children often have more space to explore and are more likely to be able to play outside or have social contact with others (Cooper 1972, p. 89). Living in apartments or high-rise buildings seems to create an institutional type of setting and leads to lack of community life and generally unsafe environments for children (Cooper 1972, p. 89).

Children who live in low-rise apartment buildings appear to play together, on landings, in stairwells, and other found spaces not specifically designed for children's play. Mothers, as long as they can hear their children, believe they can monitor their play and provide a measure of safety. On the other hand, children living in high-rise buildings are not permitted by their parents to use extra spaces for play. In high-rises parents seem anxious about letting their children play in courtyards or designed play spaces because "they would be too far away if they needed help" (Silverstein and Krate 1975).

When too many adults and children must live together in small spaces, there are natural restrictions on everyone's actions. In crowded housing children's spontaneous play and explorations may be suppressed. "You can't do that now, Uncle must sleep, he has to work at night." "That's not yours, don't touch!" "Sit still and stay out of my way," may be commonly heard. In crowded conditions children may not even have a place for things of their own. They may play "musical beds," sleeping one night with one or more members of the family and another night with others.

With many others in a home, children may have to share the attention of an adult. This may lead to their developing independence at an early age; if they have had to share the attention of adults too frequently and have not had their needs for nurturance or attention met, they may be ambivalent toward adults or even sullen and withdrawn.

The noise and confusion that result from living in crowded housing conditions may also affect the growth and learning of children. Children may be constantly bombarded by the noise of others and may be overstimulated, tired, and unable to concentrate in school.

Children living in crowded homes may need more opportunities in school for

1. Physical play and exploration of the environment. If space is limited in children's homes for physical activity, it may be that teachers would want to plan more open spaces in the classroom and play yard or use a hallway for building with large blocks or riding tricycles, or arrange for children to use a gymnasium or cafeteria for romping and running about.

2. Peace and quiet. When children live in disrupted, crowded conditions, with many others about, a teacher may want to cut down on distractions in the school. She might arrange the environment using screens to visually cut children off from one another, to help children concentrate on tasks and play.

   Inside spaces could be arranged for structure and security, providing an order that leads to peace and quiet. Objects and toys can be stored on open shelves, in order. Children know where everything is and where to put things. Rather than a neat, clean well-ordered room conveying middle-class values of neatness and tidiness to the children, it gives them a feeling of quiet and security.

3. Cooperative play efforts. Children who have lived with others, crowded into one-room apartments, have learned the "abc's of survival instead of the abc's of cooperation" (Silverstein and Krate 1975). The emphasis may have been placed on protecting oneself instead of cooperating. If this is the case, teachers may want to give children time to learn to cooperate, and actively teach them how to play together.

PLAY SPACES, PARKS, RECREATIONAL SPACES

One of the myths we have in America is that all children have plenty of opportunity to play freely and uninhibitedly. However, there are often no fields, or any space at all, for children's play.

When provisions are made for children's play, they are often inadequate and rarely used. Parks, recreational spaces, and play areas may be remembered by city planners, but these may be placed far away from where the children live, cut off from the children by highways, or inconvenient in other ways that make them unattractive to children (Gump 1975).

One group of researchers observed children in sixteen different housing estates and found that even during the summer, only twenty percent of the children were ever observed outdoors. Those children who lived in low-rise buildings seemed to be outside more often, but nearly all of the observations of children at play outdoors took place very near their homes, regardless of the type of housing or the variety of planned areas for play (Gump 1975).

Even in clean, beautifully kept suburbs, children were not found playing outside. The manicured lawns and gardens seemed to negate children's digging, running, jumping, climbing, and full exploration of their environment. It may be that all children, regardless of housing type or neighborhood, need to find opportunity for physical exercise and play in the preschool.

Living in crowded, unsafe conditions, however, is not always a negative experience. Ladner (1971) observed the development of children living in the inner city of St. Louis. These children developed characteristics that were functional and helped them to adapt to the hardships of their life. Ladner (1971) sees these children as having unqualified strengths. They are emotionally stable and well integrated, often more so than their protected, sheltered middle-class counterparts (p. 60).

Organizing the Child's Environment

In the early days of our country, teachers were hired by the community. They lived with the families of the children they taught, went to the same church, and participated in the same out-of-school activities as did the children and their parents. In those days there was no real need for teachers to mentally organize the child's environment. They were a part of the environment, they knew all about the child's home life; they knew, just as everyone else did in the community, where to go for help, what resources were available, how each child lived, what his needs were, and how to supplement the child's home life with school activities. Today, however, teachers often live far from children; they are divorced from the child and family by neighborhood, and sometimes by social class and background. When teachers are not totally familiar with the child's home life and community, they must make a special effort to become acquainted with the child's neighborhood.

Following the road from a newly opened school built on the edge of the city, a teacher observes that the homes are further and further apart as city turns into country. As the homes become more spread out they also seem to be less substantial and older. The paved road ends and a red, rutted clay road takes its place. Winding through pine and pecan groves, the teacher finally comes to the corner crossroad. Here one grocery store serves as gas station, post office, and meeting hall for the community of Moccasin Gap where most of the children in her classroom live.

Clusters of homes surround the corner crossroads. The teacher sees some of the children she knows playing in the red clay yards, swept clean. The homes are one-room shacks, on stilts. No electric wires are visible from the road to the homes, and the outhouse in back of each home lets the teacher know that running water is not a part of the child's life either. The idealistic beauty of the wisteria in full bloom, twining through the tall pine trees over the shacks, and the pink of the dogwood blooming on the surrounding rolling hills hides the poverty and misery of the area.

This teacher notices that the children do have plenty of spaces in which to play, and other children to play with. On the other hand, they have few play toys and little equipment. She plans to supplement the children's environment by introducing children to blocks, wheel toys, and other materials. She also thinks of ways to extend the world of these children, through field trips and other planned experiences.

In another area of the nation, a teacher walks through the neighborhood in which the children live. Although the school has an enrollment of 2,000 children, over eighty percent live within a five square block radius of the school. Of these, nearly seventy-five percent live in high-rise apartments and housing projects. As this teacher walks through the neighborhood, she is struck by the absence of children, or people, anywhere. It is as if everyone is hiding behind the tall, concrete walls of the buildings. On one side of the school there is a large hospital and medical center. Parking lots, student dormitories, also high-rise, dominate this area. A small shopping center, with a laundromat and quick-shop store, is located near the hospital.

There is a playground nearby equipped with modern concrete sculptures that is empty of children. It seems to be near the housing project, but it is separated from both medical center and high-rise apartments by an eight-lane expressway.

This teacher makes mental notes to plan to introduce children gradually to playing and working together. Noticing the lack of spaces for active play, she thinks about ways to increase physical activity in the school. The opportunities for using the traffic system to increase children's vocabulary, introducing them to the names of different streets—expressway, avenue—and learning about the medical center are noted.

In another neighborhood a teacher sees once splendid homes now broken into smaller apartments. How many families live in these dilapidated mansions, the teacher cannot estimate, but she does know that several children in her classroom report the same address. The leaded glass windows of the mansions and ornate stairways hint of elegance long past. Here children are playing in the streets, on the sidewalks, and in the stairways. Adults sit, relaxing, chatting with one another, on the stairs or porches. Now and then one or another will say something to the children. Small stores are nestled within the larger houses. The streets seem alive with adults and children.

These children have an easy relationship with others and seem to have a variety of play activities, even if space is limited. More large muscle activity, room for running, jumping, might be provided in school. The opportunity to observe the shopkeepers and find out about the world of commerce is here. The teacher also notes the lack of plant life—trees, bushes, flowers—and thinks this may be something to introduce to children in the classroom.

These three teachers, having visited the children's homes and community environments, plan to use this information. They think about the relation between the child's home environment and that of school and determine ways to

1. Supplement the child's home experiences at school. If children have limited areas for play at home, play space at school may be important; if they have spaces for play at home but little equipment, she might plan to supply materials at school.
2. Expand on the child's experiences in the home and the community. The children from Moccasin Gap might be introduced to the city, just a few miles from the Gap. Those children in the city could be introduced to plant and animal life not found in their immediate environment.
3. Utilize the resources in the environment. Within each of these neighborhoods there are resources for teaching children, as well as resources that can be used to meet the basic needs of the children and their families.

Community Resources

FIELD TRIPS

Teachers can find many places in every neighborhood rich with learning opportunities for the children. A new building site, grocery store, gas station, or neighborhood church—any place of interest in the environment—can be the destination of a field trip. If there are specific things children must learn in order to be safe within their environment, these could become the focus of learning experiences. In some areas, teaching children to cross streets and busy intersections may be important.

LIBRARIES

Local libraries and librarians have much to offer preschool and primary teachers. Librarians are often most anxious to show children how to obtain a library card and use the library. They will also help teachers select books for children and lend armfuls of books for use in the classroom. The librarian may also be able to obtain resources for children with special needs. Talking books, records, toys, and other equipment may be available. Libraries today also offer prints, sculpture, films, filmstrips, paintings, and many other resources for the enrichment of the lives of children.

Many services for children and families can also be obtained through the library. A library usually has information on other services in the community (and may even house some of these services). Often voter registration and voting, a well-baby clinic, or adult education classes are held at the local library. Sometimes the local school system or community college will offer courses on popular topics or sponsor activity clubs for adults and children.

More and more frequently, librarians themselves are offering services for children and families. A morning hour for mothers may be held, with stories and puppet shows for the children and discussions on child care for the mothers; or reading clubs and other activities involving books and reading may be sponsored for the older child.

OTHER SCHOOLS

The preschool is just one part of a child's total schooling. Usually there are other schools in the area that can be of assistance to children and families. When you are working in a private or nonpublic preschool, it is up to you to build a bridge to the public school. By contacting the principal of the nearby school or informally arranging to meet some of the teachers of the school, a preschool teacher can help build continuity of educational experiences for children.

Meeting with public school teachers, a preschool teacher might want to explain some of the goals and objectives of her program. She may want to ask the teachers for suggestions on what they would like to see in the preschool program. The important point is that the preschool teacher, in contacting the public school in the area, is establishing a cooperative relationship with others who will be involved with children's lives.

This friendly gesture could lead to the kindergarten or primary teacher visiting the preschool class to tell children what the "big" school will be like for them next year. An invitation for the children to visit the school, to see for themslves what first grade will be like, might follow.

Resources can also be shared between schools. The public school may open its parent education meetings or courses to the parents of the children in the preschool. Often a few more parents are welcome, and the planners of parent involvement activities are happy to involve parents with whom they may work in the future. Teachers may also share in-service activities. One more teacher at a regularly scheduled training activity is usually welcome.

Children with special needs may benefit from any contacts teachers can make with the public school. Teachers may be able to obtain resources for the child and the family and help to make the child's entrance into the public school as smooth as possible.

Other resources are possible when a preschool teacher works cooperatively with the public schools in the area. She may be able to establish a volunteer program, with older children acting as tutors for younger children, with both older and younger children benefiting from the relationship.

Establish relationships with other schools in the area. The junior high school, high school, community college, and university may all offer volunteers to work with the children, as well as other resources. The university may offer diverse free services from psychological testing and screening of early learning problems to assistance with budgeting or meal planning.

COMMUNITY AGENCIES

The community action agencies, social service, and welfare agencies in the community should be familiar to the teacher. Today's teachers, just like those of the past, are members of a team of professionals devoted to improving the quality of life for children. Jane Addams and Alice Putnam showed how early childhood educators and other professionals can work together to benefit children and families.

A teacher familiar with the services available can help families obtain needed services. It may be useful for the preschool teacher to meet with a representative of these agencies in order to help families obtain services.

HEALTH, FIRE, POLICE

These agencies can be involved in a preschool program in a number of ways. First, it may be useful to contact these agencies to obtain licensing and regulations governing the establishment of a preschool. Often this initial contact leads to agency assistance. The fire and health departments could conduct safety checks of the building and play yard, and they may offer free training in health and safety practices. Fire fighters may demonstrate the procedures used in a fire drill, and a police officer might teach the children how to cross streets safely.

Health clinics will help in the training of staff and may be contacted to meet with and work with the children. A nurse or doctor may also be able to help in screening children for health problems, or let you know whom to contact for hearing and vision tests.

CIVIC ORGANIZATIONS

The Red Cross, Lions Club, American Legion, and other civic organizations may also help preschoolers. They may provide volunteers to work with all the children, or with the child with special needs. Other organizations provide transportation for children with special needs, enabling them to receive therapy and training. In some instances the organizations donate eyeglasses, hearing aids, or other needed health equipment.

Some organizations may donate or build toys and equipment for the school. One organization in Florida outfitted an entire Head Start program with all the toys and playground equipment it needed.

The Y.M.C.A., Y.W.C.A., senior citizen groups, Girl Scouts, Boy Scouts, 4-H Clubs, and churches, all offer programs for children, youth, and families. A teacher may be able to identify the services and help families to use them.

MUSEUMS, HISTORIC MARKERS AND
CULTURAL OPPORTUNITIES

Search the neighborhood to find traces of the children's cultural heritage. It may be that the large city museum is the only place for children to discover paintings and works of art, but many communities have local museums which display the work of local artists. Visits to these museums can put children in touch with art and their heritage.

Local historic markers may also supply children with the motivation to explore their heritage. These markers designate events or places of historical importance. Children could be taken to such places of interest and told of their cultural and historic significance.

Other cultural opportunities should not be missed. The teacher should know what local plays, artists, actors, and musicians are in the area. Artists and performing artists may come to the school and demonstrate or perform for the children, civic groups may sponsor a concert or other cultural activity for the children.

Changing The Environment

Preschool teachers can and have effected change in children's total environment. In one part of the country, preschool programs brought more employment to the area, fostered positive changes in health and educational systems, and brought other benefits to children and families (State of the Child in Appalachia, 1976). The Kirschner Report (1971) suggested that Head Start successfully influenced a number of changes of benefit to the community, children, and parents.

Surveying forty-two communities with original Head Start programs, and, for purpose of comparison, communities with little or no exposure to Head Start, the Kirschner Report concluded that

1. Numerous changes occurred in Head Start communities in both education and health systems.
2. There was an increased involvement of the poor in the institutions of the community, particularly at the decision making level.
3. Grassroots organizations pressured for changes in school policies, for instance, in the Southwestern villages, the teaching of Spanish in the school, in another community, the practice of letting children bring lunch to school because they could not afford to purchase the school lunch.
4. In the South, people with low incomes in one community increased their use of public health services and health institutions; desegregated waiting rooms; assigned patients to specific doctors; and changed the hours of the health clinic— opening it for evenings.
5. Paraprofessionals were used in the school systems. Teacher aides indigenous to the area were hired to help during school and to tutor children after school.

6. Social workers were hired for the schools.
7. There was increased involvement of the poor with institutions, particularly at the decision-making levels and in decision-making capacities; increased institution employment of local persons in paraprofessional occupations; greater educational emphasis on the particular needs of the poor and minorities; and modification of health institutions and practices to serve the poor better and more sensitively.

These changes are not minor and have great impact on the lives of individuals. Lewis (1966) believes that the disengagement of the poor with the major institutions of society is a crucial element in the culture of poverty. When, however, the poor feel a part of the institutions, there is "much less of the feelings of despair and apathy, so symptomatic of the culture of poverty. . . . the people had found a new sense of power and importance" (p. 25).

Head Start is a massive program, but it did demonstrate how teachers can effect change in communities. One teacher, working alone or with a school, may not be able to do as much; however, she might

1. Identify safety hazards in the neighborhood. The need for safety patrols, crossing guards, or signal lights at an intersection might be brought to the attention of the police. Street lights might be requested from the city, or repairs for sidewalks.
2. Organize an after-school playgroup for older children at the preschool or in a local church. Establishing a playgroup is feasible; it is the type of project that may appeal to a civic organization.

Changes in a community do not happen overnight and without work. Although teachers are primarily concerned with teaching, not organizing communities, throughout the history of early childhood education, the teacher of young children has been involved in community life. A truly professional teacher takes the initiative to speak for the children in her community.

Marion Wright Edelman believes, however, that teachers of young children must do more than speak for the children in their own community.

> If the well being of children and families is to become the nation's top priority—today's promise, tomorrow's reality—you and I will have to do a lot better at our jobs, and we must not repeat the mistakes of the past." (Edelman 1978, p. 4)

Today's preschool teachers, like Elizabeth Peabody, must take up the cause of children; they must learn to speak effectively for children at all levels of political life, in the local community, state, and the nation. Teachers today can, and must, stay abreast of the issues affecting the lives of young children. As a teacher you can

1. Be aware of the legislation affecting the lives of children and families being presented before their local and state legislatures, and speak out, either for or against this legislation. Teachers can write to their legislators asking for complete copies of all bills concerning children, become familiar with these and then express their opinions about them.

2. Know what is occurring at the national level for children's health, nutrition, and education. Write to your representative expressing your views on these matters.
3. Ask your representatives at the local, state, and national level for their position on bills and legislation affecting the lives of children.
4. Involve the local politicians and state representatives with your program. Invite them to have lunch with the children at the center, or to attend a parent get-together so they will know more about preschool education.

Even though early childhood educators have a rich heritage of community involvement, early childhood teachers today still have much to do. Edelman states:

> We are just beginning. It takes time and hard work to build a broad foundation for major change. The Civil Rights movement did not begin in the sixties, it began in the thirties. We have to understand that we are engaged in an ongoing process that will grow as we grow. (1978 p. 12)

In Summary

"Human behavior cannot be understood apart from the environment in which it finds its expression" (Moos 1973, p. x). An understanding of the child's social and physical environment is necessary for teachers of young children. Teachers can use this knowledge to plan the optimum classroom and play yard environment for children.

Indoor and outdoor play spaces are arranged to provide for the intellectual, physical, social, and emotional needs of children. Indoor space can be divided into areas of noisy and quiet activities, solitary and group experiences, and centers through which to pursue dramatic play, block building, woodworking and so on. Teachers must adapt their room arrangements to their own and the children's traffic patterns to provide ease of movement and access to the various parts of the room. Imagination and creativity can transform even the dreariest facility into a stimulating, creative learning environment. Similarly, outdoor space can provide a setting in which large-muscle activity is encouraged through safe and imaginative equipment. In planning how outdoor space will be utilized, teachers should consider surfaces; traffic patterns, safety, and size. Outdoor play offers stimulating opportunities to study science, art, and music, to foster group cooperation and occasions for solitary pursuits, as well as to move about freely.

Thus, the outdoor areas are considered as important as indoor areas. As in the past, today's early childhood educator continues to use the total environment of the child in planning, and in meeting the needs of the children. Surveys of childrens' neighborhoods; familiarity with community resources such as libraries, social service agencies, police and fire departments; and involvement in political issues affecting children and their families are ways in which teachers can use and even change the total environment of the child.

Resources

There are many resources available on setting up indoor and outdoor play environments for children's learning. Among these are:

FRIEDMAN, D., and D. COLODNY, *Water, Sand and Mud as Play Materials* (rev. ed.). Washington, D.C.: National Association for the Education of Young Children, 1972.

HARTLEY, R. E., L. K. FRANK, and R. M. GOLDENSON, *Understanding Children's Play*. New York: Columbia University Press, 1952.

HIRSCH, E. S., ed. *The Block Book*. Washington, D.C.: National Association for the Education of Young Children, 1974.

JOHNSON, H., *Children in the "Nursery School."* New York: Agathon Press, Inc., 1972. First published 1928.

KRITCHEVSKY, S., E. PRESCOTT, and L. WALLING,; *Planning Environments for Young Children: Physical Space*. Washington, D.C.: National Association for the Education of Young Children, 1969.

MATTERSON, E. M., *Play and Playthings for the Preschool Child*. Baltimore, Md.: Penguin Books, 1968.

STONE, J. G., *Play and Playgrounds*. Washington, D.C.: National Association for the Education of Young Children, 1970.

Projects

1. Observe a preschool group. Note the arrangement of the room. Can you find the traffic patterns children and adults use? Which areas of the room are most popular? Why do you think children gravitate to these areas?

2. As you observe, analyze how children make choices of activities and materials. How does the physical environment help or hinder children from selecting their own activities?

3. Observe children at play on a playground, in a park, or in a school yard. What materials do the children use? Can you find children who use materials in ways that differ from the intended purpose of the material? What concepts are children developing as they play outdoors?

4. Diagram your dream preschool classroom and play yard. Think about how the room and play space will change over a year's time.

5. If you have not scoured a neighborhood for hidden treasures and resources for children's use, you might plan such an expedition. Go to a drugstore, florist, gas station, liquor store, grocery store, or any other business in the area. Ask for materials they throw away and would be willing to give you to use with children. You might find polystyrene plastic packing materials, boxes, corrugated papers of all colors, large posters, and other materials children can use.

Take another trip to identify the resources in a neighborhood for children and families. What services are available in the area of health, both mental and physical, and for social services, counseling, and other aid. Make a list of services available for children and families.

References

BALDWIN, A. L., *Theories of Child Development*, New York: John Wiley & Sons, Inc., 1967.

BARKER, R. G., and WRIGHT, H. F., *Midwest and Its Children*. New York: Harper & Row, Publishers, Inc., 1955.

BENDER, J., "Have You Ever Thought of a Prop Box?" *Young Children*, 26, 3 (1971), 164–170.

CHURCHILL, W., in *Issues in Social Ecology: Human Milieus*, p. 220, ed. R. H. Moos. Palo Alto, Calif.: National Press Books, 1974.

CANNON, G. M., "Kindergarten Class Size—a Study," *Childhood Education*, 43, 2 (1966), 9–11.

COOPER, C., "Resident Dissatisfaction in Multi-Family Housing," in *Behavior, Design, and Policy Aspects of Human Habitats*, ed. W. M. Smith. Green Bay: University of Wisconsin, Green Bay, 1972.

CURRY, N. E., "Dramatic Play as a Curricular Tool," in *Play as a Learning Medium*, ed. D. Sponseller. Washington, D.C.: National Association for the Education of Young Children, 1974, 59–75.

DEWEY, J., *School and Society*. Chicago: The University of Chicago Press, 1900.

EDELMAN, M. W., "Today's Promises—Tomorrow's Americans," *Young Children*, 33, 3 (1978), 41.

"Federal Interagency Day Care Requirements," Washington, D.C.: U.S. Government Printing Office. 1968.

FREUD, S., *The Basic Writings of Sigmund Freud*. Edited and translated by A. A. Brill. New York: Modern Library, 1938.

GETZELS, J. W., "Images and Visions," in *Learning Environments*, eds. T. G. David and B. D. Wright. Chicago, Ill.: University of Chicago Press, 1975, 31.

GINSBURG, H. J., and POLLMAN, V. A., "Variation of Aggressive Interaction Among Male Elementary School Children as a Function of Changes in Spatial Density." Paper presented at Society for Research in Child Development Annual Conference, Denver, April 1975.

GOLDSMITH, C., *Better Day Care for the Young Child*. Washington, D.C.: National Association for the Education of Young Children, 1972.

GOODLAD, J. I.: KLEIN, M. F.: NOVOTNER. J. M.: *Early Schooling in the United States*. New York: McGraw-Hill Book Co., 1973.

GUMP, P. V., "Ecological Psychology and Children." in *Review of Child Development Research*, ed. E. Mavis Heatherington. Chicago, Ill.: University of Chicago Press, 1975, 75–127.

HARTLEY, R. E.: FRANK, L. K.: GOLDENSON, R. M.: *Understanding Children's Play*. New York: Columbia University Press, 1952.

HILL, P. S., in M. McMillan, *The Nursery School*. London and Toronto: J. M. Dent & Sons, Ltd., 1919.

HOUSEMAN, J., Ecological Study of Interpersonal Conflict Among Preschool Children. Unpublished Doctoral Dissertation. Detroit, Michigan: Wayne State University, 1972.

HYMES, J., *Teaching the Child Under Six*. (2nd. ed.) Columbus, Ohio: Charles E. Merrill Publishing Company, 1974.

JOHNSON, H. M., *Children in the Nursery School*. New York: Agathon Press, Inc., 1972. First published 1928.

"Kirschner Report: A National Survey of the Impacts of Head Start Centers on Community Institutions." Washington, D.C.: U.S. Government Printing Office, 1970.

KRITCHEVSKY, S.: PRESCOTT, E.; and WALLING, L.; *Planning Environments for Young Children: Physical Space*. Washington, D.C.: National Association for the Education of Young Children, 1969.

LADNER, J. A., *Tomorrow's Tomorrow: The Black Woman*. New York: Doubleday & Co. Inc., 1971, 59–60.

LE LAURIN, and RISLEY, T., "The Organization of Day Care Environments: 'zone' versus 'man to man,' Staff Assignment;" *Journal of Applied Behavior Analysis*, 5 (1972), 225–232.

LEWIN, K., *A Dynamic Theory of Personality*. New York: McGraw-Hill Book Company, 1935.

LEWIS, A., "The Culture of Poverty," *Scientific American*, 215, 4 (1966), 19–25.

McMILLAN, M. *The Nursery School*. London & Toronto: J. M. Dent & Sons, Ltd., 1919.

MILLAR, S., *The Psychology of Play*. Harmondsworth, England: Penquin Books, Ltd., 1968.

MITCHELL, S., *Young Geographers*. New York: Bank Street College, 1971.

MOOS, R. H., "Systems for the Assessment and Classification of Human Environment: An Overview. in *Issues in Social Ecology: Human Milieus*, ed. R. H. Moos. Palo Alto, Calif.: National Press Books, 1974, 5–29.

MURPHY, L. B., and LEEPER, E. M., "Caring for Children: A Setting for Growth." Number six. Washington, D.C.: U.S. Government Printing Office, 1977.

MUSINGER, H., *Fundamentals of Child Development* (2nd ed.) New York: Holt, Rinehart & Winston, 1975.

NASH, R., and DUCHARME, E. R., "A Futures Perspective on Preparing Educators for the Human Service Society: How to Restore a Sense of Social Purpose to Teacher Education, *Teachers College Record*, 77, 4 (1976), 441–471.

PRESCOTT, E., and DAVID, T. G., "The Effects of the Physical Environment on Day Care," in *Policy Issues in Day Care: Summaries of 21 Position Papers*. Washington, D.C.: U.S. Government Printing Office, 1977.

PRESCOTT, E.; JONES, E.; KRITCHEVSKY, S.; *Day Care as a Child Rearing Environment, III*. Washington, D.C.: National Association for the Education of Young Children, 1972.

PIAGET, J., and INHELDER, B., *The Child's Conception of Space*. London: Routledge & Kegan Paul, 1948.

PIAGET, J., and INHELDER, B., *The Psychology of the Child*. New York: Basic Books, Inc., Publishers, 1969.

SHURE, M. B., "Psychological Ecology of a Nursery School," *Child Development*, 34 (1963), 979–992.

SKINNER, B. F., *Beyond Freedom and Dignity*. New York: Alfred A. Knopf, Inc., 1971.

SILVERSTEIN, B., and KRATE, R., *Children of the Dark Ghetto*. New York: Praeger Publishers, 1975.

SMITH, P., "Aspects of the Playgroup Environment," in *Proceedings of the Conference: Psychology and the Built Environment*, eds. D. Cantor and T. Lee. London: Architectural Press, 1974.

SOMMER, R., and BECKER, F., "Learning Outside the Classroom," in *Learning Environments*, eds. T. G. David and B. D. Wright. Chicago: The University of Chicago Press, 1975.

STEWART, W. F. R., *Children in Flats: A Family Study*. London: National Society for the Prevention of Cruelty to Children, 1970.

STONE, J. G., *Play and Playgrounds*. Washington, D.C.: National Association for the Education of Young Children, 1970.

WEINSTEIN, C. S., "Modifying Student Behavior in an Open Classroom Through Changes in Physical Design," *American Educational Research Journal*, 14, 3 (1977), 249–263.

WILNER, D. M., and others, *The Housing Environment and Family Life*. Baltimore, Md.: The Johns Hopkins University Press, 1962.

7

Teaching Strategies

The purpose of teaching and instruction is to bring ever more and more out of man rather than put more and more into man.
F. Froebel 1887, p. 279

Traditionally, the teacher of young children has been thought of as a guide, motivator, or leader of children's learning, rather than as an instructor. The definition of teaching—the act of imparting knowledge or skills, of giving instruction—has never seemed fully appropriate to describe the behavior of teachers of young children. Since the time of Froebel (who likened teachers to gardeners who prepare the ground, set the stage for growth with occasional, yet regular watering and fertilizing, and stand back to wait for growth to occur), the act of teaching young children has been believed to be nondirective.

Perhaps it is the very nature of the physically and intellectually active, egocentric young child that has dictated a style of teaching other than that of direct instruction. Direct instruction, lecturing and telling, may be appropriate for older children, college students, or large groups of people, but it just does not work with groups of wriggling, giggling, squirming preschool children who will matter of factly walk away from anyone attempting direct teaching.

Then too, the theories of learning psychologists and child development experts (Elkind 1978), have promoted the concept of the teacher of young children acting as a guide. Piaget's work, describing the thought processes of

144

children, leads one to perceive the teacher as a guide rather than as an instructor. Piaget states:

> The development of intelligence, as it emerges from the recent research, is dependent upon natural, or spontaneous processes, in the sense that they may be utilized and accelerated by education at home or in school, but that they are not derived from that education and on the contrary, constitute a preliminary and necessary condition of efficacity in any instruction. (1951 p. 36)

Even before the writings of Piaget had received wide acceptance in the United States, the thoughts of leaders in child development, Hall, Dewey, Gesell, Frank, and others fostered the belief that teachers of young children should be indirect, nurturing, and sensitive to the child's growth and development. Teachers, according to the theorists, were, above all, not instructors, tellers, or dispensers of information.

Indirect Teaching

When teaching is indirect, and the teacher acts as a guide, rather than a giver of information, it is often difficult to describe exactly what behaviors constitute a teaching act. A group of graduate students in sociology observed a preschool

Teaching is nondirective.

teacher in a university laboratory nursery school. When the observations began, the classroom was alive with activity. Children were everywhere, moving about, involved with one another and the materials.

A few children were working at tables, others were on the floor stretched out reading books, and still other children were building with blocks. A number of art activities were in progress. Two children were painting at the easels; others were working together to create a sculpture from cardboard boxes, scraps, paper, and wire.

The students who were observing finally located the teacher. She was in the dramatic play area, sitting with the children, talking quietly with them. Occasionally she scanned the room and communicated, with a gesture, smile, or look in her eyes, to a child in another area of the room. Even after the teacher was located, it was still difficult for the observers to keep track of her, for she, like the children, was constantly in motion. The teacher spent some time with each child during the hour, working with an individual in the block area, meeting with the children who were completing the cardboard construction, and rotating her attention to all.

To the observers, the hour seemed confusing. They could not tell, they said, when and if there was any teaching going on. After all, there was not one time during the morning when the teacher stood in front of the entire group of children and directly gave instruction or imparted knowledge.

To the teacher, however, it was a busy morning, "a time of highly pin-pointed instruction" (Hymes 1975, p. 103). When the teacher met with the observers, she described her behaviors during the morning as carefully thought out, well-planned teaching strategies. These strategies included listening to individual children, giving others feedback on the progress they were making, demonstrating or giving examples, for others providing a model for children's behavior, and reinforcing their work. She also pointed out the times that she was involved with direct instruction, for example, telling one child how to make a truck work properly.

In addition to these strategies, the teacher mentioned a number of activities completed before the children arrived, which she considered teaching strategies. These included reviewing and completing records, planning, evaluating, arranging the environment, setting up a problem in the science area, and preparing the art materials.

Teaching Strategies

Preschool teachers constantly employ a variety of strategies. Some teaching strategies are used for specific purposes. Some ideas can only be learned through telling; others can never be learned that way. Experienced teachers select the strategy to suit the child and their own purpose, as well as to fit their philosophy of education and views of human nature.

To a certain extent, what a teacher actually does and the strategy he uses will be based on his beliefs. Teachers who have been trained in and endorse the Montessori method might emphasize the proper use of materials and equipment, working only with individual children. Other teachers who endorse the behavioristic theory of learning will probably be more direct, planning lessons, directing children, and reinforcing correct responses.

A teacher who sees children as interactive beings, who values the idea that children learn through action and interaction with others and the environment, will arrange a classroom rich with materials and choices. This teacher will provide periods of time for children's exploration of the environment and plan for their interactions. Endorsing Piagetian theory, he will be concerned with children's thought processes, not the end behavior. It is the use of different teaching strategies—telling, demonstrating, modeling, reinforcing, giving feedback, questioning—that enables a teacher to transform children's ongoing activities and encounters with their environment into valuable learning experiences.

Telling

At times, even young children learn by being told. Sometimes it is necessary for an adult to tell a child, "Stop, the light is red," or "Hang your coat here," "Wait until it cools," "Hold the hammer this way." Teachers should and must at times give an explanation, state a rule, provide the name of an object, or quickly and efficiently reassure the children verbally by commenting, "Thunder makes a lot of noise, but it cannot hurt us."

There are also many arbitrary things that would be difficult and maybe even impossible for children to discover for themselves. "We read from left to right. A capital letter begins your name. The name of this insect is katydid." Children have so much to learn so quickly, that even if they could discover everything for themselves, there would still be some things, the arbitrary things, that they can learn more efficiently by being told.

Teachers relay information to children by reading a story to them, helping to look up some information in a book, showing a film or filmstrip, or playing a record. This type of telling gives children information from a source that the children could not discover for themselves.

Certainly telling is a conventional way of dispensing wisdom and knowledge; it fits the dictionary definition of teaching. Nevertheless, teachers of young children must understand that telling is usually an inappropriate teaching technique because it is

1. One-way communication and often leaves little opportunity for responses on the part of the children. Feedback from the child to the teacher can be missed if teachers do too much talking and telling.
2. A strategy for passive children. When teachers tell, the children are not really participating, exploring, and trying out for themselves. They are passive receivers of information, not learners. Telling, as a strategy, is often unsuited to the needs of active, moving, curious children.

3. Easily misinterpreted by the prelogical child whose thinking patterns are not those of the adult. Telling is a symbolic way of teaching, and as Bruner points out, it is only gradually that words can be substituted for objects not present. Bruner explains:

> . . . it is a still longer time before such remote referring words are manipulated by the transformational apparatus of grammar in a manner designed to aid the solution of mental problems or tasks requiring that a barrier be overcome. And it is still later that words become vehicles for dealing in the categories of the possible, the conditional, the counterfactual conditional and the rest of the vast realm of mind in which words and utterances have no direct referent at all in immediate experience. (1966, p. 14)

Telling seems to be second nature with many people. Most likely, teachers themselves were taught by a telling teacher. Then too, they have probably observed other teachers telling preschool children. Having experienced this strategy themselves, and observed it, it is easy for teachers to incorporate it into their teaching behaviors. Thus teachers must be cautious about using telling as a teaching strategy. When teachers find themselves in the position of telling young children they might think of ways to

• supplement their words with things, offering the children some experience, activity, or object to go along with the words.
• talk clearly to children, using concise, coherent sentences.
• use examples, relating the words to some past or present experience of the children.

Teachers, however, need not feel they have failed when they tell children something. The important thing to remember is that telling is a most common teaching strategy, but one that must be balanced and supplemented with real experiences and activities on the part of children.

Listening

Active listening on the part of the teacher serves several important functions for both teacher and children. When teachers listen to children, they are, first of all, building a climate of acceptance of the children and their ideas. By listening, the teacher demonstrates to the child that she has the support of a concerned adult who cares enough to actually listen. Further, when teachers listen to children, they gain knowledge about them that is useful in planning and evaluating learning experiences.

Listening is more than hearing. Active listening means reflecting on what a person has said and trying to fully understand the thought that is being communicated. Children know teachers are listening when the teacher's physical posture communicates attentiveness. First, the teacher should stop what she is doing and devote herself to what the child is saying. Looking directly at the child lets the child know the teacher is focusing on her comments.

As a teacher listens to a child, she can try to think of the important things the child is saying. Waiting a few seconds before responding is helpful. A few seconds of wait time lets the child realize that the teacher is thinking about her statements and ideas. Having allowed some moments to pass, the teacher may respond in several different ways.

She might recall the content of what the child has said and repeat it. "You really are afraid of thunder," "You like red," or "Tommy is bothering you." This nondirective technique is especially helpful in letting children work out their own problems and gain an understanding of their own feelings. It does increase communication and verbalization on the part of the child.

In responding to a child, the teacher might also comment on the main theme, or the important points the child made. Teachers might answer, "Yes, the paper is difficult for you to work with; your fingers are sticky from the paste."

In addition to listening attentively and responding to children, teachers should observe as well. Often some subtle body movement, a sigh or other type of nonverbal communication, gives the teacher a great deal of information about the child. The child who looks worried as he relates an experience, who pauses and stammers over a word, or ends a statement with a long sigh, often reveals much of his feelings and attitudes—feelings that cannot be expressed in words.

Questioning

A well-thought-out, carefully phrased question, asked at just the right moment, constitutes an effective teaching strategy. Much has been written about the art of questioning. Hunkins (1972), Suchman (1966), Sanders (1966), and Wittmer (1974) have studied the different types of questions teachers ask. Their work, although completed on older children, offers teachers of young children insight into the types of questions they might try as they foster children's learning.

Becoming familiar with the works of Piaget, who studied children's thinking by asking them questions, can also help teachers increase their skill in questioning. Study the kinds of questions he asked children, because questions can be used to help foster communication between a teacher and the children, to explore children's thought processes, and to foster children's thinking ability.

> When a teacher asks a question, she is providing the student with an opportunity to use the mind. If the instructor asks only questions requiring regurgitation of previously presented information, the student has only the possibility of repeating what has been memorized. However, if a teacher asks a question such as, "How would you solve the problem?" she is giving the student opportunities to use and to develop many of his mental capabilities. Clearly, the questions a teacher asks can make the difference between an antiquated educational wasteland and an exciting learning environment. (R. B. Sund and A. Carin 1978, p. 3)

OPEN-ENDED AND CLOSED QUESTIONS

Open-ended questions are powerful teaching tools. These questions call for divergent and evaluative thinking on the part of the children and have been considered *thought questions*.

Because open-ended questions ask children to use their knowledge and judgment to reach a new or divergent thought, they are believed to "lift students to higher-order thinking processes" (Hough 1970, p. 191).

Closed questions are those that ask for a specific answer and can be answered in one way. These call for convergent thought and ask the child to recall something from memory or ask for a predictable and specific answer. These questions are usually designed to "call forth from the student those knowledges, skills, or feeling states that the student is presumed to possess" (Hough 1970, p. 191).

Somehow it seems much easier to ask a child a closed question, "What color is this?" "Do you want the red paint or the blue?" "Which is the biggest?" than to think of an open-ended question that will stimulate thinking. Some open-ended questions that ask children to think for themselves might begin with

- what do you think of. . .?
- can you tell me more about. . .?
- why do you think that. . .?
- how could that happen. . .?
- what else could you do. . .?

When teachers use open-ended questions, however, they must be prepared for open-ended answers and accept the responses children give. One teacher asked children to identify the most beautiful thing in the classroom. A number of children offered answers such as the paintings on the wall, the dried flower arrangements, or the box sculpture that a group of children had completed that morning. The teacher proceeded to reject each answer and finally told the children that they were the most beautiful thing in the room because God had made each of them. In this instance, the teacher should have told the children that they were beautiful. He really did not want their opinion, and in asking, left several believing that their ideas, and possibly they themselves, were rejected.

Whether or not teachers are asking open-ended or closed questions, it is helpful to tie the questions to children's actions and experiences. Asking What did you see? How did it change? How did you do it? may help focus children's attention and expand their understanding of some phenomenon.

Both open-ended and closed questions can be used to relieve the teacher from doing too much telling. Asking, What do you think this was used for? What are the rules for the field trip? or How did the farmer do that? involves the children in a conversation and serves to communicate useful information.

Just as with any other teaching strategies, questioning can be overdone. A teacher bombarding young children with questions can be obnoxious and less than helpful. "Look," a four year old told his teacher who was continuing to bombard him with questions about his painting, "it's just a painting, there's nothing to tell about it!" A teacher who asks children too many questions can leave them feeling insecure, or even threatened. Will they be able to answer each question? What will they say? Will their answers be accepted?

There are some questions that should not be asked and are actually rude

and prying. The type of questions that ask children about private an
things, or those that place them in uncomfortable positions, sho
asked. What did your mommy do when your daddy said that? A
you did that? Who do you like best, me or Ms. Albert? are examples of ques
that are totally inappropriate and have no place in a good school for young
children.

Reinforcing

Whenever a teacher smiles at a child, gives a quick hug, wink, praises,
or on the other hand punishes and ignores some behavior or action of a child,
he is using the principles of behavior modification. Whether or not teachers
are aware of it, they are continually reinforcing, rewarding, ignoring, and
punishing children's behavior. These practices are common in day care centers,
Head Start programs, and kindergartens, in fact in every type of school from
nursery to graduate. Teachers are familiar with the principles of behavior
modification, for they themselves have been recipients of rewards or punishments. They have received reinforcing grades, awards, memberships on dean's
lists, and paychecks, or the punishment of low grades and extra assignments.

As defined by psychologists, behavior modification is a program that
systematically and precisely applies basic principles from psychological research
dealing with stimulus and response learning to teach desirable behavior, learning, or the development of skills in children and to eradicate undesirable
behaviors.

When a child receives a reinforcement for some behavior, which might
be anything from a smile or word of praise, to food, money, or a token which
can be exchanged for some desired object, it increases the probability that the
child will repeat the behavior. On the other hand, when undesirable behavior
is ignored, when no reinforcement in the form of recognition, or even punishment, is given, the child will probably not continue or repeat the behavior.
Ignoring undesirable behavior has been called the process of *extinction*. It is
the gradual weakening of a response as a direct result of nonreinforcement.
Nursery school teachers have successfully used nonrecognition of undesirable
behavior as a discipline technique. A child who is having a temper tantrum is
matter of factly ignored until the tantrum is over. The fighting, kicking, spitting,
hitting—any of the behaviors young children use to call attention to themselves—when ignored, and no longer useful to the child for gaining the teacher's
attention, will gradually disappear.

Behavior modification has been the subject of a number of research studies. Some of the studies demonstrate how teachers of young children, by
ignoring a child's deviant behavior—crawling, spitting, hitting, not attending
to a task—can eliminate the behavior. Other studies demonstrate how teachers
have used rewards and reinforcements to teach children every variety of learning or skill (Madsen 1969; Meacham 1969).

Reinforcement promotes learning and increases positive behaviors. It is a positive teaching strategy, as opposed to punishment, which is negative. Nevertheless, there are problems inherent in the use of reinforcement or behavior modification. Katz (1974) in "Condition with Caution" reminds teachers that the use of reinforcement, without an understanding of the child and his behavior, can be a dangerous practice. Teachers must ask themselves before using reinforcement, why the child is doing what he is, what is the meaning of the behavior, and what behavior they feel is preferred.

Denying children reinforcement, ignoring them, can be equally hazardous. Read (1971) points out:

> Failure to get attention and response will rouse resentment and hostility in children, too, especially in insecure children who are seeking reassurance through getting attention. Their feelings are involved in a way that makes them sensitive to failure. Situations are constantly arising in which children want attention from the teacher, or from other children, want to feel important and needed—and fail. They are resentful and hostile as a result. (Read 1971, p. 301)

The technique of reinforcement is so powerful and effective that it is the basis of animal training. Perhaps the automated animals—chickens pecking at a toy piano to receive a kernel of corn, parrots squawking out some rhyme, horses doing tricks—have led early childhood educators to view reinforcement as a mechanistic approach, not suited to teaching young children.

When reinforcement denies children's basic human motivation, when it leaves no room for children's feelings or sensitivities, then it is mechanistic. When teachers reinforce children's behavior and learning without permitting children to develop their own autonomy in learning, to use their instrinsic motivation, then the analogy can be drawn between the nonthinking, mechanistic, highly trained performing animals and the training of children.

Reinforcement is only a technique, one of the many an experienced teacher uses. Broudy (1965) puts reinforcement in the framework of the total teaching environment stating:

> It is the general quality of the teacher/student relationship as developed and maintained in the total context of the preschool experience rather than the teacher's praise of isolated success that is really important. If the teacher has created a solid relationship with each child, praise of his specific individual response is neither important or expected. By the same token, if the teacher has alienated the child, or frightened the children, praising them for responding successfully is unlikely to do much to improve the general undesirable relationships. A solid relationship is based on the children's individual characteristics, not on praise of a few, isolated, correct answers. (Broudy 1965, p. 201)

Giving Feedback

Giving feedback, letting children know how they are progressing, is in fact a type of reinforcement. The teacher, in giving feedback, is not only recognizing the child for some achievement, a demonstrated skill or behavior, but also at the same time is giving the child some explicit information about that behavior. Feedback communicates to the children something about their performance. It helps children to clarify their tasks, affirms for them that their work, or they themselves, are valid and accepted, and offers them help in evaluating and analyzing their work.

Feedback, like all teaching strategies, must begin with an understanding of individual children. The teacher must take cues from each child in order to know what type of feedback will be useful, and when. In general, feedback is considered useful when it

1. Describes what a child is doing, rather than places a value judgment on it. "You are painting with green paint, the green is bright," rather than "I like green paint."

2. Is specific instead of general. "You climbed to the top of the bars today," instead of "You did well outside."

3. Directs the child toward something she has control over and can do something about. "Put these dishes here" is more helpful than "pick up."

4. Is well timed, juxtaposed with the child's actions, and given while children are actually working or achieving.

Feedback can also be used to suggest problem solutions to children, "What would happen if?" or "Put your finger here, and see if it will work." Children can be encouraged to complete a task and stay with a project, "Where does this piece fit? Look at the puzzle, can you see a space for it?" Feedback need not be extensive, a smile, wink, nod from across the room is often all a child needs to feel confident or to continue with a task.

Modeling

Every action, nonaction, and reaction, every bit of verbal and nonverbal behavior of the teacher is noted by the children, and many of these behaviors become incorporated into children's repertoires. Children learn from copying the behavior of their teachers. Almy (1975) writes:

> Teachers may not be fully aware of the extent to which what they do becomes a pattern for the children to follow. . . . it is also evident that in the facilitating function where the teacher's exploratory and investigative attitude toward materials can be copied by the children. Furthermore one only has to observe the way children in some classrooms take care of each other and provide comfort in the time of distress to realize that the care-taking and guidance functions of the teacher can also be copied by the children. (Almy 1975, p. 21)

Bandura and Walters (1963), who have explored the behavior of modeling, believe that enough work has been completed to describe how the process, especially in the area of social learning, occurs. According to their work, new behavior units (chunks of behavior) are learned initially through observing and imitating a model, rather than being learned through the process of reinforcement. Bandura and Walters are convinced that children do learn as they observe and imitate their parents, teachers, and others around them.

According to their research, children also model the behavior of those they see on television, in the movies, or in instructional materials. The process involves children observing the behavior of a model and reconstructing their behavior to match that of the models. If children see a model being rewarded for a particular type of behavior, they are more likely to copy that behavior than if it was not rewarded. If, on the other hand, the model observed was punished for exhibiting the behavior, children will usually not reconstruct that behavior.

Parents are usually the first models children identify with and imitate. When parents are warm and accepting people, the child views their behavior as rewarding and wants to be and act like them. When the child reaches school, other people serve as models. The teacher, who has power, who reinforces emulated behavior, is a potent model.

Upon entrance into school, some children find a conflict between the models they have at home and those at school. A middle-class teacher may disapprove of a lower-class child's way of life and that can cause conflicts. Alexander (1973) claims that middle-class young children placed in a nursery school have better opportunities for identification and imitation of a satisfying nature, for they can interact both with peers and adults of similar backgrounds. This experience leads to continuing and stable behavior patterns.

Although teachers are constantly serving as models for children, there are times when they will actually want to demonstrate some activity and provide more direct modeling for children. They may model by showing how to hold a book, use a record player, telephone, or bicycle. At other times teachers might say, "Look at me while I put the pegs in the board. Now you do it," or "Watch me while I thread the needle; this is how you do it."

Knowing that children do model their behaviors on others, teachers have a responsibility to exhibit behaviors that are worthy of being emulated. The very attitudes teachers hold toward others, the environment, and learning are copied by the children. Teachers should attempt to analyze their attitudes, values, and behaviors in order to present children with those that are prosocial and will transmit the values inherent in a democratic society.

Observing

As the children work and play, the teacher maintains the active role of observer. The entire group of children, small groups working together, and each individual child receive the teacher's observation.

Observing and keeping an eye on everything and everyone at the same time, the teacher maintains control over the group, even when the children are actively involved in individual, self-initiated activities. All teachers who have worked with young children can relate a time when, somehow, intuitively, they knew something was wrong or disaster was approaching. Either the children were suddenly quiet, or a nosie, motion, or action alerted the teacher to impending trouble. Using all of her senses as she observes, the teacher uses this strategy to protect the safety of the children and to maintain order and control.

Observing is a strategy that is ongoing. Teachers observe throughout the day as children relate to each other, their parents, and the materials.

Nurturing

"Young children need to know that they are loved. Every human, even the strongest among us—shares this hunger. But young children are dependent in the extreme" (Hymes 1974, p. 42). All teachers, but especially teachers of young children, must be able to give children the nurturance, care, and affection each child needs and craves. Children, young and unsophisticated, are open in their affection and in expressing their needs. They hug, squeeze, run to greet the teacher and frequently tell her just how very much they love her.

The ability to give children the nurturance they need is a strategy of the successful teacher. Nurturance, feeling the warmth and approval of another, is a prerequisite to intellectual growth. Only as children feel secure, loved, and nurtured, do they have the confidence, support, and security they need to risk learning new things and to reach out to others.

Children can be nurtured in many ways. Teachers must be sensitive to the needs of each child and know which chiildren are made comfortable by just a smile or nonphysical expression of nurturance and which children need hugs, holding, and a pat on the back. Knowledge of the backgrounds of the children often helps teachers to understand each child's needs.

Nurturance can be demonstrated in many ways. Respecting the feelings of children; permitting them to cry, to be angry; taking the time to listen are some of the diverse ways teachers show children that they care.

Working With Groups

Some teaching strategies are useful when working with children in groups. Children, like all humans, are social beings and take great pleasure in being with others. Young children, however, have difficulty learning to work in a group. Their attention spans are short, they cannot sit still for long, and their egocentric thought gets in the way of understanding one another. Even though it is difficult for young children to work together, to become a part of a group, it is something everyone wants to, and must, learn.

Nearly everyone can recall the good feelings that came from sitting around a campfire, singing songs with a group, building a fort of boxes and scraps with the neighborhood gang, or the first time they were really working with others and actually belonged to a group. The same type of intimate, secure, amicable feelings arise when young children, who do have needs to be social, take part in a group. Brian Sutton-Smith (1975) describes the hilarity and sense of mastery children feel when they do things together, reaching social organization and developing social coordination at three years of age.

Group activities help children develop the skills of interaction that will permit them to enter into the social world. In addition, participation in a group strengthens cognitive ability. When children are together with others, they are forced to see alternative points of view and to readjust their thinking to that of the group. When children share in group discussions, they begin to recognize that others have ideas, and they may see the same event in different ways.

Group experiences for three year olds are limited to brief, spontaneous encounters. The group may consist of one or two children, together on a teacher's lap, listening to a story, or two or three children observing the rabbit chew lettuce. This group lasts for a few minutes, with children leaving and others entering.

Four year olds enjoy singing songs together, playing a circle singing game, coming together to make plans for a field trip, or talking about their block buildings. Group experiences with four year olds are also brief and flexible. Whenever the teacher asks a group of these children to come together for a meeting, it is with the full understanding that the members of the group are free to leave or to rejoin it.

Group times with five year olds can be more formal. Group meetings become regular, definite parts of the daily schedule. The number of group activities, scheduling, and the nature and length of time of each depends, in a large part, on the type of program, the philosophy of the teacher, the number of teachers available, the ages of the children, and the amount of space in the preschool. Some group activities that may become routines for five year olds are *opening, sharing and discussion, or evaluation*.

Opening

An opening time, informal and brief, can set the stage for the entire day. Calling children together to begin the day gives them needed structure, some idea of the choices that are available, and what to expect for the rest of the day. During the opening group meeting, a discussion of the events, the routines, and news of the day may take place. A news story could be written on the board and read to the children. Routines of recording the weather, recognizing birthdays, or explaining planned activities will be a part of this time.

Sharing and Discussion

During the day there will be occasions when the entire group of children will come together to discuss a special problem or to share some event. Children might be called together as a group to discuss how to get the blocks back on the shelf, keep the fishbowl clean, or work together at the woodwork. There are other times when it may be desirable to ask all of the child come together to share in a special event—observe the butterfly emerge fro the chrysalis or watch the electrician fix lights.

Children will also come together to enjoy poetry, stories, singing, or dancing. When the entire group listens to a story, music, or poem, it serves to unify the group, giving them common information that forms the base of play and other creative activities.

EVALUATING

At the end of the day, or following work time, another type of group activity is appropriate. This is a time for evaluation, a pulling together and summing up that gives children a feeling of closure. It is a time for children to reflect on and to recall the day's activities, remembering the immediate past. Evaluating the activities of the day helps to clarify children's experiences and gives a sense of continuity to the diverse and varied activities that may have taken place.

When working with children in a group, teachers have found that it is helpful to

1. Remember that these are very young children. They are learning and cannot be expected to behave like adults. Children will wiggle, squirm, stand up, dance, talk to themselves, sing, or chat with a friend. Teachers who are prepared for children who are active find it easier to accept the natural behaviors of children.

2. Keep group activities short, flexible, and spontaneous. Simply because young children find it difficult to sit still, it is wise to plan for brief meetings. Young children may focus their attention, while in a group, for unbelievably long periods of time. One librarian, a master storyteller, held the undivided attention of a group of three to five year olds for a complete hour. She tried to leave after the first twenty minutes, but the children kept asking her to stay and "tell just one more." Such times, however, are rare. Teachers will usually want to plan to terminate a group activity after a short time, perhaps three, five, or ten minutes. It is usually beneficial to end the group before the children's attention spans end. If groups go on for too long, teachers begin to fight for control of the bored, frustrated, and restless children.

3. Establish physical closeness with the children. Physical closeness is helpful in gaining and holding the attention of a group of young children. When the teacher is close to the children, she can maintain eye contact, hold one on her lap, put an arm around another—helping children to concentrate on the task at hand.

4. Begin without waiting for the group to become ready. A teacher who waits for the entire group to get ready may wait forever. Rather than waiting for the entire group to assemble, the teacher can begin with a finger play, short poem, book, song, anything that will attract the children's attention and encourage those who have not yet joined to hurry to the group.

5. See that all of the children have the opportunity to participate. It is so easy to be fooled by a group of young children. One or two highly verbal and aggressive children may give all the answers, do all of the discussing, and reach all of the conclusions. These few children can lead a teacher to believe the children are all progressing well in developing group skills.

When teachers know each child, they know whom they can ask to participate in the group, how, and when. Teachers can remind individual children to listen to another child or to think about what someone else has said. They also recognize children who must have immediate attention. Teachers might say, "Yes Albert. Can you hold your idea until John finishes?" "Will, that's interesting, but we're talking about turtles. Do you want to tell us something about turtles?" or "What do you think about that, Andrea; can you tell us something about it?" These types of comments help all children learn to participate and develop group discussion skills.

In Summary

Become familiar with a variety of strategies and be able to sensitively use the strategy that best fits you, your personality, the situation, and the children. Among the strategies used by preschool teachers are telling, listening, questioning, reinforcing, and nurturing. To a certain extent it seems as if the best strategies are those that fit the needs of teacher and children. Lowenfeld (1957) believed that how a teacher behaves, and the strategies she employs depend on at least three things. The first is the personality of the teacher—the degree of sensitivity the teacher has and the character of her relationships with the environment; second, the teacher's ability to put herself in the place of others; and third, her ability to understand the needs of those she is teaching. "It is impossible to say that any one approach may it be given the best sounding name, is good for all. At one time it may be better than another, but in the end the approach will depend on the individual teacher" (Lowenfeld 1957, p. 57)

Resources

Some references that may be useful in helping you to develop a variety of teaching strategies include

BARKER, LARRY, *Listening Behavior*. Englewood Cliffs, N.J.: Prentice-Hall, Inc., 1971.

BLANK, M., *Teaching Learning in the Preschool: A Dialogue Approach*, Columbus, Ohio: Charles E. Merrill Publishing Company, 1973.

SUND, R.B., and CARRIN, A., *Creative Questioning and Sensitive Listening Techniques: A Self Concept Approach*. Columbus, Ohio: Charles E. Merrill Publishing Company, 1978.

Projects

1. Each teacher must perfect her own teaching strategies. Some strategies feel comfortable for some people, others do not seem to fit. As you work with young children, try to practice different strategies of giving feedback, questioning, and listening. Which do you find difficult to use? Which come easy? Which do you use the most frequently?

If there are strategies that you have not perfected and are not using, you might try to remember to give children feedback, for instance, as you continue to work with them.

2. Analyze your own needs for affection and nurturance. Why have you decided to work with young children? Do you enjoy their spontaneous expressions of love? What does this mean for you as a teacher of young children? In order to help clarify your own needs, discuss your feelings with other teachers and students.

3. Write a list of questions that require children to use higher-order thought processes or that are open-ended in nature. Practice using these questions with a fellow student or teacher. Do they really seem to extend and facilitate expression of ideas and thoughts?

4. Observe in a preschool classroom. Record the instances of questioning, telling, reinforcing, nurturing, and observing. What strategy is most frequently used? Which is the most effective strategy the teacher you observe uses?

References

ALEXANDER, T., *Human Development in an Urban Age*. Englewood Cliffs, N.J.: Prentice-Hall, Inc., 1973.

ALMY, M., *The Early Childhood Educator at Work*. New York: McGraw-Hill Book Company, 1975.

BANDURA, A. and WALTERS, R.H., *Social Learning and Personality Development*. New York: Holt, Rinehart & Winston, 1963.

BROUDY, H.S., *Exemplars of Teaching Method*. Chicago: Rand McNally & Company, 1965.

BRUNER, J.S., *The Process of Education*. Cambridge, Mass.: Harvard University Press, 1966.

ELKIND, D. *A Sympathetic Understanding of the Child: Birth to Sixteen*. (2nd. ed.) Boston: Allyn & Bacon, Inc., 1978.

FROEBEL, F. *The Education of Man*. New York: D. Appleton and Company, 1889.

HOUGH, J.B., and DUNCAN, J.K., *Teaching: Description and Analysis*. Reading, Mass.: Addison-Wesley Publishing Co., Inc., 1970.

HUNKINS, F.P., *Questioning Strategies and Techniques*. Boston: Allyn & Bacon, Inc., 1972.

HYMES, J.L., *Teaching the Child Under Six*. Columbus, Ohio: Charles E. Merrill Publishing Company, 1974.

JORDAN, D. *"Early Childhood Education—It's a Science!"* in *Early Childhood Education: It's an Art. It's a Science*, ed. J.D. Andrews. Washington, D.C.: National Association for the Education of Young Children, 1975.

KATZ, L., *Condition With Caution*. Urbana, Ill.: ERIC ECE Publishing House, 1974.

LOWENFELD, V., *Creative and Mental Growth*. New York: Macmillan, Inc., 1957.

MEACHAM, M.L., and WIESEN, A.E., *Changing Classroom Behavior: A Manual for Precision Teaching*. Scranton, Penn.: International Textbook Company, 1969.

PIAGET, J., *Play, Dreams and Imitation in Childhood*. New York: W.W. Norton & Co., Inc., 1951.

READ, K.B. *The Nursery School*, New York: Wm. B. Saunders, 1971.

SANDERS, N.M., *Classroom Questions: What Kinds?* New York: Harper & Row, Publishers, Inc., 1965.

SUCHMAN, J.R., "The Child and the Inquiry Process," in *Intellectual Development: Another Look*, ed. A.H. Passow. Washington, D.C.: Association for Supervision and Curriculum Development, 1964, 59–77.

SUTTON-SMITH, B., "Play as Novelty Training," in *One Child Indivisible*, ed. J.D. Andrews. Washington, D.C.: National Association for the Education of Young Children, 1975, 227–257.

WITTMER, J., and MYRICK, R.D., *Facilitative Teaching: Theory and Practice*. Pacific Palisades, Calif: Goodyear Publishing Co. Inc., 1974.

SUND, R.B., and CARIN, A., *Creative Questioning and Sensitive Listening Techniques: A Self Concept Approach* (2nd ed.) Columbus, Ohio: Charles E. Merrill Publishing Company, 1978.

8

Communicating

Men live in a community in virtue of the things which they have in common; and communication is the way in which they come to possess things in common.

J. Dewey 1916, p. 4

Communication is the key to building understanding, trust, and mutual helpfulness between children and teachers, teachers and parents, and teachers and other members of the school faculty. "But to say that communication is the key doesn't tell much. We must know, understand and practice the ins and outs of effective communication" (Otto 1969, p. 1). Communication has been recognized as a complex process and field of study. It is a process that transmits information between people, involves interaction, is reciprocal, and involves the ability to take on the role of another (Smith and Williamson 1977).

Freud (1953) was interested in the process of communication, and his work still influences us today. Whenever you say, "Oh that really was a slip of the tongue," you are referring to Freud's idea that such slips were reflections of deep, hidden beliefs and feelings. Freud (1953) believed that all behavior had an underlying, identifiable logic, and that the unconscious directed all unexplained behaviors.

As Freud suggested, people communicate whether they mean to or not. Nonverbal communication is responsible for more than half of the meaning people assign to interpersonal communication. "Nonverbal cues can suggest to the child that she is liked and respected by the teacher. They can also

Communication is the key
to understanding.

suggest that the teacher wishes the child would go away. Thus nonverbal cues
are efficient suggestions" (Flannery 1978, p. 57).

Nonverbal Communication

Think of the messages communicated through body behaviors and manners. Gestures a person makes, physical expressions, and facial expressions all
communicate a message. It is important to understand the meaning of such
body gestures—and to recognize that gestures and movements mean different
things to different people—in order to become an effective communicator.

Eye contact is one area of nonverbal communication of interest to researchers. In general, communication is believed to be fostered when eye
contact has been established. If eye contact is too intense, or for too long a
period, people may begin to feel uncomfortable. Then too, in some cultures
children are taught that it is a sign of disrespect to look directly in another's
eyes. A teacher's demand to "Look me in the eyes," when children have been
taught that this is a sign of disrespect, can certainly hinder good communication.

There seems to be more eye contact when people are speaking than
listening (Flannery 1978). More eye contact is found when people are receiving
positive, rather than negative, feedback. Eye contact is also believed to indicate
to others that you are communicating with them and want to include them in
the conversation.

Eye contact is especially important when communicating with children,
for it helps the young child to focus on what you are saying. It is important to
remember to be at the eye level of the child. Asking a child to look up at an
adult and try to find her eyes is not very efficient. Stooping down or sitting
on a low chair places you at the child's eye level.

Facial expressions are another form of nonverbal communication. Facial

162

expressions (or lack of them), give feedback and help clarify the meaning of a person's words. Too many facial expressions, especially of a negative kind, can be distracting. Teachers often use facial expressions as they communicate with children. A wink, nod, smile, frown, or head shake may be all a teacher needs to keep control of or send a message to a group of children.

Likewise, children's facial expressions communicate. Because the verbal ability of young children is limited, their facial expressions—frowns, smiles, tears, a tightly closed mouth—let a teacher know more about their feelings than could be communicated with words.

Communicating with parents and others in the school also depends on nonverbal cues. Teachers show concern for parents by smiling, nodding encouragement or approval as the parent talks, and by maintaining comfortable eye contact. A teacher with sagging posture, downcast eyes, grim facial expression, or faraway gaze may be communicating disinterest, unconcern, or even antagonism to parents or other adults.

Clothing, cosmetics, and hair style also convey messages to children. Remember the messages communicated during the 1960s without the use of words. The hair styles, an American flag as a patch for blue jeans, and the dashiki communicated more meanings, feelings, and suggestions than words could express.

Meanings are communicated to children through a teacher's clothing. "Please wear those yellow shoes again," a kindergarten child said to her teacher in the middle of winter. Even though snow covered the ground, the child still remembered the yellow sandals worn by her teacher during the hot September days. Dressing with care tells children how much they are respected. As trite as it seems, children do enjoy pretty, bright-colored clothing, and clothing considerd stylish.

Conflict between what is acceptable clothing and what is not can arise between teachers and parents. "Teachers with unusual hairstyles may very well convey one image to the students and another to the community where short conservative hairstyles may be more prevalent, the teacher with extreme styles may be viewed with suspicion" (Smith and Williamson 1977, p. 70).

Where a teacher places herself and the distance she keeps between children, other teachers, and parents also send messages. Hall (1966) describes an eighteen-inch distance between speakers as *intimate space*, the eighteen-inch to four-foot distance as *personal space*, the four-foot to twelve-foot distance as *social distance*, and beyond the twelve-foot distance as *public distance*. Each of these distances is believed to communicate a different message. With close physical proximity, intimacy and touching are possible. If the distance between two people is great, a lot of fine verbal and nonverbal details are lost in the communicative process.

When a teacher sits with children, on the floor with the block builders, or hugs children, tucking a few around her as she reads a story, she is building good communication. She is saying, I want to be close to you, to make contact with you, to communicate.

Communicating with adults, parents, and other team members is also improved by decreasing the physical distance between you and the others. Sitting far away from parents, behind a table or desk, is saying nonverbally, I really don't want to get involved, please let's keep our distance from one another. In setting up parent conferences think about where you will sit, how close the parents will be, and what physical barriers could be removed to increase proximity and communication.

Verbal Communication

Verbal cues also send messages and communicate meanings. People use words as well as silences to communicate. Tone of voice, loudness, and strength of voice also communicate.

A soft voice is useful in establishing communication with children and in maintaining control over the classroom. Children will imitate the voice of their teacher, and if that voice is quiet, calm, and soft, a quiet gentle atmosphere will prevail. A teacher who generally keeps her voice low and soft also gains instant attention when she does find it necessary to raise her voice to give directions or to gain control over some situation.

The ability to modulate the voice to achieve different effects in tone and quality is of high value when communicating with children. Variations in loudness, changes in pitch, tone, speed, and fluency help adults and children pay attention and enter into a communicative relationship. A continually high pitched voice can grate on any listener's ears and distract from communication. On the other hand, a monotonous voice bores both children and adults.

Silences speak. Sometimes silence is used as a form of disapproval. "I don't like what you're saying, I won't respond." Other times, silence can be used to reflect on what someone has said, to think about it, and then respond with an idea that builds on the person's thought.

Language is communication. The trouble with language is that words have different meanings for different people. Hayakawa (1971) discusses all of the different meanings people can give to the word *frog*. You can catch a frog in a pond, have one in your throat, in the bottom of a vase holding flowers, or you can use the word to describe a kind of button on a silk jacket, pick the frog on a horse's hoof, or use one on your violin.

Words do carry different meanings. Most words have more meanings than dictionaries supply. When you remember that each person brings different experiences, memories, likes, and dislikes to each word, it is clear that words have great impact. In a way it is miraculous that people communicate as efficiently as they do. This is especially true when regional or cultural differences enter into the communicative process.

Lack of familiarity with the meanings of different verbal expressions in any given neighborhood or culture can cause a teacher trouble. A five year old, after moving to a Southern city, was asked by the teacher if his mother was going to carry him to school. The teacher wanted to know if the child would ride the bus, or if the mother would drive him to school. The child, however, was puzzled. His mother could not even carry him for a few moments, how in the world could she pick him up and carry him all the way to school?

Professionals also need to watch the use of educational jargon when speaking with parents or other people from the community. Rather than telling a parent her child needs more *peer association*, you might simply say how valuable it would be if the child could play with other children after school. It is unnecessary and undesirable to talk down to parents when reporting about a child's progress, or at any time. It is important, however, to be certain that the words you use mean the same to you as they do to the parent.

Saying things clearly and concisely, highlighting important and significant points is helpful. Effective use of words requires a lot of thinking and the ability to perceive what the other person is thinking. Teachers must think about the meaning of the words they use, as well as perceive the meanings others assign to them.

Specificity is also helpful in fostering good communication with children and adults alike. Using language that is too general does not communicate clearly. Asking children to clean up is much less effective than asking them to pick up the clothing, or the blocks, and telling parents their child is doing well is less helpful than sharing some specific skill the child has gained.

Ineffective speech and communication can cause problems in the classroom, school community, and with parents. Listening to children talk, you find them using *parallel speech*. They enjoy talking with one another, answering one another, but they are each speaking about different things. They are not communicating, they are simply talking together. Each is discussing a different topic, each fails to listen, reflect, and respond to what the other has said.

Now listen to adults speaking to one another while waiting for a bus, in line at school or voter registration, or in the waiting room of a doctor's office. How many adult conversations can be called parallel speech? Do adults talk about the same things, or do they converse about different things? Adults, just like children, must learn to avoid parallel speech if effective communication is desired.

Learning to communicate takes time and practice. It is a two-way process and means talking with, not at, or to others. It means that each person must be tuned in to others. In addition to clarity of speech and correct use of words, ask yourself: (1) How many times do I interrupt a child, fellow teacher, or parent? (2) Do I use language to support others, to listen, to insult, agree with, attack, or stall? (3) When do I restate what another has said? (4) When and how often do I find myself repeating things?

Communicating With Children

She could make herself plainly understood by even the smallest of children. There was no talking down to their level—no baby talk about her. The words were selected that were already known and some new ones added and explained. Never tiresome. We always wanted more—

went away hungry is no fanciful phrase as applied to Miss Peabody's teaching. . . . what she said and how she said it filled every crack and cranny of our minds. I do not remember to have ever heard a word said about not whispering or "keep still." (The Pilgrims Scrip 1911, p. 123)

Every preschool teacher would hope to be remembered as this person remembers his experiences as a pupil in Elizabeth Peabody's kindergarten. Certainly there is nothing as painful as listening to an adult talking down to or using baby talk with children. Experienced teachers have found the following suggestions useful in developing the skill of communicating effectively with children.

1. Be sure the child is listening. Children can concentrate on only one thing at a time. If you want to give a child a direction, share some information, or make a request, either call the child, or children's names, touch them, or in some other way gain their attention before attempting to communicate.
2. Remember that children's attention spans are short and keep verbal statements concise and to the point. As a general rule about what to say to children, don't say too much, is good advice (Pitcher and Ames 1964).
3. Establish a tone of expectancy. When you talk with children expect that they will attend and respond. Beginning teachers, who want to be kind and have the children like them, often say things like, "Do you want to come to lunch now?" "Who wants to hear a good story?" or "Do you want to wash your hands?" And when children honestly respond, No! they don't want to do any of those things, the teacher has a problem. Instead of asking children if they want to do things that must be done anyway, it is more effective to simply tell the child what is expected. "Come to lunch now." "Wash your hands." "Now it's time for a story."
4. Use more *dos* than *don'ts*. Telling a child, "Don't color on the table, don't run into the street, don't drag your coat," isn't as useful as telling them what to do. Often children, failing to hear the "don't," do exactly what the teacher has asked them not to do. Even if they have heard the "don't," they may not have an alternative in mind and are left not knowing what to do. Giving children an alternative is helpful. "Do carry your coat this way. Do stop at the curb. Do color on the paper, not the table."
5. Use humor. Young children are intrigued with the humor of language. They burst into giggles over silly rhymes and nonsense words. Show them you appreciate their humor, join them in their fun, and use a light, humorous touch in communication.

Pitcher and Ames (1964) offer verbal techniques that are helpful when working with children.

Two Year Olds—Use simple, concrete, and repetitive language. The repetition will help the two year old feel comfortable. Avoid verbosity.

Two and a Half Year Olds—Motivate children with questions. "Where do you hang your coat?" "How could you, how about, I wonder if," are face-saving questions designed to redirect children's behavior. Verbal expressions of affection and praise are welcome.

Three Year Olds—Children are beginning to enjoy language. Spontaneous, two-way conversations begin. Whispering is a useful technique to gain attention.

Three and a Half Year Olds—Going to extremes to match the extreme and exaggerated behavior of the three and a half year old works well. Raising and lowering your voice or varying the tone of your voice helps gain and hold children's attention.

Four Year Olds—Praise and compliments are effective, as with any age child. Frequent verbalization about expected behaviors tends to produce those behaviors. Teachers can now interpret other people's feelings or give verbal reasons why children did specific things. Positive suggestions continue to be best, but four year olds can respond to statements such as "Don't throw sand," when necessary.

Five Year Olds—Five year olds are much more adultlike in their ability to comprehend spoken language and to carry out conversations with others. They continue to appreciate humor, praise, and positive suggestions.

Communicating With Parents

Parents have always been considered in early childhood education. Margaret McMillan (1919) writes of making changes in the homes of the children attending her open-air nursery school in London.

> Teddy's mother lives in a cellar and neglects him, for long spells, when she is out enjoying herself . . . yet she is suggestible, and our Miss S. has got a hold of her somehow. . . . she has got Teddy's mother to give him his bath at the week end, and to wash his home clothing and send him in bright and sweet on a Monday morning. (M. McMillan 1919, p. 177)

Communicating with parents by "getting a hold of them" has long been rejected. Yet all early childhood programs, throughout the years, have involved parents. And it is true, many of the beginning kindergarten programs, those in settlement houses for children and their immigrant parents, had as a major goal, fostering change in parents. These programs worked just as hard educating parents in the ways of the new country as they did in educating children.

Early childhood education, however, has another history of parent involvement. The cooperative nursery schools were actually begun by parents. In these programs teachers did not "get a hold" of parents or try to change them; rather they cooperated with parent policy boards in carrying out programs for children. The cooperative schools are called "native American" by Katherine Whiteside Taylor (1978) because they originated in America, not in England or Germany as did the nursery school and the kindergarten. Cooperative nursery schools are organized by parents, "rooted in people. Parents—mothers, fathers—create them, trying to get something they know they need for their children and themselves" (Taylor 1978, p. 31). Rather than attempt to change parents, teachers and parents learn together as they cooperate to develop and implement programs for young children.

Teachers communicate with children.

The critical importance of parent involvement in schools became clarified during the 1960s. By this time research had clearly demonstrated that parents play a major role in the education of their children and that the more parents are involved in a preschool program, the greater the achievement of their children. Thus, Head Start and other compensatory educational programs have as their major goal involvement of parents in order to maximize the effect of early educational experiences for children.

Head Start, like the cooperative nursery schools, does not try to get a hold of parents to change them. Rather, Head Start views parent involvement in several different ways but always with the idea that parents and teachers are equal partners in the education of children. Parents in Head Start can be involved as volunteers in the classroom, visitors or observers, or as paid aides. They might participate in social functions, educational groups, or policy-making boards. The highest level of parent participation is considered working on a policy-making board, making decisions affecting the program in cooperation with teachers and other community members.

The success of Head Start in creating communication between parents and teachers serves as a model for all preschool programs. Children, parents, teachers, and total communities can benefit when parents and teachers learn to communicate, and cooperate.

168

Parent group meetings are one way communication can be established between teachers and parents. Depending on the needs and desires of parents in any given community and the goals and objectives of the preschool, parent meetings can be held for any number of purposes. Often the meetings will be of a social nature, giving parents the opportunity to meet one another and form a social group. In high-mobility suburban communities, or in low-income neighborhoods, parents may not have an opportunity to join with others in group situations where enjoyment and pleasure are the major goals.

Other meetings may be held for educational or advocacy purposes or for conducting business, as in parent cooperatives and Head Start programs. In Head Start, the use of group meetings—large and small, long- or short-term—has been viewed as an important means of reaching individuals and families in low-income communities. Group experiences engage the interest of parents and foster involvement in other areas of the program.

As a teacher, it may be your role to act as leader of parent group meetings. You will be given the responsibility of creating a bond between individual parents and building group structure. One of the first things the group will do is decide on goals and aims. You may have to help the group achieve these goals.

SOCIAL GROUPS

Social groups may develop before more formal groups, or they might arise from the formal task-oriented meetings. Some begin spontaneously as a group of parents wait together to pick up their children and decide to meet for a picnic on the weekend. Other groups may be initiated by the teacher, inviting parents to a coffee hour at the center or to a parent's night.

When parents first meet, some time is spent in getting acquainted. This is the time when parents feel one another out, test the group for its value to them, and make decisions about dates, times, and places of future meetings. Leadership in a social group generally emerges from the members of the group. A teacher can observe the group and identify possible leaders. Working with these people, teachers may help plan for future social events—arranging for a room, coffee, babysitting, or for entertainment—and in general assist parents in carrying out their plans.

EDUCATIONAL GROUPS

Many preschool parent group meetings will take place for educational purposes. The most successful educational groups are those in which the members participate in all stages of the group, from the planning stage to the evaluation phase. As opposed to social group meetings, educational groups are

- structured and task-oriented;
- led by a volunteer, teacher, or some expert in the field. The expert may, of course, be one of the parents.
- related to the pursuit of educational goals and purposes

As individuals support activities and meetings they themselves have planned and feel responsible for, parents should decide on the content of the meetings. Parents may want information on how to raise young children, how to handle sibling rivalry, how to develop language skills, or on first aid and safety. Other meetings might be focused on nutrition, budgeting, time buying, job interviewing, learning another language, and any other basic educational need.

Often the teacher will act as leader of these groups. Even when a speaker or expert is present, it is still up to the teacher to put parents at ease and to help them relate the information to their lives. Teachers may help to start and maintain discussions, or, when necessary, stop discussions, and, in general, foster good relations.

To lead a group effectively you can

1. meet the group's needs for dependency. Individuals will come to the group with certain expectations. They will expect someone to be in charge and expect that their time will be well spent. Some introductory activity can help meet dependency needs. You might have people interview one another and then introduce each other to the group.
2. Provide for early group success. Introductions offer one successful experience, but there are others. Try serving coffee as people arrive, or engaging in some opening ritual, that will give people feelings of success.
3. Give everyone a chance to express views and opinions. "Let's hear from the others." "That's an important point, but what do the rest of you think?" "Hold that idea till we hear from . . ." Help everyone take part in the discussions.
4. Help the group set its own agenda and develop goals and objectives. "Today we agreed we'd talk about—. Let's find out what we already know about. . ."

The purpose of these methods is to develop a feeling of safety within the group and enable each person to participate. After people feel comfortable, the group can get on with learning new things, making decisions, and solving problems (Hollister).

POLICY-MAKING GROUPS

"Parent participation and involvement goes beyond parent education and adult activities. It includes opportunities for parents to come to grips with problems that affect their lives and the lives of their families" (Child Study 1967, p. 41). In many preschool programs, such as Head Start or cooperative nursery schools, parents will be responsible for establishing policy. A teacher involved with policy-making groups might

1. Interpret the objectives of the school's program to the parents.
2. Assist in preparation of the agenda, finding space for the group to meet.
3. Recognize and encourage emergence of leadership from the parents.
4. Orient all parents to the idea of participation in the group and in the purposes of the policy-making group.
5. Help get the information and decisions coming from the policy group to all of the parents.

Group meetings are but one form of parent participation. Parents and teachers can be fully involved working in social, educational, or policy making groups and still fail to communicate effectively. The small things teachers do, often spontaneously, can communicate more about the program than expensive, complicated activities. Some things teachers can do are

1. Telephone parents to compliment them, to communicate something the child has just learned to do, or just to keep in touch, letting parents and children know you really care about them.
2. Write letters to be forwarded home. As teachers review anecdotal records of the child's work, they might write a brief note telling of the progress the child is making. Or they might attach a note to a child's artwork or other work, telling how the child completed the work, what she said while doing it, or the importance of it.
3. Create a handbook. Most schools will have a handbook describing the goals of the school, listing names of the staff, telephone numbers, times of children's arrival and departure, and any other information parents will need. Invitations to join the children for lunch or to visit any time during the day can be included.

The respect the teacher has for each individual child and her family is communicated throughout the school year and serves to strengthen children's feelings of self-worth and pride in their family. Teachers will want to refer often to the children's parents during the school day and help children to remember their parents. Teachers might say, "I wonder what your mother is having for lunch today?" "Do you think your father played this game when he was your age?" "That was so much fun, sing it again on the tape recorder, and you can play the tape for your mother when she picks you up." "Why don't you draw a picture of the building you made with the blocks, that way your grandmother will be able to see your work."

Communicating in Conferences

Informal, spontaneous ways of communicating with parents do serve a purpose. But no teacher can stop with these informal ways of communication. These are valuable but should lead to building stronger, more meaningful relationships. The parent-teacher conference is, perhaps, the most valuable means of establishing and maintaining communication between parents and teachers.

In some ways, communication between parent and teacher is easy, for they have the child in common. Each has feelings for the child, and these feelings serve as the foundation for solid communication.

Teachers will want to schedule parent conferences at times that are convenient for the parents. With most parents working, and many children living in single-parent homes, conferences must be scheduled with care. It is important to arrange the room before a conference. Placing the conference table near an attractive display of children's work, or adding a plant or flowers, communicates respect.

Before the conference, outline the points that will be covered, and have examples of children's work handy so you can discuss progress in precise terms. If work and anecdotal records are dated, then teachers are better able to supply and interpret facts about the child.

Begin the discussion with positive statements, letting the parents know how much you enjoy their child. Communicate the child's progress and strong points. Encourage parent comments, questions, and suggestions at each point. "Have you noticed how well_____"; "Did she tell you about_____"; "How did he like_____"; and other questions can motivate parents to enter the conversation.

Both parent and teacher should leave the conference with feelings of satisfaction. Both should have obtained some insight into the child's best development, his behavior, or some clarification of a specific problem; they should have reached some specific decisions about next steps to be taken or should have made a positive change in their perception of the child or themselves.

Despite the best intentions and best laid plans, difficulties and conflicts between parents and teachers will arise. Some parents may be

- critical of all schools. Some people enjoy downgrading schools and teachers in general. Many want to go back to the good old days, defining the good old days as teaching three year olds phonics, or four year olds to read. It is important for you to recognize that these parents do not speak for the total group of parents. You can be prepared to explain your position, using theory and research, without becoming defensive.
- uncertain and insecure with their own abilities. Many may feel uncomfortable in any school building. Others may be indifferent, or unconcerned about their child, or seem unable to participate as an equal in the school's activities. Sometimes it is easy to misjudge a parent's insecurity as unconcern. Parents need time to recognize that they are welcome. Keep communications open and refrain from making too quick a judgment.
- unsatisfied. Nothing is ever enough for some parents. The neighbor child is learning more at Kiddie Kollege center, or everyone is picking on Susie. You need to recognize that you will never be able to meet all of the needs of all of the parents. Sometimes you can call on other team members to help assure the parents that their child is making progress or to explain the goals of the program.

Communicating Through Home Visits

Many programs are based on home visits. Other programs require that teachers visit in the home at least twice during the year, but in any case, teachers will want to visit the children's homes. There is no right or wrong way, or approach, to home visiting. Some parents are more comfortable in their own home and find it easier to communicate with teachers on their own "turf." Others may not be ready, or willing, to invite a teacher into their home. It may be that the home visit will take place in the front yard or on the porch, rather than in the home itself. Each teacher must develop her own style of working with families in the home. One approach will work well for one teacher and family; another, for other teachers and families.

Some teachers find that an "ice breaker" is useful. They like to take something with them. Pamphlets on making toys from scraps, things to do with children, or some other booklet obtained free of charge from the government printing office, a book, toy, or record, which can be left in the home, are effective ice breakers.

During the home visit, parents, teachers, and children can talk together, informally discussing the events of school. It is a fine time to let parents know of your goals for the coming weeks, as well as a good time for parents to express their concerns about their children and the school.

As the child plays or interacts with others in the home, teachers can point out different areas of growth and development, introduce techniques of talking with children, or present other ideas about child rearing.

On a home visit teachers will learn to recognize the strengths of many families. Many families have held together through a lot of traumatic experiences. Some have had a long history of coping with daily trials, yet have managed to survive. A greater understanding of the child can also develop through a home visit.

When making home visits, as with any other contact with parents, it is important to respect confidential information. Even seemingly unimportant information gained through a home visit is personal to the family and must not be shared with others. If the information will be shared during staff discussions about the child, it is still important to recognize and respect the rights of privacy of children and families.

Communicating With Parents
of Handicapped Children

Parents of handicapped children, just like their children, have special needs. Public Law 94-142 (1975) insures that both parents' and children's needs will be met in the school setting. The law requires that each child be given the least restrictive educational environment, but also outlines certain rights of the parents of the child. The law requires that parents

- give consent prior to an evaluation of the child.
- have the right to examine all records with respect to the evaluation and educational placement of the child.
- must be given prior written notice whenever a change in the identification, evaluation, or educational placement of the child takes place.
- have the right to a due process hearing in relation to any complaint.
- have the right to participate in the development of the individual educational plan for the child.
- have the right to attend meetings to develop the individual educational plan; the right to have the meetings held in their native tongue at a time and place agreeable to them.

Even if these requirements were not law, teachers would want to work closely with the parents of children with special needs. As with all children, the child with special needs must find a consistency between the environment of home and that of school. This does not mean that the school will do things exactly as they are done at home, but that the school and home know about one another and plan for the child's adjustment to any new additions to the school setting.

Then too, the parent of the handicapped child is a valuable resource for the teaching team. The parent knows the child better than anyone else and can inform the teacher of the child's likes, dislikes, how things are done, and whenever possible, can volunteer in the classroom.

Parents of handicapped children, like all parents, want to see their child become strong and self-sufficient, well-adjusted, and able to cope with the world. As responsible people, parents of handicapped children cannot stay uninvolved in their child's life and are usually eager to establish communications with teachers and to cooperate with the school.

When working with parents of handicapped children, however, teachers must be aware of some of the attitudes surrounding children with special needs. First, many parents may feel guilty about their child's handicap. The current attention being called to the relationship between the first weeks of conception and later handicaps may leave mothers wondering if their diet, activities, or even mental attitude before they were aware of their pregnancy could have affected the infant's development.

Some parents may withdraw from society as an expression of grief over having a handicapped child. Temporary withdrawal is considered natural, but some parents may need extra support and encouragement to join in the activities of the school or to meet with other parents.

Some parents may react to their child's handicap by rejecting the child. "The behavior of the mother who rejects her impaired child is characterized as indifferent, careless, selfish, or cruel. Such behavior adversely influences the child's adjustment" (Fallen and McGovern 1978, p. 179). These parents may demonstrate their rejection by failing to keep appointments, and, in general, by showing disinterest in the activities of the school.

Overprotection of the child is another way parents have of handling a child's handicaps. By overprotecting the child, the parent denies the child the right to learn about the world and to develop her own ways of coping with the environment. These parents may need extra help to leave their child to attend meetings or to let their child participate in the activities of the school.

Establishing good communication between parents and teachers is never a simple task. Many parents, not just those of the handicapped child, have had negative experiences with schools and will distrust a preschool teacher's intentions. Teachers can be sympathetic to the parents' attitudes but must at the same time persist in developing a working relationship with them.

Being a parent is always a difficult job, whether the child is handicapped or normal. Society tells us that it is good to have children, but then when the children are here, offers little support or help in raising the children. Sometimes preschool teachers have to be careful not to make too many demands of parents, demands that could overburden a parent, or take the parent away from the family. Teachers need to recognize that asking a parent to come to a meeting, to work with a child at home, or to come to the school for a conference, is at times simply beyond the parent's capability. When this happens, teachers must offer parents support, "It's O.K., I know how busy you are. I don't know how you do all you do. I'll let you know what happened at the meeting, or I'll write a note about Ralph's progress."

Communicating with Staff

When a new teacher, or student teacher enters a school for the first time, he is entering a highly organized, sophisticated, well-established group. As a new teacher you will want to be able to express yourself, to establish yourself as an autonomous, competent teacher, but you also want to be accepted into the already established community of teachers and school staff.

Any teacher entering a new situation will be wise to take some time to observe the staff relationships. Planning for a period of time to observe and identify lines of authority, the autonomy teachers have, how the faculty communicates and cooperates, and how each member of the faculty expresses uniqueness is helpful.

Authority

Who is in authority in the school? Is anyone really in charge? Take some time to observe the principal or director in action. Does this administrator actually serve as the authority, making decisions, handling complaints of parents, and settling disputes between teachers? Does he or she protect the teachers from administrative activities that could interrupt or interfere with teaching? What kinds of communication does the person in charge establish with the teachers? What things do they wish to know about and which things are unnecessary to communicate?

If the director or principal of the school does not assume the authority, then teachers may be placed in the position of making decisions about many matters themselves. In this situation a new teacher may feel unsure of herself and feel "open to the demands and expectations of all those who were concerned about what she did with the child, in particular the parents" (McPherson 1972, p. 156). Understanding what areas you will be expected to be in charge of and which things the principal or director will handle, will be useful to the new teacher.

If the director has not actually taken charge, it may be helpful to ask for a conference to establish what you can and cannot do. Are you to handle parents, what kind of reporting should take place, what rules and regulations do you need to know about?

In looking for lines of authority, you may uncover a complicated informal structure of authority within the school. The cook may be in charge of the lunch room. She tells you when and where you and the children can eat, how long you can stay, and if and how you can use her room when it is not in use for meals. A teacher who has seniority may be the actual authority in the school. The parents go to her with problems, as do the teachers. This teacher may be the person who settles teacher conflicts and in some instances even obtains supplies because of her long-standing friendship with board members or supervisory staff. In other cases it is the janitor who has the real authority in a school. It is she who will tell you what kinds of materials you can and cannot use ("Clay and paint are much too messy") and demand that children use a different entrance on rainy days "so the front hall will stay polished."

Sometimes one of the teachers will act as representative for a group of teachers. One kindergarten teacher assumes authority for all of the other kindergarten teachers. It is he who will expect you to cover certain units, "We always do a unit on spring," and it is he who will tell you when to use the play yard, or how the children are to walk in the hallways.

Observations of the roles and responsibilities of team members and, more importantly, how these people and others perceive their roles is necessary. Understanding what is expected of you, and others, in terms of compliance and communication is very useful in becoming a member of the group. It is not that you will want to comply, but you will want to know what is expected and condoned behavior.

Autonomy

Everyone, from the two year old to the teacher, wants some degree of autonomy. Some people, in fact, enter the field of teaching because they believe there is more opportunity to be autonomous in a classroom than in other kinds of work. "Yes, I listen to all of those regulations, but when I get in my room and close my door, I do what I know is best." Teachers do appear to have more autonomy than other workers (Dreeben 1973). Bureaucratic decisions may affect a teacher's salary, when school begins and ends, and how the bus service is organized, but these decisions have little to do with the teacher's autonomy within her own classroom.

Sometimes a kindergarten teacher within a public school will have more autonomy than other teachers (Sarason 1971). Kindergarten rooms are often physically separated from the other areas of the school, and the children do not mix with others on the play yard or in the lunch room.

Then too, "Kindergarten teachers are viewed by others, and they view themselves, as a special kind of teacher AND person" (Sarason 1971, p. 19). Other teachers in the school and the principal seem to accept the idea that kindergarten children are curious, may be noisy and active, and that the quirks of the kindergarten teacher and children will have to be accepted. All of which results in a kind of social insulation for children and teachers, as well as a great degree of autonomy.

Cooperation and Communication

"Hi there, I'm Bobbie, your cohort in crime, welcome to the dumping grounds of the world." Adding, "We've really got a bunch of dummies this year," Bobbie continued her introductions to the new teacher. This type of interaction, as shocking as it appears, is one of the major ways teachers communicate with one another (McPherson 1972). McPherson (1972) believes that this type of superficial griping-jocularity, serves several functions.

> Through expanding personal experience into general experience, the solidarity of the group was enhanced and individual weaknesses overcome. The group's bonds against the outside were strengthened through quick consensus. Jocular griping thus provided both support for the teacher against outside threats and social distance from her peers in a situation rife with anxiety about her own achievement and stature. No teacher felt really safe with other teachers. Each wore a superficial mask. (McPherson 1972, p. 75)

But the jocular bantering about the "stupid kids," "the salt mine," or the "dumb parents" can be detrimental to both group and the individual. Complaints are minimized by the banter and not corrected. A teacher in need of help does not receive it; jokes and lighthearted talk conceal problems, but they cannot eliminate them.

As a new teacher you can, of course, enter into the banter, or at least understand the purposes it serves. But look for other ways to establish communication with the other members of the team. You might try to find one or two other like-minded teachers in the program you can trust. With these teachers you can establish a serious dialogue. It may be that through communicating with another teacher in the school, the two of you can identify and solve problems, set the pace for other teachers, and demonstrate that cooperative activity can, and does, take place in schools.

Not all communication within a school, however, is of the griping-banter type. As you observe the faculty in action, ask yourself how well, and often, do the team members keep one another informed. Is there an easy sharing between them? Do they show interest in one another's work? Be certain to understand your role in the more formal communications of the school. You will be expected to attend faculty meetings, share memos, and communicate in other formal ways.

Expressions of Uniqueness

> Teachers more frequently lose their jobs because they fail to conform or to deal with certain rules, such as being punctual, keeping accurate

records, maintaining discipline, or getting along with the administration and the parent than because they are incompetent as teachers of a particular area of study. (Corwin and Edelfelt 1976, p. 35)

Most new teachers will want to follow the rules and regulations of a school, yet they will also want to be able to express themselves freely.

Often it is the way a teacher expresses her uniqueness that gets her in trouble, rather than the fact that she has challenged the established way of doing things (Corwin 1973). Rebellious teachers, who attempt to express themselves by shocking and aggressively or openly challenging persons in authority, actually produce very little change in a school or community and usually leave teaching quickly (Corwin 1973).

On the other hand, teachers who carefully and quietly plan changes do succeed. Sometimes waiting for a while before expressing uniqueness or attempting to change something is effective. If you want to change certain rigid rules, wait until the time is ripe, until conditions are right. Sometimes staffing patterns will change, a vocal parent moves away, or new people enter the school, all of which give opportunities for making change. When staff members obtain more security for themselves, it is another time ripe for making changes.

Most of us can benefit by thinking about how much uniqueness we can express and under what conditions. How much discretion is necessary in any given situation, where the limits lie, and how we might go about influencing these limits are questions that should be answered before expressing uniqueness in any school setting. This type of thoughtful action can lead to an autonomy that is valued by the organization, welcomed and accepted, rather than rejected.

Change is always a slow process. You may enter a school with ideas, hopes, and optimism. You are highly motivated to provide the best for all of the children and their families, and you want to makes changes that will improve conditions right away. Remember that changing the established way of doing things cannot happen overnight, but at the same time, look for ways to do things your way without upsetting others, and always innovate when the opportunity presents itself.

Look for support from others. It may be that within your center or kindergarten unit there will be limited support for new ideas. Keeping in touch with college friends, with professors, or joining a professional teacher's organization may offer you the opportunities you need to support your unique ideas. These contacts can add to feelings of security, for they will be supportive, and at the same time they will help you build and expand on your resources.

Remember, too, as a new teacher, you need personal satisfaction and a life of hobbies, interests, friends, not necessarily connected with the school. A teacher who keeps growing, learning, who finds outlets for expression through hobbies and activities, can focus on the satisfaction and happiness of others. Focusing on others—thinking first about the children, or how the principal and other staff members feel, often leads to the relief of your own worries, anxieties, or concerns.

In Summary

Teachers are communicators, and because they are, they have the responsibility to learn effective modes of verbal and nonverbal communication. The ability to handle words, to use voice and body language to communicate is important. For example, in nonverbal communication, eye contact, gesture, and facial expression are as important aspects as pitch, tone, and specificity are to verbal communication. Specific techniques for working with children, parents, and fellow staff members can be developed. Such methods as establishing a tone of expectancy, speaking clearly, and using more do's than don'ts are effective with children. With parents, involvement through social groups, policy-making groups, home visits, conferences and so on are important to communication provided the teacher avoids a patronizing role expressed through technical jargon. Staff communication can prove supportive and informative once lines of authority are understood and new teachers receive the acceptance of their colleagues. Change may come about gradually and strengthen the teachers' sense of individual uniqueness.

Communication is not all that is necessary when building relationships with children, parents and other staff members. But effective communication is the beginning of establishing positive relationships.

Resources

The following books may be useful resources in developing an understanding of the communication process with children, parents and colleagues.

HONIG, ALICE, *Parent Involvement in Early Childhood Education*. Washington, D.C.: National Association for the Education of Young Children, 1975.

McPHERSON, G. H., *Small Town Teacher*. Cambridge, Mass.: Harvard University Press, 1972.

PITCHER, EVELYN, and L. B. AMES, *The Guidance Nursery School*. New York: A Delta Book, Dell Publishing Co. Inc., 1964.

Projects

1. Observe teachers and children interacting in a preschool setting. Note how the teacher uses nonverbal communication with children. To which nonverbal cues, on the part of children, do teachers respond?

2. Interview a teacher in a preschool, and ask her how she involves parents. Find out whether she holds parent conferences and how she maintains communication with parents between such conferences. Ask to see a sample of her reports to parents.

3. As you student teach, think about the way faculty members communicate with one another. Can you find established lines of communication? Can you identify the leaders and the followers? Think about your own role in the school.

References

A Curriculum of Training for Parent Participation in Project Head Start. New York: Child Study Association of America, 1967.

CORWIN, R. G., *Reform and Organizational Survival: The Teacher Corps as an Instrument of Educational Change*. New York: Wiley Interscience, 1973.

CORWIN, R. G., and EDELFELT, R. A., *Perspectives on Organization: Viewpoints for Teachers*. Washington, D.C.: Association of Colleges for Teacher Education and the Association of Teacher Educators, 1976.

DEWEY, J., *Democracy and Education*. New York: The Free Press, 1944. First published 1916.

DREEBEN, R., "The School as Workplace," in *Second Handbook of Research on Teaching*, ed. R. M. W. Travers. Chicago, Ill.: Rand McNally & Company, 1973, 450–474.

FALLEN, N. H. and McGOVERN, J. E., *Young Children with Special Needs*. Columbus, Ohio: Charles E. Merrill Publishing Company, 1978.

FLANNERY, G. V. and others, Communication and Society, in *Improving the Human Condition*, ed. J. E. Jelinek. Washington, D.C.: Association for Supervision and Curriculum Development, 1978.

FREUD, S., *The Complete Psychological Works of Sigmund Freud*. London: Hogarth Press, 1953.

HALL, E. T., *The Hidden Dimension*. Garden City, N.Y.: Doubleday & Co., Inc., 1966.

HAYAKAWA, S. I., "How Words Change Our Lives," in *The Language of Man*, ed. J. F. Littell. Evanston, Ill.; McDougal, Littel & Company, 1971.

HOLLISTER, W. G., *Group Participation Methods*. Boston, Mass.: Unitarian Universalist Association. Undated.

McMILLAN, M., *The Nursery School*. London: J. M. Dent & Sons, Ltd., 1919.

McPHERSON, G. H., *Small Town Teacher*. Cambridge, Mass.: Harvard University Press, 1972.

OTTO, H. J., "Communication Is the Key," in *Parents—children—teachers: Communications*, ed. R. Van Allen. Washington, D.C.: Association for Childhood Education International, 1969.

PITCHER, E. G., and AMES, L. B., *The Guidance Nursery School*. New York: A Delta Book, Dell Publishing Co., Inc., 1964.

"The Pilgrim's Scrip. Readers' Letters, Comments and Confessions," *The American Magazine* (November 1911), 123–125.

Public Law 94-142. The Education for All Handicapped Children Act, 1975. Washington, D.C.: U.S. Printing Office.

SARASON, S. B., *The Culture of the School and the Process of Change*. Boston, Mass.: Allyn & Bacon, Inc., 1971.

SMITH, D. R., and WILLIAMSON, L. K., *Interpersonal Communication: Roles, Rules, Strategies and Games*. Dubuque, Iowa: Wm C. Brown Company, Publishers, 1977.

TAYLOR, K. W., "Parent Cooperative Nursery Schools," in *Living History Interviews*, ed. J. L. Hymes. Carmel, California: Hacienda Press, 1978.

The Curriculum

Part III

Children learn through play. The curriculum is implemented as children play. You fulfill the goals for each child and for the total program through children's play activities. Chapter 9 suggests ways of using play as the major mode of children's learning.

Health, safety, and nutrition are vital when working with young children. Chapter 10 describes the goals of health, safety, and nutrition education and methods of establishing a safe and physically and mentally healthy environment.

Chapter 11 discusses the child's understanding of mathematics and science and suggests methods for extending children's experiences in these areas.

Without language facility, children will be limited in their ability to think or get along with others. Chapter 12 describes the importance of language and gives ideas for activities in the language arts to prepare children for later reading and writing.

Art and music are important parts of the curriculum. Ways to plan for children's experiences in art and music are suggested in chapter 13.

The final chapter, "Self and Others," describes children's relations with others and gives an introduction to concepts children can gain in history, economics, and geography.

9

Play

Play, like love, defies description.
B. Tyler, 1976, p. 225.

As with love, there is something fascinating, almost magical, about children's play that mystifies. Different definitions have been offered to describe children's play, and many theories about the nature and purpose of play have been advanced. Each theory explains something of children's play; yet no one theory is completely adequate. "Play appears in so many guises and a great variety of forms. Its results are so subtle and far reaching that any one definition or explanation will of necessity be partial and incomplete" (Perryman 1962, p. 146).

A look at the different types of children's play helps one understand why so many different theories have been advanced. Children, bursting from a school room onto a playground—shouting, jumping, running, exploding with excess energy—seem to give proof to the theory that play is a form of releasing excess energy. This theory, first advanced by Spencer in 1873, suggests that children, as young animals, play because they must release an abundance of excess energy. Spencer believed that nature invested each living thing with just enough strength to satisfy basic needs of hunger, preservation, and propagation. The lower the animal on the evolutionary scale, the more time and energy must be spent in satisfying basic needs. Animals who are more efficient

Play appears in many forms.

need to spend less time satisfying basic drives and thus have a lot of excess energy which requires some outlet. Play is the way children disperse this excess energy. When you observe children playing, really "letting off steam," or recognize the need in yourself to release pent-up energies, you find it easy to accept Spencer's theory of play.

Yet release of energy cannot be the only explanation for children's play. Children carefully and seriously building forts, digging houses out of hillsides, and creating primitive societies are seen the world over. Some of the children are designated to stay and "guard the fort;" others go off "hunting." Eventually the play culminates in a "war," with one group of children from a neighboring fort destroying the fort of the other. Hall (1907) proposed that all play of young children, as epitomized by fort play, occurred because children need to act out primitive urges. Basing his beliefs on evolutionary theory, Hall claimed that children played out each successive stage of the evolution of the human race. Through play, children could experience all of the prehistoric events humanity has ever known. They would have a channel through which to release wild, primitive urges that was safe and socially acceptable.

When you see giggling, laughing children at play, whether splashing in the mud or delightedly dropping object after object from the high chair tray, you are reminded of a theory of play advanced by Buhler (1935). Buhler defines play as function training, but she emphasized the special sense of enjoyment

184

that comes with the fulfillment of functions characteristic at each stage of play. Her theory is that all activity always involves enjoyment. Activity itself, pure motor activity, is the source of pleasure, play, enjoyment, and satisfaction.

Then there is the kind of play in which children pretend to be adults. They take on the role of adults they see around them, imitating every gesture and expression as they pretend to be a father cooking breakfast for a hungry, but less than cooperative, brood of children, or a mother coming home from work trying to fix dinner while handling her children's complaints. Groos (1901) believed that children play to prepare themselves for the adult world. Just as the kitten playing catch with its mother's tail prepares to someday catch a mouse, children acting out adult roles play with precision, conviction, and concentration in preparation for their own future.

Sometimes children, while playing, will slap a baby doll, toss it on a bed, and scream, "Get out of here, I hate you, you bad thing!" Or at other times children will pretend to be a baby, cuddling on a bed, enjoying the care, love, and attention the other children give. To one observing play episodes of this nature, the psychoanalytic theory of play makes sense.

This theory, developed from the works of Freud, views children's play as one avenue through which children can express deep emotions that could not safely be expressed in real life. The child slapping the doll is, according to the theory, acting out deeply ingrained feelings of sibling rivalry, and the child pretending to be a baby is expressing her desire to regress to the safety of an early time in life. "For the child, play is the vehicle for expressing his inner state, as well as the outlet for his instinctual forces" (Tyler 1976, p. 227).

Piaget (1962) has advanced yet another theory of play, a cognitive theory. Piaget relates play to the process of assimilation (in which the child interprets new experiences in familiar terms) and accommodation (in which the child changes her behavior to incorporate new information that experience has given her). For Piaget, play is the development of intelligence. Piaget's theory of play has been of great use to early childhood educators in planning curriculum and has been the subject of much research.

It is hard to define play, and harder yet to come up with one theory that is adequate to explain all play of all children. "The whole truth regarding play is still unknown. It appears to be intimately related to the whole phenomenon of life itself, and only as the complex processes of growth and development are unravelled and understood will a clear, more accurate theory of play be evolved" (Perryman 1962, p. 146).

Types of Play

Piaget views the different types of children's play and the growth of intelligence as paralleling one another. *Sensorimotor* play, characterized by exploratory behaviors, manipulation of objects, and practice play, parallels the *sensorimotor* stage of intelligence. This play begins at birth and ends around two years of age. The next stage of play, according to Piaget, is *constructive* play. Rather than the play being exploratory, it now involves building or creation. It is play with a purpose and is parallel to the *representational* stage of intelligence.

Symbolic play begins when children are around two years of age, but it is not until age four or five that children engage in symbolic play in earnest. Symbolic play occurs when the child's intelligence becomes more elaborate and organized. Children can then use symbols and refer to objects that are not present. They use language and gestures to communicate ideas.

Sensorimotor Play

From the first months of life until around two years of age, children's play is characterized by explorations, manipulations, and repetition. This repetitive kind of activity is called *functional* play by Piaget. At first babies have a limited repertoire of actions. They can look and listen, make hand movements and sound productions, but these form only their first play experiences. Play with parts of the body, then with objects, follows.

Babies need to see and hear a great deal during this time. Repetition of information is necessary. They like to see and hear things again and again and repeat their same actions over and over. When children achieve mastery of some skill—such as waving their hand in front of their eyes and watching it, or hitting a rattle and making a sound—they constantly repeat the action. Children who repeat their own actions and imitate themselves, for pleasure, are playing.

As children grow, they become capable of more varied activities, and their exploratory and manipulative play changes. They can now influence and change their environment. They can splash water, pile up sand, make mud, grasp and release an object, or pull at their father's hair. Social play also appears at this stage. The delight the baby experiences as she actually manages to grab a hunk of her father's hair shows the beginnings of social interactions. Social play involves babbling, cooing, and attempting to respond and react to the language of others. It is an important point in children's development.

From the time the baby can creep, crawl, or move around, the need for exploratory and manipulative play increases. It seems that children must actively explore and touch everything in sight. Drawers are emptied, the coffee table is cleared, as are the bookshelves. Things that were once out of sight and reach are now possible playthings for children. This is a difficult time for care givers, for the buttons found in a drawer are tasted, papers are tossed and torn, and nothing seems safe from the baby's hands. Yet this play is a necessary part of children's intellectual development, for it is the major way they have of learning about their world.

Around the age of one, children begin a new type of play. The child may pretend to feed a doll, go to sleep, use a corner of the tablecloth as a blanket; these are examples of the use of imagination in play. Now children can remember objects and things even when they are not present.

Emerging between eighteen months and two years of age, constructive play is play with a purpose.

> . . . play now assimilates the reality of particular materials to their own purposes. The materials and actions are, therefore, not restricted either by conventional standards of performance or of outcome. That is what the children produce is done to satisfy the requirements of their play rather than to match some standard of external reality. In recognition of this change from repetitive play to recognizable play with materials, which produces those results which the child intends, it will be called productive play. (Butler, Gotts, and Quisenberry 1978, p. 28)

Children enter into productive or constructive play by themselves or with others. They are physical in their play and create, build, produce, or make things. Their play lasts for longer periods of time, and they concentrate on their activities. The child does not give up functional play but builds on it and develops the beginnings of symbolic play.

Symbolic Play

Symbolic play appears when the baby can remember and use things that are not present and play as if she had cereal to feed the doll, as if the knotted rag were a baby. It is not until children are about two years of age or more that symbolic play actually begins, and not until they are three or four that this play is fully developed.

Some play is productive.

One type of symbolic play, the most highly developed, is called socio-dramatic play. This is the familiar "Let's pretend" type of play in which children freely display their social awareness by taking on the role of another and his knowledge of the social world.

They imitate the person or thing they are pretending to be in action and speech, with the aid of real, pretend, or substitute objects. Smilansky (1968) says that there must be two main elements present for play to be considered sociodramatic: (1) a reality element in which the child tries to act, take on, or even look like some other person and tries to reproduce the world of the adult and (2) the element of nonreality, the make-believe, imaginary element, with the make-believe serving as an aid to the imitation of the child. In sociodramatic play, speech serves an important function. It helps children in their pretending, with words taking the place of reality. Smilansky (1968) has observed that speech appears in four forms in sociodramatic play: (1) verbal declarations to change personal identity—"Now, I'm the daddy and you're the mommy." (2) Statements made to identify objects that are being used for something else. "This is the stove, and here is the table," the child declares pointing to the step and the porch. (3) Speech is used to substitute for an action, "Pretend I'm coming home from work," and (4) language is used to describe situations, "Let's pretend that the mother has made a cake, and now the children are coming in . . ."

Speech is also used in sociodramatic play for planning, developing, and maintaining the play and for achieving cooperation. Verbal explanations, discussions, and commands are given by children as they play. It is the type of speech that serves as actual problem solving and is a part of child-to-child interaction and the child's reality during the play. "We don't need two drivers, no bus has two drivers! You give the tickets."

Smilansky (1968) has identified six elements of sociodramatic play that are regarded as essential parts of well-developed play, These are

1. Imitative role play.
2. Make-believe in regard to objects.
3. Make-believe in regard to actions and situations.
4. Persistence.
5. Interaction.
6. Verbal communication.

Sociodramatic play is of great interest to preschool teachers. It calls on children to hold images in their minds, to symbolize, and to use language. The work of Smilansky (1968) has demonstrated that this play is also able to increase children's intelligence and school achievement. "It stimulates emotional, social and intellectual development, which is highly beneficial for the child's success in school" (Smilansky 1968, p. 12), and it "fosters creativity, problem solving, includes widening concept acquisition for new knowledge and fosters the positive skills of give and take."

How Teachers Can Help Children Play

When Harriet Johnson began her nursery school in the early 1900s, she cautioned her teachers not to interact or interfere in children's play. Rather than distract children while they were playing, Johnson suggested that teachers use the routines of dressing, undressing, and preparing children for naps or lunch to make contact. Conversing with children and teaching while children were playing were to be avoided (Johnson 1928, p. 24). Johnson was not the only educator who advocated that the teacher assume a passive role in children's play. Those who endorse the psychoanalytic view of play believe that teacher interference in children's play negates their expression of deeply hidden emotions and feelings.

If children's play can foster intellectual growth, and can even be used to predict later success in school, it seems as if teachers must take a more active role in that play.

Currently teachers have been looking for ways to foster children's play and to enhance opportunities for learning through play. Teachers, however, are not sure of just how they should do this.

> It may be that the decline of play in public schools is due to the ambiguity of the teacher's role. If teachers continue to be vague about teaching possibilities in play, it is not surprising that they invest their energies in the more structured aspects of kindergarten programs where they feel more secure." (Robison 1971, p. 333)

Teachers, aware of the possibilities inherent in children's play and the roles they could take, can be more effective. Teachers will need to (1) determine the goals and objectives they want fostered through play; (2) provide children with experiences that can be used as a foundation for dramatic play; (3) set the stage for indoor and outdoor play with room and play yard arrangement; (4) become astute observers of children; (5) enter into children's play and (6) encourage parents to provide for children's play in their home and neighborhood.

Determining Goals and Objectives

"The main problem in delineating teacher roles in play centers lies in articulating purposes or goals" (Robison 1971, p. 335). In planning for children's play, teachers might ask themselves: What goals can be fostered? Should children's vocabulary be increased as they act out roles? Should play episodes be expanded for longer periods of time?

Teachers might look at each play center or area and determine just what goals and objectives could be promoted in each. The needs of individual children in each of the areas should also be considered. Roberta loves the blocks, how can her play be used to foster a specific mathematical or scientific understanding? How many of the children, as they play with the blocks, are seeing mathematical relationships or using the vocabulary of numbers?

Once teachers decide on specific goals in each area of the room or play yard, they can then decide how to intervene in children's play. For example the teachers Robison (1971) worked with decided on the specific goals of intervening in the block area to stimulate more complex, varied, and imaginative construction, and in the housekeeping area, to stimulate richer dramatic play. The specific goals decided on were to

1. Stimulate children's production of more abundant speech, including naming of objects in the dramatic play area;
2. Encourage more varied and imaginative dramatic play;
3. Use category words and to delineate specific instances of the category in children's play;
4. Model standard syntactic speech forms and to elaborate and extend the speech forms used by the children;
5. Give children clearer definitions of family roles and relationships;
6. Encourage more imaginative forms of block play;
7. Verbalize children's actions with block play and to encourage children to talk about their block buildings.
8. Orient children's block play to aspects of reality.

Providing Experiences

Once the goals and objectives of children's play have been established, teachers will have guidelines for setting the stage for play. If children are to bring more reality to block buildings and richer, more varied imagination to dramatic play, they will need a background of experiences. The raw materials of observing people at work, watching construction workers, ticket salespersons at an airport, or the mechanic at a gasoline station, give children deeper understandings of their world to recreate in dramatic play.

Field trips to observe the social systems can be supplemented with discussions in the classroom and with vicarious experiences. The use of books, films, filmstrips, or visitors who will describe their own experiences can also provide impressions that will lead to extended, more imaginative play.

Clarifying children's experiences is also useful. As Lucy Sprague Mitchell once did, teachers can ask children to recall past experiences—"What did you see when you went on the airplane?" "What other switches look like this one?" "How do you think the street cleaner works?" "How is this truck like the one you saw?" —and to see relationships between their experiences.

Setting the Stage

Even though children enter into dramatic play without the use of props and materials, it seems as if toys, objects, and props do enhance the quality of children's play. Materials should be carefully selected to reflect children's current interests and experiences and be appropriate for the level and stage of play.

If props are too complex, or do not relate to the children's experiences, they will not be used representationally, that is, as if they were something else. A detailed fire engine can only be used as a fire engine. A wooden vehicle, without any definite details, can be used as if it were a dump truck, passenger car, or even a train and can reflect children's current interests.

If only a few materials are present, children's play does not seem to develop fully. Without props, children the world over play out the familiar theme of home and family. If, however, teachers add props suggesting a store—perhaps a scale, empty boxes and cans, play money, or a used calculator, children extend their home play to include acting as if they were shopping, running a store, or clerking. With the props children can take part in weighing "produce," adding up the bill, as well as paying for purchases and receiving change.

Observing

Observing children at play yields a wealth of information about children in general but also helps teachers find ways they can facilitate play. Through observing, teachers may note physical obstacles in the room that negate children's play, or they may observe children's play interests that will suggest props that would be helpful. Children may not be gravitating to the blocks. Teachers may see that every time a child tries to build a structure, it falls down, for the floor in the area is uneven. Moving the blocks or adding a smooth sheet of plywood to the area may increase the use of blocks. Teachers may note that some materials are not used at all because they are out of sight or simply too difficult for children to reach.

When observing, teachers can also note how each individual child handles the materials, as well as the way the children interact socially. Nonparticipants may be encouraged to take on a role, "You can be the salesperson," or the aggressive child told to settle down, "Come and rest now."

Entering Into Children's Play

Children's playtime is teaching time. All of the teaching strategies can be used to facilitate children's learning through play. Teachers can ask questions that extend children's thinking, "Why is it heavier?" offer children feedback, "You joined the pieces of wood together," or reinforce children's progress, "Nice job with the blocks!"

Additional ways of supporting children's play have been suggested by Smilansky (1968). She studied disadvantaged children's play patterns and found that they did not enter into extended sociodramatic play. Based on these observations she recommended several types of teacher interventions, with the caution that children be permitted to begin the play by themselves. If children do not know how to begin to play, or if they repeat the same play activities over and over and do not seem to know what to do next, Smilansky recommends teacher intervention. "It is our opinion that adult intervention, properly controlled, will prove to be highly effective as a catalytic agent in making sociodramatic play a pleasant and a possible experience to a child" (Smilansky 1968, p. 95).

Adult intervention can take the following forms: (1) Participation in the play; or (2) Intervention from outside the play. At times teachers will enter into the play of the children. "I'm the mother, now I'm going to fix you breakfast, while you get ready to go to school." This type of intervention serves two functions. It gives teachers an opportunity to actually demonstrate how to play and shows children the possibilities inherent in the play. The teacher's actions may become the stimulus for subsequent play activities. Smilansky and Sutton-Smith (Sponseller 1974, p. 72) have both concluded that the playfulness of young children depends on the modeling provided by the adults in their environment.

Intervention from outside children's play involves the use of all of the teaching strategies, but unlike intervention that has the teacher interacting with the children, the teacher stays out of the play. From outside, the teacher may ask a question, help establish contact between children, offer suggestions, or encourage children with praise.

Encouraging Parents

Parental influences affect all of children's learning, and especially their play. Teachers who want to capitalize on children's play as a learning medium need to encourage parents to provide for children's play at home. They might explain the relationship of play to the child's growing intelligence and encourage parents to provide conditions for play—time, space, and companions—at home. Teachers can recommend toys and materials appropriate for children to use at various ages, talk with parents about arranging for children's play spaces within a crowded home, or organize afterschool play groups. Parents should also be made aware of the value of their entering into children's play.

Nevertheless, when suggesting anything to parents, teachers must be aware of the burdens of raising children. When one teacher suggested arranging a space for play at home, the parent reminded her of some of the burdens of rearing children. "Look, I live in a two-room apartment, with four kids, I work all day. After all, I'm sending Sally to your school so she can play with other children. You do your job and I'll do mine."

In Summary

The major portion of the day in a school for young children should be spent in play. It is through play that children learn about themselves, others, and the world. Play is the way they learn concepts in science, art, music, mathematics, and language. There is no other way children can learn besides through play. Children must find the materials for play, time to play, and a teacher who understands the value of play, when in a preschool.

The principle of building the early childhood curriculum on play was put into practice in the nursery schools of the 1900s and survives today as the foundation for all early childhood programs (Biber 1977, p. 47). The idea that teachers can use the natural play activities of children to foster intellectual growth and to stimulate children's search for cognitive relationships is as valid today as it was in the first nursery schools and kindergartens.

Today, however, the idea that children must play is backed by hard research (Smilansky 1968). Research has demonstrated that children who have plenty of time to play succeed in later school experiences. On the other hand, children who have not had the opportunity to play while young are often those who find school difficult, or even fail in school.

Children who are denied the opportunity to play in a preschool are being denied their right to intellectual freedom. Play permits children to develop their own style of learning, their own ideas and ways of doing things. Every child in our nation has the right to this type of intellectual freedom, and the right to be encouraged to be curious, creative, and an active participant in his own learning. Without play, children do not have the opportunity to develop the freedom of thought required for living in a democracy (Bikson 1978, p. 69).

Resources

The following books are useful sources of information about the play of the young child.

BJORKLUND, GAIL, *Planning for Play*, Columbus, Ohio: Charles E. Merrill Publishing Company, 1978.

BUTLER, ANNIE, EDWARD GOTTS and NANCY QUISENBERRY, *Play as Development*. Columbus, Ohio: Charles E. Merrill Publishing Company, 1978.

SMILANSKY, SARA, *The Effects of Sociodramatic Play on Disadvantaged Children*. New York: John Wiley & Sons, 1968.

SPONSELLER, DORIS, *Play as a Learning Medium*. Washington, D.C.: National Association for the Education of Young Children, 1974.

Projects

1. Observe in a school for young children. Identify the different types of play—social, solitary, onlooker—and see if you can distinguish between constructive and symbolic play. As you observe, can you find evidence of children playing just for fun and pleasure, to release surplus energy, or express deep hidden psychological feelings?

2. Enter into a child's play group. How do the children react to an adult playing with them? Use vocabulary that is new to the children as you play with them. Do they repeat this vocabulary?

3. Interview a teacher of young children to find out what her goals are for children's play. How does she plan for play activities?

4. Do you think teachers can interfere in children's play? Observe children and adults together. Can you find any signs that might suggest the adult is assuming too much direction in children's play and taking over the activity by not letting children develop their own interests and ideas?

References

BIBER, B., "Cognition in Early Childhood Education: A Historical Perspective," in *Early Childhood Education: Issues and Insights*, eds. B. Spodek and H. J. Walberg. Berkeley, California: McCutchan Publishing Corporation (1977), 41–65.

BIKSON, T. K., "Intellectual Rights of Children," *Journal of Scoial Issues*, 34, 2 (1978), 69–86.

BUHLER, C., *From Birth to Maturity*. London: Kegan, Paul, 1935.

BUTLER, A. L.: GOTTS, E. E.: QUISENBERRY, N. L.: *Play as Development*. Columbus, Ohio: Charles E. Merrill Publishing Company, 1978.

GROOS, K., *The Play of Man*. New York: D. Appleton, 1901.

HALL, G., *Youth: It's Education, Regimen and Hygiene*. New York: Appleton-Century-Crofts Medical and Nursing Publication, 1907.

HERRON, B., and SUTTON-SMITH, B., *Child's Play*. New York: John Wiley & Sons, Inc., 1971.

JOHNSON, H., *Children in "the Nursery School."* New York: Agathon Press, Inc., 1928. Reprinted, New York: Schocken Books, 1972.

PERRYMAN, L. C., "Dramatic Play and Cognitive Development," *The Journal of Nursery Education*, 17 (1962), 183–188.

PIAGET, J., *Play, Dreams and Imagination in Childhood*. New York: W. W. Norton & Co., Inc., 1962.

ROBISON, H., "The Decline of Play in Urban Kindergartens," *Young Children*, 26, 6 (1971), 333–342.

SMILANSKY, S., *The Effects of Sociodramatic Play on Disadvantaged Children*. New York: John Wiley & Sons, Inc., 1968.

————, Play as a Predictor of Academic Success. Unpublished Speech. University of Maryland, College Park, Md., 1978.

SPONSELLER, D., *Play as a Learning Medium*. Washington, D.C.: National Association for the Education of Young Children, 1974.

SPENCER, H., *Principles of Psychology* (2nd ed.) New York: Appleton-Century-Crofts Medical and Nursing Publications, 1871.

TYLER, B., "Play," in *Curriculum for the Preschool/Primary Child: A Review of the Research*, ed. C. Seefeldt. Columbus, Ohio: Charles E. Merrill Publishing Company, 1976.

10

Health, Safety, and Nutrition

A very important part of the nursery school's responsibility is its provision for the health of its charges.

H. Johnson, 1928, p. 22.

Health was of primary concern to the pioneer early childhood educators. It had to be! Even in the first decade of the twentieth century in New York City, over one-third of the people who died were children under the age of five, and one-fifth of all deaths were babies less than a year old (Grotberg 1977). Some eighty percent of all children born were well at birth, but only twenty percent entered school in good health during the 1900s (Hymes 1978).

Children died because of improper food, epidemics, and from society's lack of health knowledge. A public health officer in the late 1800s wrote of the conditions of the stables and dairy barns:

> The stables were dirty, festooned with cobwebs. . . . the utensils dirty, often containing layers of sour milk with a mixture of countless millions of bacteria and the milk itself so imperfectly cared for and badly cooled that it is often soured before reaching the consumer. (Grotberg 1977, p. 62)

In 1936, some seventy-one percent of all of the cities in the country with a population under 10,000 had no sanitary control over milk supplies reaching children.

Unsanitary conditions in the streets, open sewers, the dead left unburied

Concern for health is primary.

at the curbs during epidemics—all were responsible for vast numbers of deaths. But the science of medicine was also responsible for the deaths of many children. Patent medicines contained opium and cocaine, and prescribed remedies probably killed as many children as they cured. A pill recommended for toothache consisted of "Half a grain each of opium and yellow sulphate of quicksilver" (Henderson 1870). Giving newborn children a mixture of molasses and urine as a physic was common.

Neither physicians nor lay persons seemed to have much knowledge of either preventive medicine or health care. A doctor practicing in the late 1880s wrote about the distress he felt watching children admitted to a hospital for some minor ailment, perhaps malnutrition, who died after developing one of the highly contagious diseases common to the hospital (Grotberg 1977).

Abigale Eliot, who founded the Ruggles Street Nursery School and Training Center in 1922, believed that the nursery school actually arose from the poor state of children's health. Many of the schools were organized in an attempt to improve children's health conditions.

> The studies threw the spotlight on the years before school—the nursery years—and showed them to be years of great neglect. Margaret McMillan knew education in England well, and her response to what she knew was to establish an open-air nursery school. She began her school in 1911, in Deptford, a heavily industrialized, wretched slum section in London. (A. Eliot 1978, p. 9)

Given the general state of children's health, it was not unusual for the first nursery schools to have as their primary goal the improvement of health.

196

Because of the rapid spread of infectious diseases, there were daily health inspections of children before they were permitted inside the school. Cleanliness, good food habits, napping, outdoor play and toileting were stressed. Bathing at school was a common practice. In the McMillan school, three and four years olds bathed together in large, common baths, and the two years olds, in individual tubs. For children who were five and six years of age, communal concrete shower baths, "filled with showers from above," were recommended.

Health concerns remained primary through the 1930s, for health conditions for children in our nation did not improve very rapidly. "From Pearl Harbor to V.J. Day, 280,000 Americans were killed in action and during this same period, 430,000 babies died in the United States before they were a year old. Three babies died for every two soldiers killed in World War II and this was in the early 1940's" (Grotberg 1977, p. 71).

By the end of the Second World War, sulfa drugs and the development of antibiotics eased the situation and led to the treatment and cure of acute bacterial infections that once killed. The discovery of penicillin and the ability to immunize against polio, measles, diphtheria, and other contagious diseases greatly improved the health of children.

Health conditions continue to improve for children in our country. "Good news health and safety stories abounded in 1977" (Hymes 1978, p. 5). A new vaccine was announced that is effective against a form of pneumonia to which children with sickle cell anemia are unusually vulnerable, and advances in the treatment of acute leukemia have continued. An HEW program to completely immunize ninety percent of all children against the seven most common preventable diseases: measles, polio, mumps, diphtheria, rubella, whooping cough, and tetanus has begun.

In fact, the health of young children has improved so greatly that today health is treated rather casually in preschools. Children in group care experience no greater incidence of illness than those of similar backgrounds kept in their own homes (Peters 1971). This research documents that, today, it is safe for infants and young children to be in group care—that is, group care when there is adequate staff, fully trained and capable of giving high-level care to young children.

Even though concern for the health of children has been minimized by medical technology, all schools for young children must provide for health, safety, and nutrition. Head Start, which includes medical, dental, and psychological health components, as well as health education for children, parents, and staff, remains a guiding example for all preschool programs. As in the Head Start program, all children, in every preschool, should be provided with a clean, physically and mentally safe, and healthy environment. The experiences that will enable children to establish sound health practices and habits and build a basic understanding of health, safety, and nutrition should be a part of every preschool curriculum.

PLANNING FOR HEALTH

Teachers will have to be both creative and innovative in planning for health education. There is little research available on children's knowledge of health, safety, and nutrition, or on how children learn concepts of healthy living. The *Review of Head Start Research Since 1969* (1977) points out the need to understand more about children's health needs and experiences by concluding, "This meager array of studies emphasizes the need to identify specifically the health problems and education of young children" (*Review of Head Start Research* 1977, p. 39).

Nor do children's interests guide teachers in planning for health education. Unless a child is ill, or special efforts have been made to impress upon her the importance of the subject, the average child under the age of puberty apparently does not give much thought to health as compared to other interests (Strang 1939, Wann 1962). Wann (1962) found only eight references out of six hundred recorded anecdotes of children's conversations mentioning the topic of health or body processes, such as breathing or bleeding. Compared to the number of references in children's discussions to animals, places, travel, and time divisions, the references to health were minimal.

Nevertheless, health education must be an important part of every preschool curriculum. Children can develop concepts of health, safety, and nutrition and be provided with satisfactory health care. In a preschool, children can learn concepts of

1. Body Structure and Function
2. Body Care and Grooming
3. The Need for Activity and Rest
4. Safety Principles
5. Concepts of Nutrition
6. Sound Mental Health Practices: Discipline and Self-Control

Generally, children will be expected to acquire health attitudes and knowledge through experience. Learning by doing, essential for all educational activities with young children, is even more critical in the area of health, safety, and nutrition.

Body Structure and Function

Arnold Gesell (1954) established norms for the physical growth and development of children. These norms attempted to chart the course of human growth according to significant landmarks which would signal normal, accelerated, or retarded development of the individual child. This study, replicated in 1974, concludes that growth proceeds from the

- head toward legs and feet. At birth the infant's head more closely resembles an adult's than do the infant's legs and feet. An infant's first motor control occurs

198

in the muscles that move the head. As the child grows and matures, the arms, abdominal, and finally the leg muscles come under control.

• central axis of the body outward. The baby's early movements are gross body actions. It takes about a year for the child to be able to move fingers independently or grasp objects.

• general to more specific response patterns and from gross to refined control over body.

During the preschool years children will gain nearly twice as much in height as in weight. Their body proportion will change with the trunk and head coming into proportion as the lower limbs experience rapid growth. By the time the baby is around ten months of age, she will be able to sit unaided, and by a year or fifteen months, she will be able to walk. From this point on, children develop the ability to walk sideways, backwards, upstairs, downstairs, as well as skip rope, hop, throw, and catch a ball.

Although the pattern of growth is similar for each child and follows a predictable sequence, each child is unique in his passage through the sequence. The rate of growth depends on conditions inside and outside the child's body, such as nutrition, activity, and rest.

Preschool children can begin to learn basic concepts of body structure and function. They can develop the following ideas:

1. Changes in height and weight are called growth.
2. Different rates of growth are normal.
3. As people grow, they develop skills.
4. The body has many parts, each serving a function.

Many different techniques can be used to teach children these basic concepts. The use of mirrors will attract children to recognizing parts of the body and the functions of each. Placing full-length mirrors in the dressing area, bathroom, and dramatic play areas—as well as mirrors over sinks, and magnifying mirrors in the science or dramatic play area—will draw children's attention to the structure of their bodies. As children gravitate toward exploration of the reflection of their bodies in the mirrors, teachers might focus discussions on body parts and functions. "How does your arm move?" "How many parts of your body can you move?" "How can they move?" "Bend your elbow. How does it look in the mirror?"

Vocabulary can be introduced as teachers offer children labels for body parts. Using mirrors, teachers can label children's waist, hips, calves, shoulders, joints, or wrists. Simon Says games, while looking in a mirror, are fun to play with a few children or an individual child. The teacher can give directions, "Simon says touch your toes, eyebrow, lip, eyelid," and so on.

Fun with mirrors and reflections might lead to discussions of the function of body parts. "What does your nose do?" "Ears?" "Eyes?" Even discussions about the physiological functions might take place. As children watch their chest expand or contract as they breathe, feel their heart, or examine a cut being bandaged, teachers can provide information about body processes. The direction of these discussions will depend on the interests of the child, her experiences, as well as the goals and objectives of the program.

Photographs of the children are also useful in teaching body structure, parts, function, and growth. At the beginning of the year, a photograph of each child can be taken. These can be mounted on cards, a bulletin board, or a chart for the children to handle and discuss. When the children have tired of looking at the photos or playing with them, they can be placed in the children's file to compare with photographs taken during the middle of the year and with others taken at the end of the school year.

Photographs can also be compared with baby pictures. The growth that has taken place and the changes in children's body structure can be pointed out. Children's current photographs might be compared with pictures of their parents, teachers, or older siblings in order to focus children's attention on changes that will occur in the future. Asking the adults in the school or center to bring in photographs of themselves as babies or young children and mounting these on a bulletin board provide for hours of discussion. Was their teacher really this baby? Will they grow? This activity not only provides fun for children and adults, but also helps to focus children's attention on changes that will occur in their own bodies as they grow and mature.

Weight and height charts can be made to help children see different rates of growth. The caution must be added that any comparisons made between the growth rates of children should be done matter of factly, without implying competition or placing value on the tallest, shortest, or largest child. Teachers can present in a matter-of-fact approach that all children, all people, differ in size, weight, height, and rate of growth.

Using cash register tape to measure the height of children and adults in the school provides children with a great deal of fun and learning. The tape, as long as they are tall, is a symbolic representation of their height. The tapes can be taken home, or mounted into a graph, or even placed in a booklet of "All About Me." It is fun to measure all of the people in the school with tape— the teacher, aide, director, cook, bus driver—and place these in a graph. In this way, children see for themselves that all people differ and are unique in height and weight, as well as role.

Movement exploration offers another opportunity to introduce concepts of body structure, function, and skill. Movement exploration, as a curriculum content area, differs from creative movement or exploring body movements through rhythm and music. Movement exploration stems from the content of physical education and was first developed in England and Germany. It uses guided exploration, with teacher direction, and is based on the child's solving specific problems. It is concerned with the whole body moving, exploring, seeking a solution to a stated problem (Hackett and Jenson 1967.)

Through movement exploration children can learn to name parts of the body, begin to understand the relationship between body parts, and find out the things they can do with their bodies in terms of

- locomotor movements—walking, running, jumping, hopping, leaping, skipping, sliding, and galloping.

Who am I?

name	inches	eyes	hair	weight
David	43			40
Lisa	43			45
Lesley	41			40
William	44			47
Nicki	44			39
Amanda	41			44
Randall	48			47
Adam	40			39
Andrew	41			41
Joe	41			40
Karl	43			43
Babi	44			49
Andy	42			40
Miriam	43			51
Shantel	41			41
John M.	39			40
John H.	42			39
Claire	44			41
Angela	45			49
Mrs. Leiserson				

Weight and height charts focus attention on growth.

- manipulation—catching, throwing, kicking, striking.
- nonlocomotor movements—bending, swinging, swaying, turning, twisting, pushing, pulling, and stretching.

In addition, children can be introduced to the elements of movement including

- space—direction, distance, level, the space in which the body can move.
- time—speed of movement and timing. Movement can be fast, slow, quick, or sudden.
- force—the quality of movement, heavy, relaxed, light, airy, or strong.
- flow of movement—bounding, free, flowing, or controlled.

The teacher plays a primary role in movement exploration. She identifies the particular movements and skills the children will experience, selecting those that provide a challenge but also the probability of success, and she puts the movements in sequence, by presenting the simplest first, followed by the more complex.

Instead of telling or showing children how to move, a teacher provides children with problems to be solved. Most of the problems, or challenges are introduced by a phrase such as; "who can . . . can you . . . what can you . . . how can you . . . show us . . . Who can find a new way to . . ." (Hackett and Jenson 1967, p. 4).

Sample problems that young children can solve might include

1. Can you walk forward and stop when the bell rings?
2. Who can walk quickly, or slowly, or with long steps?
3. Who can walk sideward, or backward, or walk on tiptoes, without making a sound?

Not all of these problems are introduced at one time. Children are usually given just one or two problems to solve at a time. The challenges increase in complexity as children gain experience and skills.

Children can also be asked to solve problems in pairs or small groups, with teachers asking, "Can you and a partner walk together holding hands, back to back without holding hands, or can one of you walk high and the other low, one with large steps, the other tiny?"

The same types of problems given for walking can be posed for running, skipping, jumping, sliding, hopping, or any other movement. The teacher introduces the ideas of changing speeds and directions and exploring space. Any one of the elements of movement could form the content of a session. The sessions are short, spontaneous, ending before children tire of solving problems or of the physical exercise.

Body Care and Grooming

Sometimes teachers of young children think of themselves as care givers instead of teachers, for very young children do demand a great deal of physical care. They must be helped to dress and undress and be given help as they use the bathroom. Washing hands and faces, brushing teeth, and other body care and grooming activities require adult help.

These routines, essential to health, must be completed. Each center will have its own routines for body care. Provisions for sinks, mirrors, and toilets that are child-sized are almost essential if children are to become independent in taking care of themselves. If children need help to climb onto a standard size toilet, chances are that the toileting process will continue to be a responsibility of the adult, rather than of the child. If children cannot reach sinks, get their own toothbrush, or turn on faucets, it is not realistic to ask them to take charge of body grooming and care.

If child-sized facilities are not available, teachers will try to arrange the bathroom in a way that encourages as much child initiative as possible. Small, sturdy benches or stools may be placed near the sinks for children to climb on to reach faucets. Mirrors can be placed closer to the sink, permitting children to see progress in face or hand washing, or toothbrushing. Toothbrushes are placed in plastic containers, labeled with children's names and hung on hooks. Washcloths, one for each child on a hook labeled with the child's name, help children care for themselves.

Washing hands after using the toilet and before eating, as well as washing faces and brushing teeth after eating are routines that are established and followed. As children participate in the routines, teachers can introduce them to the purpose and objective of these activities.

Brushing teeth naturally leads to discussions of teeth. "How many teeth do you have?" "Your teeth are white and clean." "Rinse your mouth." The vocabulary of upper and lower jaw, gums, and first and permanent teeth can be introduced. A visit from the dentist or other health person may reinforce the routines of hand washing and tooth brushing. An outsider, in any group, speaks with authority.

Dressing and undressing are other routines teachers must help children complete. In Johnson's program, teachers were encouraged to get children past the "meal sack stage" where children were passively stuffed into their clothing. During the dressing and undressing process, as with brushing teeth or face washing, teachers help children participate actively by calling attention to the tasks at hand. They also show them how to take a role in completing the task.

Breaking the task into small steps, "first roll up your sock, now put it on your toe, now pull the sock up over your heel," is helpful. Or offering children initial help, "Let me start your zipper," "I'll button the first button," or "Let me get that boot over the toe . . ." will help children attend to the task, and give them a good chance of completing it independently. Hildebrand offers teachers sound advice.

> The teacher's guidance during dressing should be supportive. The child should be helped with tasks he can't perform, aided with those he can almost and allowed to do the task he is capable of. Praise for accomplishment is one of the best guidance techniques. It is ridiculous to see a five year old, with an easily handled fat zipper, being zipped by a hovering adult. An observant teacher can see when frustration is about to set in and offer a little help or word of advice and demonstration. (V. Hildebrand 1975, p. 189)

The reward for children's independence in body care is severalfold. First, teachers can free themselves of tedious care-giving functions; second, children gain immeasurably in feelings of self-confidence and esteem when they can do things for themselves; third, habits and understandings established during the early years of life are believed to last a lifetime.

Activity and Rest

All children need activity and exercise, but they need to balance this activity with periods of rest. It is difficult to explain the cause and effect relationship between adequate rest and health to a young child. Johnson (1928) did not recommend it. "We do not attempt to explain to the children our demands and why we are making them" (p. 24). Rather than enter into an argument about routines that are going to be accomplished anyway, Johnson suggested to teachers that they approach teaching concepts of the need for rest to maintain health by having children rest.

> We make it a part of our procedure that each child shall accept what has to be done at these times . . . that he shall lie down and stay in his crib during his nap. This is usually accomplished just by carrying in our manner the expectation that it will be done. (H. Johnson 1928, p. 24)

Children's acceptance of the routine of activity followed by rest should eventually lead to the recognition of the relationship between rest and health. The acceptance of the routines of napping and resting, however, is a very individual matter.

In planning for rest and naps, the individuality of each child must be respected. Sleep needs vary. Even infants show a wide variation in sleep patterns and needs. Usually after the age of two, napping during the day becomes an all-or-none proposition. Sometimes forcing or permitting children over the age of two to take long naps during the day interferes with sleeping at night. Strang (1939) observed that the active, spontaneously interested and socially well-adjusted child usually did not spend as much time in sleep, or fall asleep, as quickly after going to bed as children who were more passive and showed less interest in playmates and were less spontaneous and active in play.

Individual sleep patterns continue into the preschool years. Some children fall asleep immediately when they lie down, while others take up to an hour to fall asleep. As individual sleep patterns, habits, and needs of young children follow no standard pattern, it is unrealistic to expect a group of children to exhibit the same needs for nap and rest. The child's sleep habits at home must also be considered. Children who stay up late (and many do today), and children in day care need longer and earlier naps at school. Children who go to bed early have little need for a long nap at school.

Nevertheless, the need for rest periods in any preschool program, whether half-day or full, morning or afternoon, is essential (Hildebrand 1975, p. 170).

> Overstimulation is frequently a problem in group care situations. Continued contact with other babies or children, the continued presence of equipment for vigorous activity, the number of people in the setting and their voices and actions combine to make group care highly stimulating and therefore likely to be overtiring for children. (Hildebrand 1975, p. 170)

When there is a full-day program, there probably should be the expectation, as Johnson suggested, that all children will go to their cots and rest for at least some time. During the first half-hour or so of rest, all children may be expected to be quiet and on their cots, resting as completely as they can. Then, following this time, those children who do not nap could select a quiet activity they would enjoy—reading books, playing with dolls or puzzles, or some other quiet play in another area of the room. "Teachers should remember that such activities as sand play, listening to records, painting or playing with puzzles can be restful" (Hildebrand 1975, p. 178).

Some ideas that teachers have found useful in establishing restful nap periods are

- conferring with parents in order to plan for individual needs and resting preferences.
- providing quiet activities prior to the nap period. Do not expect children to go directly from a highly active period to a nap.
- arranging the room in a way that suggests resting. Turn out lights, darken the room, and put active toys away.
- using screens, or even blankets draped over a rope stretched across a room to block children's views of one another. These screens may permit children the freedom to express their own individuality during scheduled rest times.
- eliminating distractions. Even music can distract some children. Remember that rest time is just that, not story time or listening time. Keep your voice low when directing children to rest, and assume that air of confident expectation suggested by Johnson.
- accepting habits of thumbsucking, blanket twisting, or other tension releasers. Ask parents to let their children bring their favorite resting blanket or stuffed animal with them to the center.
- adjusting schedules so children are not overtired when it is time to rest. When you notice children rubbing eyes, whining, crying, and know their schedule at home, you may want to schedule rest earlier, later, or make other arrangements that permit children to rest before they become overtired.
- giving children choices. "You do not have to fall asleep, you only have to rest for a moment," "You can put your cot here or here," "Pick the child you want to rest near," or "You may rest with, or without, a screen."

PLANNING FOR SAFETY

Accidents are the leading cause of death of children under the age of fourteen. After children are one year of age, and become mobile, motor vehicle accidents are the major cause of death. Drownings, fires, and ingestion of poisons follow motor vehicle accidents in killing more children than all illness and disease combined. Because accidents are the leading cause of death, preschool teachers must "develop a formidable accident prevention program" (Zigler 1978, p. 10).

Understanding something about children's thinking gives important clues to preventing accidents. The way children think, their need to explore all of their environment, and their inadequate motor skills contribute to their being involved in accidents.

Adults have long given up the superstitious thinking that attributes unexplained events, such as thunder, hurricanes or fires, to the work of the devil or evil forces. But children, although they may not attribute fires or floods to the work of a devil, do perceive accidents and events differently from adults—more like primitive people once did. A child may fall and hurt herself and blame the concrete pavement for hurting her. Or she may see a vehicle approaching the intersection and still enter the street, fully certain that the car will see her and stop.

Piaget has described this type of thinking as *animistic*, "the tendency to regard objects as living and endowed with will" (Piaget 1965, p. 170). A child in the animistic stage of thought believes a stone can hurt because it wants to, that a bicycle can make her fall, or that the desk can poke her.

Children's thinking is also egocentric. Piaget claims it is primitive, confused, and rigid. The child cannot take another's point of view, does not look for another way, and does not apply logic to any situation. Thus children are not concerned about traffic, for the driver is thinking only of them and will certainly see them in time to stop.

Young children's thinking has not matured enough to let them think before acting. Piaget also found that children cannot think of rules imposed on them from without, before they act. The teaching of rules must wait until children can think and then act. This is important in the teaching of safety principles, for it means that merely learning safety rules will not be successful in preventing accidents.

The inability of children to focus on more than one thing at a time is responsible for other accidents. Children, under the age of six or seven, concentrate on one thing at a time. Playing, they will run into a street to catch a ball or to greet a friend unaware of traffic.

The Need to Explore

Couple the characteristics of children's thinking with their innate need to explore the environment, and it is easy to see why they are accident victims. There is a direct relationship between the child's exploratory behavior and accidents. The more active a child is, the more likely she will be involved in an accident.

This means that the environment must be ordered and made safe for the natural explorations of children. Centers must be clean, objects—anything that the young could stuff in their noses, ears, mouths—safely put away. Bathrooms should be checked to see that floors are clean and dry. Turning hot water heaters to a lower level can protect children from burns. All cleaning products, or other poisons and medicines, should be placed out of reach of the children, preferably in another area of the center.

But another ordering of the environment has been recommended. Deutsch (1971) suggests that the environment be made safe *for* mishaps. When children have the opportunity to make small mistakes, have small mishaps, it serves as a kind of innoculation against more serious accidents. The child who has experienced a tumble on the play yard is less likely to have a serious fall down a flight of stairs. This child has experienced pain and learns to avoid hazards. Being able to handle small mishaps also increases children's confidence in their own ability to deal with accidents or the unexpected.

Physical Development

Children's physical development contributes to accidents. They are short, cannot see the top of a table, or over a fence. They are still learning body control, and once they have started running, jumping, or climbing, they cannot stop in time to prevent an accident. Their visual discrimination is also incomplete. Children's eyes take longer than adults' do to focus and it is believed that they see only a small part of the environment at any one time. All of which leads to accidents.

Teaching Safety

Teaching safety and accident prevention begins by planning an environment safe for children's play and active exploration. Teachers must be active supervisors of all children's play and activities. Alert to accident possibilities, teachers can prevent them before they occur. Teachers step in—showing a child how to climb, removing a sharp object from the sand pile, asking another child to put the truck down if running—before accidents happen.

The ultimate goal of safety education, however, is to teach children to be responsible for themselves. It means that children must improve their own skills, judgment, and thinking so they will be able to care for themselves.

> No longer a restrictive set of "don'ts," good safety education can actually give the child more freedom in his everyday action. By helping him to improve his judgment, skills, knowledge and ability to estimate hazards, it allows him more opportunities for worthwhile pursuits—even adventurous ones that entail calculated risks—with fewer mishaps likely to sideline him along the way. (Seder 1974, p. 2)

TEACHING TRAFFIC SAFETY

More children will die in traffic accidents than from any other cause. It is a part of every teacher's responsibility to help children learn traffic safety, to (1) stop before entering any area that is designated for motor vehicles; (2) listen and scan for traffic before crossing streets; (3) cross residential intersections and (4) interpret traffic signal lights (Ross and Seefeldt 1978, p. 69).

1. Stop before Entering a Street. Children can be taught to stop before entering a street. Begin by having them identify the surfaces of the school, or play yard, asking them to stop every time the surface changes. The surfaces of streets and sidewalks differ. The habit of stopping every time the surface differs encourages children to stop before entering a street.

Take the children for a walk around the school to identify differences in the surfaces of the street and the places for walkers. Always be certain to have adequate adult supervision on these trips. Children can practice stopping every time the surface changes. Curbs are other places to stop. When these are present in a neighborhood, they will signal another place for children to stop before entering a street.

Involving parents is essential in establishing the habit of stopping before entering a street. To establish any habit, the action must be repeated again and again. A newsletter to parents can help them understand and reinforce the goals of the school's safety program and encourage them to help children develop the habit of stopping before entering any street.

2. Listen and Scan for Traffic. Once children learn to stop before entering a street, they need to learn to listen and scan for traffic before crossing the street. When walking on field trips, teachers can ask children to listen and look for traffic as they stop at the curb. Teachers can ask, "Listen to the sound of the car, can you tell if it is starting? Stopping? Slowing down?" Ask children to watch the traffic and identify cars that are going fast, slow, coming toward them, or going away from them. Again, parental support should be recruited in teaching children to listen and scan for traffic, by reinforcing listening and scanning skills.

3. Cross a Residential Street. Children must also learn how to cross a street. Another trip to a quiet intersection can be taken. Children can be asked to look for signs and signals that tell vehicles and walkers how and when to cross a street. They can be asked to focus their attention on the traffic. Children might be asked: "How do drivers know what to do? Why do some cars stop while others do not? What would happen if none of the cars stopped? What does it mean when the driver of a car uses the turn signal?" Other questions, on other field trips, can help children focus their attention to the workings of an intersection.

Back in the classroom a pretend street can be constructed using tape on the floor. Using this street, children can practice crossing, remembering to look and listen for traffic before stepping into the street. A table-top map, toy cars, and people can also be used for children to practice or pretend they are crossing a street.

With adult help and supervision, you may be able to take a class to an intersection and actually practice crossing streets. It may be that the police officer or patrol captain of the school will join you for the trip.

Real experiences are indeed necessary if children are to develop the skill and habit of crossing streets without being involved in accidents. Simply teaching children slogans or songs about crossing streets and looking for traffic has been totally ineffective as a safety measure (Pease and Preston 1967).

4. Interpret Traffic Signal Lights. Traffic lights make crossing streets difficult for children. The lights and other signals at the intersection, which are meant to help children, actually confuse them. Children seem to cross streets in mid-block rather than face the complexity of an intersection.

Children can, however, be taught to interpret the meaning of the lights and signals found at intersections. Children first need to understand that red symbolizes danger and means they must stop. Placing a red tag on objects that may be hazardous in the room, school, and play yard may help children understand the meaning of red. Let the children help make the decisions where the flags should be placed. Playing follow the leader type games, with children stopping whenever the leader holds up a red flag, can also help them recognize the meaning of the symbol. Once children recognize red, the meaning of the other colors, green and yellow, can be introduced. The children can practice crossing the pretend street following red, green, or yellow signals given by one of the children. Other games might be played outdoors, with some children riding tricycles, others taking the role of pedestrians, and still others holding up red, green, or yellow signals to direct the traffic.

Children must actually cross intersections following the signal lights in order to learn to cross streets safely. Parents might be asked to follow up traffic light instruction with their children.

TEACHING FIRE SAFETY

Although the incidence of children being injured or killed in fires has dropped since the development of fire-resistant clothing, many children still die because of burns. *Project Burn Prevention* funded by the U.S. Consumer Product Safety Commission, is a program designed to provide schools with fire prevention information and to conduct a mass media campaign to prevent injury from burns to children across the country.

The program helps teachers prepare children for fires by outlining the behaviors that are to be followed in case of a fire. Children are taught to drop and roll and to carry out practice fire drills.

All preschool programs should practice fire drills in the center. Firefighters can help teachers plan and conduct the practice drills. A fire marshal in Georgia (Collins 1977) has developed the following questionnaire in order to assist early childhood educators in training children and staff for fire emergencies.

Do you have a written plan for a fire drill?
Do you conduct monthly drills based on the plan?
Have you had the basic plan reviewed by the fire department?
Have you held a meeting with the center staff about the plan?
Do you review the plan for new members?
Does everyone know how to operate fire extinguishers?
Does everyone know how to activate the fire alarm or phone the fire department?
Have you practiced drills during naptime, mealtimes?
Do you have an idea of how the children will react?
Do you have an assembly point outside of the building?
Do you have a method for accounting for children once outside?
Is there a procedure to ensure that children, once outside, do not reenter the building?

Do you hold drills with different exits blocked?
Have you given children and their parents information about fire and smoke accidents? (Collins 1977, p. 29)

Along with an active program of emergency preparedness, teachers can also introduce children to knowledge of fire and develop attitudes of respect for fire. Whenever children are cooking, or using fire, precautions must be taken. Teachers may always keep a bucket of water or sand handy whenever using fire—for instance to light a candle for the jack-o'-lantern. Whenever matches, candles, or heating elements are being used in the preschool, teachers can demonstrate proper use of fire and heat and attitudes of careful respect.

TEACHING POISON SAFETY

Tasting is one way children find out about their environment. Knowing that children will put everything into their mouths in order to learn about their world, it is not unusual that many will be involved in poisoning accidents each year. Over 117,589 children a year experience accidental poisoning in our country, and these are only the cases reported to clearinghouse control centers in forty-five states. The development of the poison control centers and of the Mr. Yuk sticker on dangerous substances has helped to eliminate many cases of accidental poisoning.

Yet children in a preschool are just as susceptible to poisonings as children at home. In a preschool setting, however, it becomes the staff's responsibility to protect children from possible accidents. Children can be taught to

- recognize the Mr. Yuk symbol and understand that Mr. Yuk stands for poisons that must not be put in your mouth.
- take medicines only from parents, adult family members, physicians, or health personnel.
- understand that some things are to eat, others are not. Using food for art materials confuses children on this point. Clear lines should be drawn in a preschool—food is to taste and eat, other substances—berries from the play yard, art materials, toys, leaves, or flowers from plants—are not for eating.

In addition, staff members can

1. Select products they will use in the center carefully, picking those that are nontoxic to children and storing cleaning products out of children's reach.
2. Never refer to medicine as candy or take medicines in front of children.
3. Keep the poison control center number by the telephone.
4. Let parents know of your plans for poison control in the preschool and involve them in reinforcing the concepts at home.

Lead poisoning could be another concern. Many schools have been or will be established in old, vacant houses and buildings. Prior to renovation of the building, the paint must be assessed for lead content. If remodeling is to be done, all work should be completed before the children are to enter the building.

If preschool centers are located near high-traffic areas, lead poisoning is also of concern. The lead content of the sand or dirt on the play yard, believed to stem from the fumes of traffic, can produce serious damage in children. It is wise to have the lead content of the dirt assessed, and prevent children from ingesting dirt or sand in the yard.

Always Be Prepared

Even though our nation has made great strides in health and accident prevention, a recent study concluded that children in a day care center in our nation are at risk (Aronson and Pizzo 1977). This study found that few child care centers in our nation were equipped to handle any emergency, nor were fire or accident drills held. The staff in many of the centers did not practice sanitary procedures in caring for themselves or for the children. Few centers had any planned program for establishing health habits or safety education.

To remedy this situation, everyone planning to work with young children should have knowledge of basic first aid. The local Red Cross or other health agency in the community will offer these courses free of charge. At least one staff member at each center should be trained in first aid. Updating the first aid information should take place regularly.

All staff should participate in training programs and be prepared to handle emergencies. The emergency plans should be posted and practiced. Who will stay with the children, who will care for the injured child, and how should be clear. A plan for transporting an injured or sick child should be prepared.

First aid equipment and a list of procedures for handling common injuries should be on hand. The list of emergency phone numbers should be permanently posted near each phone. Plans for children with special needs should also be completed.

PLANNING FOR NUTRITION

"It is urgent that teachers, while becoming deeply concerned with their pupil's health in general, should become more keenly aware of the effects of malnutrition on ability to learn" (Cravioto and others 1967, p. 75). Good nutrition is of major importance in the physical development of the brain and enables a child to benefit from the school situation. How a child feels, behaves, looks, and learns is affected by what he eats.

Malnutrition, even before a child is born, can severely limit the child's learning.

> From the day a poor child is conceived by his poorly nourished mother, he is probably unequal. His growth is likely to be slower; he is more likely to be assaulted by infections and prenatal complications and he is all too

likely to be born in a premature state, which exposes him to enormous risks of brain damage. (Winick 1968)

Many children in our nation do suffer from malnutrition, whether they live in poverty or wealth. Twenty-six percent of children under the age of six consume less than the daily recommended intake of calories, and for low income families, the figure is estimated at thirty percent (Read 1976). National surveys show larger than expected percentages of children with low height and weight for their age, especially for children of low socioeconomic backgrounds. Iron deficiency is also widespread and affects all socioeconomic classes. Overweight is another nutritional problem for children in our country. It has been estimated that nearly thirty percent of all children are overweight (Eden 1974).

A teacher's responsibility for children's nutrition is twofold. First, adequate food must be provided in programs for young children in order to fulfill nutrition requirements. The food offered at a center must not interfere with the food a child eats at home, but must be a part of her total diet, providing a balance of nutrition. Foods served at a center must also reflect children's home and cultural backgrounds, as well as individual likes and dislikes.

Second, teachers also have the responsibility for fostering knowledge of food and establishing habits and attitudes of good nutrition. Most children are not knowledgeable about their nutritional needs or sensitive to them (Smith 1975). "It is time, and past time, to get on with the essential work of helping children and their families develop sounder food habits" (Smith 1975, p. 142).

TEACHING NUTRITION

The White House Conference on Food, Nutrition, and Health (1969) emphasized that all Americans should have access to knowledge of nutrition and its relation to health. The conference identified four major goals of nutrition education. These are

1. Nutrition is the food we eat and how the body uses it. We eat food to live, grow, keep healthy, and have energy for work and play.
2. Food is made up of nutrients. Each nutrient has a specific use, the basic four food groups give a balance of food.
3. All people, throughout life, need the same nutrients, but in different amounts.
4. The way the food is handled influences the amount of nutrients in food, its safety, appearance, and taste. Food is grown, processed, and prepared.

All teaching should be in connection with children's actual experiences with food. Preparing snacks and eating snacks and lunch offer teachers excellent opportunities to introduce children to knowledge of food and to the four nutrition concepts outlined by the White House conference.

But before any teaching is attempted,

We as adults must search our own attitudes and values about our bodies and the foods we eat. Remember the maxim, "I cannot hear what you are saying because what you are doing is making too much noise." Each of us must realize that we serve as models for the children we teach. Do we respect our bodies? Do we keep them clean and in good shape? Do we eat the proper foods to keep healthy?" (Smith 1975, p. 142)

Teaching nutrition concepts is difficult. The concepts are abstract and involve complete understanding of chemistry, digestion, and physiology. Nevertheless, while children are busy preparing snacks or eating lunch, informal discussions about the reasons we eat food can take place. "It's time for a snack, your body needs some food now." "Perhaps after lunch, when you have more energy, is a better time to finish the fort." "These grapefruit sections help keep our skin and gums healthy." Even though most of the teaching is in the form of telling, the telling should be closely tied with children's actual experiences with food. Repeated experiences with foods, and information added to those experiences, may help to build preconcepts in children that will later enable them to develop the understanding that food is used by the body and that we need food to live, grow, and keep healthy.

Young children, who categorize their environment, can be introduced to the four basic food groups informally. "Find all of the pictures of fruit . . . . These all belong to the fruit group." "Here is some milk, what else goes in the milk group?" Since children are just beginning to categorize their environment and cannot categorize on the basis of two factors at the same time, they cannot be expected to fully grasp the meaning of the four basic food groups. To them, an apple is grouped with other apples, or other foods that are red, or other foods that are round. But it certainly could not belong to a group of foods including things as different as cherries, oranges, and plums.

Children who are over five, however, might be able to use the following activities to help them understand the four basic food groups and develop the

Teaching takes place as children experience.

idea that a food can be categorized with other foods that may have diverse characteristics. Jameson (1975) suggests the following activities.

1. Present the four food groups to the children using a large felt circle divided into four pie-shaped pieces with red representing the meat group; blue, the milk group; green, the fruit and vegetable group; and yellow the bread and cereal group. This is the uniform color system used by the Dairy Council. The children can color paper plates to match the felt circle. Using food models—real items, cans, boxes, wax or plastic items, or even pictures of food obtained from the Dairy Council—children plan nutritious meals, being sure to put some food from each of the four groups on their plates.

2. You can make a food train from four small cartons, colored to represent the four food groups. Label each car by gluing representative foods on the side of the carton. Using the food representations, made of wax or plastic, or picture cutouts, children can sort the food into the cartons.

When a new baby is brought to the center, or an elderly volunteer is working with children, or even at a family style lunch, the idea that everyone needs the same nutrients, but in different amounts, can be introduced. Children can discuss the things they eat now, the things they may eat when they are as old as a teenager, as old as their mother or father, or as old as their grandmother.

Of all of the concepts of nutrition suggested by the White House Conference, the concept that the way food is handled, grown, processed, and prepared changes the food may be most appropriate for young children. The concept is easily taught, for children are active participants in growing their food, processing it, and preparing it for eating. They can grow their own garden, shop for raw, frozen, or canned peas, and visit a farmer or food processing plant to see how food is grown, packaged, and prepared for sale.

Although the idea that the way food is processed influences the amount of nutrients in the food is complex and will not be developed as a concept for several years, children will be involved in processing food. They will prepare snacks for their party or a special dish for lunch.

Cooking with children has long been advocated as an activity that can teach children nutrition concepts. If cooking activities are to be used to foster concepts of nutrition, however, prior planning is necessary. "Cooking with children does not automatically teach nutrition information or help children develop sound food habits" (Smith 1975, p. 149).

Before beginning a cooking experience with children, teachers must decide on their goals. Weikart (1971) describes how a teacher endorsing the maturational theory of child growth and development may use a shotgun approach to the cooking of pudding. She might discuss how the substances change, how to divide the pudding among the children, the color of the pudding, or the amount of milk used to make it. He suggests that a teacher, oriented to the cognitive developmental approach to teaching, select one major concept on which to focus during the activity. This teacher might focus on the fact that heat changes the pudding from liquid to solid and ask children to recall other foods that change from liquid to solid when heated, or to speculate on why the material changes when heated.

To make cooking experiences more valuable for children, teachers can

1. Determine the goals of the experience prior to completing it with children.
2. Involve the children with the planning, shopping, and preliminary activities.
3. Use follow-up activities to reinforce concepts introduced during the cooking experience. Send recipe books home, use games involving the four basic food groups, and relate the cooking experience to other experiences children have with food.

Some foods can be prepared easily in a preschool. Before planning to cook, think about methods of allowing each child to participate. Perhaps it may mean inviting volunteers to work with the children in groups. It is important that children participate, rather than merely watch someone else cook.

With an electric frying pay you can

- boil rice and watch one small cup of rice expand and make enough for all to taste.
- make soup, or stew.
- cook beans and marvel at how hard beans turn soft and expand.
- pop corn.
- toast nuts, pumpkin seeds, or granola.
- sauté vegetables and observe how the vegetables change with heat and cooking.
- heat frankfurters for a picnic.
- cook applesauce.
- scramble eggs.
- fry pancakes.

When children cook, it is not necessary for them to make large quantities of food. They only need a taste to feel satisfied. Simple cooking activities might include

MAKING CINNAMON TOAST

Toast bread in toaster or on oven pan. Have each child spread their piece of bread with butter and sprinkle with a mixture of cinnamon and sugar. Use 1 part sugar to ¼ part cinnamon.

MAKING MEATBALLS

Mix 1 pound of ground beef
1 teaspoon of salt
1 minced onion
¼ cup fine bread crumbs
1 egg, slightly beaten
Two children can be responsible for mincing the onion with the help of

a volunteer, and another group can be given the responsibility for making breadcrumbs, by sprinkling stale or toasted bread between pieces of wax paper and rolling over it with a rolling pin.

All children, with hands washed, can mix the meatballs, and each can roll her own for frying. The heat of cooking will kill any germs.

After each child has rolled her meatball, fry at medium heat in the frying pan. When the meatballs are cooked, children can use toothpicks to serve themselves.

COOKING APPLE SAUCE

Each child can wash and prepare an apple of his choice by removing the stem and cutting the fruit into sections. Remove the seeds and core. Adult supervision can be provided. After the children prepare their apples, drop the apple sections into a saucepan, or the electric frying pan. Cover the bottom of the pan with water, about ¼–½ cup. Have each child add one packet, or two cubes of sugar. Cook until tender. Mash with potato masher if desired. Cool and serve.

MAKING CHEESE SQUARES

¼–½ a piece of bread for each child. Or if for lunch, use one piece of bread for each child.

¼ cup of grated melting cheese for each two pieces of bread.

1 egg white, stiffly beaten, for each eight pieces of bread.

enough butter to spread on bread.

Have one group of children beat the egg whites using either a hand or electric beater. Another group can grate the cheese using a hand grater. All children should have supervision. Then let the children butter their bread and spread the cheese that has been mixed with the egg white over the butter. Bake in a preheated oven at 400° for about eight minutes or until puffy and lightly browned.

MAKING FRUIT KABOBS

Let children create their own fruit kabob for a snack or dessert by spearing fruit with long, wooden picks. Have ready chunks of pineapples, strawberries, seedless grapes, and other sectioned fruit. Tiny tomatoes, pieces of luncheon meat, sharp cheese, citrus sections, or apple pieces could also be used.

MAKING APPLE CRISP

Have a committee of children peel and slice five or six medium apples. Put the apples into a greased casserole and pour in

1 teaspoon of cinnamon mixed in

½ cup of water

Have another committee of children mix together seven tablespoons of butter, 1 cup of sugar and ¾ cup of flour. They can use their hands to crumble this mixture. Sprinkle the top of the apples with it and bake at 350° for 30–40 minutes or until the apples are soft.

PLANNING FOR MENTAL HEALTH; DISCIPLINE AND SELF-CONTROL

How children feel in general, the way they cope with the frustrations of daily living, is a part of children's total well being and health. All children need to know that they are loved, accepted, and approved of in the preschool, but they also need to learn how to handle limits and frustrations they meet in day-to-day living. "The two are intricately related and criterion factors in the mental health of the growing individual" (Dittmann 1969, p. 6).

Aletha sits crammed in her cubby, sucking her thumb, responding in baby talk—grunting and moaning when asked to join the group or participate in some activity. David lashes out—hitting, screaming, kicking—seeming to explode when the puzzle piece jams and will not slip easily into the frame. Andrea, calmly and matter of factly, gets a sponge and wipes up the milk she has spilled.

Not all children come to preschool with the same ability to handle emotions or the day-to-day frustrations of daily living. Some, like Andrea, are even-tempered, happy, stable, and express themselves in healthy ways when faced with frustrations. Others, like Aletha, take on the role of a baby, reverting to an earlier, safer time. And then there are children like David, who explode and are simply unable to face even the smallest frustration without lashing out.

Observations of children's behaviors show a great deal of variation. Their past experiences, feelings of self, of approval and acceptance, are believed to have a significant effect on the way they learn to adjust in life.

How children cope with daily encounters of limits and frustrations is believed to stem from their experiences as infants. The physical care an infant receives is believed to contribute to later emotional adjustment. If a child's needs for physical care are not met, the child's inner needs are thwarted, and this is believed to result in an accumulation of inner emotional tensions. If stress and inner frustrations accumulate, they may create a tense way of responding that continues in later life. Adequate physical care then becomes important for relieving inner tensions and is an important part of a child's emotional development.

But children need more than physical care. Studies of children who were deprived of love and affection, but given adequate physical care, show that these children were retarded in all areas of development (Spitz 1945). These studies suggest that in addition to physical care, children need parents, or other adults, who will provide them with love and understanding, who are able to respond to them attentively and sensitively.

As children grow and mature, their emotions grow and mature. Emotions

217

proceed through a series of stages from the relatively undifferentiated emotional responses of the infant to what is termed *emotional maturity*. By the age of three months, infants seem able to differentiate between distress and delight; by two years of age, a child can express a full range of emotions, including fear, disgust, anger, jealousy, distress, delight, elation, and affection.

Providing for Mental Health

Children's emotions are different from those of the adult. They are spontaneous, close to the surface, and often brief. Once the explosion is over, the emotion is spent. Children cannot hide their feelings as adults do. They give expression to feelings in actions and by their physical appearance.

When children come to school, they are asked to face an entirely new situation. There will be new adults and children with whom to relate. "Teachers of kindergarten and primary children need to be masters of understanding and empathy. At the same time, they must assist the children eventually to accept the new relationships and new experiences" (Dinkmeyer 1965, p. 260).

Children develop the ability to cope in school gradually. When teachers make special efforts to smooth transitions from home to school, they are helping children to develop *coping mechanisms*. Some programs offer visiting days when parents and children can observe. Children can enter into the activities of the program as they wish, feeling safe and secure for their parents are near. Other teachers have found that shortened beginning days are helpful. Young children seem to be able to cope in a new setting for a few hours or so, but if asked to stay in a strange place, with strange people, without the support of adults they know for an extended period, they may become frightened, frustrated, and anxious.

Another important transition time is when children leave a program. Children may move, their parents may make other child care arrangements, or they may leave the program to enter a public school. Leaving times also require the special attention of teachers. Children who are leaving can be helped to prepare for their new situation. They can be given information about the school they will be going to, what the program will be like, and what will be expected of them.

Children who do not leave must also be considered. When a friend disappears without explanation, it may cause worry. "Where did she go?" "Why?" "Will I disappear too?" These concerns and anxieties need to be considered as teachers prepare the total group for one child's departure. The group may keep in touch with the child who has moved by sending cards and dictated letters, or pictures of the group. This establishes feelings of security for all children.

COPING WITH TEMPER

Children, like adults, have ways of handling emotions and expressing feelings. In the preschool, children need to learn new ways of expressing

Learning to cope.

emotions and feelings that are socially accepted and will not interfere with their own learning or the learning of others.

An occasional outburst of temper is natural. Everyone loses self-control at one time or another, but when children use temper tantrums—kicking, screaming, falling on the floor—as a means of getting attention and getting their own way, then teachers must intervene.

During tantrums children are often in the position of hurting themselves or others, and teachers must step in fast. Even if the child is not in any danger, removal from the group is desirable, for the tantrum may be so intense as to affect other children's feelings.

Teachers can learn the technique of picking a child up, with the child's back to them, and controlling lashing arms and legs so they will not be kicked. Taking the child to another room, a screened area, or some other place in the school, and staying with the child, or asking another adult to stay with the child until the outburst is over is recommended. After the outburst, discussions might take place on how the child could have handled emotions and feelings without using a tantrum.

The discussion lets the child know her outburst was not desirable and should give her ideas about other ways to deal with strong feelings. "I know you were angry, but you cannot scream and kick. If you want something, you must ask for it."

219

If tantrums are habitual, teachers can observe the child to identify what seems to precipitate the outbursts. Once a teacher understands when children are likely to lose their tempers, she can plan to intervene before an explosion occurs. If a child always seems to have trouble in the sandbox, block area, or when working with more than one other child, a teacher can be ready to offer the child alternative toys or to suggest ways of dealing with frustrations without resorting to a tantrum.

Young children can begin to understand and handle their own feelings. When a child is calm, the teacher might talk to him. "You seem to have trouble when———I wonder what I can do to help. Next time you think you're going to lose your temper, call me and I'll help you." Be certain you can keep your promise to the child by being near enough to help. You can check with the child during activity time, "How are things going?" or just wink, or nod, to let the child know you really are available to help (Day Care 1974, p. 56).

COPING WITH JEALOUSY

Children who are very jealous also need the help of an understanding teacher. "The most effective way to deal with jealousy is with preventative measures. If each child is treated as an individual and is not compared, some of the causal reasons for jealousy are removed" (Dinkmeyer 1965, p. 270). Sometimes children who are highly jealous need to be recognized frequently because of their need for status, either within the classroom, or at home. It is helpful to recognize the assets of each child and establish cooperative, rather than competitive, ways of working.

Sometimes young children develop feelings of jealousy when a new baby arrives. The new baby, taking the attention of the parents, may precipitate feelings of jealousy. Teachers can be helpful to these children. Sometimes they may help by discussing with the parent measures that can be taken to relieve the child's jealousy, or they might help by giving the child realistic information about the nature of newborns. Many times children are told that they will have a new brother or sister to play with and will be expecting a new playmate. When they are faced with a newborn, whom they are not allowed to hold, much less play with, they feel hurt. Having children look at their own baby pictures, reading books about babies, and discussing the helplessness of a baby compared with the abilities they have may help children handle jealousy.

COPING WITH AGGRESSION

Children who express their emotions and feelings by biting, kicking, hitting, spitting, and fighting pose real problems for adults. The child who has been bitten, or who has been hurt, elicits strong feelings of sympathy from the adult, while the child who has done the hurting evokes the adult's anger. It does not help for the adult to add strong feelings or outbursts to the situation, however, and a teacher should remain calm.

Children who kick, bite, or fight are usually frightened children. Frightened children could handle their fears by withdrawing or by attacking. By attacking, a child can deny fears and establish herself as a person who frightens others.

Or perhaps the child has come from a background where aggression is valued and taught as an acceptable way of handling feelings, or is means of survival.

Trying to understand the underlying cause of the child's strong emotions is helpful. Showing these children that they are liked and accepted, helping them to talk out their feelings instead of acting them out, may be necessary. Redirecting the child to find ways of expressing feelings of anger through dance, movement, painting, or working with clay might be used.

Many times children who lash out are overtired, overhungry or have just reached their limits of being with others. For these children, teachers can look for signs of fatigue and suggest rest or a change of pace before an explosion occurs.

Biters may pose a different problem. Sometimes young children are just teething and have aching gums. They may think it will be soothing to sink their teeth into another child's arm. Other very young children bite as a means of finding out more about their world. It is just another way they have of finding out about the nature of things. But children who bite continually and use biting as a means of expressing feelings need particular help. Biting the child back or making her bite into a bar of soap does not work.

In general, the same kinds of suggestions used to help children with temper tantrums are useful with children who bite, kick, hit, or use aggression as a means of getting their way. A teacher can observe to find out what triggers the act and intervene before the outburst occurs. She can also help these children recognize the need to establish their own controls and reinforce them when they do express emotions in socially accepted ways.

COPING WITH FEAR

All children have fears, but when children's fears get in the way of their relating with others and learning, they need help. Children's fears may stem from (1) their undeveloped thought processes and limited knowledge of how the world works; (2) threats of punishment, or (3) the fears of others—parents, siblings, peers—that they have internalized as their own.

Some children are able to discuss their fears with an adult. Even three year olds can express themselves. One child, who expressed fear of going to the babysitter's told her mother, "You put me in your big beautiful car and take me to the nursery school, then you put me in your big car and take me to my house, then you put me in your car and take me to the babysitter's, and I don't know why you take me away all the time." The mother readjusted her schedule and arranged for the child to stay at the nursery school the full day, rather than being taken from place to place.

Children who cannot talk about their fears may be able to handle them better if parents or adults talk about them. "The dark cannot hurt you. I know you are afraid, but here is a small light to keep on at night. Let's read this book about day and night to find out what happens at night."

Other children who are afraid of trying new things can be offered encouragement and support in the form of direct guidance. "Let me help you. Push the pedal with this foot, now put your other foot here and push," or "I'm here to help you, you won't get hurt." This kind of direction and encouragement is specific and enables a child to try, as well as succeed at, something new and helps eliminate fears.

Modeling nonfearful behavior may also be helpful. Children who are afraid of water, thunder, or insects may imitate a teacher who handles such things matter of factly and unafraid.

Gradually children are taught ways to express and handle strong feelings, emotions, and fears, and the ability to adjust to daily frustrations. Teachers have an important job in building children's coping ability and mental health. Just as they foster children's concepts, skills, and attitudes toward physical care, grooming, and nutrition, they influence children's mental health, helping them develop a solid base of self-understanding that will permit them to handle the frustrations of daily life.

In Summary

Health is a state of complete physical, mental, and social well being, not just the absence of disease. Whenever young children are together, whether in a day care center, nursery school, Head Start, or kindergarten program, a primary concern of the teachers must be for the health, safety, and complete well being of the children. The improved health conditions of contemporary America do not relieve teachers of the responsibility to work diligently to protect children from disease and accidents. The pace of modern American life makes it imperative that they work at the same time to teach children to assume responsibility for the maintenance of complete physical, mental, and social well being. As you design your health, safety, and nutrition curriculum, ask yourself:

Is the total program related to children's thinking. For instance, have I remembered children focus on one thing at a time and have trouble following safety rules or planning ahead?

How have I provided for children's growth and development? Do I recognize when they are able to achieve independence in dressing and body care or grooming?

Do I plan for a balance between rest and activity? Are children recognizing and accepting the need for both activity and rest?

Are children fully involved in food preparation and developing sound nutritional habits?

Are the children growing in physical skill and body control?

Are they learning positive mental health practices? Are the children growing in their ability to recognize strong emotions, and to handle their feelings in positive ways?

Resources

A number of organizations have free or inexpensive materials designed to teach children about health, safety, and nutrition. The following organizations might be contacted for a list of the materials they offer free of charge, or for a small fee.

U.S. Department of Health, Education and Welfare
Washington, D.C. 20201

Your state department of education

Your state department of motor vehicles

U.S. Department of Transportation
Federal Highway Administration
Washington, D.C. 20590

Consumer Product Safety Commission
Washington, D.C. 20207

National Safety Council
425 North Michigan Ave.
Chicago, Illinois 60611

American Automobile Association
8111 Gatehouse Road,
Falls Church, Va. 22042

Bicycle Manufacturers Association of America
1101 15th Street, N.W.
Washington, D.C. 20005

Aetna Life and Casualty
Audio Visual Resources
Hartford, Ct. 06156

Projects

1. Take a walk through a school for young children. Note the way the school has been made safe for children. Check to see if the exits are marked, where fire extinguishers are kept, and how routine fire and accident drills are conducted. Are there hazards in the school building or yard? What additional things could you do to safety proof the building and yard for children's use?

2. Interview children to find out what they know about the traffic system. Ask them what the traffic lights mean, where they should cross streets, and how they should cross streets. Have them identify people who could help them in crossing streets safely.

3. Observe during nap times at several day care or nursery schools to find out how different teachers arrange for children's rest. What things do all teachers do? How do the teachers meet the needs of individual children for rest?

4. Interview four or five young children to find out what they know about health and body care. You might ask them why they need to wash hands, brush teeth, or wear clothes. What attitudes do they reveal about health?

References

ARONSON, S. S., and PIZZO, P., "Health and Safety Issues in Day Care," in *Policy Issues in Day Care: Summaries of 21 papers*. Washington, D.C.: U.S. Department of HEW, 1977.

COLLINS, R. H., "Planning for Fire Safety," *Young Children*, 32,5 (1977), 28–33.

CRAVIOTO, J.; GANOA, C. E.; and BIRCH, H.G.; "Early Malnutrition and Auditory Visual Integration in School-Age Children," *The Journal of Special Education*. 2 (1967), 75–82.

Day Care Serving Children with Special Needs. Washington, D.C.: U.S. Department of HEW, 1974.

DEUTSCH, M., "Socio-Developmental Considerations in Children's Accidents," in *Behavioral Approaches to Accident Prevention*. New York: Association for the Aid of Crippled Children, 1961, 90–102.

DITTMANN, L., *Children in Day Care with Focus on Health*. Washington, D.C.: U.S. Department of HEW, 1968.

DINKMEYER, D.C., *Child Development: The Emerging Self*. Englewood Cliffs, N.J.: Prentice-Hall, Inc., 1965.

EDEN, A.N., *Growing up Thin*. New York: David McKay Co., Inc., 1974.

ELIOT, A. A., "America's First Nursery Schools," in *Living History Interviews: Book I: Beginnings*, ed. J. L. Hymes, Jr. Carmel, California: Hacienda Press (1978), 7–27.

GESELL, A., "The Ontogenesis of Infant Behavior," in *Manual of Child Psychology* (2nd ed.), ed. L. Carmichael. New York: John Wiley & Sons, 1954.

GROTBERG, E.H., ed. *200 Years of Childhood*. Washington, D.C.: U.S. Department of HEW, 1977.

HACKETT, L.C., and JENSEN, R.G., *A Guide to Movement Exploration*. Palo Alto, California: Peet Publications, 1967.

HENDERSON, W.A. *Common Sense in the Kitchen*. New York: Hurst & Co., Publishers, 1870.

HILDEBRAND, V., *Guiding Young Children*. New York: Macmillan, Inc., 1975.

HYMES, J.L., *A Look at 1977: Early Childhood Education. The Year in Review*. Carmel, California: Hacienda Press, 1978.

JAMESON, D.D., "What Do They Know from Bacon and Eggs? *Childhood Education*, 51, 3 (1975), 139–41.

JOHNSON, H., *Children in "the Nursery School."* New York: Agathon Press, 1928. Reprinted, New York: Schocken Books, 1972.

PEASE, K., and PRESTON, B., "Road Safety Education for Young Children," *British Journal of Educational Psychology*, 37,3 (1967), 305–313.

PETERS, A.D., "Health Support in Day Care," in *Day Care: Resources for Decisions*, ed. E. Grotberg. Washington, D.C.: Office of Economic Opportunity, 1971.

Project Burn Prevention. Protect Someone You Love. Washington, D.C.: Consumer Product Safety Commission, 1978.

PIAGET, J., *The Child's Conception of the World*. Totowa, N.J.: Littlefield Adams & Co., 1965.

READ, M.S., *Malnutrition, Learning and Behavior*. Bethesda, Md.: NICHD, Office of Research and Reporting, 1976.

Review of Head Start Research Since 1969 and Annotated Bibliography. Washington, D.C.: U.S. Department of HEW, 1977.

Ross, S., and Seefeldt, C., "Young Children in Traffic: How Can They Cope? *Young Children*, 33,4 (1978), 68–74.

Seder, S., *Teaching About Safety. Volume 3, Pedestrians*. Chicago, Ill.: National Safety Council, 1974.

Spitz, R., *Hospitalization: An Inquiry into the Genesis of Psychiatric Conditions in Early Childhood*. New York: International University Press, 1945.

Smith, N.B., "Child Nutrition in a Changing World," *Childhood Education*, 51, 3 (1975), 142–146.

Strang, R., "Health and Safety Education," in *The Thirty Eighth Yearbook of the National Society for the Study of Education*, ed. C. Washburne. Bloomington, Ill.: Public School Publishing Co. (1939), 85–95.

Wann, K.; Dorn, D.; and Liddle, E.Z.; *Fostering Intellectual Development in Young Children*. New York: Teachers College Press. Columbia University, 1962.

Weikart, D. and others, *The Cognitively Oriented Curriculum*. Urbana, Ill.: University of Illinois, 1971.

White House Conference on Food, Nutrition and Health. *Final Report*. Washington, D.C.: Government Printing Office, 1970.

Winick, M., "Malnutrition and Brain Development," *Journal of Pediatrics*, 74 (1969), 667–679.

Zigler, E., "America's Head Start Program: An Agenda for Its Second Decade," *Young Children*, 33,5 (1978), 4–14.

11

Science and Mathematics

*Much of the knowledge children absorb is best acquired by exploration
in the real world where they may freely, actively, construct their vision
of reality, rather than be passively instructed about it.*

E. A. Chittenden, 1969, p. 12.

Of all of the theories of learning, and of all the people who influenced early
education, none has had as great an effect as Jean Piaget. Piaget, a Swiss
psychologist at the Geneva School of Psychology, has been studying children's
thought processes for over forty years. His work has primarily described children's thinking and is based on observations of children, beginning with his
own three, and later expanding to hundreds of other children.

Piaget's work, and work completed by others, seems to suggest that there'
are certain stages of mental growth through which all children pass. Science
and mathematics educators have utilized knowledge of these stages in planning
to teach young children concepts from math and science.

Stages of Intellectual Growth

Mental development during the first eighteen months of life is considered
highly important. It is during this time that all of the cognitive substructures
that will serve as a base for later intellectual development (and even for emo-

226

Children learn as they explore the environment.

tional and affective responses), are formed. From birth until around eighteen months of age, children's thinking is termed *sensorimotor intelligence*. Children learn through sensory motor actions and reactions to and with their environment, acting only on things that are present in the environment.

Language is just developing, and the child lacks the ability to symbolize. That is, children during the sensorimotor period do not have representations by which they can evoke persons, or objects, in their absence (Chittenden 1969, p. 3).

The next stage of intellectual growth, termed *preoperational*, occurs around two years of age. The preoperational stage is sometimes divided into two parts; the preconceptual phase—from two to four years of age—and the intuitive phase—from about four to seven years of age.

These years of preoperational thought are of highest concern to early childhood educators. These, of course, are the years children will be in preschool; however, they are important for other reasons. First, this is the time when language appears, when children can by means of a signifier, language, symbol, mental image, or gesture represent something that is not present. It is a giant step in children's thinking ability and permits them to learn, to expand their environment, to think.

Now children can communicate with others, and their world contains not only the objects and things present, but also the ideas, concepts, and objects in the world of others. Through communication with others, children can adjust their ideas and thinking.

During the preoperation stage of thought, children are learning language, as well as social, physical, and logicomathematic knowledge. To Piaget, each of these differ. Social knowledge comes from information given by others, Customs, morals, and values are examples of social knowledge. Physical knowledge is knowledge about objects in external reality and logicomathematical knowledge is knowledge about relationships between objects.

Physical knowledge about a pencil includes the facts that the pencil is blue, it rolls when pushed, has a point and lead. But when two pencils are together, the twoness is a relationship created mentally by the individual who groups the objects. This is the logicomathemical knowledge of which Piaget speaks (Kamii and De Vries 1976, p. 5).

For Piaget, each child, each individual, must construct his own knowledge. There is no way children can be taught knowledge. Instruction, in the formal sense of the word, is out of place. "From the teacher's point of view, then, the young child embodies two puzzling qualities—while he readily learns a great deal, he is paradoxically, rather difficult to teach" (Chittenden 1969, p. 19).

The Role of the Teacher

Does this mean that teachers should just sit back and wait for children to develop physical and mathematical concepts? Not necessarily. Although Piaget stresses that children must learn for themselves, we do know that children will need certain experiences in order to develop. It is up to teachers to provide these experiences for children and help them use experiences to construct their own knowledge.

Action. Piaget has always stressed the need for activity in order to learn. As early childhood educators have long advocated, children must be active learners. The work of Piaget calls special attention to the role of activity in sensorimotor and preoperational intelligence. Only as children carry things about, observe them, and try them out can they learn. Piaget puts it this way, "Knowledge is not a copy of reality. To know an object, to know an event, is not simply to look at it and make a mental copy, or image, of it. To know an object is to act on it" (Piaget 1965, p. 8). Teachers of young children then, must provide children with activity.

Repetition. Who has not seen a toddler, upon first learning a skill— perhaps walking backward or putting a puzzle together—repeat the action over and over again? Anyone who has worked with children knows that they demand to hear the same story again, to repeat the same song, to do the same things again and again. Piaget believes this repetition is required for learning. Even though the action may seem the same to an adult, children modify their actions each time. As children repeatedly act on the environment they begin to differentiate the properties, size, shape, and weight of objects; they learn. Teachers must give children the opportunity to repeat their actions and activities.

Variation. Although children need to repeat the same actions, they also need variety. The greater the variation in their environment, the greater the learning. The variety and the repetition work together to enable children to form concepts. Basic abilities to handle quantity and number or science concepts stem, not just from manipulating, but from variety. As children act, they see that the large Styrofoam blocks are lighter than the small wooden blocks or that a tiny ball is heavier than a larger ball. Teachers have a role in providing children with variety, not only in objects to manipulate, but in the way they do things and in the routines of the school as well.

Objects. The role of the physical world appears to be especially critical to the development of mathematical and scientific knowledge. "Objects are essential here, as in scientific thinking, but the child is learning from the actions he performs on them, the act of counting; the act of grouping; and not from the properties of the objects" (Chittenden 1969, p. 16). Teachers must provide children with objects on which to act.

Self-regulation. Piaget firmly believes in the need for children to direct themselves in their own learning. "In the area of logicomathematical structures, children have real understanding only of that which they invent themselves, and each time we try to teach them something too quickly, we keep them from reinventing it themselves (Piaget 1969, p. vi). Teachers who let children select their own activities help children build new knowledge onto their past knowledge. When children are free to choose their own play activities, they have a greater sense of mastery and control that permits them to learn.

None of these ideas are new to early childhood educators. Biber, Froebel, Montessori, and others knew them. The work of Harriet Johnson, Rachel and Margaret McMillan, and others, clearly demonstrates the role of the teacher. The principles that children should be self-directing and have opportunities to act and react repeatedly on objects and on the environment are inherent in their programs.

The function of the teacher was to provide for these activities and to introduce children to variety, to novelty, in order to startle children's thinking with variation, presented in context of the familiar, and to arouse children's curiosity.

Teachers use language to help children learn. With language children can discuss their activities and ideas with others. Language also helps children consolidate what they already know. But direct instruction is inappropriate. Especially in the area of mathematics and science, the teacher's role is one of helping children to initiate activities, and then, through language and repeated activities, to enable children to consolidate the experiences gained through activity into knowledge.

SCIENCE

"The more I observe preschool children and read about the observations of others, the more convinced I become that sciencing is an appropriate activity for young children" (D. Neuman 1972, p. 216). A teacher who does not believe that science is an appropriate subject for children will probably have a difficult time. Children demand science for they are naturally curious, eager to explore, discover, learn, and create anew. Even the most casual observation of children yields the information that they are driven by an inquisitiveness that demands that they look into, behind, under, and around all of the wonderful objects and things with which they come in contact (Navarra and Zafforoni 1960).

Healthy children are driven to master their world. "With young children, science is continuous wondering, finding out, knowing. Science is thinking and doing and making the two go together" (Holt 1977, p. 2). If children have not been hurt, they are eager learners, doers, and scientists.

Science is the process of finding out about the world through exploration and the use of the senses. Pestalozzi (1746–1827) believed that the learning environment for young children was totally built around children's sense perception and their sensory activities. His ideas influenced Froebel's kindergarten curriculum, and Froebel designed play activities to develop children's sense perceptions and activity within their environment. An environment organized around sensory experiences was the basis for Montessori's curriculum for preschool children.

Science, a way of thinking or arriving at new knowledge, belongs in every school for young children. The process of science occurs in a classroom with children constantly searching and attempting to find explanations for their environment. In this setting science is a "continuous search for unity in the wide variety of nature" (Deitz and Sunal 1976, p. 126).

The Role of the Teacher

Teachers of young children may have a hard time keeping children from actively exploring their environment and acting as scientists, but they will have an equally difficult time deciding on the goals and objectives for their science program, and on what their role should be. They can, of course, select a curriculum developed by experts in the field of science education, but most prefer to develop their own approach, one that fits their style and the needs of their children. Teachers can develop an awareness of the science that goes on constantly, the resources available, and the content areas of science.

230

Teachers are often surprised to find out they are so heavily involved in science activities. As a teacher you can make yourself aware of what you are already doing. "Give yourself some credit for it. Respect it. When Cindy is holding her head as her bandana is whipping in the wind you say, 'Listen to your scarf. It's snapping. Isn't that great?' But now you say to yourself:

> I have started a science experience. I have focused Cindy on feeling and sound, on the effect —maybe she will think about the cause. I have taken something very personal to this child, right now, and we have shared it. Maybe I have helped her to wonder, instead of being bothered or upset. And I have shown that I'm ready for Cindy's reason, wherever that takes us. It could be nowhere, anywhere, out to the airport to see the wind sock or inside to get a bag and make one. (Holt 1977, p. 20)

To make yourself aware of the opportunities for science, as well as the science that is already going on, you can put a notebook in your pocket and record all of the science interests of the children, noting every time you and the children react or interact in an event that could be called science (Holt 1977). You might find yourself recording children playing in mud puddles, blowing bubbles with soapy water, wondering why the water in the sun dries before that in the shade, or watching your breath on a chilly day.

Science takes place throughout the day.

*This scheme is based on that of B. G. Holt in *Science With Young Children*. National Association for the Education of Young Children, 1977. Reprinted with permission: National Association for the Education of Young Children.

As you record, or observe children's interests and interactions with science, you might also think about the different approaches you can use. Sometimes you may use a problem-solving approach, at other times, you may focus on a scientific, discovery, or process approach.

PROBLEM SOLVING

Sometimes you will use a problem-solving approach when teaching science. You may actively confront the children with problems that need solving. Some materials may be specifically selected for the problems they will cause. A kite might be brought to the play yard on a windy day or plants allowed to die from lack of water.

SCIENTIFIC APPROACH

At times you will use the scientific approach as you ask children to identify problems and to formulate hypotheses. "What do you think will happen if . . .? "Why are the trees moving . . .?" Once the problem is identified, a teacher employing the scientific approach asks children to collect information that will be used to solve the problem or to reach a conclusion. "Let's find out about_____" "Look again, what else do you see?" "How many legs does it have?" Finally, children are asked to draw conclusions. "This is an insect." "The wind makes the trees move."

DISCOVERY APPROACH

There are other times when learning by discovery will be stressed. Rather than telling children, a teacher will ask them to find out for themselves. They are given many experiences that permit them to discover the facts and concepts of science for themselves.

PROCESS APPROACH

Focusing on the techniques of the process of science, a teacher will ask children to develop skills of observing, classifying, measuring, communicating, quantifying, inferring, predicting, and reaching conclusions. Rather than teaching specific information, teachers stress the process of science.

These approaches are similar in that each suggests that children are active learners and must participate in their own learning. Remembering to focus on each of the approaches helps provide balance to a science program.

Developing an Awareness of Danger

There is a film, which is often used in teacher training, that shows a child standing on a chair, stirring boiling soup. The narration describes all of the scientific learnings that come from making soup. One student, as she viewed the scene, commented, "Sure, children can learn all of that from making soup, that is, if they're not burned to death first! In science, as in every other activity in the preschool, the safety of the children must be considered. "The health and safety of children should be paramount considerations for all of the areas of the curriculum. There are some special concerns in science" (Holt 1977, p. 56).

Although all activities involving young children must be analyzed for health and safety hazards, children must be especially protected when participating in science activities. When exploring the world, the natural and man-made environment, children are bound to come face to face with dangers and hazards.

Living things, of great interest to children, can be hazardous. Children must be taught to approach all insects, reptiles, animals, or other living things with caution and respect. Plants and other life must also be respected. Children may be tempted to touch and taste whatever form of plant life they discover. But tasting some berries, leaves, and flowers can be dangerous.

Even encouraging children to sniff things to find out about their world can be dangerous. Smelling unknown substances, such as ammonia, can be very dangerous. Children should be taught to sniff materials cautiously, without inhaling deeply.

Teachers must be especially careful when children with handicaps are involved in science. They must consider the abilities of the individual child and the special needs for protection of the child while exploring any substance or other living thing.

Collecting Resources

Before beginning to teach science, teachers also need to become aware of all of the resources available. Just as teachers develop awareness of the science they are teaching, the approach they use, and the dangers present, they also need to develop an awareness of all of the resources, indoors and out, in the school and community, at their disposal.

Teachers can begin by making a list of all the science equipment currently in their schools. There could be magnets, mirrors, tools, boxes, jars, and other materials. Outdoors there might be a variety of plant and animal life, rocks, fossils, water, sand, and soil.

Some additional equipment should be obtained before children come to the school. Having on hand the ingredients for a terrarium and aquarium, for instance, is helpful. Other materials can also be constructed and prepared before beginning to teach.

INSECT CAGES

Capturing insects is a popular pastime of young children. If respect for all living things is to be fostered, a place for the insects should be prepared. Insect cages permit children to study the captured insect for a time and then release it. A handy insect cage for temporary examination can be constructed from two ends of plastic bottles. Cut the ends from the bottoms of the bottles, leaving about a two inch rim. Take a piece of wire or plastic screening, roll it up and place one of the ends of the bottle at each end of the screen. Let the screen unroll and you have created a handy insect cage. A branch, leaves, water, or plants can be placed in the bottom of the cage to permit insects to perch, or maintain life in their temporary home.

Ants also provide many hours of concentrated observation for children. Large food jars can be cleaned and filled with sand or dirt and a colony of ants. Cover the outside of the jar with dark paper for a few days. Place a cap from a discarded bottle filled with sugar water, and a few bits of food on the top of the sand. In a few days, remove the paper from the outside of the jar, and you and the children can enjoy watching ants working in tunnels and experience observing an entire ant village at work.

ANIMAL CAGES

Simple animal cages can be prepared from discarded wooden fruit or vegetable packing crates. Line the box with half-inch galvanized wire and the bottom of the cage with a galvanized sheet of metal or a discarded cookie pan. A leaking aquarium can be used as a home for reptiles or other small animals by converting it into a terrarium. A sandy bottom, with a few succulent plants, makes the aquarium into a suitable habitat for toads, lizards, or chameleons. Filling the bottom with dirt, rocks, and a cookie tin of water turns the same aquarium into a home for small turtles, frogs, or other amphibians. A piece of wire can be molded to fit around the top as a cover for the cage.

SCALES

Scales should be waiting for children's use. A number of scales can be constructed for inside and outside work. One form of a balance scale can be made from a wooden coat hanger. One each end of the hanger, aluminum pie tins are suspended. The hanger is then hung anywhere, on anything, for children's use as a balance scale.

Other balance scales can be constructed from carboard milk cartons. Fill the carton solidly with paper to provide a sturdy base for the scale. Obtain a plastic ruler with holes along one eldge. With a brad, or small nail, attach the ruler to the top of the milk carton so it is balanced. Attach a small aluminum tin to each end of the ruler with pipe cleaners.

MATERIALS FOR PLANTS

All children will, at one time or another, collect seeds and enjoy watching things grow. If a teacher has prepared ahead of time, she will be ready to meet children's interests in growing things. Flat wooden, metal, or even heavy cardboard boxes can be used for flats and filled with soil. These will be handy for starting seeds or small plants. Old leaky aquariums can be used to grow either desert plants or small woodland plants. Clear plastic sandwich boxes are good containers for sprouting seeds or growing molds. Glass jars, flower pots, and discarded plastic containers can all be kept handy for growing plants or starting seeds.

BIRD FEEDERS

Rather than keep insects or animals trapped inside the classroom in unnatural environments, teachers can encourage children to study life outside. A number of different types of bird feeders will attract birds, as well as squirrels and other small animals to the preschool. Any object that can be hung from a branch, or other high place, to avoid attracting rodents, can be used as a bird feeder.

A coconut, hollowed out and wrapped with twine to form a hanger, is a handy receptacle for bird seed and food. A hole in the coconut lets small birds into the feeder and keeps squirrels and larger birds out. A flowerpot filled with bird food and suspended from a tree, a log with holes for mixtures of suet and seeds, a pine cone stuffed with peanut butter and rolled in bird seed are all handy bird feeders.

SCIENCE BOXES

Making science boxes can also help teachers to capitalize on incidental events and turn these events into science experiences. A box or sturdy plastic container can be used to hold all of the materials useful in helping children to explore a specific concept. For instance, you might fill one box with materials that will be used to explore the concept of air. The box might contain straws, bubble pipes, light handkerchiefs tied to weights for parachutes, small pinwheels, balloons, or any other small objects that will be used to help children explore the properties of air.

Other boxes could contain things for use in water—things that might sink or float; to explore light—prisms, magnifying glasses, mirrors; or magnets—all types of magnets, metal filings in a jar, and other things that can be magnetized. Still other boxes could contain materials for exploring the properties of electricity, tools, shells, rocks, clocks, or gears.

PURCHASES

Some science materials will have to be purchased. Just because children will have scales made from coat hangers does not negate their need for using accurate, exact scales. At least one balance scale and a bathroom scale should be available for children's use. Magnifying glasses of different sizes and strengths must be purchased. Cameras, stop watches, tape measures, flashlights, trundle wheels, telescopes, and perhaps, a microscope will be useful.

Tapping Resources in the Community

Teachers should also be aware of the science resources in the community. Take an inventory of the museums in the area, the places of interest for observing and learning about science, and of the people available to work with children. The local librarian, 4–H club leader, agriculture extension agent, or persons from organizations such as the local garden club, ecology, or wildlife club might be willing to work either with you, or with the group of children.

Do not forget high school or junior high students who can work with children. One preschool teacher, who did not understand the principle of electricity, asked a junior high student to work with her and the children. Together they hooked up batteries and constructed motors that ran with electricity. Senior citizen clubs or organizations of elderly volunteers might also have resources to help teach science. A retired astronomer, aerospace engineer, or entomologist could offer children a wealth of information and understanding.

Deciding on Content

Now that the equipment and resources are gathered, and you have identified all of the resources possible in the environment, it is time to decide on the content of the science course. From the vast array of organized knowledge in science—meterology, astronomy, mathematics, engineering, agriculture, biology, botany, zoology—teachers must select content for children's learning. "You stand between the great traditions of adult science and the great mysteries of young children's learning. You will not only guide the experiences; you will choose some of them" (Holt 1977, p. 79).

In selecting content for a science course, teachers can remember that the most effective sources of every learning experience are those that are

1. Closest to the child. This means the most immediate in terms of time, nearest in actual physical proximity, and closest to their interests, level of development, and past experiences.
2. Available for children's active exploration, actual manipulation and hands-on experiencing.
3. Related directly to the needs of the child, and those that help foster the goals of the program (Holt 1977, p. 79).

You can also remember that it is not necessary to present children with everything or to be overwhelmed by the complexity of all of science. Each teacher is responsible for only a small portion of the total of children's learning. It is also helpful to remember that many of children's experiences with science will be used as a base for later scientific understanding. This base is essential for later learnings, but it is on a simplistic level, an exploration or experimentation level, not a complete, scientific, conceptual level of understanding.

Balance is also necessary. Children's interest in living things often directs a great deal of attention to plant and animal life. This is not wrong at all, but you can also remember to introduce children to ideas in other areas of science that provide a balance to the total program. Children need to have some introduction to the total scope of science and to ideas that will permit them to understand the interplay of all of life and the forces at work in the total environment.

When science is defined as finding out about the world through exploration of the senses, then the content must include everything to which the child reacts, and interacts with. The child's world is the near as well as the far away. Young children can and do explore, experience, and interact with living things, the earth, things beyond the earth, man's attempts to utilize the environment, and physical and chemical forces (Craig 1947).

LIVING THINGS

It is natural for children to be interested in life. They spend hours, fascinated by the workings of a colony of ants or playing with a worm. There is so much to be attracted to; a child's world is filled with living things. Things they want to know. Children can develop concepts of the variety of life, conditions for life, and the interrelationships between all living things.

You might want to start by focusing on the idea of living and nonliving things. Children are confused about what constitutes life. Three year olds attribute life to anything that does or does not move. At this stage children think things move because they want to and can do anything they want. Children believe all things are conscious at this stage, even if they do not move.

Next, children restrict consciousness, or life, to only those things that do move. During this stage, cars, planes, rivers, and clouds have life and consciousness. This stage usually lasts until children are seven to nine years of age. The final development of the concept of life is more reflective. Children distinguish between movement imposed from outside and that which stems from life.

In relation to actual experiences, teachers can help children sort out living and nonliving things in the environment. Teachers should provide children with experiences that will enable them to move to the next level of thinking. A teacher can focus children's attention on the conditions necessary to sustain all life.

As you and the children observe life, you could ask them what things plants need to live or the things that animals, including themselves, need to sustain life. Children can observe living things and reach the conclusion that living things need air, light, water, food, and warmth to sustain life. The dependency of living creatures on one another and on other forms of life might be explored.

The worms grown in the worm farm are used to feed the reptiles, some insects are used to feed other living animals, and we, ourselves, eat many plants and animals. The need to conserve and respect all life is fostered as relationships between forms of life are clarified. No flowers, trees, or leaves should be destroyed without purpose, and only that which can be used to foster other life should be taken from the environment. As worms are used to feed the reptiles, or leaves picked to feed the caterpillar, the idea that all of life is related, and that we, like all other forms of life, depend on one another can be strengthened. You can point out to the children how all living things are affected by other life. "What does it eat?" "What would happen if there were no trees?" "Why does it need clean water?" "Who else needs water?" "What would happen if there were no water?"

To further the concept that life is related, you can have children compare and contrast living things observed in the environment. "How are you just like the squirrel? How is the bird like the squirrel? How are they different?" Or you can have children begin to classify different forms of life, beginning with things that are living and nonliving. Then progress to things with fur, or scales, things that eat plants, or other animals, things that live in, on, or above the ground, farm animals, zoo animals, insects, reptiles, or circus animals.

Individual booklets can be constructed from a few pieces of paper stapled together with a construction paper cover. The topic of the booklet can be any category of life. Children fill the booklets with pictures cut from magazines, pictures they draw, or dictated stories. Wall charts can be constructed for the class as well, with children placing one of their pictures on the chart for the group to enjoy. This type of activity should be reserved for older five years olds.

Learning centers can be constructed around the topic of living things and give children another experience in categorizing their environment. Boxes, pockets, a flannel board divided into spaces with felt strips, and pictures of living things mounted on heavy cardboard or paper are all you need for a multitude of learning stations. Children can sort the cards into the pockets, or boxes, that have been labeled, CIRCUS ANIMALS, FARM ANIMALS, or ANIMALS EAT PLANTS, and so on. Children can check themselves for correctness by turning the cards over and checking to see that all of them have the same mark or color symbol on the back for each pocket.

Pictures of living things—plant life, insects, trees, flowers, animals, fish, and birds—on heavy cardboard provide children with material for other activities and games. Children can simply sort the cards into different piles, or they might advance into playing matching games with each other.

Eventually, as children are exposed to living things, the beginnings and endings of life are experienced. Children may watch the caterpillar laying eggs or the guppies giving birth to live young and begin to question how life begins and how they were born. Children receive a lot of information about life and death from their environment, but they are not always able to sort out this information and form accurate concepts. One child, discussing the birth of a baby sister, said to the other children in the sandbox, "I don't know where babies come from, but I do know you have to have eggs."

Teachers will want to find out what the parents have told children about life and death and the types of information parents believe children should have. Then teachers need to find out what children already know about the topics. Asking children "What do you think?" will help uncover their concepts and knowledge. Once you understand children's level of thinking, you can provide experiences that will correct misconceptions or help them to clarify their ideas.

A teacher should try to answer children's questions frankly, but "she will not burden them with more information than they want at any one point, . . . make sure that they are given information when they want it. The information is needed in small doses, with time to digest it, and with many repetitions" (Read 1976; p. 253–254).

Throughout children's experiences with living things, teachers can remember to strengthen children's powers of observing, classifying, and inferring. Every child will observe, but with only limited accuracy. Observing is

> a skill born of interest, training, practice and evaluation. Awareness has to be directed to those features which concern the problem in hand and this is what makes demands on the teacher's skill. For example, children will watch a blue tit at a bird table and show pleasure and excitement at its antics. yet if they are asked subsequently which food the creature selected, or by what means it clung on to the apparatus, they often find they must look again, and with more detailed, particular attention. (Brearley 1970, p. 28)

To strengthen children's powers of observation, you might ask them to focus on just one thing at a time, "Look at the legs," or "How many colors can you see in the wing?" Also try to get children to focus observations for extended periods of time, so they will notice details, similarities, and differences. All senses can be used, but in observing living things the senses of hearing, smelling, and seeing will be used primarily. Children will not be able to touch a squirrel or a snake, but they can be asked to project how the squirrel or other living thing they are observing would feel. "Can you tell how it might feel?" "Would it be soft? Silky? Fluffy? Smooth?"

Four stages in observing have been identified by Forman and Kuschner (1977). They suggest teachers ask children to (1) identify parts of the thing or object children are observing; (2) look at the object or thing from different angles; (3) contrast it with a familiar object; and (4) relate structure to function.

When children are asked to do these things, they will also be using the other processes of science. They will be inferring, relating new information to that already gathered, and they can be asked to draw conclusions.

Some observations children make will be brief and spontaneous, seemingly over before they begin. Others will be extended over long periods of time. Children who become involved in watching the caterpillars may demand other information. Further experiences with insects and vicarious information given through books, films, or filmstrips can expand and deepen their skills of observing, classifying, inferring, and concluding.

HUMANS' ATTEMPTS TO UTILIZE THE ENVIRONMENT

Children can begin to develop the concept that humans control their own environment. They will see people making roads, leveling hills, or creating ponds. They themselves may plant and maintain a garden and use inventions and discoveries of people to control the environment of the classroom.

Planting and maintaining a garden teaches children many things, not only how they can control their environment. "The garden is the place to teach and illustrate some of the knowledge much needed in the education of children" (Parsons 1910, p. 3). "Through planting gardens children can be introduced to the laws of nature, economy, conservation, the physical properties of tools and the life cycle" (p. 4). As children dig, plant, and nurture their own garden, attempt to provide adequate moisture, and control insects and pests, they actually experience the problems, as well as the satisfactions, of controlling and utilizing their environment.

Planting a garden can also be used to introduce children to the uses of tools. The principle of the shovel, hoe, or other tools can actually be experienced.

In the school room children will use other tools invented by people. They will use scissors—"Who do you think first used a scissors? What would happen if you didn't have a scissors? How do they work?"

Children can find other things in the room that are the result of inventions and discoveries. They might find pencil sharpeners, electric lights, pencils, or crayons. The things they play with, their toys, may be the result of people's inventions. Five year olds might examine the things in the room and decide what they are made of, how people made them, where people found the metal, wood, or other material, and how that material was changed to create the objects.

From these experiences children can gain the concept that people invent and discover uses for materials found in the environment. Some things are used for fun and enjoyment, but other things are used to keep people healthy and safe. In the school, children may explore the heating and cooling plants as well as the trash disposal and sanitation systems.

The importance of control over the environment for health and safety can be explored. Children do participate in cleaning up after lunch, in keeping their room clean and safe by wiping up spills, picking up toys, and conserving materials.

Wise use of resources should be fostered. People use natural resources for their benefit, but they must also use them carefully. Conserving paper, paste, and paint, caring for paint brushes and other materials should be stressed. Scraps are saved for use in collage, lids are placed on paint jars, and dried clay is reprocessed by adding water.

People are not always successful in controlling their environment. Sometimes insect pests will take over the art cabinet, or a garden will be destroyed overnight by an attack of beetles. At other times the inventions of people will break, and children will experience the discomfort of a chilly or very hot school, or school will be cancelled until the heating and cooling plant can be repaired.

BEYOND THE EARTH

"Star light, star bright, first star I see tonight," children recite. But what do children know of the stars? Of the things beyond their earth? With the sun, moon, stars being far from them, how can they actually experience things beyond the earth?

Children can, however, observe the things beyond their earth. They might be given homework assignments to look at the moon every night for a month. In the classroom they can record the shape of the moon and notice how the moon's shape will change during the month. Reference books can add information about the moon.

Discussions of night and day can take place. Children might be given another homework assignment and asked to notice a sunset and report to the others what they observed. Or they could watch a sunrise. The different things people do during the day and at night can be the focus of other discussions.

A trip to the local planetarium, perhaps at a high school or university, might stimulate children's interest in the sun, moon, or stars. A resource person could show children how to use a telescope to further their interest in looking beyond the earth.

Some children may have traveled in an airplane. This kind of experience could lead to a discussion of how people leave the earth and of space travel. Five year olds who show an interest in space travel may be given props, old boots, a piece of discarded machinery, or hoses to help them play astronauts.

Realistically, children's experiences with things beyond the earth will be limited. Nevertheless, their interests should be supported with as many real experiences as possible and with appropriate vicarious experiences—information given through books, films, or resource persons.

THE EARTH

The concept of the earth as the place where humans live offers yet another body of knowledge for children's exploration and experiences. The study of geology, meteorology, ecology, and geography are all included in the study of the earth. As children learn about their social world they will take trips into the community to observe land forms and to explore the surfaces of the earth. They will learn to map their world and to classify and discuss the things that live on the earth.

Often, however, children fail to realize that air is a part of the earth, not separate from it. Children can experiment with air and begin to form concepts about it. Always remember, however, that these activities are experiments and explorations. Teachers may not know where to go next, but they can follow the cues the children give. Do not push experiments on children; do not impose your ideas on them. You can introduce experiments and then see where children's questions, ideas, and interests lead next. You could introduce children to air with some of the following activites.

Air can keep things out, it can be poured, it can be used to pick things up, or to hold things up. With drinking straws children can use air to push things. They might blow (push) a ping-pong ball across a table, keeping it moving as a team effort, or they might push thin paint across a piece of paper to create a design. Children can also use straws to pull things up. As they drink juice or milk let them experiment with their straws. When they suck on the straw, see how long it takes for them to taste the liquid. They will suck for a moment before the water rises, for they must first remove the air from the straw so the air pushing on the surface of the glass of liquid will be strong enough to let them draw the liquid up into the straw.

If children blow into the straw, they will see bubbles in their cup. Other things when placed in water will create bubbles. Children might try experimenting with different objects and a container of water to find out which will create bubbles. A sponge, piece of chalk, some rocks, a crumbled up rag, and paper will all release air bubbles that children can see. The idea is to let the children decide which things in their environment will create bubbles in water and which will not. Ask the question, "Why" and see what children say.

Water play is another area where children can be introduced to the properties of air. Children might try to fill a container by pushing it straight down into the water. The water will rise only so far. You might place a tissue in the end of the container and push the jar upside down into the water and lift it straight out. The children can speculate on why the tissue remains dry. The idea is that even when jars, containers, or boxes look empty, they are not—they are filled with air. This type of experience should, however, be initiated by the children's interest or be closely related to their own self-directed play with the water.

When you are ready to empty a tub, another experience using air is possible. Children can bail the water from the tub, bucket by bucket, or they can use air pressure to empty the tub. A piece of hose or tubing and a container at the bottom of the tub are the materials needed. Place the rubber hose in the tub of water. Hold one end of the tube in the container to be emptied; put the other end into the empty pail, holding a finger over each end. When you remove your fingers the water should flow from the tub into the container at the bottom because of the air pressure on the surface of the water in the tub.

Air can do many other things. Perhaps children can examine the toys in the center and those at home to find toys that use air in one way or another. Balloons are helpful in learning about air. Air will fill the space in the rubber container and create a balloon. Or you can place a light book over a balloon, then blow into the balloon to see how air can lift things.

Air can lift heavier things than books. You can give children bicycle pumps to play with. They will enjoy the use of the pumps in dramatic play as well as in exploring the properties of air. The pumps can be used to fill tires on bicycles and other wheeled toys. Take the children to a gasoline station or demonstrate with a car on the play yard, using air to inflate a deflated tire. Air in the tires holds things up, even something as heavy and big as a car.

Some things tossed into the air fall to the ground quickly; others float gently to the ground. What makes this difference? Can the children find things that float to the ground and those that quickly fall? Examine the objects that floated to the ground and see if you can find out how they differ from those that just landed with a thump. The air trapped in feathers, a handkerchief, under a piece of cloth or paper holds these objects up longer than objects that do not trap air.

Children can also discover that all living things need air. They might try experimenting with plants, sealing one in a tight jar, giving indirect sunlight, water, and soil, but not air. They also learn to keep insects and other animals in cages that are open to air.

In addition, children can explore the way they use air. Have them inhale, feel their chests, and let the air out. They might listen to one another breathing with a stethoscope. Safety principles might be added to the discussion of breathing, and the places people cannot find air could be identified. The fact that people use safety precautions when swimming, boating, or playing near water—because people cannot find, or use, air in the water—might be pointed out. The danger of small, closed spaces, where air will be used up quickly, could also be discussed.

The child's understanding of the earth, and the air that is a part of it, depends a great deal on how the adults help interpret experiences. If children have had teachers who help them experiment with objects in the environment, who build on children's natural interests in the forces of the environment by planning clarifying experiences and adding language, children will begin to develop accurate concepts of the world about them.

PHYSICAL AND CHEMICAL FORCES

Experiences for young children with physical and chemical forces are more elementary than those for older children. Perhaps the greatest contribution of experiences with physical and chemical forces is that these introduce children to the idea of change.

Being adaptable, able to think about change, is central to children's cognitive development.

> In the everyday world the child is attuned to process, the sensitive to change is simply more likely to be adaptive, and therefore more likely to think intelligently. Such a child will resist the temptation to associate everything with every other thing, an endeavor bound to overwhelm the mind and make the mind go random. (Forman and Kuschner 1977, p. 54).

Kamii and De Vries (1978) suggest that teachers give children objects and things that they can act on and with. To Kamii and DeVries knowledge of physical and chemical forces stems from children's actions. They believe you should provide children with things that can be pushed, pulled, rolled, twirled, tilted, spilled, sucked, kicked, swung, dropped, or jumped on; things that can be put in water, sifted, sponged, or drained.

All of the activities in cooking, art, music, shadow play, and woodworking offer children opportunities to do things to and with the objects they find in their world. As children cook, or work with the materials of art, you can help them to think about what is happening. Focus their attention on what they are doing, what they have observed, and ask them to predict what will happen (Kamii and DeVries 1978).

Most physical and chemical forces can be observed directly in the classroom. Children can experience change as a solid—butter—turns to liquid when making popcorn; magnets and electricity; chemical changes as jello powder turns to liquid and then to a solid; and the physical properties of simple tools—hammers, levers, nails, screws, and wheel toys.

Other forces can be observed by taking children on a field trip. They might see a bulldozer cutting a hill down, or a baker making dough into bread.

In Summary

The content of science and children's interest in science are broad. So broad, in fact, it is hard not to build a science program that is based on a shotgun approach—a little here, and a little there, with no unity between experiences and with unclear outcomes. Collect and prepare resources within the classroom, and take advantage of community facilities and volunteers. As you work with children, keep a record of the science activities that have gone on. Keep track of the experiences used to introduce children to specific concepts; vary your approaches so that children sample discovery, scientific problem solving, and process methods of experiencing science. Go over your records and check for a balance between the content areas of science. Cover human manipulation of the environment, the earth and beyond, and physical and chemical forces. Children are so interested in living things that you may be tempted to begin and end the science experiences children will have with this topic alone. Remember that children do need experiences with every area of science in order for them to develop fully. As you evaluate your science program, ask

- are individual as well as group interests being covered?
- are you fostering the concept of the interrelatedness of all science experiences?
- are children progressing in using the processes of science? Is each experience helping children to develop skills of observing, classifying, comparing and contrasting, inferring and drawing conclusions?
- how does each experience contribute to children's thinking? Will it foster magical thinking or does the experience fit into the child's conceptual framework?

There is really no great rush.

> Concepts and words come gradually, or as a social accomplishment to children's own involved activities. His or her own discoveries at every step of the way are real and true. They are not contrived or predetermined fact—earning sessions. They are not lessons. Information first emerges because the child and the earth get together. If that one adult is around to share the moment, she or he can also provide the vocabulary for discussion . . . then the discussion adds a way for the child to handle and remember an experience, therefore to reexperience. (Holt 1977, p. 15)

MATHEMATICS

"The three year old is ready to begin counting. He knows we have three rabbits, for he feeds them and watches them in their house. He counts the shelters too, and the birds in the aviary—there are only three" (McMillan

1919, p. 123). Young children are ready to begin work with mathematics when they enter a preschool. In fact they come to school with many concepts of numbers gained through daily living. They count, "I'm this many years old—one, two, three—" holding up three stubby fingers; solve problems—"You only gave me three, we need one more"; and experience mathematical relationships—"I'm taller than you, but Sara is taller than me."

Surveys show that children indeed acquire mathematical ideas before the age of five (Gesell, Ilg, and Ames 1974). Most children can count to ten; some can count by tens. Others know the meanings of first, can recognize numbers to ten, and even write a few of them. Five years olds will be able to give simple answers to addition and subtraction combinations and have some knowledge of coins, time, measurements, fractions, and geometric shapes.

Today's children apparently develop the same mathematical understandings from incidental living as did children decades ago. (Gesell, Ilg and Ames 1974). The mathematical abilities of today's children, like those of the children in the 1940s, are influenced by age, intelligence, the socioeconomic status of the family, and children's experiences. Children's skills and abilities in mathematics increase as their age, intelligence, and socioeconomic status increase.

Today, however, educators know a lot more about children's number world. The work of Piaget provides teachers with insights into children's mathematical understandings. Although Piaget's work does not tell us what and how to teach, it does describe the stages through which children pass as they learn about numbers and some of the difficulties they are likely to encounter at different age levels (Lovell 1971, p. 1).

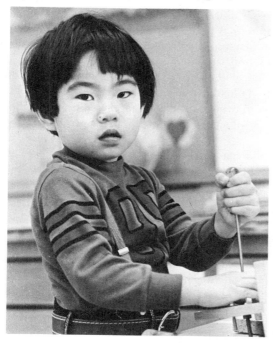

Children use mathematical concepts.

Piaget's Idea of Number

The time between two and seven years of age is characterized by *preoperational thinking*. Children at this time are governed by perception, rather than by logical reasoning. They have not learned to conserve; that is, they do not yet understand constancy of quantity across arrangements. When children are presented with seven cubes, they cannot understand that there are still seven cubes when these are placed in a circle or all clumped together. Children or adults who can conserve see that the cubes do not change in number just because they have been arranged in a different way on the table top.

Children under the age of seven or eight understand that a piece of wire twisted into a different shape is still the same piece of wire, but they do not understand that it is the same length. Around seven years of age children's thinking changes. "You haven't added any wire, you haven't taken any away, it's the same." Piaget sees this ability to conserve as a necessary condition for all rational activity (Piaget 1965, p. 3).

Because children cannot conserve, "one must not think that a child understands number simply because he can count verbally" (Piaget 1969, p. 104). In the child's mind, spatial arrangements are linked with numerical evaluation. There "can be no question of operatory numbers before the existence of a conservation of numerical groups independent of spatial arrangement" (Piaget 1969, p. 104).

To move children from this prelogical thinking to adult thinking demands experiences and action. Mathematical concepts, according to Piaget, are constructed from ideas children form as they act on objects and experience situations. For example, it is believed that only as children place the same seven cubes in different shapes on a table top for themselves, rearranging and arranging under different situations, will they develop the idea that the number of cubes remains constant, despite their actions on them. Children developing concepts of shape, for instance, must learn that the color or texture of an object is not relevant; or children learning to conserve must learn through experience that the spatial arrangement of the objects is irrelevant to the number of objects.

The work of Piaget has led to some generalizations about the role of teachers in mathematics. First, there is the recognition that no amount of verbal counting or drill will enable a child to construct the idea of number (Kamii and DeVries 1977). Number concepts are not directly teachable, rather teachers should

1. Provide continuing opportunities for children to manipulate materials. Accurate generalizations are more likely to be made as a result of experiences with a wide variety of materials and objects.
2. Intervene with language as children explore materials, helping them to focus on relevant mathematical ideas. The role of teacher language in helping children to clarify, refine, and extend their ideas is critical.
3. Encourage children to play together, to work and solve problems together. Piaget believes that social interaction is essential for children to coordinate and group their thinking into a coherent structure or whole.

246

When children are confronted with an idea that conflicts their own, they are motivated to think about the problem again, and either revise their idea or argue about it. Therefore, an important principle of teaching is to bring disagreements to children's attention by asking for many opinions or by mentioning casually to a child that someone else has a different idea. (Kamii and DeVries 1976, p. 17)

4. Encourage children in a general way to put all kinds of objects, events, and actions into relationships (Kamii and DeVries 1976). Children need many experiences seeing, and experiencing, relationships between time—"There are seven more days till my birthday"; with one to one correspondence—"Here's one for you and one for me!" and with things like shape, "Why are bottle caps and necks both round?"

5. Understand children's thinking processes. Piaget became interested in children's thinking when he administered items that would appear on Binet's test of intelligence. It was not the correct answers that intrigued him, but children's incorrect answers. Listen to children, try to understand how they are thinking and why. Without this kind of insight, teachers cannot know what kinds of experiences to give children, the language that will help them clarify understandings, or why the child has made an error. Although new teachers may think this is an impossible task and want specific guidelines, it is something teachers must create for themselves. "Our knowledge of the growth of human thinking is as yet insufficient to provide a basis for scientific pedagogy, and an intuitive understanding of children on the part of the teacher must complement what we know of them in a scientific sense" (Lovell 1971, p. 22).

Planning for Math

"In planning any instruction one must choose content and instructional strategies that are based on the characteristics of the learners and the subject matter" (Gibb and Castaneda 1975, p. 96). Agreed that any mathematics instruction must be built on children's experiences, sensory opportunities, appropriate language, and seeing and experiencing relationships, the problem of what to introduce to the children, and how to organize mathematical content, remains. Gibb and Castaneda (1975) have organized a series of topics and abilities in mathematics that can give children the opportunity to develop concepts in mathematics, as well as "build the young child's trust and confidence in his own perception and cognition, his trust in his own ability to learn, and his image of himself as a learner and as a valued human being" (1977, p. 97).

Included in the activities and experiences are those related to pre-number—classifying, comparing, and ordering; measurement; shape and space; and numbers.

Pre-Number Activities

Classification, comparing, and ordering are important aspects of children's cognitive development. Children only develop a sense of order of their world when aided by the ability to recognize that certain objects can be categorized because of similar qualities or attributes.

In order to classify, children must not only observe, but also think. They have already had many opportunities to observe and classify their environment before they come to preschool. At home they put the forks together, separate from the spoons, in a drawer; put all the cookies on one plate; all their toys in a box; or all of the blocks on a shelf.

At school many other opportunities present themselves for children's experiencing. Teachers can ask all of the children with buckle shoes to get their coats, just those who have something red on to sing the song, or all the children to keep all of the things they can draw with on one shelf. Children can, in direct relation with their experiences, learn to put things together that are alike, or those that belong together, and to tell why they have grouped things as they have.

In order to determine just what classification skills children do possess, you can present each individual child with a collection of figures, plastic letters, buttons, or other small, easily handled objects. Tell the children to put all of the things together that belong together, and then observe how children follow this direction. Children should progress through the following stages:

1. Sorting into graphic collections with no kind of plan in mind. Children may put all of the letters together, and then, ending with a blue letter, may put blue buttons in the group. When the group is completed, they cannot tell why the things belong together, only that they do.
2. Grouping with no apparent plan. When asked why all of these things go together, children will respond with some reason, unfamiliar to the adult. "All of these things make me think of my Auntie."
3. Sorting objects on the basis of two criteria. All of the green and square buttons here, all of the pink and round ones here.
4. Grouping on the basis of criteria given to them. "Put a pile of objects that are all the same size here, or put the letters here."

Once aware of children's skills in classification, experiences designed to promote the next stages in the process can be provided. Authorities agree (Piaget 1965; Lovell 1971; Gibb and Castaneda, 1975) that the greater the range of perceptual experiences, the more likely it is that children will grow in their ability to classify.

Teachers might provide children with

• boxes of scrap materials—velvet, tweeds, linens, cotton—cut into uniform shapes, for feeling, sorting, and manipulating.
• greeting cards representing many occasions for children to classify according to holiday or event, or by picture, design, size, shape, or other criteria.
• lotto games, dominoes, and board games offering children opportunities for classification.
• a button box full of all types of buttons, for sorting and grouping.
• plastic farm animals, zoo animals, trucks, cars, small people, for grouping any-way children desire.
• collections of rocks, sea shells, seeds, leaves, beans, for feeling, sorting, and classifying.

• a box of marbles of all different colors, sizes, and types.

Giving children some type of sorting tray aids them in their work. Egg cartons, any box that has dividers is helpful. Plastic glasses glued to a heavy piece of cardboard and a flannel board with yarn divisions are other useful sorting trays. It is not necessary for children to use these trays, but their presence seems to give children suggestions for use of the materials.

Children work with the materials without guidance at first. After the children have explored and experimented with the materials, teachers may want to discuss differences and likenesses between objects, and lead children to think of other similarities besides those of size, color, or shape. Teachers can also add verbal labels as they work, identifying attributes, purposes, or position labels to help children in the acquisition of concepts. Throughout the classification activities, teachers permit children to talk with one another, argue, and discuss their experiences.

As children continue with their activities, teachers can introduce the idea of sets. "Look, you made a set of blue cars," or "This is a set of green marbles, can you make a set of red ones?" The idea is to let children know that a set can be named by describing or listing members of the set. The name of a set determines its membership. Teachers can help children see that one object can be a member of several different sets, as well as to name sets for themselves.

COMPARING

As children create sets, they will be comparing attributes of objects. "Comparing is the process by which the child establishes a relation between two objects on the basis of some specific attribute" (Gibb and Castaneda 1975, p. 102). Children seem to compare things naturally as they explore their world. "This is the softest," or "Take the biggest." Often these spontaneous comparisons revolve around the concepts of big or little. Teachers will want to lead children to making comparisons on the basis of other attributes. Children can use blocks, sand and water play, or art activities to develop the language of comparisons and the ability to make comparisons.

Blocks offer children numerous opportunities to make comparisons As children build, they may refer to their own height in relation to the blocks or to the buildings of others. Teachers might ask them to build something as long as the truck, the same length, or shorter than another object. Children can make comparisons on the basis of number. "How many arches are there?" "You have two double blocks, Susan has four." With blocks, comparisons can be made on the basis of height, shape, size, or number.

Playing with sand and water offers other opportunities for comparisons. The different size containers, with differing shapes, colors, and volume, lead children to making comparisons on the basis of how much, how much more, or how much less. Teachers might focus on comparing sizes of two containers, finding out which container holds the most, the least, or which is the lightest and heaviest.

Art activities, play with clay, paints, and crayons can all be used to introduce children to the vocabulary of comparison. Textures, colors, lengths, and shapes are each involved in children's artwork and can be pointed out as the basis of comparisons.

Daily experiences can be used to foster comparison of numbers, such as counting cookies or snacks. During dressing and washing, the idea of more and less, or of one shoe for each foot, one sock for each foot, or the fact that there are as many hooks as toothbrushes can be used to help children compare number.

Other activities that might be structured to lead children to making comparisons on the basis of numbers are

- give one child three objects, another two. Have them place their objects on a table, one at a time. Then ask the children who has the most.
- ask children to set tables, put paintbrushes with paint jars, or give each child one glass of juice or one cracker.
- compare number of dolls and doll dresses, cowboys and horses, or trucks and drivers.

To assess children's growth in making comparisons you can present them with a number of easily handled objects and ask them how these are alike and how these differ. Children should move in their ability to make comparisons on the basis of

1. Attributes and identities known to them, such as color and size;
2. Height and length;
3. Amount, which requires that children can set up a one-to-one correspondence between members of sets.

ORDERING

Ordering is another pre-number skill. By the time children are three or four years of age, they have some idea of ordering. Many of their toys, the nesting blocks, building towers, rings in graduated sizes, all are based on the principle of ordering (Lovell 1971, p. 24).

In school, children can be presented with additional types of materials that will increase their experiences with ordering. Sets of rods of differing lengths; Montessori materials that require ordering of pegs, colors, or sounds; blocks, tinker toys, and other materials can be used for ordering. After children have freely explored these materials, teachers might ask them to

1. Find the shortest or the longest rod or tinker toy stick.
2. Pick, from three objects of differing heights, the one that is the shortest, and describe the remaining two objects.
3. Describe how a series of objects, arranged from shortest to longest, differs from one another.
4. Arrange a group of objects from shortest to longer.

Children's ability to use measurements develops from their experiences in classifying, comparing, and ordering. As children actually compare the weight of two objects, find a block as long as their box, or see that the blue bucket holds as much sand as the red bucket, they are using concepts of measurement.

Children's ability to understand measurement is directly related to their ability to conserve matter. Children must understand that the length of an object remains the same whatever changes occur in its position. This involves their ability to understand that measurement can be expressed as a multiple of any number of units. It will not be until a child is six, seven, or even eight years old, that the full concept of measurement, with the ability to use systematic measurement, is developed.

This does not mean that preschool-age children should not have experiences with measurement. "The experiences derived from activities involving measurement, which the child carries out at a teacher's suggestion, provide the basis out of which understanding arises with the growth of thinking skills" (Lovell 1971, p. 104). The important thing to understand is the extent to which children are able to carry out a measurement task. To determine children's understanding of measurement of weight, capacity, and length, teachers can

1. Present children with two sticks of equal length, placed like this ————, and ask children if they are the same length. Then place the sticks like this ————, and ask them if they are still the same. Preoperational children will believe that one of the sticks is now longer than the other.

2. Assess children's abilities to measure capacity by presenting them with a pitcher of colored water, two containers of the same shape and size, and a third container of a different shape and size. Have the children pour water into the two containers that are the same until there is the same amount in both. Have the child confirm that the water is the same in each of these containers. Then take one of the containers and pour the contents into the third container that is a different shape and size, and ask children if the containers still hold the same amount. Children under the age of seven or eight will believe that there is either more or less water in the third container, because this container is a different shape or size than the others.

3. Determine children's ability to conserve weight by giving them a piece of clay that is rolled into a ball. Have the children weigh the ball of clay. Now ask them to make a snake, or a pancake out of the clay ball and ask if the ball of clay and the snake will weigh the same. Conservers will see that the clay is the same weight, simply made into a different shape. Nothing has been added, nothing has been taken away.

Children can be given experiences with measurement that will help them develop the idea that things can be measured. These should be

leisurely enough to allow them to build concepts both of the properties to be measured and of the appropriate units . . . the teacher should be in no

hurry to use standard units, rather she should make sure that each experience related to measurement contributes to a general concept of the
process of measure and to the concept of measurement. (Gibb and Castaneda 1975, p. 104).

All types of activities can help children understand measurement. Children could be given bits of ribbon or string and asked to find things in the
room as long as their piece of string, or to put their ribbon around objects,
across the tops of other objects, or up or down still other objects. Children
might find out how many times they must place their piece of string end to
end to measure a wastebasket or table.

Other things can be measured by using hands, feet, or other body parts.
Children can find out how many times they must place their feet, one in front
of the other, to get across the room, a hallway, or play yard. A trundle wheel
can also be used by the children as a means of measuring the room or play
yard.

Woodworking provides excellent opportunities for children to use measurement. Children must find nails that are long enough to penetrate the two
pieces of wood they wish to join, or wood that is just the right length for their
project.

Concept of capacity can be developed through sand and water play. The
vocabulary of how much, how much more, and how much less goes hand in
hand with the play. Sand and water play also help build concepts of weight
when scales are added to these areas. With simple scales, children can become
involved in weighing buckets of sand or containers of water.

With balance scales children can weigh all types of materials—rocks,
shells, pine cones, acorns, nuts, or bolts. Other activities with measuring weight
involve

- weighing children to find out who weighs the most, the least, and how many
weigh just the same.
- weighing food materials for cooking.
- using balls of clay, changing the shape of the clay, and measuring the clay
before and after the shape has changed.

Measurement should involve as many real life, natural experiences that
arise from children's needs as possible. "Let's fill the aquarium. Count the
number of pails of water." "How long should we cut the material for the
curtains?" "Get a block just as long as this one," or "You need to balance it
with something that weighs just the same amount, try the book." It will take
children many experiences before they gain the concepts of measurement. Yet
introduction to measuring, when used in connection with actual experiences
repeated over and over again, can give children a feeling of mastery over their
environment, and the preconcepts they will need when introduced to actual
standard units of measurement in later years.

Most children will enter school with some concept of shape and space. They can tell you that their mother has a pin the same shape as yours, or that they want the square cookie. By five, children seem to be able to recognize the basic shapes of square, circle, and triangle, although they will not be able to name them. To assess the individual child's awareness of concept of shape and size, give him a series of attribute blocks of various shapes, and have him pick out the blocks that are round, square, or triangular in shape.

Concepts of shape can also be developed in connection with daily experiences. Children might recognize the shapes of the blocks or the shapes they use in their artwork. Materials used for ordering and classifying can be compared on the basis of shape. Lotto and board games and bingo and car games can also be used to let children match on the basis of shape.

Field trips can be taken to call the attention of children to shapes. The children might go outside and look at the school building, identifying the shapes they observe on the building. They might identify the shapes of flowers, leaves, or insects on the play yard.

Concepts of space develop as children explore space with their bodies. The area of movement exploration gives them ample opportunities to experience all dimensions of space.

Numbers

Because young children count and use number words, it is easy to think they actually comprehend numbers. To explore children's actual concept of number, teachers can present them with ten easily handled objects. Beads, buttons, cubes, toy cars, other counters can be used. As the ability to do rational counting also implies the ability to count by rote, the former is tested first. Ask the children to

1. Count the beads, or counters on the table. They should be told to touch them if they wish. If the child loses one-to-one correspondence before arriving at ten, the last number in correct association gives an indication of her ability to count using one-to-one correspondence. (One-to-one correspondence means that children are able to pair the term *one* with the first object, *two* with the second object, and so on.)

   Children may be able to mouth the names correctly, even move a finger from one object to another, and still have no understanding of counting. It must be emphasized that it is futile to teach children to count by rote; in doing so they are not learning arithmetic. Real counting implies that the child is aware that she is pairing the term one with the first object; two with the second (Lovell 1971, p. 35).

2. Tell, when the counters are arranged in sets of two, three, five, and six, which set contains the most, the least, or which set has more.

3. Tell how many counters there are when all ten are placed in a row.

4. Hand you the first, second, or last counter.

These activities give some idea of children's concepts of number. Many children will count to ten, but will skip objects, or count the same one a number of times. "This tendency shows that the child does not feel any logical necessity to put objects in an order to make sure he does not skip any or count the same one more than once" (Kamii and DeVries 1976, p. 7).

Children should not be hurried into counting, otherwise their number concepts will be similar to those of parrots in a zoo who have learned to peck out correct numbers without any concept of what counting means. "In order to develop counting as a meaningful process, the child must be asked to count only with number names that are meaningful to him . . ." (Gibb and Castaneda 1975, p. 117).

Children can, in connection with their experiences, count the number of rabbits, fish, or insects, or the number of children at the table. Kamii and De Vries (1977) give suggestions for meaningful counting experiences for young children. These include counting

- children who ride a certain bus;
- children who are absent;
- the number of girls, or boys;
- the number of votes for a given topic.

Group games, such as "Hi-Ho Cherry Oh!", "Candy Land," and "Chutes and Ladders," are also given as suggestions for meaningful counting activities. Card games, dominoes, ten pins, and aiming games are also useful. Workbooks, kits, and rote drills are meaningless. The stuff of learning is children's manipulation of materials in the environment. Children must be motivated to learn, to construct the world of numbers for themselves (Kamii and De Vries 1977, p. 49).

In Summary

Built on children's play activities, their experiences, and sensory opportunities, mathematics instruction is a part of all activities in the preschool. Teachers should remember that children's thinking at this age is preoperational, not logical. Because children can count by rote, teachers should not assume that preschoolers understand numbers and can conserve. In relation to children's actual experiences and activities, teachers find opportunities to foster children's ability to classify, use measurement, compare, order, and become acquainted with shape, space, and number.

It is important to remember that all instruction in mathematics must be based on children's actual experiences. Teachers must find out what children actually know and then build on it. When children play, work with one another, or manipulate materials, teachers can introduce the ideas of mathematics. The use of language, play, and socialization with others are thought to be necessary. Gibb and Castaneda (1975) believe that mathematics instruction should be based on experiences and sensory perceptions, permit children the maximum use of oral language, and be designed to permit children to build confidence in their own perception and powers to seek out information and draw their own conclusions.

Resources

Science resources include the following:

B., HOLT, *Science With Children*. Washington, D.C.: National Association for the Education of Young Children, 1977.

Science 5/13

"Using the Environment: 1 Early Explorations"
"Change, A Unit for Teachers; Stage 1"
"Using the Environment: 2 Investigations"
"Beginnings: Early Experiences"
"Science From Toys"
"With Objectives in Mind"

The Science 5/13 series is available in the United States from Macdonald Educational, 850 Seventh Avenue, New York, New York, 10019.

An excellent resource for mathematics education is

The Thirty-Seventh Yearbook of the National Council of Teachers of Mathematics, *Mathematics Learning in Early Childhood Education*, 1975.

Projects

1. Before beginning to teach young children it is very helpful to explore their understanding of science and mathematical concepts. Use the assessment suggestions given for mathematics with young children. As you question children about their understanding of these concepts note how their thinking differs from that of adults.

2. Observe children during free play or activity time. How many times do they use mathematical or science terminology as they play? What encounters with math and science do they have as they play? What should your role as a teacher be?

3. Update your own understanding of science and mathematics. Read Jacob Bronowski's *The Ascent of Man* (Boston: Little, Brown and Company, 1973) or the Time-Life series on science and mathematics. In which area of math and science do you feel you are most deficient? Make it a point to take a course, read, or work with another teacher to fill this gap in knowledge.

4. Make at least one piece of science equipment to use with young children. Suggestions for scales, insect cages, or single concept boxes are given in the section on science.

References

ALMY, M.; CHITTENDEN, E.; and MILLER, P.; *Young Children's Thinking*. New York: Teachers College Press. Columbia University, 1966.

ASHLOCK, R., "What Math for Fours and Fives?" in *Childhood Education*, 43, 8 (1967), 469–474.

BREARLEY, M., ed. *The Teaching of Young Children*. New York: Schocken Books, 1970.

CHITTENDEN, E. A., "What Is Learned and What Is Taught," *Young Children*, 25, 1 (1969), 12–20.

CHURCHILL, E., *Counting and Measuring*. Toronto: University of Toronto Press, 1961.

CRAIG, G. S., *Science for the Elementary-School Teacher*. Boston: Ginn and Company, 1947.

DEITZ, M., and SUNAL, D., "Science," in *Curriculum for the Preschool/Primary Child: A Review of the Research*, pp. 125–153, ed. C. Seefeldt. Columbus, Ohio: Charles E. Merrill Publishing Company, 1976.

FORMAN G. E., and KUSCHNER, *The Child's Construction of Knowledge: Piaget for Teaching Children*. Monterey, California: Brooks-Cole Publishing Co., 1977.

GIBB, G., and CASTANEDA, A., "Experiences for Young Children," in *Mathematics Learning in Early Childhood Education. Thirty-Seventh Yearbook*, pp. 95–195. Washington, D.C.: National Council of Teachers of Mathematics, 1975.

GESELL, A.; ILG, F. L.; and AMES, L. B.: *Infant and Child in the Culture of Today*. Rev. Ed. New York: Harper & Row, Publishers, 1974.

HOLT, B. G., *Science with Young Children*. Washington, D.C.: National Association for the Education of Young Children, 1977.

KAMII, C., and DE VRIES, R., *Piaget, Children and Numbers*. Washington, D.C.: National Association for the Education of Young Children, 1976.

KAMII, C., and DE VRIES, R., *Physical Knowledge in Preschool Education*. Englewood Cliffs, N.J.: Prentice-Hall, Inc., 1978.

LOVELL, K., *The Growth of Understanding in Mathematics: Kindergarten Through Third Grade*. New York: Holt, Rinehart & Winston, 1971.

MCMILLAN, M., *The Nursery School*. London: J. M. Dent & Sons, 1919.

NEUMAN, D., "Sciencing for Young Children," *Young Children*, 27, 4 (1972), 215–226.

PARSONS, H. G., *Children's Gardens for Pleasure, Health and Education*. New York: Sturges & Walton Company, 1910.

PIAGET, J., *The Child's Conception of Number*. New York: W. W. Norton & Co., Inc., 1965.

PIAGET, J., and INHELDER, B., *The Psychology of the Child*. New York: Basic Books, Inc., Publishers, 1969.

READ, K. B., *The Nursery School: Human Relationships and Learning* (6th ed.). Philadelphia: W. B. Saunders Company, 1976.

Science 5/13, London: Macdonald Educational, 1972.

Science Curriculum Improvement Study, SCIS Sample Guide. New York: Rand McNally & Company, 1970.

12

Language and Reading

Nevertheless, I believe that there is a kind of reflective intelligence that emerges as soon as the child acquires language . . .

D. Elkind, 1976, p. 115.

Does a child develop language as the result of a growing ability to think? Or is thinking a result of the child's developing use of language? Piaget (1955) believes that language and thought are very closely related—parts of the same process. To others, Vogotsky (1962) for instance, language is a mediator of thought, and although language and thought are related, language is the hand-maiden of thought. It is language that gives power to thinking.

What is not disputed is the close relationship between thought and language. Growth in command over language is linked with thinking. It is through language that people most frequently study children's thought processes (Russell 1956).

Today, most intelligence tests are based on observations of children's language. Success in language means more than just scoring high on an intelligence test. Children who enter preschool with language facility have a greater chance of achieving in the school. It does not matter which program is implemented in the school, what the goals and objectives are. Children will be required to use and understand language in school.

If children have inadequate skills in listening and speaking, they will have inadequate skills in reading and writing. Without the ability to understand

257

what someone says, the ability to speak, read, and write, children are severely limited in our society.

Children without a finely developed language facility will fail in the business of school and society, and they will also fail in social relationships. Like thinking, social growth is interwoven with language power. How children relate with others—children, teachers, other adults—and handle themselves in a social situation, depends, in a large part, on their ability to be able to express themselves clearly, to communicate and understand language. Of utmost importance in any social relationship is the ability to express feelings, thoughts, or ideas with precision.

Feelings of self-esteem are also closely related to language facility. Soon after children are born, they learn that language produces results. Some language makes for good feelings of approval, affection, and security; other language means anger, disapproval, distrust, and anxiety.

Developing Language

Everyone agrees that language is necessary for children if they are to develop their full potential, socially, emotionally, and intellectually, but not everyone agrees on just how children go about learning a language. Some believe that children are "prewired" for language, and that language development is largely

Children listen, speak, and use the printed word.

a process of maturation. Others suggest that children's language behavior is learned as the child's total environment reinforces different patterns of language usage. Still others believe that language is the result of a biological interaction between child and environment.

Nativistic Theory

No matter what culture children are born in, no matter where they live, or what language they hear, the onset of language is consistent. Children the world over attain language at the same time and continue through the same sequence of language development. There seems to be a type of synchronization between language and motor development. When a baby begins to sit up, around five or six months of age, she also begins to babble in consonant sounds. At two, a child can run and climb stairs with one foot forward and speak in two phrases, whether growing up in China, Russia, Spain, or the United States (Lennenberg 1967).

According to the nativistic theory, every child has a built in "language acquisition device" (Chomsky 1965). This device is a type of preknowledge of language. The environment provides the models of language, but the language mechanism, or prewiring, enables children to analyze the language heard, so that from a sample of language, they are able to discern the pattern, structure, and rules of language (Mc Neill 1970).

Behaviorist Theory

Behaviorists also believe that children have an inborn mechanism that enables them to learn language, but this mechanism lets children make a stimulus-response connection and articulate speech sounds. Skinner (1957), describes several ways speech patterns might come about. Speech might be learned as an *echoic response;* that is, an imitation of a heard stimulus that a parent or other adult has rewarded. Language might be learned as a result of a *mand;* the child may make a random speech utterance that sound enough like the current need of the child that the parent rewards the sound by supplying the need. Or language might be acquired by a *tact;* a child may make a particular verbal response while in the presence of, or in contact with, a given stimulus and is rewarded for doing so.

Research supports the idea that children learn language through reinforcement (Staats 1971). Humans continually reward and punish each other through language and continually reinforce certain language patterns over others, influencing one another's verbal behavior.

Social Theory

Piaget (1955) sees language as the result of a biological interaction between man and environment and an adaptation process called *accommodation* and *assimilation.* Children pass through a number of developmental stages, each characterized by certain types of language organization and behavior. Piaget believes that language develops along with the child's capacity for logical thought, judgment, and reasoning and that it reflects these capacities. As the child's internal organization changes, he must interact with the environment and absorb these elements into his internal structure before the next stage can take place. Heredity, growth, and experience contribute to the learning of language.

Learning to Speak

It seems a miracle that children learn to speak. Think of how difficult it is for us to learn another language. Yet children, within a few short years, learn to understand, speak, read, and write a language.

Babies begin speech by cooing. By three or four weeks of age a baby will coo and babble and perhaps even squeal. At this age babies can be comforted by the voice of their parents or care giver. At around three months of age, cooing makes way for more ambitious sounds; babbling develops into *da da, ya ya, ga,* and *ba* sounds. This babbling is the beginning of all articulation, and babies use both vowel and consonant sounds as they babble.

Soon babies learn to understand the speech they hear. Very quickly children will be able to wave bye-bye, dance when someone asks them to, and play pat a cake. They show in other ways that they can understand and recognize a few words. Usually this occurs around eight months of age. The first words of the baby usually result from babblings. When the care giver hears babbles she thinks she recognizes, she repeats them and reinforces them. Babies begin with a *ma ma* sound in nearly every culture, which is reinforced by mother, who believes she has heard her name. The important thing is that by around nine to twelve months of age, babies will attempt to communicate with syllables. Babytalk is actually the child's attempt to articulate syllables, or words, that mean something. Sometimes meanings are assigned to sounds that only the care giver understands. *Too too* may stand for dog, or *pa pa* for the child's favorite stuffed toy. What matters is that meaning is now being assigned to sounds, and that others are reponding to the sounds.

From one year to two years of age, children will use increasing amounts of speech. From the first two-word sentence that appears around eighteen months of age, children begin to form sentences, and their words and babblings fall into patterns. Their speech is imperfect, sometimes clear only to the parent or care giver, but it is speech. It communicates, and the sounds have meaning.

By two and a half years of age, children have doubled their vocabulary, and speech continues in rapid development. By three years of age, children should have nearly 8,000 words at their command, and learn nearly fifty new words each month.

Two and three years olds carry on monologues. No one needs to be near, or listening; they do not care if anyone responds to their speech or not. They just carry on, babbling away, speaking to themselves. Piaget calls this talk *egocentric monologues*. Three and four year olds enjoy talking with one another, although they still use monologue speech. But with more than one child it is now a collective type of monologue. Children seem to have mastered all of the important rules of language by the time they are four.

Five year olds use speech realistically, almost like adults. They are well socialized, speaking and responding to others. Although speech is still far from perfect, children learn new words daily. Sentences increase in length and complexity, and the verbs, pronouns, prepositions, and other parts of speech have been sorted out.

Individual Differences

While the course of language development is similar for all children, individual differences in the rate of development are striking. Some two year olds speak fluently; others, not at all.

Children will learn the language they hear in their home and neighborhood. Some children may enter the preschool without a word of English because another language is used at home. Other children may speak English that differs from standard English. Children growing up in rural New England, Appalachia, and regions of the south and southwest have dialects that differ from those of children growing up in the eastern United States.

Children growing up in lower socioeconomic backgrounds have patterns of language that also differ from children who grow up in middle-class backgrounds (Hess and Shipman 1965). In homes of lower socioeconomic backgrounds, a restricted code is used. Children are told no, few explanations are given for demands, and little language is used to discuss abstract ideas. In upper economic backgrounds, children are encouraged to speak, they are given long explanations for rules, and elaborated patterns of usage of speech are used to discuss abstract ideas (Bernstein 1962).

Research suggests that languages simply differ from one another (Cazden, Baratz, Labov, and Palmer 1971). Children use distinctive regional or cultural language patterns or have developmental differences, but these differences do not mean that one language is better than another, only that the language patterns and usage differ.

Research has also shown that languages are inherently equal in the complexity of their grammatical and logical structure. Each has a highly structured set of rules of sound and syntax, and all languages are used for interpersonal communications. Different cultures may vary in what topics are appropriate to talk about or what words or gestures mean, but all language has the potential to deal with any topic.

The diversity of cultures in America is a strength. Children feel more secure, and the parents, whose words and ways are no longer demeaned, are more positive in their ideas of education for their children when the language they bring to school is respected. This does not mean that children do not learn to use the standard language of school and society, only that great care is taken to preserve their heritage, protect their pride, and recognize their individuality through valuing the language patterns they bring to school.

We now know that chidlren's experiences influence language development. When children come to a preschool they are presented with a great variety of experiences. Each of these experiences is used to expand and extend their language, the major goal of many preschool programs. The language arts—listening, speaking, reading, and writing—promote growth and development. The more experiences children have in preschool programs to speak and listen, to see the value of reading and writing, the better.

THE LANGUAGE ARTS

"There are bound to be words to go with the things and ideas that are to be spoken or thought about" (Davidson 1971, p. 19). Before children can put words with things and ideas, they must have experiences. They must have something to think about and to talk about. Experiences serve as the base for all language arts, for without experiences no symbolic learning can take place.

Everyone needs experiences in order to learn. Think about your first college registration, the first time you traveled to a different country, the first time you faced a group of young children. You may have prepared yourself for the experience by reading what others have written, or you may have gathered some information by discussing the event with others. Nevertheless, until you actually experienced these things for yourself, your knowledge was incomplete, inadequate, and perhaps inaccurate.

The younger the person, the more important are firsthand experiences. As children experience, taking in impressions through the senses, they are building a fund of information with which they begin to form knowledge of the world. With a background of experiences, children can gain some meaning from the language of others.

Experiences alone are not enough to complete children's learning. There must be some connection between the child's experiences and the symbols of language.

> There must be discussion and explanation that bring out the meaning of the objects and situations that have come to her attention. Thus concepts grow, the child acquires a vocabulary and she learns to understand the use of sentences competently. Experience, whether actual or second hand, requires interpretation through language if it is to be accurate and fully understood. (Dawson 1966, p. 27)

Every experience in the preschool involves language, and the purpose of experiences is to make the need for language real and necessary for the child. From the moment the child arrives, language is being used to add meaning, to clarify and expand children's experiences. Teachers build the atmosphere that encourages children to actively experience, an atmosphere that encourages talking, arguing, discussing, listening, and reading about their experiences.

Sometimes it is the teacher who is the talker. The teacher takes center stage and seems to say to the children, "I'm the talker, the entertainer, you're the audience, now listen!" In other schools the teacher seems to say, "Participate, act, experience, and talk, talk, talk—express yourself, use language with your experiences."

Role of the Teacher

Teachers play an important role in fostering growth of the language arts. They set the stage for learning, experiencing, and for language. Teachers will clearly want to identify the goals of their language program by planning carefully to include all of the areas of the language arts: listening, speaking, reading, and writing. Most preschool teachers can identify common goals for their language arts program. These include

- providing experiences that will give meaning to the symbol of language and a reason for using language;
- developing children's vocabulary and their ability to communicate orally with others;
- increasing children's ability to speak in complete sentences;
- developing children's understanding of the relationship between the written and spoken word;
- developing in the children an interest in appreciation of books;
- developing children's ability to listen to the language of others and to comprehend the spoken and written word.

In order to foster these goals, teachers must understand their role. The type of teacher talk and the quality of the talk are critical. "Adults can talk to children in ways which are uniquely beneficial to their language and cognitive development . . . but what counts is the quality of adult/child talk, not just the quantity, and the organizational conditions within which high quality talk is likely to occur" (Cazden 1971, p. 153).

Low level talk is that of giving directions, commands, or routines (Tizard 1972). This kind of teacher talk has been shown to be less effective in fostering children's language than talk that is informational, about something the child is doing, or about a child's past experiences (Tizard 1972).

Shifting the teacher talk away from that of an interviewer, "What is the color of the truck?" to that of a resource person also seems to foster children's language (Cazden 1971). Teachers who ask children questions that call for genuine requests for information, for discussion and reflection, rather than just a specific response, seem to increase children's language.

When adults expand on the ideas children express, they are also fostering speech (Brown and Bellugi 1964). If a child says, "Truck, truck" the adult can respond by saying "Yes, the dump truck is carrying sand," or if a child says "Doggie, doggie," the teacher might respond, "The dog is barking at the kitten over there," reinforcing children's ideas, and at the same time expanding on their ideas, giving them something else to think and then speak about.

Teachers are also in the position of acting as reinforcers of children's talk. It has been found, however, that teachers tend to like reinforcement themselves. Teachers tend to gravitate to those children who are highly verbal. Those who already speak well and fluently seem to attract a teacher's attention more than those children who do not speak as well. Because children with less adequate skills really need the interaction with the teacher, it is important to remember to spend a lot of time with children whose language facility is less adequate than the others.

Listening and Speaking

Children come to school with fairly well developed listening and speaking skills. They will not learn to listen and speak at school, for they have already learned the basic structure of language at home and in the neighborhood. But the school can increase children's listening and speaking skills.

Listening and speaking cannot be separated in a preschool. Someone speaks; the others listen. Oral language and listening go together, and together they build the base for future success in reading and writing.

Children listen for different purposes in a preschool. Sometimes they will listen to receive directions and information; at other times, for pleasure and enjoyment. It is the goal of the teacher to increase children's listening ability from merely hearing the spoken word to gaining meaning and understanding from the words spoken.

Children's speech can also be enhanced and developed in the preschool. Most children love to talk. They enjoy speaking and have plenty to tell others. Yet some are too shy to tell things to others, and there will be some who don't have the language facility to speak at all. Whatever level children are at, the experiences of the school can help them increase vocabulary and skill in oral expression.

SHARING AND DISCUSSIONS

When the classroom is organized to encourage activity and play, children share and discuss their ideas with others constantly. They chat together as they snack, eat lunch, play together at the water or sand table, or make plans for tomorrow's activities. Comfortable with this type of informal sharing of ideas and experiences, children can also be introduced to sharing in a group.

First listening and speaking activities as a group are informal. Perhaps two or three children have gathered to watch the caterpillar crawling along, or those sitting at a table working puzzles will begin a discussion. The teacher asks questions and guides the discussion, adding pieces of information, reflecting on children's ideas, encouraging each to express himself fully.

Other types of more formal sharing and discussion sessions will take place. Perhaps a visitor will come to the class, or the children will wish to share and discuss something with the entire group.

Before children are asked to listen to someone, they need to understand something of what will be expected of them. If a speaker is to visit the class, the teacher might prepare the children by telling them some things they should do when the visitor is there. Reminding them to listen for certain ideas and of the fact that the visitor will talk and they must listen might be helpful. The teacher might have the children dictate questions to ask the visitor or list the things for which they will want to listen. The teacher might tell the children something about the person, and the subject that will be discussed. Reading a book about the topic or giving children some experience that can serve as a base for abstract listening is also helpful and may enable children to reflect on what they are hearing.

When outsiders come to the class, they too, need preparation. You might share with them facts about the children, reminding them that children have short attention spans, will be better able to listen if some prop or picture is shown, and will want to do a lot of talking themselves. The speaker also needs to know what questions the children have and the things they will be listening for.

Opening the day with a show and tell period has been customary in preschools. Too often, however, these sessions end up as bring and brag, with children who have nothing to bring either making something up or stealing something to share with the others. There are some things that need to be shared with the total group. To help the group listen, teachers can prepare they by saying, "Rachel is going to tell you about living in Paraguay. Listen to find out how she . . ." The child who is going to speak to the group also needs help. "What will you tell the children?" is a question that may help the child organize her thoughts and ideas before speaking to the group.

Instead of the usual show and tell, teachers can encourage children to tell others about their experiences in the classroom. Children might tell

1. How they made something, how to play a game, how to do a trick, or how to use a toy.
2. Why the plants died, the fish needs water, or why they will be taking an airplane flight.
3. Where the nurse's office is, the library, or park.
4. What happens at the nurse's office, what something is used for, or what their drawing means to them.

As children speak to others, the skills of listening can be developed. Children can be helped to listen critically and analytically. "What did you find out about———? What else do you need to know? Did the doctor answer all of your questions?"

There are many other activities that help foster listening and speaking skills. Teachers have used telephones, tape recorders, and even television to stimulate children's listening and speaking activities.

Discarded telephones, obtained from the public relations office of the phone company, stimulate children's ability to carry on a conversation. When speaking over a telephone, children must use words that communicate, for the listener cannot see any nonverbal cues to help him understand what the other is saying. Telephones can be placed in the dramatic play area, office area, or other places for children's use.

Some teachers use the demonstration telephones to teach five year olds how to dial the operator for help or to reach Information. One teacher of five year olds had each child learn to dial. After the children mastered the skill, they called their parents at work or home.

Tape recorders, language masters, and listening jacks are all useful in fostering listening and speaking skills. Children could tape record themselves telling a story, singing a song, or reciting a poem. Groups can record and then listen to poems, songs, or chants.

Some teachers have recorded the sounds of the office, cafeteria, play yard, or street and replayed these to the children. Children then identify the sounds on the tape, telling where they occurred. It is fun to keep a recorder on while children are playing in the dramatic play block, or wheel toy areas. Listening to the tape, children will identify their voices and recall the events recorded on the tape.

Teachers have also recorded children's favorite stories, songs, or poems on tape for independent listening. Children can listen to the tapes over and over again. Listening to tape recordings or records requires greater listening skills on the part of the children than listening to a person speak. When someone is speaking there is eye contact and a person to whom to relate. When listening to a record or recording, there is only the voice.

As children are known to view over forty hours of television a week, it seems as if this experience should also be used by teachers to foster the goals of the program in the area of language arts. Teachers might spot shows of interest and value to the children and forward notes home, recommending these to parents as possible television selections. If a documentary about the desert will be on television during children's viewing hours, the teacher might suggest that the children view the show, if possible. The teacher can then follow up the viewing by having the children plant a desert garden, introducing some reptiles, or discussing what it might be like to live on a desert. Reference books, films, and filmstrips might extend children's ideas of desert.

At times television can even be used in the classroom, not as a group listening activity, but to observe special events or occurrences. This does not mean that children would watch an entire presidential address, parade, or space shot, but the group could gather to get a sense of the current event by viewing for a few moments.

When children watch a lot of television, they need to develop skills of critical viewing. Teachers, as they hear the children discussing various shows, might ask, "Do you really think that could happen?" "Was that a real show or pretend?" "Why do you think that happened?"

Listening and speaking activities can be used to enhance the entire curriculum. Science, math, even traffic safety, can be explored through listening and speaking activities. To increase children's knowledge of the physical world, take them on a field trip in the school building to identify all of the sounds they hear near the office, cafeteria, or street. Ask them to examine the different sounds their feet make as the surfaces of the school floor and play yard change. Outdoors children might try to find ways of making an interesting sound, or they can experiment with the quickest way to get a message across the field. Is it through signalling, shouting, or using a speaking tube (a length of garden hose with funnels attached at each end)? (Science 5/13, 1977, pp. 25–26).

At other times children might try to find places within the school, or play yard where they can produce echoes. At the street corner, while learning about traffic safety, they can try to identify whether cars are approaching or going away from them, through listening. Returning to the classroom, children can talk about their listening experiences and collect words to describe sounds. For example they might dictate a book or class chart about:

> Sounds in the middle of the field.
> Sounds at night.
> Sounds of my school.
> I like noise.
> Near the street.
> At the swimming pool (Science 5/13, 1977, p. 25)

As listening and speaking take place constantly, it is up to the teacher to evaluate children's progress on a continual basis. Teachers will know that their program in the language arts is effective if children are able to

1. Initiate conversations with adults and peers, use all parts of speech, speak in complete sentences, and use new vocabulary;
2. Use words that have been introduced in school, use words with feeling, expression, and appropriate voice modulation;
3. Use a telephone;
4. Take part as both listener, speaker, and discussant in group sharing sessions;
5. Attend to the speech of others, reflect on the speech, and repeat the main ideas.

Literature

"The frosting on the cake" (Broman 1975, p. 323) of the language arts is children's literature. Reading to children or being read to remains one of the greatest pleasures of life. Nothing compares to the quiet, thoughtful wonder of children listening to *Dawn* by Uri Shulevitz, or the giggling fun, tickle-to-the-toes delight of listening to just one more *Curious George* story.

Children's literature offers children much more than "frosting." It serves many functions. Literature introduces children to new vocabulary, and the opportunity to listen to language used to lift spirits and expand thinking. As children listen to stories that are well told, or read, they are developing attentive listening skills, and when they discuss the story together, they develop skills of critical and evaluative listening.

By discussing stories and reliving them through play, children's speaking abilities are fostered. The vocabulary they learn by listening to their favorite story is repeated as it applies to their own activities. One three year old told another, whose tricycle was stuck in the sand, "Exert yourself"—repeating the phrase used by the sparrows in *Peter Rabbit*, who implored Peter to exert himself and escape from the tangles of the blueberry net.

Reading literature to children, however, does much more than simply increase vocabulary and listening skills. It expands their life. Through literature children can learn, at least vicariously, what it might be like to live on a houseboat in China or to get a new umbrella for your birthday.

Literature offers children insights into their own behavior. Things, ideas, people, and events not present in a child's own life are presented. The way people handle their own behaviors and feelings in the stories gives children an awareness of the range of human emotions.

When children identify with a character in a story, they can vent their own emotions and gain insights into their own feelings. They can feel very angry when reflecting over the injustice of being sent to bed without supper as Max was in *Where the Wild Things Are*, and they can feel just as brave as Max as they listen to him commanding the wild things to "Be Still!" The safety and warmth that come from listening to *The Bundle Book* or to *Runaway Bunny*, serve as a security blanket for children whose needs for emotional support are great.

Appreciating Literature

One goal of every preschool should be to foster children's appreciation of literature. Leaving preschool, each child should be driven by a desire to read books, to use books, to love books. Appreciation means that children will exhibit a heightened interest in books—they will go to books, choosing books over other activities, and ask for books to be read to them. It also means that children will recognize books—"Hey, here's another book by Sally and Jane's daddy" and develop a sensitive awareness to books.

HEIGHTENED INTEREST

Children who appreciate literature begin to seek books as a resource for living; they can relate their feelings and imaginative responses to the vicarious ones found in books. Incorporating literature into every content area, coordinating it with each experience, teachers foster the understanding that literature is invaluable as a resource for living. Incorporating literature into every content area, coordinating it with each experience, teachers foster the realization that literature brings a depth and range of meaning into each learning experience, and is invaluable to full participation in life. Whatever the content area, there is a contribution a book can bring. Books offer children vicarious experiences and insights into a fuller range of meaning, while serving to unify learning experiences. Children who are developing a heightened interest in books will seek out books about airplanes and airports as they construct an airport with blocks; those children interested in the ant hill on the playground will demand reference materials and books on ants.

RECOGNITION OF BOOKS

An appreciative child will begin to differentiate between books, selecting one over another, developing definite preferences for specific types of literature. When children have had exposure to many books they will soon begin to say, "Where's that riddle book?. . . I want some fun," or "I wanted this book because it makes me feel good." They will show their enjoyment of books by responding with interest, laughter, and feeling as stories are read to them.

Children also give recognition to specific works and authors. As teachers read to children they might tell them the name of the person who wrote the book and something about that person. "Robert McClosky is Sal and little Jane's father; he wrote this book about his daughters." Children might even dictate thank you letters to favorite authors, and perhaps receive a reply.

Recognition of books also develops as children become authors themselves. Individual or group stories are recorded by the teacher. Booklets are duplicated and forwarded to children and families to enjoy. What a marvelous sense of accomplishment and recognition occurs in a child when the teacher reads the book the child has written or dictated to the other children!

SENSITIVE AWARENESS

Sensitive awareness is one characteristic of appreciation (Dewey 1916). Dewey believed that appreciation can only result as children directly experience the sense of a thing. Direct experiences, designed to develop children's awareness of senses, and opportunities for children to respond directly to sensory impressions are essential in fostering the appreciation of literature. Literature itself offers the possibilities of many sensory responses and provides the vehicle for children's direct experiences.

You can taste marmalade and butter to see if the king used good judgment in A.A. Milne's *The King's Breakfast*. And how can children really appreciate *The Biggest Bear* if they have not tasted for themselves the overpowering, throat-swelling sweetness of maple sugar candy? Until you yourself have rolled in the snow and saved a snowball for a later day, how can you really identify with or appreciate Keats's *The Snowy Day*?

Other stories demand different types of experiences. You might march to Milne's "Buckingham Palace" or skip to a story of "Skip to My Lou." Acting out stories gives children one more opportunity to directly experience a story. When children take on the role of a character in a story, they employ their entire bodies and all of their creative imagination to interpret the meaning of the story for themselves.

THE TEACHER

Appreciation of children's literature is directly related to the teacher's attitudes toward books. Teachers who use a book to prop up an uneven table leg or for a pillow in the doll's bed are showing disregard for books. Shabby and torn books should be replaced or repaired. Teachers who value literature themselves, and want children to value books, never exile a child to the library area as a punishment or as a means of stopping a highly active child from boisterous play.

The library area itself should be a place of beauty. This ever-changing area of the room can be a place of varied activities. Magic carpet squares, or pillows can invite children to sit awhile and browse. Flowers, puppets, flannel boards, story props, and other real life objects can reflect the current interests of the children and become a part of the library corner or area.

Story time is also important. Stories should be thoughtfully chosen for children. They are not just grabbed and read because "I don't know what else to do with this group!" or because "it's time for a story, you need calming down." Children quickly sense when stories are used for fillers and begin to develop the attitude that literature is not very important in and of itself, but is only useful when there is nothing better to do.

Selecting Literature

It is important to select books that meet children's interests, needs, and their level of maturity. There is a wide range of literature available, with many thousands of books being published each year. Only a handful, however, prove to be worthy of young children's attention. It is up to the teacher to make wise selections.

It is good to begin with books that offer children something familiar. This does not mean that a book such as *The Story of Ping* is inappropriate because it takes place on a houseboat in China, rather, it means that teachers look for books that offer children portrayals of human emotions to which they can relate. Perhaps the very popularity of *The Story of Ping* is based on just that—everyone, the world over, in any kind of house, can identify with the boy on the houseboat who let Ping return to his family, or with Ping, who was lost and then happily reunited with his family.

Books that are simple and those that have repetitive phrases are popular with very young children. Mitchell (1950) believed that children did not need fanciful tales and were more interested in stories that dealt with their everyday life. Perhaps this is, in part, because of the ability of children to identify with stories about things they are familiar with, but also because children need help in understanding the complexities of their world. Informational books offer children help in dealing with everyday topics whether about getting dressed, growing up, a new baby, or going to bed at night.

A wide variety of books is also necessary. No one wants to keep children at the same level. Books can expose children to events, things, and people that are far from them. Children also need single concept books, poetry, and fiction.

Careful selection of children's literature also means that teachers screen books for racial, ethnic, and other stereotypes. Sometimes one believes it is impossible to find any one book completely free of all racist, sexist, or ageist stereotypes. Yet children can be exposed to a variety of books, those portraying minority members, women, and elderly persons in a variety of roles and situations. This means giving children access to a variety of books about different people. From this selection of books, children should have the opportunity to develop nonstereotypic ideas of older persons, women, and people of all cultures, backgrounds, and races.

Reading to Children

Literature can be presented to children in many different ways. Sometimes children will be introduced to the literature of poetry in a spontaneous manner. A number of flies in the room might precipitate a teacher's saying, "Flies walk on the ceilings and straight up all the walls," introducing children to the poetry of Dorothy Aldis. Or someone else might begin the chant, "Hundreds of cats, thousands of cats," from Gag's *Millions of Cats*. In addition to these informal sharings of literature, teachers plan several times during each day for reading to children.

These are times that are sacred. Nothing is permitted to interfere with them. Perhaps there is even a special place—the story corner, the play yard, the story tree—reserved for reading stories. A story circle, blanket, or even a ribbon placed in a circle, can set the special tone for story reading.

Before reading, or telling a story to children, you must be very familiar with the story. You will want to be familiar with the story so you will be able to give emphasis to the high interest points and use voice modulation and control to enhance parts of the story. Some teachers read the story over a tape recorder so they can hear themselves and critique their techniques. Others read the story to their friends or relatives and get their reaction.

Sometimes the story will be read to the entire group of children. At other times, especially when working with children four and under, the story will be read to a small group, gathered around or on the teacher. When reading to the entire group, teachers sit in front of the children, at their level, holding the book in a way that permits children to see the illustrations.

Advance organizers might be given. You can simply say to children, "This is a story about———, or listen for———." At other times props can be used as advance organizers. A caterpillar might be observed before reading a book about butterflies, or a branding iron shown prior to reading a book on cowboys. Sometimes a riddle or question can be posed to stimulate children's interest in the book.

As the book is read to the children, permit them to interrupt, and give them time to really look at the pictures. Do not be afraid to repeat the story. Reading the same book over and over again gives children the opportunity to achieve mastery over it, to know the book as their own. A love of literature comes only after books are totally familiar to children.

Telling stories is another way to present literature to children. Children must perfect their listening skills when a story is told; and teachers, their ability to communicate orally with children. When a story is told, without a book, children must respond directly to the spoken word, without the help of illustrations or pictures.

Following Up

Much of the value of literature lies in the follow-up activities that take place after the reading or telling of a story. Once children know a story as their own, they should be able to give expression to their ideas. Only as children bring their own expression to the story will it become a part of them. Creative dramatics, puppets, and dramatic play, as well as art and musical expression, permit children to bring meaning to the literature they have heard.

Creative dramatics does not just happen with young children. They need many beginning experiences with creative dramatics before they will be able to act out an entire story. Sometimes the entire class or a small group of children can act out a poem or story using pantomime. "Here We Go Round the Mulberry Bush," with children taking turns acting out different actions, "This is the way we brush our teeth," or "Did you Ever See a Lassie?" gives children practice with pantomime.

Sometimes all of the children will act out a nursery rhyme with each child choosing to be either Jack or Jill. Or each will act out the role of Little Nancy Etticoat. Or some can be horses and the others the king's men, as the entire group tries to put Humpty Dumpty together again. The teacher reads the poem or nursery rhyme as the children act out the roles they have chosen.

From these beginnings children can take on the roles of characters in the stories they hear. In *Caps for Sale*, one child can call out the words of the salesperson as the others act out the roles of the monkeys. Favorite folk tales, *The Three Pigs, Three Billy Goats Gruff*, are other good stories to introduce children to creative dramatics.

When children act out stories, a teacher may serve as the narrator, holding the play together, "Now the wolf comes in, what does he say?" or prompt the children to recall other parts of the story.

Puppets are another way children can take a part in creative dramatics. The puppet need be nothing more than a sock pushed on a child's hand, a paper bag, or a paper cut-out figure mounted on a popsicle stick. The stage—a table turned on its side—lets children hide while acting with the puppet.

Puppets can be used for other purposes. With a puppet, and the safety of the stage to hide behind, the shy child might tell the others how she walks to school, what her brothers and sisters do, things she did on vacation, or the way to cross the street. Puppet shows can be put on for other children or another class to enjoy. Or they can just be one activity children can select during free play time.

Children give meaning and expression to the literature they have heard in other ways. They can draw, paint, or construct representations of favorite stories, or parts of a story, and they can use flannel board cutouts to retell the story to one another.

In Summary

A primary goal of all preschool education is to foster children's language. The entire day, whether in a day care center, kindergarten, nursery school, or Head Start program is directed at increasing children's ability to use and understand language in a manner that respects regional, cultural, and socio-economic differences in family backgrounds.

Language begins with experiences. When a preschool program is based on activities and experiences, children have feelings and ideas to express and then communicate with others. Wondering over a moth emerging from a co-coon, building a police car out of boxes and blocks together, or listening to the fire fighter tell about her work, are examples of experiences that give children a common base for listening and speaking.

To evaluate your program in language arts you might ask yourself:

• Do I establish an atmosphere that encourages children not only to speak but also to listen to one another? Do I take care in talking with children, never being condescending, but using exact, descriptive terminology? Do I take the time to seriously listen to all children?

• What things are in the room for children to wonder over and then talk about? Are there clocks to take apart, puzzles to put together, eggs that may hatch?

• Is there a special time each day set aside just for the enjoyment of poetry and stories? Do I encourage children to use books by themselves, with others, or arrange for them to take books home?

• What special activities do I plan each day to foster children's listening and speaking? A puppet show, discussion or conversation?

• Are there spaces in the room where children can engage in serious conversation together? A quiet area at the library corner, or a table and chairs set aside by a screen for quiet conversation?

READING

"But do you teach them to read?" is a frequently heard question as parents try to decide in which preschool they should enroll their child. Today many more parents believe that children are ready to read upon entrance in a preschool program; they feel that their children have had many more experiences by the time they enter a preschool or kindergarten program than did children of former generations. Children today have had opportunities to play with friends, they have traveled and had many enriching experiences in their own homes. What's more, they have even learned the alphabet and numbers from watching television.

Educators, like parents, are also asking the question, when should children be introduced to formal reading? Certainly the past decades, focusing on the cognitive growth of the child, fostered concern for beginning reading instruction prior to the first grade. Bruner's statement in *The Process of Education* (1962) "Any subject can be taught effectively in some intellectually honest form to any child at any stage of development," and the work of Bloom, *Stability and Change in Human Characteristics* (1964), postulating that the first four years of a child's life are most critical for later intellectual growth, "offered a new conception of young children's capacity for learning, along with persistent reminders about the critical importance of an intellectually stimulating early environment" (Durkin 1976, p. 18).

In spite of all of the interest in the question of when children should be taught to read, there is little evidence that gives a definite answer. Some studies show that early reading instruction is effective; yet others suggest that reading should not be taught until children are much older, around seven or eight years of age.

One of the more prominent of the studies suggesting that early reading instruction is effective is the Denver Kindergarten Experiment (McKee, 1966). Four thousand children were included in this study which assessed the success of teaching kindergarten children to read. The study concluded that five year olds, who were taught to read in kindergarten, were, at the end of first grade, superior to children not taught to read in kindergarten. Children who were taught to read in kindergarten did not have greater emotional disturbances, or visual deficiencies than children who were not taught to read early. This led to the conclusion that five year olds are not handicapped by early exposure to the types of reading activities introduced by the experiment.

Another study followed through to the third grade children who had begun to read before entering the first grade (Durkin 1976). The children who had learned to read during the preschool years maintained their reading gains and were not hindered in academic or emotional achievement in later years.

There are those, however, who believe that reading instruction, when started too early, can actually harm children. "The risks of delaying instruction too long seem much less than the possible disadvantages of forcing instruction

274

on a child who is still far from his optimal readiness for the subject of instruction"
(Jensen 1969, p. 15).

When children are forced to read before they are physically or mentally
ready, two kinds of adverse effects could take place.

1. Children may learn the subject matter or skills by means of cognitive structures
   they have, but because these structures are not complete, and are less optimal
   than adult structures, the learning is much less efficient. Children may be able
   to repeat facts, or recall words and numbers as a parrot would by means of rote
   memory, but they will have no ability to transfer this learning to later learning.
2. The second kind of adverse effect of beginning instruction in any subject before
   the child is ready is referred to as the *turning off* effect. "This amounts to an
   increasing inhibition of the very behaviors that promote learning, and I believe
   it becomes so extreme that it may eventually prevent the child from learning
   even those things for which he is not lacking in readiness" (Jensen 1969, p. 10).

Many school learning problems could be prevented, according to Jensen,
if teachers paid more attention to readiness during the primary grades. It is
during the preschool and primary years that children's learning, due to a lack
of readiness, is most easily turned off through extinction.

> The high rate of reading failures and other deficiencies in basic scholastic
> skills found among high school graduates in groups called disadvantaged
> can hardly be explained in terms of deficiencies in basic learning abilities.
> It would seem necessary to invoke turn-off mechanisms at some early stage
> of their school to account for some of their marked educational deficiencies."
> (Jensen 1969, p. 16)

Readiness to Read

If a child's readiness for formal instruction appears to be a critical factor
in early reading instruction, then attention must be focused on the concept of
readiness. There are at least two ways of thinking about readiness. The first
idea of readiness is that of *maturational* or *growth* readiness. The readiness
of a child to learn anything—climbing steps, smiling, talking, walking, as well
as reading—is based on the child's own internal physiological mechanisms and
his sequential growth. Certain organized patterns of growth of neural structures
must occur before teaching or enriching experiences can effectively contribute
to development (Gesell and Ilg 1974).

The other idea of readiness sees learning as the major factor. The *cumulative learning* theory suggests that all human brains have the capacity for
acquiring stimulus-response connections or habits. Mental development is
viewed as the learning of an ordered set of capabilities in some hierarchical or
progressive fashion, making for increasing skills in stimulus-response differ-
entiation, recall of previously learned response, and generalization of transfer
of learning (Jensen 1969). Both theories, the cumulative learning theory and
the maturational theory of readiness, recognize that there are some things,

such as the growth of the eyes and brain, or physical growth, that cannot be influenced by teaching. These things—ability to sit on a chair, hold a book, focus the eyes on words—must wait for children's growth and development.

There are other things, however, that can be influenced by teaching. If the skill of reading is analyzed and broken into hierarchies, then teachers can identify all of the subskills children need to develop to acquire the skill of reading (Gagné 1965).

It has been demonstrated that children, in order to master the skill of learning to read, must have mastery over oral and aural language. They will have to be able to listen to and understand spoken language and be able to speak language before they will be able to read. In order to read with comprehension, children also need to be able to recognize written words, understand their meanings, and be able to visualize, criticize, and think about what other people have written.

LANGUAGE FACILITY IN LISTENING AND SPEAKING

"Interrelationships among the different aspects of language are a reminder to teachers that the ability to read does not sprout in a vacuum; it grows out of prior abilities to listen and speak" (Durkin 1970, p. 6). Children will have larger listening vocabularies than speaking vocabularies, and they will be able to understand the meaning of more words than they can say, but the larger their listening and speaking vocabulary, the greater the likelihood of success in reading.

Effective listening and speaking skills are the goals of all preschool programs. They provide the basis for reading readiness activities. Without opportunities for listening, speaking, and seeing the relationship between the spoken and written word, children will have a difficult time learning to read. All preschool programs must provide children with opportunities to:

- talk and dictate stories and experiences, giving depth of meaning to their artwork, constructions, and activities.
- listen, view, discuss, make books, and report on their experiences in the social studies, science, and quantitative aspects of the program.
- plan together, learn new words as well as the meanings of words known to them, and carefully listen to songs, sing songs, and play word games.
- think about what they see, hear, and do, and be able to think critically about what others say, dictate, and write (Van Allen 1961 p. 13).

Auditory Discrimination. Auditory discrimination is one of the essentials of listening skills. Some children will enter a preschool program with a fine sense of listening. They love the sounds of words and will giggle for hours over some silly rhyme someone has chanced upon, "Silly, filly, dilly, nilly, there goes Billy. . . ." Over and over they will remember the rhyme, giggling, laughing, snickering over their wonderful word joke.

Some children will recognize that words can sound alike or begin alike. "Hey, her name begins just like mine, listen, Shelly, Sheri . . . Did you hear it?" Most five year olds have mastered the ability to distinguish between sounds in words, but some children, perhaps those from non-English-speaking homes, may have difficulty in focusing on differences between sounds of English words. All children, however, can participate in games and activities designed to increase their ability to hear similarities and differences. Some activities used to foster auditory discrimination are

1. Listening games in which children identify the two words that begin alike, have the same rhyming sounds, or end alike. It is best to work with individual children or small groups and to use one word, followed by two or three other words, asking children to clap when they hear the word that either begins, ends, or rhymes with the first word spoken.

   This game can be played during those transition times when you are waiting for the bus to arrive, the doctor to come, or for your turn to enter the cafeteria. Short, sometimes spontaneous, taking just a few minutes, this kind of game can focus children's attention to the sounds of words.

2. Reading plenty of nursery rhymes, encouraging children to learn them, to sing and act them. When children have a repertoire of numbers of poems and nursery rhymes, you can begin, "Hippety hop, to the barber . . ." leaving out the last word. Then follow up with "Hippety hop, I just can't . . ." for the children to fill in with another rhyming word.

3. Clapping or beating on a drum the number of syllables in children's names. Develop until children can recognize their first, then their first and last, names when the syllables are clapped.

4. Playing I Spy. "I spy something that begins with the same sound as Roberta. I spy something that sounds just like block. It is round, you tell time with it, what is it?" Children take turns asking others what they spy.

Oral Language Facility. Oral language and beginning reading are related, but oral language facility is also significantly related to reading achievement in the upper grades (Wilson and Hall 1972). Children need to be familiar with a large number of words in order to succeed at reading. They need to understand that words represent places, things, and people; that some words are used to represent movements; and that others describe things and movements. In addition, children also need to understand the meaning of the functors—connecting words.

Even the simple understanding that each child and each adult in the school has his own name can help prepare children for reading. You can begin by calling all children and others in the school by their names and encouraging children to do the same. Rather than answering to "Teacher, teacher," tell children your name.

When children have learned one another's names, they can begin to focus on last names and nicknames. It is also important for children to realize that their mothers and fathers have names. As homework have the children ask their parents what their names are and find out if they have nicknames. Often children's last names open up a whole exploration of cultural heritages. A McCormick, Saracho, or Smyanski may be able to tell the meaning of his name, and stories of his heritage.

Children should be familiar with the names of things, objects, and places, as well as people. They could take a look at the things in the room and try to figure out why the things are named as they are. What is a mobile? You and the children have constructed one, but what does the word mean? Where did it come from? What else do you know that is mobile? This same kind of exploration might be done with other things in the room, as children's interests and maturity level permit. Are they ready to think about the words aquarium, terrarium, astronaut, or automobile and trace their meanings?

The story *Brown Bear, Brown Bear, What Do You See?* by Bill Martin (1969) is an excellent book to use to introduce children to the names of things in the school and neighborhood. After children have enjoyed the animals and colors in the book and have repeated the phrases over and over, they can play the game with the names of things in the room.

You start by saying, "Children, children what do you see? I see an air vent looking at me," and point to the air vent. Taking turns, you and the children can name all of the other things in the room. You might include such things as the venetian blinds, the thermostat, and linoleum tile, as well as more common things, such as a table top, desk, window, or curtain. The game can be continued outside where you can point out trees, cars, street lights, and plants.

Verbs, the movement words, are accented as children explore all of the ways they themselves can move. Movement exploration activities can extend children's speaking vocabularies as they find out how many ways they can jump, glide, slide, climb, where they can move, and the quality of their movements.

Descriptive words are often lacking in children's vocabularies. Teachers can introduce children to adverbs and adjectives by describing things to children in increasingly descriptive, discriminating ways. Rather than labeling a bottle as big or little as children play with sand or water, describe it accurately, "Use the wide-mouthed jar," or "Take the tall, narrow container." You can use descriptive words as children dress, "Susan's boots are buckle boots," "Your coat is soft," "This scarf is fluffy."

As children have experiences such as a trip to the park, have them describe the things they have observed. "How did we walk to the park?" Writing the words on a list the teacher may record, We walked quickly, carefully, slowly. At the park we saw squirrels. The squirrels were frisky, quick, furry, funny, jumpy, brown.

Nouns and verbs, adjectives and adverbs are the content words of the language. But children also need to understand the meaning of the words that are called functors: the prepositions in, on, under, before, after, and the conjunctions and, but, when, or, because. It is hard for children to understand these words if they have never actually experienced them. How can a child understand the word *or* if she has never been given a choice between one thing and another? Teachers need to be certain that children experience the functors by asking them, many times, for many different purposes, "Do you want this or that?" They also need to experience the other functors, in connection with their experiences. "*Since* it's raining we'll . . . *although* we planned a picnic . . . *if* the weather . . . *after* we eat . . . Wash your hands *because* . . . or put the blocks *on* . . ."

You can explore children's understandings of these words by playing games. Have the children place an object, perhaps a toy dog or doll, in, under, behind, or in front of another object.

AN UNDERSTANDING OF THE RELATIONSHIP BETWEEN THE SPOKEN AND PRINTED WORD

Auditory discrimination and the ability to express ideas with words are but two of the prerequisite skills for reading. Children must also be able to connect the spoken word with the printed word. A teacher knows children have made this connection when she asks, "Do you have time to take dictation now, I have a story that needs writing so it won't be forgotten."

From the very first day of school, children should be encouraged to express their ideas, dreams, and thoughts, not only through song, dance, and art, but also through words. As they express these ideas, teachers write them down. Teachers can begin the process by writing children's names on their cubbies, artwork, and other places in the room. Writing can be added to children's play activities. Gradually, as teachers observe children at play, they add signs and other writing to enhance the play. A sign added to the block building, "This is the airport." Or a sign is made for the children playing store, "Cookies for Sale." "The teacher's continuous use of the written word is one of the most important stimuli she provides. This tool, the written word, must be used abundantly in our classrooms with young children" (Hymes 1974, p. 98).

Many opportunities for writing in the preschool occur naturally. Teachers write notes to themselves, "I'll put that on the board so I won't forget," or to the children, "This note is for you, so you won't forget to get ready to leave early," or "Olivia's mother is coming early today." Teachers also need to let children see them writing notes to other teachers, parents, and using writing for other functions—recording attendance, keeping records, and communicating information.

Four and five year olds may be ready to begin dictating stories to explain their artwork or their own stories. Following a trip to the zoo, or some other experience, children will dictate their own stories about the trip. These can be put into a booklet called "At the Zoo" or "In My Neighborhood."

When children share in a common experience—perhaps going to the grocery store, listening to a visiting fire fighter, or raising baby chicks, the need for writing becomes greater. They may need to write an invitation to the visiting person or a letter asking if they can observe at the store on a given day. Following the experience, a thank you note and stories describing the experience can be dictated. The dictation might be written on large charts, so children can actually see their words being translated into written form.

The teacher who wants children to make the connection between the spoken and written word will act as a secretary, taking dictation. He will make lists for the children as they describe their experiences, or things they want to find out about, and will record the things they have said, "I like the way you said that, I'm going to write it, so it won't be forgotten."

Many projects will demand writing. A recipe for making jam, popcorn, or butter is written. It is not the intent of these charts and recipes to teach children to read, only to see that there is a relationship established between the spoken and written words. Records of daily activities can also be kept. A record of "Our Garden," with words illustrated by pictures of the progress and sequence of keeping a garden; a record of "Our Playhouse," describing the events that led to the completion of the house; or "Our Chickens," recording the events leading to the hatching of eggs, lets children see the need for written language.

News items—a new baby in the family, new shoes, a visit from the nurse, or a child moving—are written on a board or chart. The story will be read to the children as a news item, something that will be of interest for them to know. Sometimes teachers can write the news on the board before children arrive and observe the children trying to decipher the news for the day. "I'll bet it's about the nurse, you know she's coming today."

Children may dictate diaries of their own, recording accounts of their pets, their day at school, or experiences at home. They may be able to dictate poems, stories, or letters to their parents for special occasions. Children sense the importance of their dictation when teachers type their words. Typing letters to parents or greeting cards adds to the experience.

Five year olds might enjoy dictating riddles that can later be read to the group for solving. Plans for a party, for the day, or for any event can be written as children dictate their ideas to the teacher.

Using every opportunity to write spoken words builds the understanding that

- what children think about they can say,
- what they say can be written or dictated,
- what has been written can be read, and
- children can read what others have written (R. Van Allen 1961, p. 6).

This experience, called the *language experience approach* to reading, gives children the chance to share their ideas and experiences with others, and it develops their ability to tell or illustrate their experiences, clarifying them as they communicate with others. As children discuss group experiences they interact with one another and see that what they say can be written and then read back to them.

When children dictate a story of their trip to grandmother's, it gives them an opportunity to organize their thinking so it can be shared with others. They must think about their experiences as they recall the details. They must select those details that are important to share with others. This forces them to organize their thinking and fosters effective communication.

Making books, and having people read these books to others, lets children see that reading is speech written down. And through all the activities, children develop an awareness of the purposes of language.

THE ABILITY TO RECOGNIZE THE WRITTEN WORD, TO DECODE SYMBOLS, WHILE RELATING THESE TO THE SPOKEN WORD

"In the pre-reading period, provision for visual discrimination training is a major responsibility of the teacher" (Wilson and Hall 1972, p. 105). In order to be able to read, children will need to be able to visually discriminate between letter and word forms. Although there is nothing a teacher can do that will help children's eyes mature more quickly, there are activities that have proven useful in helping children to develop the ability to discriminate between letter and word forms. Children can be provided with

1. Puzzles, beginning with simple three-piece puzzles, progressing to multipieced puzzles. An assortment of puzzles of different levels of difficulty should be present to meet the needs of individual children.
2. Pegboards and pegs, as well as cards with sample designs printed on them, for children to copy. The pegboards can be used with or without cards, but when cards are used, the designs should range from simple to complex.
3. Shape, lotto, bingo, and matching games. Beginning with picture lotto and matching shapes, children can progress to playing with lotto games that require matching of numerals, letters, or other symbols.
4. Card games with numbers, letters, or pictures. Children match the two that are alike or make up their own games.
5. Sets of pictures cut from magazines and mounted on cardboard, with parts of the pictures missing. Children try to identify the missing part.
6. Pictures cut from activity books and mounted on cardboard with things hidden in the picture. Children try to find all of the animals, or whatever, hidden within the picture.

Teachers can check children's ability to discriminate between pictures, symbols, or letter and word forms by using old workbooks or reading readiness books, or by making up their own games. They can give children a picture of a group of letters and ask them to point to all of those that are the same or put children's printed names with a group of others and ask them to pick out their own names. Using old workbook pages, teachers can ask children to mark the letters that are the same, the picture that is different from the others, or to find the two designs that are alike.

THE ABILITY TO UNDERSTAND THE MEANING OF THE WORDS, TO THINK, VISUALIZE AND CRITIQUE WHAT AN AUTHOR HAS WRITTEN

Parents sometimes comment, "I sure hope she won't be bored in your preschool, you know she's reading." There are some preschool children in every group who will be able to recognize an advertising slogan, different brands of cereals, or read a few words. Yet even these children, if they cannot

The written word.

think about the meaning of the words, are not reading. Without comprehension, reading is not taking place.

The process of comprehending what an author has written involves a number of related mental abilities rather than a single mental process. Comprehension suggests at least three different, but related, mental abilities. First, children must be able to literally understand what an author has written, then they must be able to interpret the author's ideas, and finally they must be able to solve problems, critique the writing, make judgments, and evaluate the author's ideas.

Literal Understanding. In connection with children's own experiences with stories they have heard, films they have viewed, or television programs they have watched, teachers can build children's ability to understand what others have written. After a story, a talk by a visitor, or a child's report, teachers might ask children to recall the details of the event. "What was the name of the girl in this story?" "What did she do?" "What did the fire fighter tell us?"

The main ideas of the story or discussion could be recalled. "What do you remember from the fire fighter's talk?" "What do you think this story tells us?"

All of children's experiences with language will aid them in developing the ability to understand words. As they listen and respond to others and discuss common experiences, they are developing the ability to bring meaning to a sizable number of words.

282

Interpretative Understanding. For children to interpret an author's ideas, they must be able to think about what a person has written and reflect on these ideas. To be able to interpret, children must think about what they have heard or read in terms of their own experiences and ideas. The child must be able to mentally manipulate the ideas and information at a cognitive level. Interpretation means children will be able to modify the content of a story, analyze the story, reconstruct and infer relationships from the story, and predict outcomes. They should be able to estimate and determine implications of the message of the story. In order for children to develop interpretative thinking skills, teachers might

1. Ask children to tell a story they have heard, in their own words.
2. Have children paint, draw, or construct the story using art media, or act the story using puppets, dance, or music.
3. Suggest that children draw a picture that would give the story a different ending or to pick a new name for the story.

Children's ability to interpret what others have written or said will depend on the maturity of their mental structures. Their thinking abilities will be greatly influenced by the background of experiences they have had, as well as their own understanding of spoken and written words.

Problem Solving, Critical Thinking. Finally, children will develop the ability to read critically and to make independent judgments about what they have read. Critical thinking and problem-solving abilities begin as children are given many decisions to make. They are able to decide for themselves who they will play with, how much they will eat, and what they will play. Children who have a background in making decisions, in judging the merits of one thing over another, are ready to make judgments about the things they are told and the things that are read to them.

Following a story, teachers can ask children to tell which part they liked the best, and why, or to illustrate their favorite character with some art material. Children could tell which part of the story they thought was the funniest, that frightened them the most, or the part they did not like at all.

Children should also be able to challenge what others have written or illustrated. "Do you think all older people act as helpless as the woman in this story?" "Do you know any older women who do not act this way?" When children are presented with stereotypes in the materials of the school, teachers must challenge these to stretch the children's thinking.

Reading two versions of the same story permits children to evaluate and make judgments about what people have written. Two different versions of the story, "The Gingerbread Boy," let children make comparisons, decide which version they like the best, and introduces the concept that there are many different ways people can express the same idea.

Handwriting

Handwriting is as individual as a fingerprint. Everyone accepts the fact that adults have individualistic styles, manners, and ways of writing. Authorities discriminate between samples of handwriting, and people are convicted or freed on the basis of a sample of their handwriting. Many teachers seem to accept the fact that adults have personalized ways of writing, yet fail to permit children the same privilege. "Traditionally, handwriting instruction has been taught to the entire class, and has been the last of the areas of language arts to become individualized" (Barbe and Lucas 1974, p. 209).

In the preschool, the teaching of handwriting must be an individualized activity. Although studies show that children under the age of four are interested in the writing process and even attempt to write by themselves (Durkin 1976), not every young child will be interested in writing, or will be able to write at the same time as others in the class.

Yet most children do have a natural interest in handwriting. They eagerly squiggle writing in discarded record or receipt books and scribble a letter to include with the one their mother has written to grandmother. They mark on a paper and call it their list to Santa, or squiggle lines on a drawing and tell their teacher, "This is my name; this says, Zelda had baby kittens, and here are her kittens."

Readiness for Writing

A lot of the activities of the preschool help prepare children for writing. Many experiences are planned to strengthen the muscles children will use in writing and to help them gain control over the tools of writing. All of the paper, crayons, paints, scissors, small blocks, pegboards, fingerpaints, chalk, and pencils found in the preschool give children experiences in practicing and developing control over materials and muscles used in writing. When children have not had a background of experiences with these materials at home or in a preschool, Durkin (1976) recommends that even first grade children be given the opportunity to scribble with crayons and paper "to get a feel for these materials and to experience pencil power" (p. 142).

Once children achieve this pencil power, either in preschool or the first grade, their scribbling and drawing can be channeled into readiness experiences for writing. Preschool children who have had plenty of experiences with all of the art materials, with drawing and painting, may be introduced to the idea that papers have a top and a bottom. When children ask for their name or the story of their painting to be written on paper, teachers can introduce them to the idea that writing moves from the left side of the paper to the right. In this way you will expose children to the fact they will read and write from left to right.

As children draw and paint, they are using all of the strokes of writing. They draw circles, ovals, straight and slanted lines. To foster readiness for

"I can write my name!"

writing, a child can be shown all of the different lines in his artwork, or the work of others and be asked to discuss how these are alike and different.

The beginnings of writing, and the actual amount of writing that occurs in a preschool will depend on the individual child's intellectual, physical, emotional, and social maturity (Leeper, 1974). A teacher can usually tell when children are ready for some type of instruction by observing. A child who is ready for instruction will begin to write her name on work, write things as she plays, and show in other ways that she is interested in learning to write.

When children begin to write their own names, teachers have the responsibility to show them the correct way to form the letters. Manuscript printing, rather than cursive writing, is recommended. Manuscript is based on the circles and lines children already have been producing in their drawings and paintings, and it more closely resembles the print in books children will be reading. It can be helpful to send a copy of the child's name home in manuscript printing, so parents will understand how to help their child at home if they wish.

As children begin to write, reversing letters, making and repeating errors, it seems only sensible and kind to help them. Leaving children to discover for themselves can lead to poor writing habits; and the habit of illegible writing might last a lifetime. "Handwriting that is taught by teachers untrained in any method of teaching it other than that they know how to write themselves, too often has produced in otherwise capable children, a casual attitude toward the need for legibility" (Barbe and Lucas 1974, p. 208).

"Beginning with a child's name is useful, for this seems to be a favorite, not only with the group, but with adults too" (Durkin 1976, p. 143). To assist children in preschools, teachers can make name cards from heavy cardboard for each child. Duplicate sets can be used in the game, or library area.

Some preschool and kindergarten teachers have found the use of small individual chalkboards and chalk an enjoyable, fun way of practicing writing and forming letters. The chalk and the chalkboards are always available and ready for use with the individual children. As writing is such an individualistic skill, few children will be ready for the boards at the same time, so there is no need to have more than a few. Using the chalkboards, teachers can write children's names at the top of the board, and let children practice writing their name below. Letters can be formed, erased, and practiced again and again.

Children can also practice writing letters or their names with paint brushes and water on the playground. They can use the name cards the teachers have made for a guide, or teachers can write children's names with water and brushes on the pavement. The entire experience is informal, fun, spontaneous. There is nothing informal, however, about the help the teacher gives each child. She knows when each is ready to have his work corrected, when to introduce another skill or technique, and when to let the child practice without guidance.

Montessori suggested the use of sensory materials and had children trace the letters and their names in trays of sand. Giving children cookie trays filled with fine sand for tracing letters is an enjoyable activity. This, or writing with sticks in the play yard dirt or sand, can also be used to demonstrate the correct way to form letters.

Kindergarten children may also be given pencils, ballpoint or felt-tip pens. These tools can be placed in the office dramatic play area, housekeeping play area, or any other dramatic play area such as a post office, doctor's office, or store. A good supply of paper and pens should always be available in the writing area.

Durkin (1976) believes that writing should be tied to the reading experiences of the children. The language experience approach, writing children's names as they speak them, certainly offers children a connection between the printed and spoken word. Durkin, however, in recommending that the language experience be used, also recognizes the individuality of the teacher, and the children:

> Nothing in the recommendation, however, suggests it is the best or the only method. In fact, the more I visit classrooms, the more firmly convinced I become that there is no such thing as one best way to teach anything. What is successful and of interest to some children can either be boring

or frustrating for others. And a method that works well with one teacher seems doomed to immediate failure when used by another." (Durkin 1976, p. 139)

In Summary

Language is an important part of the young child's life. Without facility in language children are limited intellectually as well as socially. Without the ability to manipulate and understand words, children are limited in their ability to receive information from others, from books and other printed materials, or to develop ideas and communicate these to others.

As children grow in their ability to speak and listen to others, the need for written language emerges. In a preschool, children see teachers record their words. Teachers write thank you notes, keep records of all kinds, and record children's poetry and stories. From this base of dictating and watching adults write lists, announcements, invitations, or whatever, children develop confidence in their ability to express themselves and readiness for the processes of reading and writing.

In addition to facility in listening and speaking, readiness to read includes perceptions of the connection between the printed and the spoken word as well as decoding ability. Furthermore, reading involves literal, interpretative, and critical comprehension of the material. Not all preschool children will have developed these skills, but teachers can utilize discussions, games, questioning, and classroom experiences to help each child progress. Care must be taken so that children are not forced to read before they are physically or mentally ready to do so.

Writing skills emerge as children develop and strengthen their small muscle control. Many preschool activities, such as painting and cutting, prepare children for writing. When children begin to write their own names, teachers should be ready to assist them to form letters properly so that the children learn how to hold a pencil, to write from left to right, and to avoid poor writing habits. Children should be permitted the same individuality in handwriting style that is customarily accorded adults. In preschool, teaching writing should not be presented to the entire class as a group activity. By being alert to the individual needs of the children, teachers can make both reading and writing a creative and enjoyable part of the preschool curriculum.

Resources

The following texts and other resources will be useful in developing a deeper understanding of the process of learning language and the ability to read.

CAZDEN, COURTNEY, *Language in Early Childhood Education*. Washington, D.C.: National Association for the Education of Young Children, 1972.

DURKIN, D., *Children Who Read Early*, New York: Teachers College Press, 1966.

DURKIN, D., *Teaching Young Children to Read*. Boston: Allyn & Bacon, Inc. 1975.

PIAGET, JEAN, *Language and Thought of the Child*. New York: Meriden Books, 1955.

For help in selecting children's books, the following are suggested.

Council on Interracial Books for Children, Inc.

The Horn Book Magazine

Reviews of children's books appear regularly in *Childhood Education*, the journal of the Association for Childhood Education International, Washington, D.C. and *Young Children*, the journal of the National Association for the Education of Young Children.

Projects

1. With classmates or teachers you know, discuss the following topics. When should children be taught to read? (Do you understand your own feelings about the time children should be taught to read?) What experiences should children have in their homes that will prepare them for reading? What conditions are found in good preschools that help foster children's readiness for reading?

2. Do you remember the first time you actually read? What were your felings at this time? Do you remember how you were taught to read or just the feelings that surrounded you at the time? What is the relationship between feelings of self and success in reading?

3. Review a number of children's books, and select one to read to a group of children. What were the criteria used to make your selection? What were the children's reactions to the book? List some of the possible follow-up activities children might enjoy after the reading of the story.

4. Observe in a number of preschool settings to note the types of verbal interactions teachers use with young children. Which of these techniques appears to foster language development and usage? Which do not seem as effective?

5. Observe young children at play. Record each instance of their trying to write, or showing an interest in writing. What does this interest mean for teachers of young children? How could you build on this interest without pushing children into a skill for which they are not yet ready?

6. Children in preschools are not reading children. Yet they demonstrate their interest and readiness to read in a number of ways. Observe young children at play and note instances of them "reading" to one another or trying to use the printed word in their play.

7. Take dictation from children. Try taking down children's spoken words in a number of situations. As children play, see if you can capture some of their imaginative language on paper and read it back to them. Another time ask a group of children to dictate a story or letter, and ask an individual child to dictate something for you to record in writing.

8. Can you explain to parents the value of taking children's dictation?

References

BARBE, W. B., and LUCAS, V. H., "Instruction in Handwriting: A New Look," *Childhood Education*, 4 (1974), 207–210.

BERNSTEIN, B., "Social Class Linguistic Codes and Grammatical Elements," *Language and Speech*, 5 (1962), 221–240.

BLOOM, B. S., *Stability and Change in Human Characteristics*. New York: John Wiley & Sons, Inc., 1964.

BROMAN, B., "Storytelling: The Frosting on the Cake," *Childhood Education*, 51, 6, (1975), 323–324.

BROWN, R. and BELLUGI, U., "Three Processes in the Child's Acquisition of Syntax, *Harvard Educational Review*, 34 (1964), 133–151.

BRUNER, J., *The Process of Education*. Cambridge, Mass.: Harvard University Press, 1962.

CAZDEN, C., "Children's Questions: Their Forms, Function and Role in Education," *Young Children*, (1970), 202–220.

CAZDEN, C.; BARATZ, J.; LABOV, W.; and PALMER, F.; "Language Development in Day Care Programs," *Day Care: Resources for Decisions*, ed. E. H. Grotberg. Washington, D.C.: Office of Economic Opportunity, 1971, 153–173.

CHOMSKY, C., Aspects of the Theory of Syntax. Cambridge: M.I.T. Press, 1965.

DAVIDSON, J., "Unspeakable Ideas," in *The Language of Man*, ed. J. F. Littell. Evanston, Ill.: McDougal, Littel & Company, 1971.

DAWSON, M. A., and NEWMAN, G. C., *Language Teaching in the Kindergarten and Early Primary Grades*. New York: Harcourt Brace Jovanovich, 1966.

DEWEY, J., *Democracy and Education*. New York: The Free Press, 1944. First published 1916.

DURKIN, D., *Children Who Read Early*. New York: Teachers College Press. Columbia University, 1966.

———, *Teaching Them to Read*. Boston: Allyn & Bacon, Inc., 1970.

———, *Teaching Young Children to Read*. Boston: Allyn & Bacon, Inc., 1975.

ELKIND, D., *Child Development and Education: A Piagetian Perspective*. New York: Oxford Press, 1976.

GAGNÉ, R. M., *Conditions of Learning*. New York: Holt, Rinehart & Winston, 1970.

GESELL, A.; ILG, F. L.; and AMES, L. B.; *Infant and Child in the Culture of Today*, (rev. ed.) New York: Harper & Row, Publishers, Inc., 1974.

HESS, R., and SHIPMAN, V., "Early Experience and the Socialization of Cognitive Modes in Children," *Child Development*, 36 (1965), 869–886.

HYMES, J. L., *Teaching the Child Under Six* (2nd ed.). Columbus, Ohio: Charles E. Merrill Publishing Co., 1974.

JENSEN, A., *Understanding Readiness: An Occasional Paper*. Urbana, Ill.: ERIC Clearinghouse on Early Childhood Education, 1969.

LEEPER, S. H. and others, *Good Schools for Young Children* (3rd ed.). New York: Macmillan, Inc., 1974.

LENNENBERG, E., *Biological Foundations of Language*. New York: John Wiley & Sons, Inc., 1967.

LABOV, W., "The Logic of Nonstandard English," in *Language and Poverty: Perspectives on a Theme*, ed. F. Williams. Chicago: Markham Publishing Co., 1970.

Martin, B., *Brown Bear, Brown Bear What Do You See?* New York: Holt, Rinehart & Winston, 1969.

McKee, P.; Brzenski, J. E.; and Harrison, M. L.; *The Effectiveness of Teaching Reading in the Kindergarten*. Mimeographed. Denver, Colorado: Denver Public Schools, 1966.

McNeill, D., *The Acquisition of Language*. New York: Harper & Row, Publishers, 1970.

Mitchell, L. S., *Our Children and Our Schools*. New York: Simon & Schuster Inc., 1950.

Piaget, J., *The Language and Thought of the Child*. Translated by M. Gabian. New York: Meriden Books: The World Publishing Co., 1955.

Russell, D. H., *Children's Thinking*. Waltham, Mass.: Blaisdell Publishing Co., 1956.

Saville-Troike, M., "Language Kinstruction and Multicultural Education," in *Multicultural Education*, ed. C. A. Grant. Washington, D.C.: Association for Supervision and Curriculum Development, 1977.

Science 5/13. London: Macdonald Educational Ltd., 1977.

Skinner, B. F., *Verbal Behavior*. Englewood Cliffs, N.J.: Prentice-Hall, Inc., 1957.

Staats, A., "Linguistic-Mentalistic Theory Versus an Explanatory S-R Learning Theory of Language Development, in *The Ontogenesis of Grammar: A Theoretical Symposium*, ed. D. Slobin. New York: Academic Press, 1971.

Tizard, J., "Child Welfare Research Group: Report on Work Carried Out 1967–1969," in *Day Care: Resources for Decisions*, ed. E.H. Grotberg, p. 153.

Van Allen, R., and Allen, C., *An Introduction to a Language Experience Program*. Chicago, Ill.: Encyclopaedia Britannica Press, 1961.

Vygotsky, L. S., *Thought and Language of the Child*. Translated by E. Hanfmann and G. Vakar. Cambridge, Mass.: The MIT Press, 1962.

Wilson, R., and Hall, M., *Reading and the Elementary School Child*. New York: Van Nostrand Reinhold Company, 1972.

13

The Arts

At ages four to seven, nearly every child with a supporting environment is overwhelmed by his own creativity and is full of inventiveness. For all youngsters, these are the free years.

H. Gardner, 1973, p. 256.

Young children are full of their own inventiveness. Children are so spontaneous, so joyous in their approach to life that they overwhelm adults with their creative abilities. Children express their feelings and ideas freely as they paint with bold strokes of the brush or dance uninhibitedly in a sunbeam. The very inventiveness of the young demands they find opportunities for creative expression in their schools.

Many strategies for building and supporting children's natural creativity have been advanced over the years. Generally it is believed that children are best able to create when the teacher supports their expression within the context of a free and unstructured program. The provision for firsthand, sensory experiences as the foundation for creative thought is also believed important.

Teachers' Attitudes

The attitude of the teacher seems to be very important. Teachers who are spontaneous themselves, who value spontaneity and originality of thought in others, seem to be able to support creativity. Those teachers who accept

291

and are respectful of imaginative or unusual ideas seem to foster art (Torrance 1965). Studies also suggest that children who are able to work without teacher evaluation are able to perform more creatively (Torrance 1965).

It is risky to be different; yet when you ask children to create, you are asking them to bring a new and different response to something. You are also asking them to reveal inner feelings, emotions, and ideas. In order to do this children must feel secure. You can show children you support their creativity by

1. Focusing on the different ways children respond to the same experience, valuing each response. The child who paints a sheet of paper entirely yellow and tells you this is the fire engine finds the same level of approval as the child who paints a representational, detailed picture of the yellow fire engine. Let children see that uniqueness is valued. "Look, Jerry uses the string this way. Who has another way to use it?"
2. Recognizing all children. Display the work of each child, or comment on the dance, music, or expression of each. Think about this recognition. Make it specific to each child's work or effort. A "good," or "nice," is sometimes too general. But comments such as, "That's really yellow!" "What a smooth dance," or "Your song makes me think of Christmas bells" lets children know you have really thought about their creation.
3. Giving children the freedom, materials, and time in which to create. Creation takes time, giving the children large blocks of free activity time permits them to give full expression to their ideas.

The Failings of Structured Programs

Programs that support creativity in the arts cannot be dictatorial. In a highly structured environment the teacher does the thinking for the children and makes choices for them. Children neither have the opportunity to select the skills they wish to master, nor the materials with which to work. All of the children do the same thing. Their products, completed under the direction of the teacher, are all alike. There is little opportunity to express unique ideas, feelings, or emotions when the teacher tells you what to paint, how to dance, or what to model with clay.

The ditto sheets, patterns as well as some readiness workbooks and programmed curriculum kits also negate children's creativity. These materials do the thinking for the children. Individual differences and expression are not wanted. All of the children do the same thing. The fact that some may complete the task before, or after, others does not meet individual needs or allow for individual expression.

With these types of materials and a teacher who directs all activities, children learn that conformity, not creativity, is valued. It is useless, in this kind of program, to occasionally ask children to give unique expression to some idea through art, music, or dance. The environment, the teacher, and the program have already informed the children that their ideas are not wanted or valued.

Children are full of their own inventiveness.

Experiences

What should a child paint if he has nothing to express? What should a child dance, sing, or write about if she has not had some experience to convey? Children need many fulfilling, rich, and rewarding experiences to bring content to their movement, dance, music, and visual arts.

All children have experiences. They walk in the rain, feel the snow on their faces, push a spider from their arms, feel the pavement under their running feet. Dewey says, "Experiences occur continuously, life is full of experiences, yet not everything can be considered an experience" (Dewey 1916, p. 34).

Teachers must do more than just permit children to be involved in the mechanical process of living. Everyone can remember some moment in life—a first date, broken leg, graduation, seeing a whale for the first time—that is recalled as a *real* experience. These are times of tremendous personal importance, times that stand out as being complete, full, and distinctive moments in life.

Preschool teachers cannot make all of life stand out. Nor would they wish to, for no one could handle life if every moment met the criteria of a real experience. Yet teachers do help children to become aware of and sensitive to their environment and help them to really experience.

REFLECTING ON EXPERIENCES

Dewey (1916) spoke of experiences as having a backward and forward connection, having an element of reflective thought about them. Without this

293

reflection, without any perception of the relationships or continuities to which it leads, an experience is not complete. If children do not learn to reflect, to see the connecting links between what is done and the consequences, to see the relationships between experiences, they will not have deep inner thoughts, emotions, or ideas to express through the arts. You can help children by

1. Focusing attention on experience in a way that calls up thoughts and feelings. "What does the spider's web make you think of? Where did you see that shape before? How is it just like lace? Look at the sparkles of dew on the web. How does that make you feel?"
2. Introducing additional experiences. Having observed the web, you could then read a story of a spider, or ask children to pretend they are spinning a web or to make their own web of string and paint.
3. Providing verbal labels for the experience. "This is the center of the web. This part of the spider is called a spinneret. These are the spokes."

BEING SENSITIVE TO EXPERIENCES

Highly creative people are blessed with a sense of heightened awareness. You can help children develop this sense of heightened awareness by

1. Encouraging children to use all of their senses. "Let's look at the web with the magnifying glass. Feel the web. Smell it."
2. Call attention to details. "Does the spider have eyes? Ears? What are these hairs for?"

PROVIDING A RANGE OF EXPERIENCES

Schools for young children are places where things happen. There are raw and natural materials of clay, mud, water, sand, and wood. These foster children's experimentation, and children can use them in any way to fit their own needs. There are growing things, animals that produce young, grow, and die. There are magnets, magnifying glasses, and stop watches. You can add to children's experiences by

1. Taking field trips into the neighborhood and community.
2. Introducing children to the experiences of others through books, movies, and filmstrips.
3. Providing additional materials to experiment with through art—wood and wind chimes or interesting materials to paint with or on.

THE VISUAL ARTS

"Art, however we may define it, is present in everything we do to please our senses . . ." (Read 1956, p. 15). All who observe children creating art know the deep personal involvement children bring to the task. As children draw, paint, model, or construct, they give expression to their thoughts and, as a result, experience pleasure and the deep personal satisfaction of accomplishment. accomplishment.

Pleasure and the deep personal satisfaction of accomplishment are but two of the values of the visual arts. Eisner (1974) believes that the major role of all aspects of the visual arts is the ability to foster children's (1) awareness of self, (2) knowledge of others, and (3) knowledge of the world about them.

AWARENESS OF SELF

Through the visual arts children come to know themselves. The visual arts permit children to give form to thoughts, perceptions, and vague feelings. "As the child becomes able to handle symbolic media, to make and perceive symbolic expression, his awareness of his feeling system is tremendously enriched" (Gardner 1973, p. 163).

When children produce art, they learn to control their emotions. They recognize that they can handle their negative as well as their joyous feelings through positive action. They can tear paper, pound clay, squish fingerpaints on a table top—all releasing feelings without harming self or others.

Self-assurance and confidence develop as children learn to control the media of the visual arts. Producing visual art gives children opportunities to develop fine eye-hand muscle control. It gives them a feeling of control over the world about them. Threading needles, controlling paint, using scissors, and crayons help children develop control over their own bodies and materials.

Experiences in the visual arts are valued for the self-understanding and confidence they foster. Secure in their ability to organize their thoughts and in their ability to control their bodies and the world, children are ready to reach out to form relationships with others.

KNOWLEDGE OF OTHERS

Art activities are often enjoyable social occasions. Sharing clay, chatting as they build with the blocks, children learn skills of relating to others. Art offers opportunities to learn to take turns at the easel, share materials, take responsibility in cleaning up, and conserve materials. The cooperation, sharing, and give-and-take that occur during art are important for children's social development.

More importantly, however, are the opportunities children have to learn that others have a point of view that may differ from theirs. After a trip to a farm, zoo, or supermarket, children will reproduce their perceptions in the visual arts. Comparing children's drawings, paintings, or models gives the group concrete, dramatic examples of how different people express the same experience in different ways. Children actually see that their point of view is not the only one and learn to appreciate, understand, and accept the fact that others, who have experienced the same event as they, may view and express it in a different way.

Knowledge of others is also extended as children examine the art of others far from them in time and place. Exploring the details of an African mask, the beauty of a Mexican bark painting, or a wood carving from South America, children have an introduction to lives of others far from them. Art, which represents and reproduces the values, attitudes, and life of a society either past or present, gives children a vision of that society. As children examine the art of others and think about why and how it was made, they develop a sense of the cultural and ethnic heritages of others.

AWARENESS OF THE WORLD

Paints spread, drip, dry, and chip. Clay becomes hard and then pliable again when placed in water. Paper tears but can be folded to stand up. Paste changes form and texture as it dries. Through the arts children learn about the physical properties of things in their world. Concepts from the physical sciences can be introduced as children observe bubbles coming from the chalk dipped in water, or as they experience the marvelous solvent qualities of water.

Seeing and feeling visual relationships, children learn more about their world. They closely examine the wings of a grasshopper, marvel at the colors caught in soap bubbles, or feel the texture of a rock. Then they see and examine visual relationships in their artwork and in the art of others. Teachers help children pick out shapes, colors, textures, form, lines, and patterns in their artwork and the work of others.

Mathematical concepts are also present in the visual arts. Children work producing two- and three-dimensional art products. They explore space and solve problems of how to use it. Length and width measurements are involved as children produce art. Size, shapes, numbers are experienced when children create art. Observing and evaluating the work of others, children begin to learn about parallel lines, diagonals, patterns, circles, and rectangles. Children match and compare and use every possible mathematical concept as they discuss their art and the art of others.

Concepts from the social sciences abound as children create visual art. They themselves become producers and consumers. They produce art and consume materials. How the materials arrive at the school, who pays for them, how they are made and delivered might be the basis for a study of economics. The laws of supply and demand and conservation of materials enter into art and are a natural introduction to principles of economics.

It is no secret that producing and evaluating art require the use of language. Listen while children paint or draw. They hum, sing, or carry on a monologue describing their work. Pounding clay or hammering nails often leads children to burst out in song. As children begin to develop the ability to talk about their art, they learn new words. Every time children handle art materials or observe things in their environment, they can learn to use the terminology of art using words that describe texture, line, form, and color.

Art is a highly valid, important part of children's preschool experience. Teachers who fully understand the contribution the visual arts make to children's language, mathematical concepts, knowledge of the world, self, and others have a better perspective for planning the goals and objectives of their program.

Planning to Teach the Visual Arts

Planning to teach the visual arts begins by deciding on the goals and objectives of the program. Understanding the need for motivating experiences and how to select materials are also required.

Selecting Objectives

Goals and objectives for art are based on the values visual art holds for children. The content of art provides another source of objectives. In general, a well-balanced visual art program should include objectives from the four content areas of art: (1) seeing and feeling visual relationships, (2) producing works of art, (3) knowing and understanding art objects, and (4) evaluating art products.

The Fine Arts Department of Florida State University identified the following goals and objectives for a visual arts program.

All children should

- have intense personal involvement in and response to visual experiences.
- perceive and understand visual relationships in the environment.
- think, feel, and act creatively with visual art materials.
- increase manipulations and organizational skills in art performance appropriate to their abilities.
- acquire knowledge of our visual art heritage.
- use art knowledge and skills in their personal and community life.
- make intelligent visual judgments suited to individual experience and maturity.
- understand the nature of art and the creative process

Specific, or educational objectives, can be selected and designed for individual children, programs, or even specific activities. Examples of specific objectives might be that children will be able

- to make a design out of an arrangement of colors, using repetition, pattern and line.
- to use the emotional qualities of color and shape to convey a specific mood or feeling.
- recognize and point to actual textures or surfaces.
- to point out shapes in their own art work and the work of others.
- to use the side of a crayon to make a mass.
- to use lines in a variety of media.
- to perform, from the inception of an idea, to the creation a design, to the finished product, an object of clay.

These are simply examples of the types of specific objectives that are consistent with the theoretical foundations of art and that foster a number of specific values. All are based on the content of art. Although these are sample

297

objectives, it seems critical that teachers be able to determine and specify their own goals and objectives for children's art. Without clear ideas of the goals and purposes of art, the full potential of art cannot be realized. Without specified, carefully thought out objectives, art activities become unrelated and based on whim, rather than logic and reason. Eisner (1972) states that the value of setting goals and objectives is important because it encourages curriculum makers to think "with precision about what they are after" (p. 154).

> Since instructional objectives describe the ways in which students are to behave, or the competencies they are to display after working through a curriculum, the careful statement of such objectives mitigates against the fuzzy thinking and language that too often makes goals in the field appear more like slogans than like statements having any real meaning. (Eisner 1972, p. 154)

On the other hand, you should remember that objectives are tools, not laws. There are many outcomes of art activities that can never be stated or predetermined. Art does not always lend itself to the predictable, nor do young children. Further, learning opportunities that arise as children create visual art cannot always be specified in advance. Art is an individual experience. Making each child conform to specified objectives would negate the opportunity for children to express their own uniqueness. Eisner (1972, p. 152) concludes, "When the objectives are treated with discretion, rather than with passion, and when they are used with those activities that are intended to yield predictable consequences, they are useful tools."

Using Motivational Techniques

Before children can produce visual arts, they must be motivated. Linderman and Herberholz call it "winding up the mainspring" (1974 p. 34), and most art educators would agree that an element of motivation is required before children can create visual art. In a way, motivation occurs as children live and have true experiences. The daily sensory and reflective experiences children have are the basis for producing art. Any experience a child has can be used to give her a source of ideas, feelings, or emotions to draw on and express through the visual arts. Motivational activities might include

LANGUAGE ACTIVITIES

Reading a poem about the fog creeping in on cat's feet or a story of a steam shovel provides children with images they might express through the visual arts. Children are not asked to reproduce the images drawn by the poem or story, but the poem or story can serve them as a source of ideas. You could help children by asking them to think about the poem, recall the parts of phrases they like the best, relate it to some experience of theirs, or to think about the character they thought the bravest or the part that frightened them the most.

Often the very nature of the media, the paints, clay or chalk, provides motivation for children. Exploring and experimenting with media, children discover possible ways to use it to express their unique ideas. You could ask children to drop dry powder paint on paper dampened with a sponge, try dipping dry chalk into a pan of water before use, or to color with the edge of a crayon.

ART

The art products of others offer motivation for children's art production. Children could examine ceramic sculptures, discuss how the artists created these and how they could use their clay in the same way. Schwartz and Douglas (1967) found that showing children ceramic pieces provided a unique motivational experience for four year olds. They introduced children to the sculptures, discussed with the children how the artist might have created the piece, and then demonstrated some of the techniques of the artist with clay in the classroom. As a result, children's attention span at the clay table increased dramatically, as did their verbalizations about their own art products. The complexity, detail, and dimensionality of the children's clay products also increased following the motivation.

SENSORY EXPERIENCES

Firsthand, sensory experiences will be the most important type of motivation. The more children see, hear, taste, and smell, the more they take in through their senses, the more they will have to express through the visual arts. A basic approach to increasing children's capacity for using their senses is to direct their attention to the objects, things, and events in their environment. Asking children questions, organized in a way that children will have to search for answers (Linderman and Herberholz 1974) is useful. Looking at an insect, you might ask, "Does it have a nose? What are the feelers used for? What sound does this cricket make? How?"

Demonstrating the power of directed observations to influence children's art production, McWhinnie (1974) has asked children to complete two drawings of a tree. The first drawing is completed after children are told to "Draw a tree." The second is done after children's attention has been focused on a tree, either one in their environment or a painting or drawing created by an artist. Children are asked to look at and feel the bark, to see the branches, examine the way the leaves are attached to the branches, to feel and smell the leaves. Without fail, the first drawing of a tree is stereotypic, usually a green circle on a brown stick. The second drawing, completed following a direct observation of a tree, is individual, detailed, precise, and complete.

Selecting Media

Many teachers, perhaps reflecting the culture and values of our society, attempt to present new and different media daily. Children paint with marshmallows, draw with candles, or paint with food colors. Some believe that preschool programs are judged by the number and variety of media with which the children are presented. "The more media they provide, the better they think they are; the more varieties of media their children experience, the better they assume the learning to be. Most teachers are on a perpetual hunt, not only for media, but also new ones" (Barkan 1966, p. 426).

It may be, however, that less is better when working with young children. The practice of presenting children with endless new and different media has been questioned. "Does this seemingly infinite variety of materials and equipment really enhance children's learning? Or does it merely reflect the American propensity for conspicious consumption?" (Almy 1975, p. 257).

Young children have not nearly experienced all life has to offer. Everything is new, exciting, and stimulating to them. The basics of paints, crayons, paper, paste, and wood are full of marvelous possibilities for the young. Put yourself in the child's place, and you begin to realize that there really is no need to have a new medium daily, for the whole world is new.

When children are introduced to a variety of media, on an endless basis, they have little time to develop the skills required to actually master and control any medium. It takes time and practice to learn control and mastery. Control over the medium is absolutely essential if children are to develop the skills required to express their feelings, emotions, and ideas through visual art.

Paints are basic.

Children Produce Visual Art

All children the world over, go through the same stages in producing art. The same schemes appear in the art of children in the United States, Mexico, Israel, Paraguay—any country in the world. Beginning with random scribbles that are actually the result of pure motor action and not an expression of anything, children learn to control scribbling and eventually produce symbols that represent objects, ideas, people, and things in their world.

Theories of Why Children Produce Art

For many years people have been trying to explain why all children, the world over, draw in the same predictable ways. The theories—although each is different—offer an explanation for why children produce art and also suggest strategies for teachers.

DEVELOPMENTAL THEORY

The developmental theory has been one of the most influential of all theories for teachers. This theory suggests that children's art progresses through developmental stages, which are based on children's overall development. From 1830, when Ebenezer Cooke first drew attention to the successive stages of development found in children's drawings, to date, with Viktor Lowenfeld's *Creative and Mental Growth of the Child*, teachers have based their objectives for art activities on the idea that children's art is developmental.

According to this theory, art depends on children's growth, thus there is no need for teacher intervention. The teacher provides materials and acts as a guide. Teachers who endorse this theory of instruction base goals and objectives of their art program on children's growth. Any attempt to specify goals, other than that of fostering growth and development in an indirect way, seems inconsistent.

COGNITIVE THEORY

According to the cognitive theory, children draw what they know. Production of visual art, the distortions children draw in size, shape, and form, are believed to represent the child's level of thinking. Florence Goodenough developed the Goodenough Draw A Man Test, which supports the idea that the amount of detail and accuracy in children's drawings reflects their thinking.

Teachers who endorse this theory base their art program on increasing children's knowledge and awareness of the world. As children gain in understanding, grow, and have more and more experiences, they increase their fund of concepts and thus their visual art increases in both detail and accuracy.

301

PSYCHOANALYTIC THEORY

Proponents of psychoanalytic theory claim that children draw what they feel, and that their art is a reflection of deep, inner emotions. Art comes "from deep down inside" (Cole 1966). This theory holds that children's artwork is influenced by emotions, feelings, and inner psychological drives. The reason children draw daddy so tall is not because that is what they know, but because they feel daddy is so powerful and looms so large in their emotions.

Basing a program on psychoanalytic theory, teachers would select goals for art to free children for expressing and releasing inner feelings. They would select fingerpaints, clay, and tempera as appropriate materials. The role of the teacher would be one of guide and supporter.

PERCEPTION-DELINEATION THEORY

June McFee in *Preparation for Art* advances another theory to explain why children draw. She believes that children's art is based on a number of factors, not just one. The readiness of the children, including general physical, intellectual and perceptual development; the psychological environment in which they are working; their ability to handle detail; their intelligence, categorizing, and delineation skills; their ability to manipulate media, creative ability, and ability to design qualities of form; all are believed to be factors in the production of visual art.

This theory provides teachers with a comprehensive and useful base for determining and selecting objectives for art education. Objectives could be selected to foster growth in each of the areas believed to influence children's art. Some objectives might be selected to foster general physical and perceptual development; others, to provide a sound psychological environment; and still others, to increase children's control over the media.

PERCEPTUAL THEORY

Another theory suggests that children draw what they see, not what they know or feel. Arnheim (1954) believes that children do not see objects as the sum of observed parts, but that they see perceptual wholes or total images structured by the brain on the basis of retinal impressions. To Arnheim, perception is learned, or at least can be improved through training in visual discrimination. Thus teachers would attempt to strengthen and improve children's visual perception by asking them to look at and observe their environment more closely.

COGNITIVE-DEVELOPMENTAL THEORY

Piaget relates children's art to the child's ability to understand the permanent existence of objects. Unless a child understands that objects have a permanent existence, she has no image through which to evoke the past and anticipate the future. Children must be able to recall what is absent in order to think about it, and this evocation requires a symbol to stand for what is not here and now. Representation is the means by which human beings organize their experiences of the world to further understand it.

Cognitive-developmental theory bases development on two distinct types of experiences. One is the sensorimotor and the other, experiences that bring content to the child's expression. Teachers who endorse this theory would base goals and objectives of art on those two kinds of experiences.

No one theory is best. Each has influenced art education for young children. It would be unusual to find a preschool program based on one theory alone. In fact, the different theories, although varied and distinct, have similar characteristics. None suggests that a teacher interfere directly with children's art production, nor does any suggest that children follow adult patterns or color in lines drawn by an adult. Each theory recognizes the need for children to express their own ideas and to do their own thinking in a supportive environment. Tables 13-1 through 13-6 describe the stages, objectives, and teaching strategies of various art forms for children, to guide the teacher.

TABLE 13-1

Modeling

Materials	Stages	Objectives	Teaching Techniques
Potter's Clay *Salt Dough* 1 part salt 2 parts flour water to mix *Corn Starch* 1 cup salt ½ cup cornstarch ¾ cup water Stir and cook over medium heat until thickens, when cool, knead until smooth. *Baker's Dough* 1 cup salt 2 cups flour ½ cups water Knead until mixed, can be baked in oven at 350° *Sawdust* 2 parts sawdust 1 part wallpaper paste Water to mix Model and let dry for food like product	Manipulates, explores, squeezes, makes pancakes, coils, balls, punches and pounds clay. Names products. Begins pulling out parts, adding on legs, arms and parts to product. Product has meaning to the adult.	The child will be able to express his own thought in clay; the child will create from the inception of an idea, to the finished product, an object from the modeling materials.	Permit children period of manipulation, explorations. Provide stimulation, sharing products made of ceramic materials, talks about how the artist might have created the object. Add sticks, dowels, other tools to modeling material as needed for children to add texture to their product. When child begins to add parts, demonstrate technique of slipping.

Knowing, understanding, and evaluating art begins with the teacher, for children will imitate the attitudes and the actions of the teacher. Your own understanding of art, the way you evaluate, treasure, or reject it, will be imitated by the children.

Before beginning to teach children to know and evaluate art, you should assess your own attitudes, values, and knowledge of art. Only as teachers know and understand art, especially that of the young child, will they be able to demonstrate the sensitive awareness required to teach children to evaluate art.

Recognition of the stages children's art progresses through helps you to know and reinforce the progress children are making. It also gives you a base

TABLE 13-2

Drawing

Materials	Stages	Sample Objective	Teaching Techniques
Crayons boxes of crayons, eight colors in each box a box of crayon scraps chunky crayons additional crayons of varied colors such as pink, white, lime, or mauve. *Chalk* pastels craypas charcoal chunky chalk *Pens Pencils* marking pens, felt point pens, ballpoint pens, colored pencils. *Paper* paper of every kind, cardboard, box lids, colored and manila paper. *Other Materials to Draw On* pieces of wood, sandpaper, cloth, wax paper, and other materials.	Manipulates, explores. Cannot control scribbles. Controls scribbles. Names scribble when finished. Recognizes symbols and repeats them in drawings to "make" something. Uses symbols to represent things with increasing detail and realism. Has a plan in mind before beginning to draw.	The child will be able to recognize lines in her drawing.	Encourage children to become aware of the environment and open to sensory experiences. Provide motivational experience. Do not expect child to sit and create without experiences as the base of creativity. Permit children adequate time to manipulate and explore materials. Encourage children to work independently by arranging materials for self-selection. Help them to concentrate on a task and complete drawings. Show, or model, ways to use drawing materials to achieve different effects. (using a crayon or piece of chalk on its side, instead of on the point).

for discussing their art. Discussion of children's art—describing their products, pointing out textures, lines, form, content, and color—is one way you give recognition to children's work.

Comments that recognize children's newly developing skills give children specific feedback about their progress and help them begin to develop knowledge about the content of art. You might comment on how a child pulled clay from the lump to form an object, or how a child used a symbol to represent some idea in a painting or drawing. This type of recognition lets children know a teacher cares about their art.

Teachers who praise children's art indiscriminately are not helping children learn to evaluate art. Further, children do sense when their art products are the result of messing around, and when the products represent thought, time, and hard work. If a teacher praises all products in the same manner, children sense insincerity, and the teacher's credibility is reduced.

Teachers also recognize children's art by taking care of it. There should be some place in the room for children to dry their paintings, to store three-dimensional products, and to keep things protected until it is time to go home. Some products, those that have special meaning to the child, can be mounted

TABLE 13-3

Painting

Materials	Stages	Sample Objective	Teaching Technique
Tempera paints in shallow containers paints in containers in a six-pack to carry out of doors or other places in the room Brushes—assorted types with short handles.	Manipulates and explores.	The child will be able to perceive and discuss color forces in his own paintings and the works of others.	Permit free exploration of materials and time for manipulation of materials.
	Explores with colors, mixing together.		
	Paints without control.		Provide motivation in the form of experiences.
Water color paints with brushes and containers of clear water Assorted papers—large paper on easel, brown paper on floor or wall, small paper for water color paints.	Develops control over media, repeating symbols to represent reality.		Demonstrate specific techniques — placing paper on easel, hanging papers up to dry.
	Paints with idea in mind, representing experiences realistically.		Arrange materials to allow children free selection, independent use.
Finger Paints Purchased finger paints or mixture of liquid starch and powdered paint in squeeze bottles Finger painting paper, shelf paper, or table tops that are washable.	From exploration to creation of shapes, controls use of fingers, hands, and arms to express emotions, feelings, and ideas.		Engage children in conversation about their products and the products of others.

before the child takes them home. Strips of construction paper, taped or pasted to the back of a picture, make a fine frame. Other paintings can be mounted in a tripod tagboard frame or placed in booklets letting children and their parents know that the art products are treasured.

Some spaces in the room, hallways, or school can be set aside for displaying children's artwork. Seeing their work decorating the school gives children a sense of satisfaction, as well as adding charm and beauty to the school. When children's work is displayed, children can see for themselves that others

TABLE 13-4

Fabric

Materials	Stages	Sample Objective	Teaching Techniques
Sewing large blunt needles, plastic or darning assorted threads and yarn material to sew on, loosely woven, burlap, mesh screening.	Explores then sews with design and pattern in mind. Practices threading strips in and out of plastic mat.	The child will be able to recognize the possibilities of expression through use of texture.	Provide materials, ready for children's independent use. Demonstrate how to thread a needle, tie a knot at the end of the thread, and other techniques. Step in to help and offer guidance before children become frustrated in working with new media.
Weaving plastic mats with precut slots for practice weaving sessions, plastic or paper strips to weave with cardboard with slots at each end for yarn to stretch across as on a loom yarn and popsicle or other straight sticks for weaving.			Encourage children to discuss texture, color, line, and form in their products and the products of others. Provide for display of children's work. Demonstrate how to weave using plastic mats for practice. Use paper mats, found materials, and paper strips for weaving. Once children understand principle of weaving, permit free exploration of material and encourage imaginative thinking. Teach principles of weaving.

have different ideas, solutions, and viewpoints, but that all views are respected.

Children who are used to having their work displayed and to discussing their work with the teacher can begin to share their work with others. When children begin to talk to others about their work and show their work to the group at circle time, teachers know that group evaluations can begin. The sensitive guidance of the teacher is important as she leads children in discussing their work with others. The sharing of artwork with others could begin by asking children to tell

1. How they completed a specific part of a drawing or painting.
2. Why they used the colors they did.
3. Which part of the painting or construction they like the best and why.
4. The story behind the painting, picture, or clay object.

The audience, the other children, can be encouraged to comment on the works being shared. Teachers might guide the discussion by focusing on the shapes, colors, textures, and lines in the products, how the pictures make the children feel, or what the pictures make them think about.

TABLE 13-5

Paper

Materials	Stages	Sample Objective	Teaching Techniques
A variety of papers, all shapes, textures, colors and sizes	Practices randomly with scissors and explores paper and paste.	The child will be able to recognize form and shapes.	Provide scissors that do cut and arrange materials for children's access.
Scissors, with left-handed scissors for those children who need them	Uses paper, paste, scissors to create shape and form. Names forms.		Teach safety habits when using scissors and fasteners.
Paste—strong white glue, library paste, and mucilage	Has preconceived idea for product and ability to execute plans to complete product.		Teach children possibilities of tearing instead of cutting materials.
Staples			
A variety of fasteners—brads, pipe cleaners, needle, and threads.			Use collages or cut-out works of famous artists, such as the Matisse cut-outs, as motivation for art work. Show the children the prints of such works, discuss how the artist constructed the collage or cutout, and encourage children to create their own collages.

Being able to evaluate artwork is the highest level of visual art children can achieve. To be able to evaluate art means that the children, just like the teacher, must be aware and knowledgeable of art. Surrounding the children with beauty is one way to lead them to appreciate and evaluate their own art.

Attractive, stimulating but orderly rooms are a must. Cold bare expanses of walls and monotonous arrangements can only depress children and teachers alike. Children could take part in setting up beauty corners or nooks of their work and other items. Pieces of cloth, a selection of vases, rocks, shells, feathers, vegetables, or flowers can be provided for children to arrange with their artwork in pleasing displays. As children arrange a beauty nook, they learn sensitive appreciation that permits them to know, understand, and evaluate art.

Children also need to become acquainted with the artwork of others. Just because children are young is no reason to deny them the pleasure of great works of art. Rather than displaying shabby cardboard pumpkins, Santa Clauses, and the like, the teacher could select prints of masterpieces to display in the room. There are many sources of inexpensive prints that can be used in classrooms. Often weekly magazines or newspapers will include prints of famous paintings or drawings. In addition, it is possible to purchase inexpensive prints or to borrow them from the school media center or library.

TABLE 13-6

Construction

Materials	Stages	Sample Objectives	Teaching Technique
A variety of junk materials including paper scraps, wood, cloth, beads, feathers, paper tubes, cardboard boxes, and anything else that is being discarded.	Explores and manipulates randomly. Control over materials. Creates realistic objects and products from the junk, wood, or wire.	The child will be able to create three-dimensional products and explore space.	Provide opportunities to explore materials. Demonstrate techniques of joining materials together to prevent children becoming frustrated. Name shapes and describe children's products using vocabulary of shape and space.
A box to keep the junk in.			
Materials to permit children to fasten junk together to form shapes, such as staplers, paste and glue, hole punch, pipe cleaners, or wire.			
Wire coated with plastic for wire construction.			
Woodworking tools, wood and table for woodworking.			

Some prints can be mounted or framed and hung in the room. Children like to be included in the hanging of the picture, selecting the place on the wall, deciding when to change the print, and choosing on the next print that will be displayed. Prints that are owned by the teacher can be mounted on cardboard and placed in the library area or on a game table for the children to handle and talk about. One teacher happened on a torn book illustrated with Arthur Rackham prints. She cut the prints from the tattered book, mounted them on construction paper, and left them on the library table. The children spent hours, stretched out on their stomachs, arranging the prints on the floor, rearranging them, discussing and evaluating these intriguing works of art.

Once a collection of prints and famous art is begun, it is easy for teachers to reach for a print of a famous painting to display instead of an Easter bunny. The prints can be used to introduce songs, poems, and stories, or to motivate children's artwork.

Finally, the prints can be used to learn to know, understand, and evaluate art. Linderman (1974) suggests that the critical process of looking at and describing works of art can be learned by young children. This process might consist of

- asking children to describe the subject matter of the picture. "What do you see in this picture? What are they doing? How can you tell? What do you think will happen next?"
- helping the children to identify the qualities of line, shape, texture, and color in the print.
- asking children to interpret the work of art, "How do you think the artist felt when he did this? What idea was she trying to tell us? How does it make you feel?"
- encouraging the children to make aesthethic judgments. "Do you like it? Why or why not?"

It may be that teachers can introduce the children to the artist by telling them the name of the person who painted the picture or made the sculpture and something of interest about the artist's life. The culmination of experiences in the visual arts is discussion, evaluation, and judgment of art works. Encouraging children to freely discuss and give their responses to their own artwork and the works of others is a long, slow, continual process. Nonetheless, it is a stimulating adventure for all.

In Summary

"To think clearly and act intelligently, people must examine and compare the bewildering possibilities around them. They must separate the important from the unimportant. The art process is one means of doing this" (Cohen and Gainer 1976, p. 19). Art serves many functions for young children. It enables them to gain control over self and learn about others and the world about them. As children produce art they must separate the important from the unimportant. It is a way for them to bring order to their world and to express their own feelings and thoughts about the world.

All children need experiences before producing art. The needs to reflect on and be sensitive to experiences are present. It is not just that children experience but that they develop the ability to utilize all their senses to bring meaning to experiences and that they learn to think about experiences.

Understanding stages of art, why children produce art, and how to plan motivational experiences is necessary for teachers of young children. Wise selection of materials is also required. The highest level of art education is the ability to know, understand, and evaluate art. Here you have a critical responsibility, for your attitudes, values, and actions influence children's evaluation of art.

MUSIC

"Music is a joy. It sharpens and delights the senses. In the classroom, teachers value music for creative movement, song and dramatics, expression, as a change of pace and as a release for tension and energy" (Kuhmerker 1969, p. 157). Froebel set the stage for music in early childhood education when he introduced his gifts of songs and the book *Mother Play* to the kindergarten (Weber 1969). Since that time, music has been a joy and delight for early childhood educators and children alike.

Music, an integral part of every childhood program, is intricately interwoven in the growth and development of the child. Children's responses to sound and rhythm are as natural as growth itself. As the baby grows, the enjoyment of sounds, music and rhythm expands and develops. Learning through the senses, babies find sounds, rhythms, and music to be fun, a natural way to learn about their world.

It does not take long for babies to recognize their parent's voice. It is singing, humming or laughing, a lilting voice that can quiet a distressed, fretful infant. Later babies turn to find the source of sound from a music box, bells strung on a cord near their crib, or wind chimes. Before a child is a year old, he can play along with the sounds he hears, giggling, burbling, moving, listening with pure enjoyment to the simple songs, "Patty Cake," "This Little Piggy," or "Thumbkin."

And very soon children begin to create music themselves. They experiment with creating the sounds they hear, blowing bubbles with their mouth, repeating over and over, "Da da da" or beating a spoon against the highchair, making a racket, but also their own rhythm of sounds.

As soon as children begin to walk, or even sooner, they respond with their entire bodies to the sounds they hear. The two year old, barely able to stand solidly, sways awkwardly to a song heard on the radio. By four or five the

Children make music.

same two year old is whirling and twirling, dancing uninhibitedly to music.

Music is familiar to children entering a preschool. It can provide unity to the school day when used spontaneously and informally and can extend, expand, and build on children's skills, knowledge, and concepts.

No time of a preschool day is without music. Music is an integral part of most programs. Singing, moving to music, and enjoying a break by listening to music permeate the entire day. "Musical experiences for both adults and children defy time limits, exacting goals and expressions" (Andrews 1976, p. 34). Music holds the school day together. It is an important part of the total program, it can

1. Lighten a tense situation. When tempers flare and tension mounts, a teacher can use a song to lighten the mood, to help children release tensions and feelings. Even beginning to hum, or starting to sing, "Here we are together, together, together" relieves tensions, redirects hostility, builds feelings of togetherness, and helps get children back on the track of cooperating and working with one another.

2. Ease transitions. Those times of the day between lunch and nap, between cleanup and story, between snack and going outside, and the routine times, when you do have to clean up or get everyone dressed to go home can be eased with song. Using the tune of "Picking Up Paw Paws" teachers might sing, "Putting on coats, putting on boots, now it's time to go home." Or at cleanup time, using the same

311

tune, "Picking up blocks, putting in the box, now it's cleanup time," happily involves children in a meaningful way while getting the job done.

3. Set the tone at the beginning and end of the day. Welcoming children with a song or beginning the day with group singing sets the mood for good feelings throughout the day. Saying goodbye with another song, "Goodbye everybody, yes indeed, yes indeed," lets everyone know and feel that school is a welcoming place, full of good feelings for all.

4. Aid the child with special needs. "Because music is a pleasurable and nonthreatening experience for most children, it can sometimes be used to help children with special needs feel comfortable while learning" (McDonald and Ramsey 1978, p. 31).

Music also enhances the total curriculum, and fosters children's skills, concepts, and knowledge. Music can

1. Build auditory discrimination and memory. Through music children learn to distinguish between sounds. They pick out sounds that are alike and ones that are different, and they remember a series of sounds, repeating the series with a drumbeat or in song.

2. Foster concept formation. What better way to teach concepts than through song? It takes a lot of practice for young children to internalize concepts, and music can happily provide that practice. Greenberg (1972) and Pruitt and Steele (1971) both report the success of music and songs in increasing children's concept formation. Cognitive skills such as right-left discrimination, color identification, counting, and body image were increased through music.

3. Extend children's language facilities. Children enjoy play with words and use music and song for pleasure, but this pleasure leads to developing vocabulary. New words are introduced through songs, and children find new ways to describe their world. The structure of the songs themselves, the rhyming words, repetition, are not only enjoyed, but help children with their language development.

4. Introduce children to others. Through folk songs, chants, and dances, children can come to experience the heritage of others who may live far from them. When children sing, dance, and enjoy the songs of others, they can better understand people everywhere.

5. Foster self-concepts. "Touch your shoulders, now your toes" and other songs help children learn the names for parts of the body. As they dance and move to music, children find out what parts of their body can bend and how to make their bodies swirl, twirl, swoop, and move to rhythm. Music provides a release for feelings and emotions; some songs are sad, others happy, some funny, some thoughtful, some pensive. Perhaps music, which permits all to achieve and succeed, does most to foster self-esteem and help children feel good about themselves.

6. Expand children's social skills. The importance of learning to sing with a group, to be a part of a group, cannot be overestimated. Singing together in a circle, all making the same motions to "Hickory, dickory, dock, the mouse went up the clock" or playing some musical instrument in the rhythm band, helps children learn how to become a participating member of a group.

7. Extend understandings of many concepts in science, math, and other content areas. Songs about the weather, raindrops falling, and chickadees flying away one by one focus children's attention on scientific concepts. As children move through the room like animals, or mimic the sounds of insects, they become familiar with the things living in the world.

8. Build creativity. All music activities can encourage children to bring new and different responses to the classroom. When teachers ask, "Who can think of another way to do this? What else could we sing? What other instrument would fit? How can you dance to let others know how you feel?" they are encouraging and strengthening the ability to children to think creatively and give expression to their own individual experiences.

Music is so important in the entire preschool and primary curriculum that it is often easy for teachers to forget how important music is in and of itself. Although music is a spontaneous integral part of the curriculum for young children, it should also be separate. There should be some time set aside each day for teaching music, a time that is carefully planned around selected goals and objectives designed to extend children's interest in music, their ability to create, make, and enjoy music, and their musical skills and understandings.

Smith (1968) has demonstrated that when nursery school children participated in music training, their interest in music, vocal skills, and general music achievement increased. This achievement was maintained through grade school and continued as the children entered high school. After just one year, nursery school children who had received group training learned to sing more accurately than older children. They showed a similar accelerated development in rhythmic and listening skills. The children who had participated in the training later showed an intense interest in further music study. By third grade, all but two children in the training group were studying piano, and they all showed a higher level of achievement at the sixth grade than children without the training.

This study is important for nursery school teachers, for it demonstrates that children can be taught the fundamentals of music and increase their interest in learning more about music. At the Tanglewood Symposium (Broudy 1968), it was concluded that children were not being taught music as such in the schools. Children were found to reach the upper grades deficient in musical skills and with a less than positive attitude about their ability to participate in musical activities. After the symposium, teachers were encouraged to teach music as an aesthetic art and to plan specific experiences for the development of children's cognitive, aesthetic, and creative musical expression.

The time to begin teaching music is in the preschool. The children are receptive to the joy and pleasure of music. It is natural to them and they are open to developing new skills and techniques. But it is not that natural for early childhood teachers. Few early childhood educators have a solid background in the fundamentals of music, and many are frankly uncomfortable with their own skills in producing music.

Teachers faced with identifying specific goals and objectives for children's musical learning may need help. Perhaps a music teacher in the school or community could work with the classroom teacher as a resource person. The music teacher might identify the specific skills and understandings children of various ages should be able to achieve and offer suggestions for fostering these understandings.

When a music resource person is available, she can also provide children with musical instruments. She may be able to accompany their singing with guitar, piano, or violin. The music teacher and classroom teacher should work together and build on one another's goals and objectives. When a music teacher is a regular member of the team, she can make suggestions for the spontaneous and informal use of music. The classroom teacher will want to help the music teacher plan for her time with the children. He can identify children who need special attention, the concepts and ideas the children are working to develop, and their general interests.

If a music teacher is not a part of the preschool team, then the teacher must look to other resources for determining the goals, objectives, and methods of the music program. Textbooks, songbooks, and music books offer suggestions for sequential activities based on the abilities of children of various ages. Teachers can also look to theory as a foundation for planning musical experiences.

Modes of Learning

From Enactive to Symbolic

Bruner describes three different modes of knowing (or understanding) and processing information from the environment (Bruner 1966). These modes of learning, based on the work of Piaget, are (1) the enactive—through action and manipulation; (2) the iconic—through perceptual organization and imagery (aural, kinesthetic, and visual); and (3) the symbolic—through words and other symbols.

> Recognition of three modes of cognition rather than one, the symbolic, places the preverbal aspects of intelligence in perspective. They assume stature not only as ways of knowing accessible to the child before he has language skills, but also as means of substantiating symbolic systems in later learning. (Aronoff 1969, p. 8)

Recognition of the three modes of learning also gives teachers a plan for organizing musical experiences for children. Children begin learning through action and manipulation and then through perceptual organization and imagery—the very ways in which a young child knows music.

Emile Jaques-Dalcroze, a Swiss educator, in the early 1900s developed a system of music education organized around three components; *eurhythmics* (rhythmic movement), *solfege* (singing a melody with syllables), and piano improvisation, which incorporate the three modes of learning.

Congruent with Bruner's idea that children begin to know the world through action and manipulation, through the enactive mode of learning, Dalcroze considered the physical body a musical instrument for interpreting the sound and pulse of music. He began teaching eurhythmics to children of four. One of the initial activities introduced was the simple exercise in which the children tiptoed around the room to piano accompaniment. When the music stopped, the children would freeze. Dalcroze believed that this exercise helped children develop the understanding of the difference between sound and silence.

As the children progressed, they learned to stay in step with the music, to adjust their steps to the music, making them larger or heavier when louder music was played, smaller and quicker for soft music. As the tempo changed, children adapted by slowing down or increasing speed. Legato, flowing music resulted in smooth movements, while staccato, jumping music caused quick, light movements.

The method receives acceptance from music educators today. It begins with movement, a natural beginning for children's learning, develops good muscular coordination, stresses body action, facilitates eye-hand-body coordination, and produces good listening habits. "Children would be much better prepared to enter their general academic studies as well as advanced music studies" if Dalcroze methods were incorporated into all nursery and kindergarten classrooms (Willour 1969, p. 74).

> Viewed in retrospect, Jaques-Dalcroze's objectives were always toward dual growth—cognitive and affective—through music. . . . From the very beginning [he] emphasized the interrelatedness of time, space, and energy in movement, these considerations became the means of focusing on the expressive potential of the musical elements in synthesis. (Aronoff 1969, p. 170)

Carl Orff (b. 1895), a German composer and educator, also believed that music education begins with movement. Orff began with children's body responses and actions. He believed in an imaginative and spontaneous approach to the teaching of music based on three principles: (1) rhythm is represented in all living things; (2) speech, movement, and music form an integrated whole in each person; (3) no child is nonmusical.

Rhythm, for Orff, is approached in a nonintellectual way, with hand clapping, knee slapping, and other body movements used as beginning responses. The emphasis is placed on the child's body movement, and each child is made aware of the different parts of the body and the ways they can move. Informality and originality are encouraged. Later, rhythmic patterns of one word, then two, and eventually entire phrases, are included. This results in the formation of a rhythmic repertoire of responses within each child.

Another music educator, Zoltan Kodaly (1882–1967), developed his ideas of music education after the communists took control of Hungary in 1945. "If you really want to lift people from their misery, give them something permanent for themselves, which can never be taken away from them, and which can bolster them in time of trouble and lift them in time of joy" (Bacon 1969, p. 54). From this thought, and to this end, Kodaly developed a music curriculum beginning with three year olds in nursery schools.

Instead of starting with rhythmic movement, Kodaly taught children simple folk music. After children could sing the authentic Hungarian folk music and songs, they then progressed to learning to read and write music. Only after children were able to recognize and reproduce folk tunes, were they introduced to the visual representation of songs.

Three and four year olds sang nursery songs, stepped, clapped to the beat of songs, and played simple percussion instruments. They were taught to recognize differences between loud and soft, identify familiar melodies, and were introduced to the concepts of high and low pitch, fast and slow tempo. By the time children were four years old, they were expected to know over twenty songs and be able to identify known songs simply by hearing the clapped rhythm of the melody.

The Kodaly curriculum spirals from the very first simple folk songs and concepts to more complex concepts. As children grow they are introduced to rhythmic clapping, hand signals (a different signal for each member of the musical scale), charts of rhythmic counting and clapping, and charts of the hand signals.

This sequential instruction toward the acquistion of musical skills and literacy has been successful. Bacon (1969) reports that now, after fifty years of the method being used in the Hungarian schools, most Hungarians up to the age of about twenty-eight in Hungary can read and write music as easily as their own language. Not only that, children who have had the Kodaly music instruction as a daily activity show greater achievement in nearly all other academic fields, especially math and reading.

The three curricula, the Dalcroze, Orff, and Kodaly, have similarities. Dalcroze's and Orff's are based on the child's rhythmic movements, but all three spiral from the simple to the complex, based on sequential hierarchies of skill and concept development. Each sees children as active participants in the curriculum, enjoying and creating music as they move through the stages of the curriculum.

Teachers today can build their music curriculum on some of the same ideas. They can begin with the enactive. The movement of children provides a natural base of experiences with music. From this base children can give expression to their ideas and feelings through music. Of course this assumes that children are given experiences which they can express. Without experiences or ideas children will be lost when asked to express themselves. From expressing themselves through movement, children can be introduced to the more complex content of music, learning to listen and then to sing and read music.

The teacher's attitude in planning musical experiences for children seems important. Shelly (1976) stresses that teachers should create a musical environment in which children can learn by

- having a flexible schedule so that music can be brought in whenever the occasion arises.
- letting music be informal, welcoming the children's ideas.
- allowing a lot of repetition.
- working with individuals as well as small groups and the total group.

• appreciating each child's divergent ideas, accepting all children at their own level, but encouraging all to participate.
• fostering creativity by asking children, "Can you think of another way . . . ? How else could you . . . ? What would happen if . . . ?"
• allowing time for free exploration and manipulation of all music materials.
• providing many and varied sensory experiences which will stimulate and challenge children to use higher levels of thinking and encourage children to perceive, associate, relate, and make value judgments.

Movement and Rhythm— The Enactive and Iconic

Children's motions begin with large muscle, random actions that later give way to rhythmic moving for short periods of time. Young children can move quickly before they can control their bodies in slower movements. With experiences in movement and maturation, children can make sustained, smooth movements and can adapt their body movements to contrasting, changing accompaniment (Leeper 1974, p. 380).

Space, time, and freedom are essential when planning to foster children's rhythmic movement. Space is necessary for children to feel free to experiment with their bodies without being inhibited by others or some piece of furniture. Time is essential. Teachers should plan to set aside some time in the schedule each day for children's rhythmic activities.

Freedom for movement stems from the teacher's attitude as much as it does from having space and time.

> The process of encouraging a young child to discover the dance within involves an adult creatively interacting with the child. It assumes the adult's respect and admiration for what the child is doing, and the belief that the child's ideas and responses are just as interesting, even though not as complex, as those of an adult. (Stinson 1977, p. 50)

Respect for children's actions can be developed by starting with the children's own rhythmic movements. Rather than asking children to move to the music or to move across the room as bears or ducks, teachers begin by building on the child's own natural movements. This is exactly what Dalcroze did when he followed a child's walk across a room with a drumbeat. Teachers might say, "This is how your feet sounded when you ran across the yard, listen . . ." or, "This is the way your body went when you rolled over and over" repeating the sounds with a drum or other rhythm instrument.

Building on the movement of the children means that the teacher must be an astute observer. In order for a teacher to extend the children's explorations, Stinson (1977) suggests that adults ask themselves questions when observing the children.

"What is the name of the movement?"
"What part of the body is emphasized?"
"Is the child tense, relaxed?"

"Is the movement strong, heavy, or light, fast, slow, or in between?"

"In which direction is the movement? Does the child use one spot or the entire floor?"

"What is the child's spatial relationship to other parts of the environment?"

"What does the shape remind you of—a worm, willow tree, elephant?"

Using these questions, teachers have a framework for giving children feedback and extending their skills.

> After really looking at the child, the next step is for the adult to tell the child what was observed . . . not just commenting "good" or "nice" but concentrating on just one or two specific points at a time. For example, "your toes go so lightly on the floor!" Comments like this help children develop vocabulary, as well as direct their attention to particular aspects of movement. Comments that are specific direct children's concentration to particular aspects of movement and heightens awareness and clarity of a child's movement. (Stinson 1977, p. 51)

Only after children have had the opportunity to find out for themselves what parts of their body they can move and how they can move, and feel the deep appreciation of their work through the teacher's specific comments, should they be asked to move to music. When music is introduced, it is done gradually and begins with children establishing their own pace and using their own ideas.

Sometimes children may be introduced to one sound or instrument at a time, exploring and experimenting what they can do with their body to imitate or reflect the sound. A teacher observing a small group of children sitting on the floor believes the children would be receptive to a change of pace and selects a maraca from the music corner. "Sitting on the floor in a small group the teacher plays the maraca, 'how does it make you want to move? Wiggle!' From this introduction the children might begin to wiggle their fingers, arms, legs or any other part of their body" (Music Educators 1973, p. 37).

Then, they could be asked to stop when the maraca does, to wiggle glued to one spot on the floor, wiggle different parts of their body, wiggle all over the room. The culmination would be asking the children to move as the instrument is played in different rhythms, tempos, or intensities. The teacher might also add a drumbeat, claps, or chants.

Other instruments could be introduced in the same manner so children become familiar with making their body respond to different sounds. Throughout the experiences the use of verbal labels is useful. Sounds can be termed loud, soft, fast, slow, staccato, gentle, legato, and so on. As children develop concepts of moving to the sounds and being able to differentiate between them, they may take turns playing the instruments for each other to move to.

From this beginning children can be introduced to musical selections. Always ask the children to listen to the record or piece of music before having them respond to it. Ask them to listen carefully, thinking about the sounds they hear. During what parts of the music would they move softly and swiftly across the room? What parts would call for different types of moving?

Moving to music is a complex process. Children must have knowledge of different sounds, the abilities to distinguish between them and to conceptualize movements. It takes time, teaching, and practice on the part of the children. And it also takes children who are comfortable with themselves and others, children who will dare to diverge, who feel free to express themselves, adapting their own bodies to the pulse or beat of the music.

Props can be added to children's movement explorations. "Now we have a brand new area in which to experiment with creative movement!" (Rosenberg 1963, p. 14). For the youngest children, perhaps the two and three year olds, sitting on the floor rolling balls back and forth is pleasant. The teacher and children can pick up a chant to the rhythm of the balls.

As children play with the balls, or balloons, the teacher can again pick up the beat of their play with a chant or follow it with a drum. Children might dribble, bounce, hold, and catch the balls or balloons. By the time children are five or six years old, they will be able to follow the beat of a drum or rhythm of a song, holding the balls on certain phrases, bouncing for others, or bouncing steadily with the beat of a drum (Rosenberg 1963, p. 15).

Colored scarfs sway, twirl, and swing as children use them with their movement. Scarfs are good to bring out when waltzing, swirling music will be played and are enjoyed by the children as they transform them into veils, shawls, or other parts of clothing.

Hoops can also be used creatively. These can be constructed from sections of plastic hose stapled together with a dowel (wooden stick) to join the ends of the hose, forming a hoop. These are inexpensive to make and provide the children with additional ideas for movement. Three year olds may place the hoops on the floor and curl up inside of them, other children place the hoops in a pattern and dance through them, still others use them to give added expression to their dance. They twirl them high in the air, at their sides, or around themselves, all in time to the beat of the music.

Some teachers have found that children, four or five years of age and older, enjoy and benefit from shadow movement. With a strong light, perhaps a slide projector without the slides, highlighting a wall in a darkened room, children can practice moving in front of the light and observe their shadow movement on the wall. Children can move by themselves, to music, or the accompanying beat of a drum; with partners or even in groups. Children enjoy watching their shadows change as they move closer to the wall or away from it.

Although moving is an enactive and iconic mode of knowing and learning about the world through action, perception, and imagery, children's movement can grow to become a symbolic mode of learning. Sometimes the props, the scarfs, hoops, perhaps ankle bells or capes, lead children to dancing as if they were queens, kings, or fairies.

From this type of beginning children use rhythm to act as if they were trains, airplanes, sailboats, or animals, symbolically representing through their movement some object, thing, or event they have experienced in the environment. For children to dance or move symbolically means that a broad, varied background of experiences has been provided. Children have visited the zoo and observed the animals moving, or they have watched different vehicles in the traffic stream, or had vicarious experiences observing plants, animals, and life through books, movies, and filmstrips.

Teachers can support children's moving from the enactive to the symbolic with the use of experiences and language. They might ask children to "Pick an animal you liked at the zoo and move as if you were that animal"; "Move as if you were carrying a heavy load"; "As if you were happy, sad, walking in the rain or snow"; "Move as if you were walking under water." These suggestions are given only after the children have grown from the enactive mode of learning, and they are always based on some experience the children have had.

Children can explore the use of various dance movements to act out their ideas. Sometimes the class may be privileged to have observed a dance troupe in the neighborhood, or they may have seen a movie of a ballet and know that stories are told through movement and dance. Children with this experience will have fun acting out stories they enjoy through dance. Dancing out stories is one way to tell others your ideas. It is like telling a story or drawing a picture, only this time you are telling the story in dance. Children can dance out stories as they make them up as a group.

Other stories can be danced based on experiences children can only imagine and cannot experience for themselves. They may dance out the story of going to, and walking on the moon, or under the ocean, or dancing as if they were some animal. Children can also create dance to tell the story of a painting they have seen, or a picture in a book, or a folk tale.

Listening—The Iconic

Listening involves perception and the organization of perceptual responses. It corresponds to the iconic mode of knowing. Even though the iconic mode of knowing follows the enactive, listening (in the content of music), comes before anything else.

Listening is one of the abilities the infant is believed to possess at birth. Babies respond to sounds from the moment of birth, and soon after, they are capable of responding to the human voice and exploring the environment in an attempt to locate the source of sounds. McDonald (1978) believes that music should be included daily for infants as well as for older children because infants are so responsive to the sounds around them. At two months of age an infant will lie motionless, with fixed attention to the sound of singing or the playing of an instrument (Michel 1973). And although babies cannot sing, they try to produce the sounds they hear at a very early age (Ostwald 1973).

By the time the child is nearing two years of age, or even before, she will enjoy listening to songs sung by others, or songs on a record. Two year olds enjoy making their own music, either with mechanical, found objects or with their own voices. Three year olds begin to be able to listen, for short periods of time, to songs and stories in a group. They can identify the differences between instruments and pick out sounds on the piano or in a recording.

Four and five year old children will be able to listen for longer periods of time and can repeat the sounds they hear. Children who have reached four or five years of age and have a solid background of listening experiences will be able to pick out the sounds of specific instruments from a recording. These children will enjoy making their own sounds and can apply the concepts of loud, soft, happy, sad, light, heavy, fast, and slow either to music they create themselves or music created by others.

Five year olds can hear pitch and match a pitch vocally. As they progress in listening experiences, they advance from the ability to make gross discriminations between sounds to fine ones. The Music Educators National Conference has compiled a list of objectives for listening. By five years of age, according to the conference, the child should

- listen to music
- act out what he hears in music
- distinguish between slow/fast, loud/soft, high/low
- recognize familiar melodies
- identify familiar orchestra instruments. (Morgan 1955, p. 72)

Children listen to music.

Most children love to explore sounds. They are usually highly motivated to create their own sounds. Most enjoy exploring the things they can do with their own voice. They make up silly rhymes, repeating them while pounding the clay, digging in the sand, or painting at the easel. To the uninitiated these silly rhymes may seem irrelevant and at times irreverent, but they are serious business for children.

These chants are a part of children's egocentric speech, described by Piaget as repetition and monologue, in which children intend to communicate only with themselves (Ginsburg and Opper 1969). This speech later leads to socialized speech which is intended to communicate with others. Teachers can build on children's natural interest in words and chants by letting them create the chants and enjoy giggling over them.

Poetry, E. Lear's "A was once an apple pie," and songs, such as "I Went to the Animal Fair," as well as nonsense poems, songs, and stories that play on and with words build on children's enjoyment of sound. About the time that children enjoy listening to poetry and songs, they will be able to repeat rhythms and sounds they hear.

Echo clapping, tapping out patterns with rhythm sticks, keeping time to a beat, and even playing a melody on bells or piano can be introduced. Children can produce sounds with their own bodies. Ask them to find out all the different sounds one part of their body will make. How many sounds can they make with their tongue? With their hands, clapping them together flat and then cupped, then slapping them on their legs, chest, or arms, or with their fingers?

Instruments produce a variety of sounds. Children can tap a drum on its side, tap with their fingers on the edge of the drum, tap the edge with the drumstick, run their fingers across the drumhead, or use sticks or their hand to pound flat on the drumhead and produce still other sounds.

As children grow in familiarity with making sounds and are able to discriminate between them, they begin to imitate the sounds around them. They might try to repeat the sound of the church bells, traffic, or children playing in the yard, and they can collect specific instruments to accompany different songs and recordings.

To help children discover more about sounds, sound carrels can be built. A carrel can be a discarded cardboard box, big enough for one child to sit in, a tent for a child to crawl inside, or an empty laundry soap can (approximately three feet high and two feet in diameter) with a hole cut in the side (Music Educators, 1973). Children can enter these carrels and explore sounds using mechanical objects, found objects, rhythm instruments, or their own voices vithout disturbing the others or being distracted by the sounds in the room.

Different sound makers could be categorized in baskets for children to use in the carrels. These baskets, placed next to the carrels, could contain found objects from the kitchen—spoons, lids, pans, graters; objects from a woodshop—sticks, bamboo pieces of various lengths, wood blocks; or metal pipes of different sizes. Bells, rattles, drums, maracas, and other rhythm instruments can also be placed near the carrels.

Exploration of sound continues as teachers encourage children to begin to classify sounds and sound makers. Teachers can ask

- How many things make a striking sound?
- Which instruments produce ringing sounds?
- What makes scraping sounds?
- Which instruments produce long, short, or smooth sounds?

Throughout all of children's experiences with sounds, the vocabulary of music should be used. It seems as if children are first able to understand the concept of loudness and are able to distinguish loud from soft sounds. This is followed by the ability to differentiate duration from pitch. Even five year olds, however, will confuse the terms high, loud, and fast; low, soft, and slow (Shelly 1975, p. 205).

Teachers of young children can be aware of these possible confusions and provide children with experiences to help them sort out the right word for the right sound. Shelly (1975) suggests the activity of filling jars with different levels of water. Blowing across the top of the jar containing water produces a sound. As the water level in the jar is lowered, the sound becomes deeper and is called low. The lower the water level, the lower the sound. Step bells, or a xylophone placed on end to make a musical stairway, also illustrate the higher the sound the higher the step. Vocabulary to describe the timbre, rhythm, melody, tempo, and intensity of sounds can be introduced and used.

June Wright, a nursery school teacher, uses the following activities to help children she teaches become familiar with the vocabulary and concept of rhythm, melody, and tempo:

1. Clap and say a simple rhythm, perhaps the rhythm of the child's name or her favorite nursery rhyme. Have the child clap the rhythm with you. For variation, play the pattern on a drum or with rhythm sticks.
2. Play a musical selection with a slow beat and one with a fast beat, explaining which is which. Let the children clap the beat with their hands, slap it on their thighs, and stamp it with their feet to begin to identify which is slow and which is fast.
3. Demonstrate loud and soft with your voice, and have the children imitate. Play a record with a steady beat and vary the volume; encourage the children to clap loud or soft with the music.
4. Use three or four rhythm instruments with which the children are familiar. Have one child turn his back while the teacher or another child plays one instrument. Have the child turn around and play the same instrument. The teacher can advance to playing two or three instruments in sequence and having the child repeat the sequence.
5. Tell the story of the three little bears as a *sound story*. Use the xylophone or piano and play low C for Papa bear, G for Mama bear, and high C for Baby bear. Play up the scale as the bears and Goldilocks go upstairs and down the scale as they come down (turning the xylophone on end to foster the understanding of high and low sounds). Let the children decide on a sound for knocking on the door, the chair crashing. Ask them to extemporize a tune for Goldilocks' sleeping

and one for the bears as they walk in the woods. Other stories can be told as sound stories, such as *Three Billy Goats Gruff* and *The Three Little Pigs*.

6. Let the children move to a record—freeze in place when the record stops. Vary the action with children putting their hands on hips or some other motion when the music stops.

7. Use two instruments. When you play one, the children walk forward; when you play the other, the children walk backward. Encourage the children to take the same number of steps as the number of beats in the instrument (J. Wright 1978, p. 6).*

Rhythm instruments have a long history of use in the kindergarten. They were supposedly introduced by Patty Smith Hill and Anna Bryan who advocated the use of found objects as rhythm instruments so that children could explore a variety of different sounds.

From this beginning with instruments, the rhythm band became a part of the kindergarten curriculum. In a rhythm band, children select different instruments and together beat time to a song. When four or five year olds are introduced to the concept of a band, they should be creating music, not just noise. It takes introducing the children to one instrument at a time and a lot of planning and cooperation to form a rhythm band. Children singing together or listening to music may be asked to accompany the song with drums or rhythm sticks. Following practice with several children playing bells, sticks, or drums to a song, additional instruments can be added. A full band, with each child playing an instrument, is the end result. Using a tape recorder will help children evaluate their band. They can listen to the recording and then try playing again, until they produce music.

Most programs will have at least a few good musical rhythm band instruments. A set of tone blocks, a step xylophone, bells, and a good drum are probably necessary for children to hear sounds of quality. Rhythm band instruments can, however, be constructed by the children, and often, when children participate in making the instruments, their interest increases.

Having created their own band, children will enjoy listening to records or performances by musicians. Visits from musicians, professional or otherwise, will expand the children's musical understanding. By seeing and hearing a violin, children have a base for listening to a recording of a violin or an orchestration of a piece of music. Children have enjoyed listening to recordings of "Peter and the Wolf," "The Sorcerer's Apprentice," and music from composers ranging from Bartók and Debussy to Prokofiev and Ravel.

Singing—The Symbolic

Who has not heard children chanting as they observed children the world over? The preschool child skips along, chanting, "Skip, skip skip, up, down, up, down," or digs in the sand, accompanying the activity with "Sandy cup, sandy cup, sandy cup, filling up, fill, fill, fill."

*Reprinted with permission from June Wright

These chants begin spontaneously and are sung in a minor third (sol–mi) (Shelly 1975, 207). They are melodic and use repeated tones. Because children sing happily, without example, singing can be a natural part of any preschool experience.

Teachers can use children's natural chanting as the beginning of song in the preschool. They can either repeat the chants back to the child, "Swinging up, swinging down," or make up chants to go with the actions of the children. "Sammy is rocking back and forth, back and forth, back and forth," or "Kirsten is jumping, jumping, jumping, up, down, up, down, up, down."

Building on children's natural chanting as a means of beginning singing, teachers can also remember that whatever can be said can be sung. Singing directions, singing the child's name as a reinforcement, giving feedback through song, and singing through the routines are natural ways to teach song. "Sing your day" (Music Educators 1973, p. 42).

> Building the singing voice as a natural way of expressing one's ideas removes the pressure from having to sing a tune correctly. The child needs to explore his singing voice and to use a variety of pitches with words to express his own feelings and ideas. Very soon the child will develop his own tunes into patterns that result in songs. (Music Educators 1973, p. 43)

Two and three year olds are especially responsive to hearing their own chants repeated by the teacher. These chants can be sung back to the children and repeated at group singing time. The young child enjoys singing a made-up chant about herself, or singing a made-up song in connection with some activity. Even if a teacher is cautious about making up songs to accompany children's activities, she can still adapt different songs to meet the occasion. For example, making pudding is a fine time to create a new version of "Mulberry Bush."

Soon the children will be joining in, repeating the teacher's chants, or their own. Two and three year olds, enjoy learning to sing a few simple nursery rhymes, folk songs, and other songs that are simple and have a lot of repetition. Recalling that children's chants are sung at the sol–mi range, teachers can select songs in the range between middle A and middle C, because these are the tones most easily sung by the preschooler.

Two and three year olds also enjoy singing along with familiar finger plays. Two Little Blackbirds, Five Little Chickadees, and Open Shut Them can be introduced. Some children will participate in following along with making the gestures, gradually adding the words and singing the entire song.

Young children enjoy songs about themselves, "Mary Wore a Red Dress," "What Should We Do When We All Go Out?" and others about things that are close to the child are valued. "The egocentric songs about himself or parents, pets, toys at home, color, and numbers become his way of knowing" (Music Educators 1973, p. 42). The complexity of songs becomes a matter of growth. The range of the melody and the complexity of the words increase as the children grow, experience, and mature.

By the time the child is five, she should have an extensive repertoire of songs. Folk songs, nursery songs, action songs are all a part of the child's portfolio. Now children enjoy singing in groups. "Skip to My Lou," "On Top of Old Smoky," "Paw Paw Patch" and so many others are enjoyed. Sheehy (1959) suggests that children begin with folk songs and patriotic songs. Then teach holiday songs, humorous songs, lullabies, and action songs, with the words directing the child as he sings and listens.

Smith (1969), who demonstrated the validity of teaching young children music, suggests that the first songs presented to children be *directional* in tone, songs with tunes that go up and down. A song with a limited range of three or four notes is a step higher than directional songs. Songs involving a total of three or four adjacent tones in a repeated melody pattern are considered *limited range songs*. Smith then proceeds with songs in the *lower range stage*. These literally are those that lower and deepen children's vocal range. These are followed by songs in the *upper range*, with subsequent expansion to include higher pitches.

Smith (1969) cautions the classroom teacher against a repertoire consisting entirely of songs of one range because individual children will be at different levels in the continuum. They are apt to be frustrated if the teacher does not vary the songs.

"But I can't sing! How can I teach singing?" is a familiar statement among beginning teachers. Let's observe in a school for young children for a moment. Here is Ms. Smith. She is sitting on a low chair and calls children to her. They come into the room ready for a quiet activity and sit around her on the rug. Ms. Smith doesn't play the piano, although there is one in the room, but she does know how to use an autoharp.

She begins, using a chord on the autoharp, singing children's names in a chant, "Here comes Aletha, here is Mary, how are you today." "Sing about me, sing about me," calls out one of the boys, and Ms. Smith makes up a song, using the same sol–mi chant about Willie. Next the children sing a few folk songs. Ms. Smith does not sing loudly, she keeps her own voice and the autoharp soft. The children do most of the singing.

Today she is introducing a new song. She has been singing it to herself for several days, and she has sung it during activity time a number of times. Now she sings it again. Instead of playing the authharp, she uses the tone blocks to help keep her voice in tune. The song is sung all the way through then repeated once again. The children begin singing with her, some of the children, that is. Tomorrow the song will be sung again during free play and at singing time.

As long as the children see and know the teacher enjoys music, hear their chants repeated, and feel they are respected, it is not really necessary that a teacher be an accomplished singer and musician. Teachers who are unsure of their own abilities can

1. Use a recording to introduce a song to children.
2. Practice the song before presenting it to the children, learning it thoroughly.

3. Teach the song to a child, or a few children who can carry a tune, and use these children as helpers when they introduce the song to the entire class.

4. Use a rhythm instrument, step blocks, xylophone, or autoharp to help keep themselves on pitch.

5. Use hand motions, moving their hands up and down with the melody of the song. The hand movement helps to keep the voice on track.

Teaching children new songs often occurs spontaneously. As Ms. Smith did, teachers sing during play time, work time, when the children are entering the classroom, or going home. It is natural to begin singing, "Snow is falling in my garden, lightly dancing all around," when you see the first snowflakes of the winter gently falling through the window. Then when the children are together at singing time, the song is already familiar. Many will be able to sing along; some can sing snatches, but all will enjoy hearing a familiar song once again.

Children who are reading or nearing beginning reading are ready to begin to be introduced to reading music. At times the teacher will show the children the music in the book or make a chart of the notes of a best-loved chant. When children sing the song, or chant, the teacher can follow with her hands, showing children that the notes represent the tune they are singing. It is not expected that children will learn to read music, but the preschool or primary teacher can introduce children to the concept that music is written, just as stories are.

Maria Montessori (1967) once called music the universal language. Singing is so natural to the children, it is only natural that the teacher responds with the children. "Sing with them, and they'll sing with you and you'll sing together as you march along!"

In Summary

You don't have to be a musician or an artist yourself to enjoy music with children. Closely tied to children's growth and development, music is a joy! Music serves to lighten the day, lift spirits, and bring pleasure. Children are so full of creativity that music is not only an integral part of their growth, but also an integral part of all programs for young children.

Whether the Dalcroze, Orff, or Kodaly methods are used or not, teachers should take a developmental approach to music instruction. They might organize preschool music experiences around the enactive, iconic, and symbolic modes of learning so that the children's needs and abilities can be met appropriate to their levels of growth.

Listening and moving to music, making music, and singing are vital and important parts of the curriculum. Music introduces children to knowledge of instruments, as well as skills of listening. But music is vital in and of itself, and for itself.

Resources

Several texts are available to provide coverage in depth of art and music in early childhood education.

BOORMAN, JOYCE, *Creative Dance in the First Three Grades*. New York: David McKay Company, 1969.

COHEN, ELAIN PEAR, and RUTH STRAUS GAINER, *Art: Another Language for Learning*. New York: Citation Press, 1976.

HERBERHOLZ, BARBARA, *Early Childhood Art*. Dubuque, Iowa: Wm. C. Brown Company, 1974.

NYE, V., *Music for Young Children*. Dubuque, Iowa: Wm. C. Brown Company, 1975.

Projects

1. Collect drawings by children two, three, four, and five years old. Analyze the drawings to determine how they differ and see what progress children make in drawing as they grow and mature.

2. Visit a classroom and note the ways children express their ideas, feelings, and emotions through the visual arts and music.

3. Collect some paintings by young children. With another teacher or friend, discuss the following statements as you examine the paintings:

  a. Children draw what they know.
  b. Children draw what they feel.
  c. Children draw what they see.

Can you find evidence in the paintings to support each of these statements?

4. Begin a card file of art and music ideas that can be used when you work with young children. The journals, *Young Children, Childhood Education, Arts and Activities,* and *The Music Educators Journal,* offer many ideas.

5. Observe children during a music session. Note the way children participate in singing. Do they each participate in active singing? Which children do not sing but seem to enjoy being with the group? Which take the lead? What other individual differences in their participation in music do you observe?

References

ALMY, M. *The Early Childhood Educator at Work*. New York: McGraw-Hill Book Company, 1975.

ALSCHULER, R., and HATTWICK, L. B., *Painting and Personality: A Study of Young Children*. Chicago: University of Chicago Press, 1947.

ANDREWS, P. A., "Music and Motion: The Rhythmic Language of Children," *Young Children*, 24, 3 (1969), 157–163.

ARNHEIM, R., *Art and Visual Perception: The Psychology of the Creative Experience*. Berkeley: University of California Press, 1954.

ARONOFF, F. W., *Music and Young Children*. New York: Holt, Rinehart & Winston, 1969.

328

BACON, D., "Kodaly and Orff: Report from Europe," *The Music Educators Journal*, 55, 8 (1969), 53–56.

BARKAN, M., "Transition in Art Education," in *Readings in Art Education*, eds. E. W. Eisner and D. W. Ecker. Waltham, Mass: Blaisdell Publishing Co., 1966.

BROUDY, H. S., "The Case of Aesthetic Education," in *Report of the Tanglewood Symposium*, ed. R. A. Choate. Washington, D.C.: Music Educators National Conference, 1968.

BRUNER, J., *Toward a Theory of Instruction*. Cambridge, Mass.: Belknap Press of Harvard University Press, 1966.

COLE, N. R., *The Arts in the Classroom*. New York: The John Day Co., 1966.

COHEN, E. P., and GAINER, R. S., *Art: Another Language for Learning*. New York: Citation Press, 1976.

DEWEY, J., *Democracy and Education*. New York: The Free Press, 1944. First published 1916.

EISNER, E. W., *Educating Artistic Vision*. New York: Macmillan, Inc., 1972.

GARDNER, H., *The Arts and Human Development*. New York: John Wiley & Sons, Inc., 1973.

GINSBURG, H., and OPPER, S., *Piaget's Theory of Intellectual Development*. Englewood Cliffs, N.J.: Prentice-Hall, Inc., 1969.

GOODENOUGH, F., *Measurement of Intelligence by Drawings*. New York: Harcourt Brace Jovanovich, Inc., 1926.

GREENBERG, M., "A Preliminary Report of the Effect of a Music Curriculum with Preschool Head Start Children." *Council for Research in Music Education: Bulletin* 29 (1972), 13–16.

JACQUES-DALCROZE, E., *Rhythm, Music and Education*. Translated by H. F. Rubinstein. New York: G. P. Putnam's Sons, 1921.

KUHMERKER, L., "Music in the Beginning Reading Program," *Young Children*, 24, 3 (1969), 157–163.

LEEPER, S. H., *Good Schools for Young Children* (4th ed.). New York: Macmillan, Inc., 1974.

LINDERMANN, E. W., and HERBOLZ, D. W., *Developing Artistic and Perceptual Awareness*. Dubuque, Iowa: Wm. C. Brown Co., 1974.

LOWENFELD, V., *Creative and Mental Growth*. New York: Macmillan, Inc., 1957.

McDONALD, D. T., and RAMSEY, J. H., "Awakening the Artist: Music for Young Children," *Young Children*. 33, 2 (1978), 26–31.

McFEE, J. K., *Preparation for Art* (2nd ed.). Belmont, Calif: Wadsworth Publishing Co., Inc., 1970.

McWHINNIE, H. J., "Viktor Lowenfeld: Art Education for the 1970's," *Studies in Art Education*, 4 (1972), 8–13.

MICHAEL, P., "The Optimum Development of Musical Abilities in the First Years of Life," *Psychology of Music*, 1, (1973), 14–20.

MONTESSORI, M., *The Absorbent Mind*. New York: Holt, Rinehart & Winston, 1967.

MORGAN, H. N., *Music in American Education: Music Educator's Source Book*. Number 2. Washington, D.C.: Music Educators National Conference, 1955.

Music in Early Childhood. Washington, D.C.: Music Educators National Conference, 1973.

OSTWALD, P. F., "Musical Behavior in Early Childhood," *Developmental Medicine and Child Neurology*, 1973. 15, 1 (1973), 367–375.

PIAGET, J., *The Child's Conception of Reality*. London: Routledge & Kegan Paul, 1955.

PRUITT, H., and STELLE, A. L., "Music by Head Start Teachers for the Educationally Disadvantaged, *American Music Teacher*. 20, 6 (1971), 29–30.

READ, H., *Education Through Art*. New York: Pantheon Books, 1956.

ROSENBERG, M., *It's Fun to Teach Creative Music*. New York: The Play School's Association, 1963.

SHEEHY, E. D., *Children Discover Music and Dance*. New York: Holt, Rinehart & Winston, 1959.

SHELLY, S., "Music," in *Curriculum for the Preschool/Primary Child: A Review of the Research*, ed. C. Seefeldt. Columbus, Ohio: Charles E. Merrill Publishing Company, 1975.

SMITH, R. B., "The Effect of Group Nursery School Music Training on Later Achievement and Interest in Music: A Ten Year Progress Report," Music Education and Child Development Division. University of Illinois, 1968. Unpublished Manuscript.

SCHWARTZ, J. B., and DOUGLAS, N. J., "Increasing the Awareness of Art Ideas of Culturally Deprived Kindergarten Children Through Experiences with Ceramics," Final Report Project Number 6-8647. Washington, D.C.: U.S. Department of HEW, 1967.

STINSON, S. W., "Movement as Creative Interaction with the Child," *Young Children*, 32, 6 (1977), 49–51.

TORRANCE, E. P., *Rewarding Creative Behavior*. Englewood Cliffs, N.J.: Prentice-Hall, Inc., 1965.

WEBER, E., *The Kindergarten*. New York: Teachers College Press, 1969.

WILLOUR, J., "Beginning with Delight, Leading to Wisdom: Dalcroze," *The Music Educators Journal*, 56, 1 (1969), 73–75.

WRIGHT, J., "Music for Young Children." College Park, Md.: University of Maryland. Unpublished Paper, 1979.

14

The Social World

The socially competent child is willing to try out new things—new toys, new relationships, new space, new people, and one would expect to see this growing over time.

A.G. Hilliard III. 1978, p. 12.

Children who are socially competent are driven by a desire to find out more and more about the world in which they live. Children who know who they are and feel good about themselves want to learn about others, how others live and interact and find out how their world works. Learning about people and all of their interactions with others and the environment is a lifelong project. It grows and expands as the child grows. It begins in infancy and ends only when life itself ends.

The social studies—that part of the curriculum concerned with people and all of their interactions with others and the environment—offers teachers an organized body of knowledge, skills, and attitudes suited for teaching children social competence. Through the social studies children should begin to develop the self-understanding required to learn about others and their world.

Infants first learn who they are, and then they learn about others and their world. The processes of learning about self and others cannot be separated. "A child cannot learn the ways of society by being apart from people. Others wittingly or unwittingly, teach through their guidance, examples, responses and emotional attachments" (Elkin 1960, p. 5). Piaget calls this social knowl-

331

Children learn who they are.

edge. But before children can gain social knowledge and learn the ways of society, they must first learn about themselves.

Knowledge of Self

Children's self-concept is the foundation on which they will build their future relationships with others and the world. Social studies begins by fostering the self-concept. Children who have developed adequate self-images are able to relate freely and positively with others as their world expands. The more adequate children feel about themselves, the more likely they are to feel a sense of oneness with their world.

When babies are born they cannot differentiate between external objects and parts of their own body. It is not until nearly eight months of age that babies can distinguish between themselves, objects, and others in the environment.

How concepts of self develop is influenced by interactions with others. Even though children must learn that they are separate from their care giver, they are still very dependent on that person for their very life. How others care for the baby is believed to be critical for the development of self.

People who have examined the relationship between early care and later adjustment in life have concluded that infants must have their needs for comfort, tactile stimulation, contact, and physical needs fulfilled if they are to develop self-concepts that permit them to interact with others and form lasting relationships (Harlow and Harlow 1965; Bolwby 1968; Spitz 1945). Infants who have been separated from their mothers and reared in institutions where the needs for comfort and contact were not met were not able to learn or interact effectively with others. Deprivation of love and care during the early years of life is believed to prevent the formation of a positive self-image.

Piaget (1969) views the interaction between child and care giver a little differently. He believes that the formation of the self-concept is not necessarily related to the mother so much as it is to stimulating interactions with a care giver.

> Even before the formation of a self complementary to, and interacting with others, we witness the elaboration of a whole system of exchanges through imitation and the reading of gestures. From this time on, the child begins to react to persons in a more and more specific manner because they behave differently from things and because they behave according to schemes which bear some relation to the schemes of the child's own actions. Sooner or later there is established a kind of causality whose source is others, in as much as they produce pleasure, comfort, pacification, security. (Piaget and Inhelder 1969, p. 24)

For Piaget then, the essential factor in the development of a self-concept is not the mother's love, but the interactions and the quality of interactions between care giver and child.

The process of building a self-image is gradual and continual. Others—in addition to the child's primary care giver—influence the development of self-understanding. Siblings, neighbors, and peers also interact with the child, and these interactions help to form the self-concept. When children enter a preschool there are others who will influence the development of self. Teachers, and another set of peers, now interact with the child. "Self discovery then, is a continuing process, not appearing at a specific time, but continuing throughout all developmental stages and phases (Dinkmeyer 1965, p. 123).

Self in School

Preschool teachers have a unique role to play in fostering children's self-concepts. As children leave their home and enter a preschool, they will shift some of their dependency needs to the teacher. How the teacher interacts with children and the kind of atmosphere she builds will influence children's self-images.

When teachers have small groups of children to work with, they will have the opportunity to foster special relationships with each child. Group size has been found to influence children's feelings of self, as well as their interactions with others. When there is a smaller group, and an adequate number of adults present, there is less distress on the part of individual children and more time spent in interactions between adults and children (Summaries of 21 Papers 1977).

Developing a special relationship with each individual child will help teachers plan experiences that foster success. The more children experience success, whether in stacking blocks, cleaning a table, or making friends, the more likely they will be to view themselves as persons who can and do learn. Failure, criticism, and discouragement, which come from being faced with tasks that are too complex to complete successfully, tend to lower children's feelings of self-confidence.

If small numbers of children are present, teachers can also plan to give them responsibilities they can handle. This means, however, that teachers must know each child so well that they know just how much to challenge the child and which responsibilities children will be able to handle without difficulty. Doing too much for children, the things they could do for themselves, keeps children dependent on others and lowers their feelings of self-esteem.

In a small group each child has an opportunity to feel special. Each feels, and knows, that she has a special contribution to make to the group. Teachers can identify the special talents and capabilities of each child, capitalize on these, and help each child to develop confidence and become a participating member of the group.

Learning About Others

"A child who is learning and building feelings of self worth is one who is able to become involved with the ongoing life in the classroom" (D'Evelyn 1970, p. 16). Just as teachers have a special responsibility to foster children's feelings of self-confidence and worth, they have a special role in teaching children to relate to others.

Children are social. They show their interest in others early in life. Babies, even under four months of age, will smile, coo, and gurgle when their mother or care giver approaches. Before their first birthday, children will attempt to interact with others (Mueller 1971). Two year olds have been observed playing and interacting with others in child care centers, and they appear fairly successful in their interactions (Greif 1977).

Preschool groups provide opportunities for children to be together, and they play an important role in social development (Greif 1977). In a preschool group, children are able to

- take an active role in selecting their own playmates;
- learn two distinct types of social interaction patterns—with adults, and with children;
- participate in activities that only children can engage in;
- be in a child centered environment where they have the freedom to interact with others and things in ways they select (Greif 1977, p. 158).

Because of these things, children in a preschool group are believed to be able to develop a larger repertoire of social skills than those children who do not have an opportunity to interact with peers in a school setting. Social skills, however, do not automatically develop just because children are together in a group. "With limited knowledge of how social interactions work, children's techniques and methods are not usually well developed. The goal of good schools for young children is to provide children with these methods and techniques that permit them to learn to live with others" (Leeper 1974, p. 61). Children need a succession of situations, of activities, that will help them learn the skills of working and living with others.

One reason children need help in learning to relate to others is because they are not able to put themselves in the place of another. Because they do not understand that others have feelings, can be hurt, or want things to be a different way, children may have difficulty interacting with others. To help children take on the role of others, teachers might

1. Ask children, "How do you think Roberta felt when you pushed her?" and try to relate whatever experience occurred to some past experience of the child. "Do you remember how you felt when_____?"
2. Connect children's actual experiences with their feelings. "How did you feel when that happened?" "Why were you angry when Jennifer took your truck?" "Did it make you feel happy to share the toys in the sandbox?"
3. Help children to understand their own feelings in context of their actions, "You're happy because you helped him," or "You feel sad because_____"
4. Try to have children put themselves in the place of others. "What would you do if you were_____?"

Children's self-concepts must be protected when they are in a group. Only when they feel secure and loved themselves, can they reach out to interact with others. Children must also be protected within the group. They cannot take on the role of others or enter into social relationships if they are frightened of being hurt. Because of children's undeveloped social skills, they may grab at others, push, or shove to get their way. Teachers must be ready to stop such behavior and let all children know clearly that they are not permitted to hurt another, nor will anyone else be allowed to hurt them.

Direct teaching has also been useful in helping children develop social knowledge. Sometimes teachers simply tell children, "This belongs to the group, you must share it." "When the timer goes off, you must leave the wagon and let someone else have a turn." Children can also be helped to reach a compromise. "Let's see, you both want to be the father. What can we do? John, you will be the father now and then Raoul will be the father."

As children work and play together in the preschool, they learn the pleasure that comes from being with others. Gradually children begin to do things together, to become a group. Many activities are planned to foster children's ability to work with others. Children can

1. Plant or maintain a garden or participate in some cooking activity—making bread, soup, or pudding—that will require the help of more than one.
2. Create a puppet show or act out stories. Many children will have to work together in order to put on a puppet show or recreate a story.
3. Construct a play house, a rabbit hutch, or some other piece of equipment for the room. Children will need to plan together to decide how they will build the item,

what materials they will use, who will be responsible for which tasks, and who will work together to complete the task.

4. Paint, draw, or cut and paste murals, make curtains for the room, or draw on a piece of material with waterproof pens to create a fabric design that their teacher will later fashion into a skirt she will wear to school.

Teachers Build Group Feelings

Teachers serve a major function in helping children become participating members of a group. The teacher is the person who establishes the classroom climate of trust and mutual respect, and it is she who models cooperative and helping behaviors.

Teachers can

- establish rapport by communicating nonverbally with a smile, an arm around a shoulder, or by holding a child.
- acknowledge children when they give comfort to one another.
"That was kind of you to help Susan." "Thank you for sharing with Alex."
- interpret a child's feelings and try to clarify another child's intent so that children can receive help.
"Chris has his arm around you because he thinks it makes you happy." "Tina was trying to help you ride the bike."
- express positive encouragement of independence as well as helping, after having assisted a child several times.
"I think you are able to do that for yourself."
- notice when a child needs to limit the amount of time spent in cooperation with others.
"I'll finish this, you can choose something else to do."
- praise a child who helps or comment when another child praises him or herself. The child might say "I helped Alicia and it was fun." The teacher reinforces, "I'm glad you are happy."
- praise themselves when help has been offered to provide a model.
"I'm glad I helped you carry the heavy block. It's too heavy for one person." (R. Marcus and M. Leiserson 1978, pp. 29–39)

Games Build Group Feelings

Playing simple organized games will help children become a group. Whether the games are active or quiet, played on a table top or in a gym or play yard, children will have to work together, following the same set of rules. Games of any kind offer children practice in becoming observant of the rights of others, taking turns, and recognizing their own responsibility to the group. When playing games together, children must learn to adjust their thinking and take on the role of another.

"Hey, watch out, you can't do that now, you have to be the duck!" Children correct one another when taking part in organized games, and they learn to concentrate on what others are doing, in order to play.

Children under four years of age are not likely to care much about organized games. They may, however, enjoy simple circle games such as Ring Around A Rosy, Farmer in the Dell, or imitative games such as Did You Ever See a Lassie, Punchinello, or Looby Loo. For children under the age of four, these games begin and end spontaneously, with whatever group of children wish to play. Children can enter or leave the group as they wish.

Children four years of age or over can take part in more complex games. These games, however, should not have any hard and fast or complicated rules. Usually children will adjust the rules to fit their own whims and fancies. Nor should games require a large number of children to play. Rather, the games chosen should be for a flexible number of children, appropriate for three or four, or fun for seven or eight.

Children should not have to wait a turn, and all should be able to participate throughout the game, without having to do a great deal of standing around and waiting. Games that are based on teams, winning and losing, are not appropriate for young children.

When teaching a new game to children it is usually best to start right in and explain what to do as you play the game. Children cannot remember a long list of things to do, and they will not sit still and listen to a long explanation of rules ahead of time. It is a good idea to say to a couple of children, "Take my hand and let's make a circle, and I'll teach you how to play." Then start out directly to play.

Teachers should play the game with the children, giving directions and guiding them as they play. Often a teacher will be able to teach the game to a group of children, who will in turn teach it to others.

Games should be short, and usually children enjoy playing two or three different games before going on to another activity. Some games children over four years of age may enjoy are

SKIP TAG

One child skips around a circle and tags some other child's outstretched hands. The child tagged skips in the opposite direction. When they meet, they shake hands. The first child goes to his place and the second child proceeds as did the first. Suitable music might be played as children skip. Children might march instead of skip.

ROUND AND ROUND THE VILLAGE

Children stand in a circle, hands joined. One (or more) walks around the circle as the group sings or chants:
Go round and round the village (repeat three times)
As we have done before.
Then at the next verse, children raise their arms and "It" goes in and out under their arms.
Go in and out the window (repeat three times)
As we have done before.

On the last verse "It" chooses another child to become "It" by standing in front of her.

Now stand before your partner (repeat three times)
As we have done before.

CAT AND KITTENS

One child is selected to be a mother cat; three or four others are chosen to be kittens, and they hide. As soon as they are hidden, they meow to the mother cat who goes to find them.

BUZZ HIDE IN SIGHT

While "It" is out of the room, or hiding her eyes, another child (or leader) hides a small object in plain sight. When "It" returns to the room, the others give clues by buzzing or clapping when "It" goes near the object. The children clap or buzz louder when the child gets closer to the object.

BASKET BALL

Children stand in a circle and take turns trying to throw a ball into a basket placed in the center of a circle.

TOSS BALL

Children stand in a circle. The leader calls the name of a child and immediately throws the ball into the air. The child whose name has been called hurries and tries to catch the ball on the first bounce.

Once children are able to relate successfully within their own group, their social world can be widened and expanded to include others. There can be joint ventures with other groups within the school—parties, field trips, or other activities—and children can reach out to others who work in the school, inviting them to participate in some activity, listen to a new song, or share the pudding they have cooked.

Knowledge

"Children are born, too, into a world of complex human relations where grown-ups love and hate, help and fight one another, where people live and work in groups" (Mitchell 1950, p. 32). Because children's social world expands beyond that of the classroom, preschool teachers also have the responsibility of helping children develop an understanding of the wider world. Children who have knowledge of their complex world feel more secure and can reach out to others, those near to them and those far away.

Through trips into the community, to see and observe the adult world, children's social knowledge can be expanded. The idea of trips into the community is not new. In 1887, Froebel wrote:

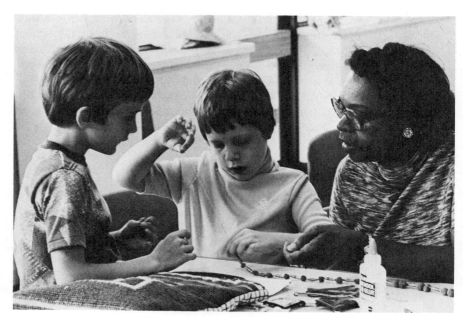

Children learn about others.

> Parents and school-teachers should remember this—and the little
> should, at least once a week, take a walk with each class—not driving them
> out like a flock of sheep, nor leading them out like a company of soldiers,
> but going with them as a father with his sons, and acquaint them more
> fully with whatever the season or nature offers them. (F. Froebel 1887, p.
> 163)

To Lucy Sprague Mitchell, the field trip was the base of the social studies
program. "The social studies program for kindergarten, grades one and two,
is based on trips . . . providing stimuli for classroom activities and guiding the
selection of reading materials, visual aids, songs, etc." (Mitchell 1950, p. 204).

Trips provide children with firsthand opportunities to learn about their
world. Through field trips children

1. Have contact with adult models in the world of work.
2. Observe social systems, such as banking, garbage collections, traffic control, fire
   and police protection, and other systems.
3. Use the methods of the scientist as they gain skills in observing, collecting information, inferring, and drawing conclusions.
4. Have a mutual experience to recreate in dramatic play or to express through
   music, dance, art, or literature.
5. Are stimulated to gain new ideas and are motivated to further learning.

A walking field trip, close to the children's school, is recommended. If
children are to learn about *their* world, no purpose is served going beyond
that world. It is not that a field trip far from the school, perhaps to a zoo or

museum, is not of value, it is just that walking trips, around the school, serve to foster daily motivation. On a trip far from the school, children may be confused by being bombarded with too many stimuli. Rather than focusing on the purpose of the trip, they may only think about the bus ride or worry that their mother will not find them.

When children take weekly walking trips, they can focus on the purpose of the trip, free from distractions. Sometimes a walking trip will be taken rather spontaneously; other times the trip is planned well in advance.

Planning the Trip

Yet planning is the key to all successful trips. It is important that the purpose of the trip be clear to both you and the children, and that there is a relationship between the trip and children's experiences in the classroom. The purpose of the trip will depend on a number of things. The children's interests and background, as well as their level of maturity, must be considered. Their knowledge of the social world and their misconceptions or gaps in knowledge can also serve to direct their teacher's plans. Then the possibilities of the environment must be considered.

> By watching and listening to her group a teacher can pick out the highlights, the points of emphasis, and learn what to reject and what to accept and build upon. It is desirable that each trip have some relationship to the one before it, as each act of a play develops out of the preceding one". (Lucy Sprague Mitchell 1950, p. 204)

Once the purpose of the trip has been decided on, definite planning takes place. Teachers should visit the place first, to look it over and make certain that children's interests and needs will be fulfilled by the trip. Safety should be considered; the things children will need to know before making the trip and the special things that children should watch for can be identified.

The time of day, how far away the place is, and the weather conditions will also be considered. Children can walk distances if the sun is not too hot, and if there is a resting place along the way. Teachers can carry a jug of water, juice, and paper cups, or other snack, for children to enjoy as they rest in a park or shady area. A supply of tissues, adhesive bandages, and other emergency items can also be carried.

Adult volunteers will be necessary. Usually one adult to every three or four children is suggested for a field trip. Depending on the purpose of the trip and the distance from school, older children from the school may even serve as helpers.

Parents need notice of the trip. Parents need to know where their children will be at all times. However, when trips are taken within the school building, yard, or within one block from the school, parents need not give their permission. They only need to know that these trips are routine and expected. If, however, children are to go further than the immediate neighborhood, parental permission should be obtained. Following the regulations of the individual school, teachers will let the parents know, not only where the children will be going, but also the purpose of the trip.

Children too need to be prepared. They may need some background information about the place they will visit and help in focusing on the purpose of the trip. Asking the children to dictate a list of the things they want to find out about on the trip or the things they will ask when they get there helps them keep the purpose of their trip clear.

Taking the Trip

Teachers are active on the trip. They keep children together, protect them from hazards, and teach them. Using any or all of the possible teaching strategies, teachers ensure that the purpose of the trip is fulfilled. On the trip teachers may

1. Sing marching songs to keep children involved, and together, as they walk.
2. Repeat safety rules, "Remember when we get to the corner, and the surface of the area changes, we must stop."
3. Use a map, or make a map, and show children how to follow it.
4. Let the children take time to observe the things around them. Take the time to let children find out about the things in which they are interested.
5. Help children focus their attention on the purpose of the trip. Take pictures of the trip, or tape record the sounds of the place you are visiting. Bring along the dictated questions, or list of things children wanted to find out about, to refresh children's memory.

After the Trip

For young children, the time following the trip may be more important than the trip itself. It may be that immediately after the trip children will need to rest. A snack, quiet time, or time for children to reflect on their experiences is required. Then follow-up activities can take place. These include

• opportunities for creative expression through art media, song, dance, movement, or literature.
• discussions about the trip.
• books, films, or filmstrips that expand on children's knowledge of the place they have visited.
• opportunities to recreate the roles they have observed on the field trip through play. New props can be added to the dramatic play area to enable children to act out the roles they have observed.

Fostering Knowledge of the Social World

Nearly every social studies concept can be fostered by a trip into the immediate community. Concepts from the area of geography, history, and economics are gained through trips to the community.

Several key concepts from the field of geography can be fostered through trips to the community. The ideas that the earth is the place where we live, that the earth moves, and that people locate themselves on earth are key concepts that provide the focus for some trips.

Children believe that the earth made itself, or that giants or God made the earth. People, or the mountain itself, made the mountain, so people can go skiing (Piaget, 1951). Field trips to the community will permit children to build the foundation on which logical thought can develop. Trips can be taken to observe the land forms in the area. Children might be able to see hills, valleys, ponds, or streams. The fact that the surface of the earth is made of water and land can be seen.

Other trips may be taken to observe the surfaces of the earth following different weather conditions. After a rainstorm or ice storm, the children can examine the changes in the land and water. Children might be able to observe the effects of erosion following a rainstorm, or the dryness that results in the earth when there is no rain.

Young children will not be able to develop complete concepts of the nature of the movement of the earth. Field trips can be taken to observe

1. Weather conditions. You can go outside to observe clouds on a windy day, rain, or snow. You can measure the shadows of the building or other landmarks on the play yard at different times of the day and discuss how the shadows change during the day. On another trip you might have the children stand in the sun and then in the shade and make comparisons between these experiences.
2. Changes that occur as the seasons change. A trip through the neighborhood can be taken to identify all of the signs of spring, winter, summer, or fall. Some of the changes will be the result of nature and weather conditions; others people will make.
3. The difference between day and night. This can be a trip children take with their parents. Have them find out how night is different from day, and discuss the differences in school.

Locating places and things on the surface of the earth is an important concept in geography. Concepts of location go hand in hand with concepts of direction. Children will use directions to locate themselves in space and to locate their homes and school. Beginning with trips taken within the school building, ask children to

1. Walk to the cafeteria or office, and tell how they would locate their room from this point in the school.
2. Take a walk around the school building to find the signs and numbers that tell where the building is located. Have them look for signs and symbols on streets and other buildings. These are the symbols that enable people to locate things in the world.
3. Go outside the school, cross the street, or walk far enough from the school so children can view the entire building. Ask children to locate their room from this

viewpoint. Or have them point out the office, nurse's room, or other parts of the building.

4. Locate stores and other landmarks in their neighborhood in relation to the school. Take a walk to the park, or any nearby place of interest. Draw a simple map to follow, and have children note the signs and landmarks that tell them where they are as they walk along.

Maps are one tool people use to locate themselves and others on the earth. Maps, however, are an abstraction of reality and constitute an extremely complex idea for children. If you use them in connection with children's experiences, you will introduce children to the purpose of maps. After a field trip using a map, children can

1. Construct a map using blocks of their school room or yard.
2. Play with maps, including a table-top map of a toy village.

HISTORY

As children explore their immediate environment, key concepts from the study of history can be fostered. Concepts of the past, change, and the continuity of life are among those that can be introduced to children through field trips.

Change occurs right within the school. As children walk through the school, their attention can be focused on the things that change and on the immediate past. Room arrangements, decorations, art displays, and the building itself change. Children can be helped to recall the immediate past and discuss the changes that occur.

Walking through the neighborhood, children can observe signs of change with the seasons, or changes that people make or have made. With each change, a house painted, roads built, houses torn down or renovated, you and the children can discuss what is happening, why, and how things have changed.

Visits to historic markers in the community, to museums, older homes, or other places of interest are often possible. If museums are too far away for the children to walk to, the museums may send a representative to the school with a small display or exhibit. Or you might bring tools and objects used in the past to the school. After using a hand eggbeater and an electric beater, children can draw inferences about a way of life that is now history. Observing things and objects used in the past or older homes in the neighborhood, children can form hypotheses about how people once lived, and about the things that have changed. They can discuss how they will use things and live in the future.

Visiting an older neighbor, a grandmother of one of the children, or some other older person in the community is also helpful in fostering concepts of the past, change, and the continuity of human life. Children can be asked to visit or interview an older relative within their family. They might find out how the old people lived when they were young, the things they enjoyed doing as children, and what their life is like now. Although many things change over time, many human things—feelings, likes, and dislikes—stay the same. There is a continuity to human life that children can experience as they visit older people in the community. Children might speculate on the changes that will occur as they grow. The fact that they will still be the same person, only older, may be stressed.

ECONOMICS

Children can be introduced to concepts of scarcity and plenty, the meaning of producers and consumers, and the advantages of division of labor through field trips. Each of these has been identified from the study of economics (Minneapolis Public Schools 1967). Field trips into the community will offer children opportunities to form concepts of economics.

Children begin to understand the meaning of being a consumer by going to stores to make purchases. If they are producing something together, perhaps a playhouse, a trip can be taken to a nearby hardware store to purchase needed supplies. Groups of children will be given responsibility for one purchase. One group may be asked to purchase roofing materials for the playhouse, another nails, and yet another the wood. In this way children see the relationship between consumers and producers, for they play both roles.

At other times small groups of children may be sent to the store to make a purchase for the total group. A group or four or five children, with an adult, might be asked to purchase a fish for the aquarium. They will take the group's wishes and make their purchase accordingly. When the group returns, they will report to the class, describing how and why they made their purchase. When children recognize that this type of experience will be available to each, they are willing to wait their turn for a special trip and special responsibility.

Frequently, however, children fail to realize that they consume services as well as products. Other trips might be taken to a doctor, dentist, library, city building, or office to observe people at work in service to others. How people pay for the doctor, dentist, librarian, school teacher, and county clerk might be discussed. People pay taxes to use the services of police and street cleaners, to build and maintain roads. This is difficult for young children to conceive. Nevertheless, through direct experiences, they can build the realization that people consume services as well as goods, and that people pay for both goods and services.

When children are consumers, they must make choices. Knowing what things they want and which they need helps them to make wise decisions. Many times during the school day, as children are given choices, teachers might remind them to ask themselves whether this is something they want or really need. "Which things are necessary?" "Is this something you really must have, or just want?"

Another time a trip can be taken to the stores to observe the diversity of jobs people hold. At a grocery store there may be clerks, baggers, shelf stockers, and managers to watch. In other stores or shopping centers, children might see people who fix cars, pump gas, wash windows, sweep floors, type, or answer phones. You can ask children why they think different people do different jobs, and what would happen if everyone did the same thing.

The world of work is open to children for observation in nearly every neighborhood. If children live in a rural area they may visit a farm, dairy, or orchard. Those living in a city can visit factories and food processing plants. Through repeated trips, children will begin to develop the concepts of division of labor, producer, and consumer.

Skills

Preschool children have many skills. They have learned, within a few short years, to walk, talk, play, and learn. They have gathered information and drawn conclusions about the world they know. In school, children should have the opportunities to sharpen the skills they already have and to strengthen their skills as learners.

Field trips help children develop the skills of

- locating, organizing, and evaluating information;
- acquiring information through listening, discussion, observations, and vicarious experiences;
- communicating orally;
- and working with others.

Children learn about their world.

On a field trip children can collect information. They can observe life around them, locate information in their environment, and organize and evaluate the information collected. Upon returning from the trip, children will find they need additional information to answer questions or to help them understand the things they have observed.

Now the value of books, the library, and resource persons enter into children's lives. There is always a reference book handy in which to look up information or to add facts to children's observations. Sometimes the reference materials serve to help children repeat their experience vicariously. A trip to the dairy may be relived as children look at pictures in a book or view a film.

A resource person may be useful. Perhaps the children have other questions, not answered by the trip. As they play, discuss their experience, and listen to how others interpret the same experience. Disagreements and questions will arise. A resource person, the police officer, doctor, or fire fighter, might be invited to the class to further children's acquisition of information.

After children have collected information, they must find some way to organize it. The paintings, booklets, and puppet shows created after a trip are one way children organize information. As they paint, draw, model, construct, or dictate stories, they are summarizing their ideas, putting things into categories, and organizing information.

Field trips provide opportunities for children to work together. They each have had the same experience, although each will perceive it differently. The experience serves as a base for their common play activities and helps them to develop the ability to work with others.

Children use all of the skills of locating, acquiring, and sharing information (Wann 1962). Children can see relationships between trips, their ideas, and the ideas of others. They classify and organize the information they have obtained. When children do these things, they are thinking. Skill development in locating, acquiring, and communicating information is actually thinking development. When children practice these skills, they are learning how to learn.

Each day teachers can check to see how many times, in how many ways, they have motivated each child to use the skill of thinking. Did they, for instance, promote children's ability to locate and evaluate information? How did they ask children to communicate that information, and what opportunities were present for children to work together to expand and clarify the information?

Attitudes

Knowledge of the world is not all children need in order to perpetuate a democratic society. The attitudes and values of democracy are also transmitted by the school. Some believe that schools are not in the business of teaching children attitudes and values. "After all," people say, "the home and church are the places for children to learn their values, not the school."

Yet the fact is that children will learn values and attitudes from all of their experiences and from all of the information they receive from their environment. During the preschool years, children learn their attitudes from others around them. Before they enter school, children identify and imitate their parents. When in school, there are other significant people to imitate. The school's staff—teachers, principals, custodians—as well as the peers in the school provide models for children to identify with, and imitate.

Even though schools purport to teach children basic skills and knowledge, they do influence children's attitudes and values. Attitude learning and modification have been demonstrated at every level of school. Because the experiences children have in school influence attitudes and values, teachers must be aware of the attitudes they demonstrate, how children form attitudes and values, and what values the school should transmit in a democratic society.

Attitudes are defined as a state of "readiness, organized thought, experience that exerts a direction of dynamic influence upon individual's respones to all objects and situations with which they are related" (Mussen and others 1969). Attitudes and values influence the way children feel about something, their emotional response toward that thing, and define how they will act and behave. There are believed to be at least three components of attitudes: (1) the cognitive—in part a person's attitudes are made up of the knowledge a person has about an object, person, idea, or thing; (2) affective—attitudes have to do mainly with feelings a person has about the thing; and (3) action—for attitudes predispose a person to act in certain ways (Klausmeier and Ripple 1971).

Clarifying Attitudes

Children imitate their teachers. They often love their teachers and want to be just like them. Teachers, therefore, must understand the values and attitudes they are transmitting to the children. "Teachers set the atmosphere of the class, dictating by their actions and thoughts what is important and what is not" (Seefeldt, 1977, p. 261). Teachers might ask themselves

1. Do they know where their values and attitudes stem from?
2. Why do they feel the way they do?
3. Did they always feel this way, and who else feels this way?

These questions have been suggested by Louis Raths (1966) to help children in the process of value clarification, but they are equally useful for teachers who must be certain of their own value systems. Raths's scheme for value clarification, based on Dewey's belief system is:

I. Prizing one's beliefs and behaviors.
    1. Prizing and cherishing.
    2. Publicly affirming when appropriate.
II. Choosing one's beliefs and behaviors.
    3. Choosing from alternatives.

4. Choosing after consideration of consequences.
5. Choosing freely.
III. Acting on one's beliefs.
6. Acting with a pattern, consistency, and repetition. (Raths 1966, p. 35)

Learning Attitudes

Children learn their attitudes. The stimuli in the environment provide them with the materials from which they form attitudes and values. Pleasant feelings, success, and reward have been shown to produce favorable and lasting attitudes. Unpleasant feelings, failure, and punishment lead to unfavorable attitudes and even to the extinction of previously favorable attitudes.

Louis Raths (1966) believes that a secure classroom atmosphere is necessary in order for children to develop positive attitudes. The stages people go through in value clarification suggest classroom practices that permit children to choose freely from alternatives or express their attitudes in words and actions.

Thus children must feel psychologically safe to talk about their feelings and beliefs. Teachers can listen to children expressing their beliefs and ask questions that might help them to clarify these beliefs. James Raths suggests that the following questions might be asked:

> Are you glad you feel that way? Have you thought of any other ways of doing that? Have you felt this way for some time? What are some examples of what you have in mind? What are some things that are good about the way you feel? Is this idea so good everyone should feel the same way? Who else do you know feels that way? (Raths 1962, p. 35)

Values in a Democracy

The question of what attitudes the school should be promoting can no longer be ignored. "It therefore becomes one of the major tasks of the school to change undesirable attitudes, to strengthen existing desirable ones and to work toward the development of new attitudes by providing appropriate learning experiences" (Khan and Weiss 1973, p. 761). Educators cannot afford to ignore attitudes. Although there would be great disagreement if schools were to foster specific attitudes of religion, politics, or government, there are attitudes inherent in a democratic society that must be cultivated in all schools. These are

1. Valuing the dignity and worth of each individual.
2. Universal participation in rule setting and maintaining of rules.
3. Freedom of speech, opportunity to express ideas and feelings.
4. The rights of each individual for protection and happiness.

5. That everyone has a responsibility for protecting the rights and happiness of others.

Children's Attitudes

Young children possess definite attitudes about the rights and worth of others. Not all of these attitudes are those valued by a democratic society. Although in a democracy the dignity and worth of each individual is valued, not all children believe this. Prejudices appear very early in life.

Research conducted during the 1950s showed that children become aware of different races by the age of three or four. Many children rejected black children, with many blacks rejecting their own race by saying they were most like the white dolls, or preferred to be just like the white doll (Goodman 1952). More recently (1977), research has demonstrated that children still prefer the Caucasian race, but that with the recent past history of civil rights and the end of some of the more flagrant segregation practices, there is less evidence of children rejecting their own race, and of children giving negative comments about blacks, Chicanos, or other minority members (Rohwer 1977).

Children also hold less than positive views of foreigners. A ten-year study by Lambert and Klineberg (1967) confirmed the fact that children begin to identify foreign people early in life. By the age of five children have formed decided opinions about foreign people, recognize differences more than similarities, display a particularly narrow similarity of outlooks, and withhold expressions of affection from foreign people.

This study offered an explanation of the process in which children learn about others. Lambert and Klineberg (1967) believe that children

- learn about others in view of the way they learn about their own group. The manner in which the concept of their own group is taught to chidren has important consequences in how they learn about others. If our country is stereotyped, and the characteristics of our country exaggerated, then children will also stereotype foreign people.
- mark certain foreign groups as outstanding examples of people who are different. Early training in national contrasts appears to mark certain groups as different.
- have the impression that foreigners are different, strange, and unfriendly; they have an overall suspicion of foreign people.
- think of themself in racial, religious, or national terms. The self-concepts of children of specific groups reflect that chidlren are taught at a very young age to distinguish between cultural groups.
- learn about others through parents, teachers, and members of the community.

To help chidren develop positive attitudes toward others of all races and ethnic backgrounds, teachers can (1) help children to feel secure within their own group; (2) increase children's knowledge of others; and (3) focus on the similarities between all people rather than the differences.

Children who are fearful and insecure are those who hold prejudices against others. Putting down others or showing superiority toward other groups helps the insecure, frightened child feel safe. If all children feel safe, welcomed, and respected, they will have little or no need to make others feel unworthy or inferior.

Increasing knowledge about another group often helps dispel stereotyping of that group. Curricula have been successfully demonstrated that teach young children to value those who differ from them racially or culturally (Kerckhoff and Treulla 1972). These curricula focused on giving children information about others, reading stories, recognizing similarities in all people, and highlighting the idea that although some people may look different, they are very much like every other person.

Emphasizing that all people, everywhere, have the same needs, feelings, and desires may be helpful in dispelling stereotypic thinking. Boys and girls differ, yet they are alike in many ways. Both boys and girls like to build with blocks, cook, sew, paint, and play with others. White children may differ from black in skin tone and hair structure, yet both are the same. Both feel, have the same needs, and enjoy doing the same things. Asking children to find out how others are just like them and finding similarities in feelings and attitudes between groups may help children to value the pluralistic society in which we live, and the many different people that make up that pluralistic society.

Summary

Social studies can introduce preschool children to geography, history, and economics. Through field trips and other enriching activities, teachers can acquaint children with the social as well as the physical environment. In addition to building knowledge and thinking skills, social studies curricula can develop children's attitudes and values consistent with those of a democratic society in a world of nations.

All of the activities of the social studies, learning about self, others, and the world should build socially competent children. Children who are growing in competence are those who

1. show interest in the environment, and a willingness to take risks to learn new things.
2. have a world view that is the product of their own unique interaction with the world.
3. have acquired social skills and school skills.
4. building a store of relevant information about the environment and world around them in the immediate neighborhood and the world far from the immediate surroundings.
5. active learners.
6. can accurately perceive their environment.
7. experience a sense of continuity in growth.
8. have a growing sense of personal and group identity.
9. encounter objects and experiences that expand at a rapid rate. (Hilliard 1978, pp. 12–13)

Resources

Free materials useful in teaching social studies are available from a number of sources. The Government Printing Office offers numerous publications that might be useful for teachers of young children. Ask that your name be added to their mailing list and request catalogs of publications that might be helpful for teachers of young children. The address is

Superintendent of Documents
U.S. Printing Office
Washington, D.C. 20402

Free materials can also be obtained by writing:
Educator's Guide to Free Curriculum Materials in Social Studies
Educator's Progress Service
Randolph, Wisconsin 53956

Salisbury, Gordan,
Catalog of Free Teaching Materials
P.O. Box 1075
Ventura, California 93003

Another resource of teachers is the *Yellow Pages of Learning Resources: Resources Directory Area Code 800*. This book illustrates how the community can be utilized as a resource for children's learning and offers suggestions for numerous field trips. It is available from the MIT Press, Cambridge, Massachusetts.

A book on attitudes and values useful for teachers is *Values Education*, the 1971 Yearbook of the National Council for the Social Studies. It gives an overview of values education and helps teachers sort out their own attitudes and values. It is available from the National Council for the Social Studies, 1201 Sixteenth Street, N.W., Washington, D.C. 20036.

Several organizations have materials available on economics education for young children. These are

Center of Economic Education
Oregon State University
Corvallis, Oregon 97331

Economics Education Project
Minneapolis Public Schools
Minneapolis, Minnesota

Joint Council on Economic Education
2 West 46th Street
New York, New York 10036

351

Projects

1. Begin a card file of all of the possible places in the neighborhood of the school that can be used for field trips. List the address, name of a contact person, and phone number on the card. Record what concepts could be fostered through the trip, what the children will see, any safety hazards to be aware of, and what the children will receive. This card file will be useful in planning and taking field trips.

2. Take a walk in and around the school building. Note places for learning and children's exploration. What can children learn from visitng the school office, cafeteria, or parking lot?

3. Observe in a classroom for young children. How do children interact with one another? Do they show empathy toward one another? What plans does the teacher make to help children interact with one another?

4. Explore reference materials to find those that can build on children's actual experiences with their environment. If the school is in a city, find books which help explain life in the city. If the school is in a rural area, find books about rural life. Pictures and illustrations can also be used as references for children. Begin a picture collection or file. Posters, photographs, and other materials can be collected and kept handy for children's learning. The local chamber of commerce and city or state government offices may have free materials available that can be used to help children better understand their world.

5. Review social studies texts designed for use with kindergarten or primary school children. Analyze the texts to determine how women, older persons, and minority members are portrayed. How do the authors of the text suggest they should be used with children? How would you use these?

References

BOWLBY, J., *Child Care and the Growth of Love*. Baltimore, Md.: Penguin Books, 1968.

D'EVELYN, K. E., *Developing Mentally Healthy Children*. Washington, D.C.: Elementary, Kindergarten, Nursery Education Association, 1970.

DINKMEYER, D. C., *Child Development: The Emerging Self*. Englewood Cliffs, N.J.: Prentice-Hall, Inc., 1965.

ELKIN, F., *The Child and Society*. New York: Random House, Inc., 1960.

FROEBEL, F., *The Education of Man*. New York: D. Appleton and Co., 1887.

GOODMAN, M., *Race Awareness in Young Children*. Reading, Mass.: Addison-Wesley Publishing Co., Inc., 1952.

GREIF, E. B., "Peer Interactions in Preschool Children," in *Social Development in Childhood: Day Care Programs and Research*, ed. R. A. Webb. Baltimore, Md.: Johns Hopkins University Press, 1967.

HARLOW, H. F., and HARLOW, M. K., "The Affectional Systems, in *Behavior of Nonhuman Primates*, Vol. II, eds. A. M. Schrier, H. F. Harlow, and F. Stollnitz. New York: Academic Press, 1965.

HILLIARD, A. G., How Should We Assess Children's Social Competence?" *Young Children*, 33, 5 (1979), 12–13.

KERCKHOFF, R., and TREULLA, S., "Teaching Race Relations in the Nursery School. *Young Children*, 27 (5) 1975, 240–274.

KHAN, S. B., and WEISS, J., "The Teaching of Affective Response," in *Second Handbook of Research on Teaching*, pp. 759–805, ed. R. M. W. Travers. Chicago, Ill.: Rand McNally & Company, 1973.

KLAUSMEIER, H. J., and RIPPLE, R., *Learning and Human Abilities* (3rd. ed.). New York: Harper & Row, Publishers, 1971.

LAMBERT, N., and KLINEBERGE, O., *Children's Views of Foreign Peoples*. New York: Appleton-Century-Crofts Medical and Nursing Publications, 1967.

LEEPER, S. H.: DALES, R. S.: SKIPPER, D. S.: and WITHERSPOON, R. L.; *Good Schools for Young Children* (3rd. ed.). New York: Macmillan, Inc., 1974.

MARCUS, R. F., and LEISERSON, M., "Encouraging Helping Behavior," *Young Children*, 33, 6 (1978), 24–45.

Minneapolis Public Schools. *Economic Education*. 1967.

MITCHELL, L. S., *Our Children and Our Schools*. New York: Simon & Schuster, 1950.

MUELLER, E., "The Maintenance of Verbal Exchanges Between Young Children," *Child Development*, 43 (1972), 930–938.

MUSSEN, P. H.; CONGER, J. J.; and KAGAN, J.; *Child Development and Personality*. New York: Harper and Row Publishers, Inc., 1969.

PIAGET, J., *The Child's Conception of the World*. London: Routledge & Kegan Paul, 1951.

——— and INHELDER, B., *The Psychology of the Child*. New York: Basic Books, Inc., 1969.

RATHS, J., "Clarifying Children's Values," *The National Elementary Principle*, 42 (1962), 35–39.

RATHS, L.; HARMIN, M.; and SIMON, S.; *Values and Teaching*. Columbus, Ohio: Charles E. Merrill Publishing Company, 1966.

ROHWER, G. K., "Racial and Ethnic Identification and Preference in Young Children." *Young Children*, 32 (1977), 24–33.

ROHWER, W. D., AMMON, P. P., CRAMER, P., *Understanding Intellectual Development*. Hinsdale, Ill.: The Dryden Press, 1974.

SEEFELDT, C., *Social Studies for The Preschool/Primary Child*. Columbus, Ohio: Charles E. Merrill Publishing Company, 1977.

SPITZ, R., *Hospitalism: An Inquiry into the Genesis of Psychiatric Conditions in Early Childhood*. New York: International University Press, 1945.

Summaries of 21 Papers: Policy Issues in Day Care. Washington, D.C.: U.S. Department of HEW, 1977.

WANN, K., DORN, M., and LIDDLE, L., *Fostering Intellectual Development in Young Children*. New York: Teachers College Press, Columbia University Bureau of Publications, 1962.

Index

A

B

T

V